Houghton Mifflin

Reading

Teacher's Edition

Grade 2

Delights

Senior Authors J. David Cooper, John J. Pikulski

Authors Kathryn H. Au, David J. Chard, Gilbert G. Garcia,
Claude N. Goldenberg, Phyllis C. Hunter, Marjorie Y. Lipson,
Shane Templeton, Sheila W. Valencia, MaryEllen Vogt

Consultants Linda H. Butler, Linnea C. Ehri, Carla B. Ford

 HOUGHTON MIFFLIN

LITERATURE REVIEWERS

Consultants: Dr. Adela Artola Allen, Associate Dean, Graduate College, Associate Vice President for Inter-American Relations, University of Arizona, Tucson, AZ; **Dr. Manley Begay,** Co-director of the Harvard Project on American Indian Economic Development, Director of the National Executive Education Program for Native Americans, Harvard University, John F. Kennedy School of Government, Cambridge, MA; **Dr. Nicholas Kannellos,** Director, Arte Publico Press, Director, Recovering the U.S. Hispanic Literacy Heritage Project, University of Houston, TX; **Mildred Lee,** author and former head of Library Services for Sonoma County, Santa Rosa, CA; **Dr. Barbara Moy,** Director of the Office of Communication Arts, Detroit Public Schools, MI; **Norma Naranjo,** Clark County School District, Las Vegas, NV; **Dr. Arlette Ingram Willis,** Associate Professor, Department of Curriculum and Instruction, Division of Language and Literacy, University of Illinois at Urbana-Champaign, IL

Teachers: Sharon Blount, Meadowbrook School, Gladstone, MO; **Gloria C. Holmes,** Math/Science Academy at Harrison Park Elementary, Grand Rapids, MI; **Betsy Kennedy,** Liberty School, Scottsdale, AZ; **Brenda Smith,** Glendover Elementary School, Lexington, KY; **Huoag Thai,** Buchanan Street School, Los Angeles, CA; **Karol L. Yeatts,** Leewood Elementary School, Miami, FL

PROGRAM REVIEWERS

Linda Bayer, Jonesboro, GA; **Sheri Blair,** Warner Robins, GA; **Faye Blake,** Jacksonville, FL; **Suzi Boyett,** Sarasota, FL; **Carol Brockhouse,** Madison Schools, Wayne Westland Schools, MI; **Patti Brustad,** Sarasota, FL; **Jan Buckelew,** Venice, FL; **Maureen Carlton,** Barstow, CA; **Karen Cedar,** Gold River, CA; **Karen Ciraulo,** Folsom, CA; **Marcia M. Clark,** Griffin, GA; **Kim S. Coady,** Covington, GA; **Eva Jean Conway,** Valley View School District, IL; **Marilyn Crownover,** Tustin, CA; **Carol Daley,** Sioux Falls, SD; **Jennifer Davison,** West Palm Beach, FL; **Lynne M. DiNardo,** Covington, GA; **Kathy Dover,** Lake City, GA; **Cheryl Dultz,** Citrus Heights, CA; **Debbie Friedman,** Fort Lauderdale, FL; **Anne Gaitor,** Lakeland, GA; **Rebecca S. Gillette,** Saint Marys, GA; **Buffy C. Gray,** Peachtree City, GA; **Merry Guest,** Homestead, FL; **Jo Nan Holbrook,** Lakeland, GA; **Beth Holguin,** San Jose, CA; **Coleen Howard-Whals,** St. Petersburg, FL; **Beverly Hurst,** Jacksonville, FL; **Debra Jackson,** St. Petersburg, FL; **Vickie Jordan,** Centerville, GA; **Cheryl Kellogg,** Panama City, FL; **Karen Landers,** Talladega County, AL; **Barb LeFerrier,** Port Orchard, WA; **Sandi Maness,** Modesto, CA; **Ileana Masud,** Miami, FL; **David Miller,** Cooper City, FL; **Muriel Miller,** Simi Valley, CA; **Walsetta W. Miller,** Macon, GA; **Jean Nielson,** Simi Valley, CA; **Sue Patton,** Brea, CA; **Debbie Peale,** Miami, FL; **Loretta Piggee,** Gary, IN; **Jennifer Rader,** Huntington, CA; **April Raiford,** Columbus, GA; **Cheryl Remash,** Manchester, NH; **Francis Rivera,** Orlando, FL; **Marina Rodriguez,** Hialeah, FL; **Marilynn Rose,** MI; **Kathy Scholtz,** Amesbury, MA; **Kimberly Moulton Schorr,** Columbus, GA; **Linda Schrum,** Orlando, FL; **Sharon Searcy,** Mandarin, FL; **Melba Sims,** Orlando, FL; **Judy Smith,** Titusville, FL; **Bea Tamo,** Huntington, CA; **Dottie Thompson,** Jefferson County, AL; **Dana Vassar,** Winston-Salem, NC; **Beverly Wakefield,** Tarpon Springs, FL; **Joy Walls,** Winston-Salem, NC; **Elaine Warwick,** Williamson County, TN; **Audrey N. Watkins,** Atlanta, GA; **Marti Watson,** Sarasota, FL

Supervisors: Judy Artz, Butler County, OH; **James Bennett,** Elkhart, IN; **Kay Buckner-Seal,** Wayne County, MI; **Charlotte Carr,** Seattle, WA; **Sister Marion Christi,** Archdiocese of Philadelphia, PA; **Alvina Crouse,** Denver, CO; **Peggy DeLapp,** Minneapolis, MN; **Carol Erlandson,** Wayne Township Schools, IN; **Brenda Feeney,** North Kansas City School District, MO; **Winnie Huebsch,** Sheboygan, WI; **Brenda Mickey,** Winston-Salem, NC; **Audrey Miller,** Camden, NJ; **JoAnne Piccolo,** Westminster, CO; **Sarah Rentz,** Baton Rouge, LA; **Kathy Sullivan,** Omaha, NE; **Rosie Washington,** Gary, IN; **Theresa Wishart,** Knox County Public Schools, TN

English Language Learners Reviewers: Maria Arevalos, Pomona, CA; **Lucy Blood,** NV; **Manuel Brenes,** Kalamazoo, MI; **Delight Diehn,** AZ; **Susan Dunlap,** Richmond, CA; **Tim Fornier,** Grand Rapids, MI; **Connie Jimenez,** Los Angeles, CA; **Diane Bonilla Lether,** Pasadena, CA; **Anna Lugo,** Chicago, IL; **Marcos Martel,** Hayward, CA; **Carolyn Mason,** Yakima, WA; **Jackie Pinson,** Moorpark, CA; **Jenaro Rivas,** NJ; **Jerilyn Smith,** Salinas, CA; **Noemi Velazquez,** Jersey City, NJ; **JoAnna Veloz,** NJ; **Dr. Santiago Veve,** Las Vegas, NV

CREDITS

Cover

Cover photography Nick Vedros, Vedros & Associates.

Photography

Theme Opener © Tim Flach/Stone/Getty Images. **T104** © Dan Guravich/CORBIS. **T250** Getty Images. **T314** © Hulton Archive by Getty Images.

Assignment Photography

55F © HMCo./Parker/Boon Productions. **T146, T214, T239, T341** © HMCo./Michael Indresano.

Illustration

All kid art by Morgan-Cain & Associates.

ACKNOWLEDGMENTS

Grateful acknowledgment is made for permission to reprint copyrighted material as follows:

Theme 4

From *Aero and Officer Mike: Police Partners,* by Joan Plummer Russell. Text copyright © 2001 by Joan Plummer Russell. Photographs copyright © 2001 by Kris Turner Sinnenberg. Published by Caroline House, Boyds Mills Press, Inc. Reprinted by permission.

"The Little Fly and the Great Moose," by Janeen R. Adil from *Spider* Magazine, August 1999 issue, Vol. 6, No. 8. Copyright © 1999 by Janeen R. Adil. Reprinted by permission of *Spider* Magazine.

From An Octopus is Amazing, by Patricia Lauber. Text copyright © 1990 by Patricia Lauber. Used by permission of HarperCollins Publishers.

Theme Big Book

From Caterpillar to Butterfly, by Deborah Heiligman, illustrated by Bari Weissman. Text copyright © 1996 by Deborah Heiligman. Illustrations copyright © 1996 by Bari Weissman. Reprinted by permission of HarperCollins Publishers.

STUDENT WRITING MODEL FEATURE

Special thanks to the following teachers whose students' compositions appear as Student Writing Models: **Cheryl Claxton,** Florida; **Patricia Kopay,** Delaware; **Susana Llanes,** Michigan; **Joan Rubens,** Delaware; **Nancy Schulten,** Kentucky; **Linda Wallis,** California

Amazing Animals

OBJECTIVES

Phonics *r*-controlled vowel *ar*; *r*-controlled vowels *or, ore*; words with *nd, nt, mp, ng, nk*; base words and endings *-s, -es, -ies* (nouns); vowel pairs *oa, ow*

High-Frequency Words recognize high-frequency words

Reading Strategies monitor/clarify; question; summarize; phonics/decoding

Comprehension drawing conclusions; text organization; cause and effect

Fluency build reading fluency

Vocabulary dictionary entry words; using a thesaurus; parts of a dictionary entry

Spelling vowel + *r* sounds in *car*; words ending with *nd, ng,* or *nk*; more long *o* words

Grammar words for nouns; singular possessive nouns; plural possessive nouns

Writing invitation; writing times of day; poem; using *I* and *me*; news article; adding details; process writing: research report

Listening/Speaking/Viewing giving a talk; discussing a factual topic; giving clear directions

Information and Study Skills interviewing; using a glossary; using directions

Amazing Animals

C O N T E N T S

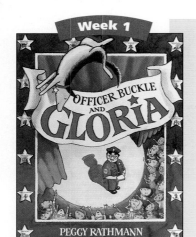

Week 1

PEGGY RATHMANN

Fantasy

Below Level   *On Level*   *Above Level*   *Language Support*

Nonfiction

Below Level

On Level

Above Level

Language Support

Theme 4

Week 3

THE GREAT BALL GAME
◄ A MUSKOGEE STORY ►

RETOLD BY JOSEPH BRUCHAC
ILLUSTRATED BY SUSAN L. ROTH

Folktale

Below Level   *On Level*   *Above Level*   *Language Support*

Theme Wrap-Up
Monitoring Student Progress

Little Grunt
and the
Big Egg

A Prehistoric Fairy Tale

Tomie
dePaola

Fantasy

Mighty
Dinosaurs

Nonfiction

Focus on Genre — BIOGRAPHY

Below Level   *On Level*   *Above Level*   *Language Support*

Leveled Theme Paperbacks

Leveled Bibliography

BOOKS FOR INDEPENDENT READING AND FLUENCY BUILDING

 **To build vocabulary and fluency,** choose books from this list for children to read outside of class. Suggest that they read for at least thirty minutes a day, either independently or with an adult who provides modeling and guidance.

Key

 Science

 Social Studies

 Multicultural

 Music

 Math

 Classic

 Art

 Career

Classroom Bookshelf

WELL BELOW LEVEL

A Snake Mistake
by Mavis Smith
Puffin 1998 (32p) paper
Jake the snake eats two light bulbs he mistakes for eggs.

 Amazing Lizards!
by Fay Robinson
Scholastic 1999 (32p)
Rhyming text introduces readers to the colorful world of lizards.

 Dinosaurs
by Grace Maccarone
Scholastic 2001 (32p)
Simple, rhyming text describes different kinds of dinosaurs.

 Waiting for Wings
by Lois Ehlert
Harcourt 2001 (32p)
In a field of flowers, caterpillars turn into beautiful monarch butterflies.

BELOW LEVEL

 Spectacular Spiders
by Linda Glaser
Millbrook 1998 (32p) also paper
A girl describes the spiders in her garden.

 Crocodile and Hen
by Joan M. Lexau
Harper 2001 (48p)
Clever Hen outwits hungry Crocodile in this tale from the Bakongo people of Africa.

Harley
by Star Livingstone
SeaStar 2001 (64p)
A woman trains a llama named Harley to protect her sheep from coyotes.

Dolores and the Big Fire: A True Story
by Andrew Clements
Simon 2002 (32p)
Dolores is a timid cat, but saves her owner from a house fire. See others in series.

ON LEVEL

*****Martha Speaks**
by Susan
Meddaugh
Houghton 1992
(32p) also paper
Martha the dog learns to talk when the letters in her alphabet soup go to her brain.

 *****Biggest, Strongest, Fastest**
by Steve Jenkins
Houghton 1995
(32p)
Fun facts about record holders of the animal world.

 The Good Luck Cat
by Joy Harjo
Harcourt 2000 (32p)
A Native American girl worries when her cat Woogie disappears.

Megatooth
by Patrick O'Brien
Holt 2001 (32p)
Megalodons were giant, ancient sharks big enough to prey on whales.

Wings: A Tale of Two Chickens
by James Marshall
Houghton 2003
(32p)
Sensible Harriet has to rescue silly Winnie from the clutches of Mr. Johnson, a fox.

 What Do You Do with a Tail Like This?
by S. Jenkins and R. Page
Houghton 2003 (32p)
Animals can do many incredible things with their eyes, ears, noses, feet, and tails.

Breakout at the Bug Lab
by Ruth Horowitz
Puffin 2001 (48p)
A giant cockroach named Max escapes from a bug laboratory, setting off a madcap search.

Buster and Phoebe
by Lisze Bechtold
Houghton 2003 (48p)
A clever dog named Phoebe teaches the new puppy, Buster, all about bones.

ABOVE LEVEL

 The Lizard and the Sun
by Alma Flor Ada
Doubleday 1997
(32p) also paper
A brave lizard helps return the sun to the people in this Mexican folktale.

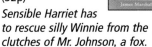

---

*Included in Classroom Bookshelf, Level 2

Chester the Worldly Pig
by Bill Peet
Houghton 1965 (48p) also paper
Chester the pig wants to be a circus performer.

A Hare-Raising Tale
by Elizabeth Levy
Aladdin 2002 (54p)
A basset hound sniffs out the mystery of what happened to a pet rabbit belonging to a third-grade class.

 Zebras
by Anthony D. Fredericks
Lerner 2002 (48p)
Each and every zebra, a dweller of the African savanna, has a different pattern of black-and-white stripes.

 Crows! Strange and Wonderful
by Laurence Pringle
Boyds Mills 2003 (32p)
Crows, among the smartest birds on earth, have a language of at least twenty-five sounds.

BOOKS FOR TEACHER READ ALOUD

 Anansi's Feast
by Tololwa Mollel
Clarion 1997 (32p)
The clever spider Anansi gets his comeuppance in this Ashanti tale.

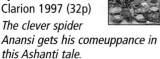

The Beauty of the Beast
Jack Prelutsky, Selector
Knopf 1997 (112p)
Poems celebrate all kinds of animals.

 Puss in Boots
by Fred Marcellino
Farrar 1990 (32p) also paper
A clever cat gains a fortune for his master. **Available in Spanish as** *El gato con botas.*

 The Little Red Ant and the Great Big Crumb
by Shirley Climo
Clarion 1995 (32p)
A small ant discovers her strength.

 Doctor De Soto
by William Steig
Farrar 1982 (32p) also paper
A mouse dentist and his wife outwit a fox who wants to eat them. **Available in Spanish as** *Doctor De Soto.*

 Mystic Horse
by Paul Goble
Harper 2003 (32p)
This story of an abandoned horse and the boy who loves him is based on a Pawnee legend.

 Roadrunner's Dance
by Rudolpho Anaya
Hyperion 2000 (32p)
Rattlesnake gets his comeuppance when a new animal called Roadrunner makes the roads safe.

 Calabash Cat and His Amazing Journey
by James Rumford
Houghton 2003 (32p)
A West African cat sets out to find where the world ends.

Technology

Computer Software Resources

- **Get Set for Reading CD-ROM**
  Amazing Animals
  Provides background building, vocabulary support, and selection summaries in English and Spanish.
- **Curious George® Learns Phonics**
  Provides interactive phonics practice. Houghton Mifflin Company
- **Curious George® Learns to Spell**
  Provides interactive spelling practice. Houghton Mifflin Company

Video Cassettes

- **Officer Buckle and Gloria** *by Peggy Rathmann. Weston Woods*
- **Chickens Aren't the Only Ones** *by Ruth Heller. Spoken Arts*
- **Doctor De Soto** *by William Steig. Weston Woods*
- **Sharks** *by Gail Gibbons. Live Oak*

Audio

- **Tyrannosaurus Was a Beast** *by Jack Prelutsky. Weston Woods*
- **Hot-Air Henry** *by Mary Calhoun. Listening Library*
- **Chester the Worldly Pig** *by Bill Peet. Houghton Mifflin Company*
- **The Littlest Dinosaurs** *by Bernard Most. Live Oak*
- **CD for *Amazing Animals*.** *Houghton Mifflin Company*

Technology Resources addresses are on page R49.

Education Place®

www.eduplace.com *Log on to Education Place for more activities relating to* Amazing Animals, *including vocabulary support—*
- e • Glossary
- e • WordGame

Book Adventure®

www.bookadventure.org *This Internet reading incentive program provides thousands of titles for children to read.*

Accelerated Reader® Universal CD-ROM

This popular CD-ROM provides practice quizzes for Anthology selections and for many popular children's books.

Theme Skills Overview

	Week 1	Week 2	Week 3
Pacing Approximately 5–6 weeks	**Officer Buckle and Gloria** Fantasy pp. T20–T93 	**Ant** Nonfiction pp. T106–T175 	**The Great Ball Game** Folktale pp. T176–T243
Reading Phonics Comprehension Fluency Information and Study Skills	🔊 *r*-Controlled Vowels *ar* T 🔊 *r*-Controlled Vowels *or, ore* T **Review: Syllables** *-tion, -ture* **Guiding Comprehension** 🔊 **Drawing Conclusions** T 🔊 **Monitor/Clarify** 🔊 **Decodable Text:** *A Park for Parkdale; Arthur's Book* **Social Studies Link:** A Map Interviewing T	🔊 **Words with** *nd, nt, mp, ng, nk* T 🔊 **Base Words and Endings** T 🔊 **Review** *r*-Controlled Vowels **Guiding Comprehension** 🔊 **Text Organization** T 🔊 **Question** T 🔊 **Decodable Text:** *Hank's Pandas; Marta's Larks* **Music Link:** Song Lyrics Using a Glossary T	🔊 **Vowel Pairs** *oa, ow* T **Review:** *nd, nt, mp, ng, nk* **Guiding Comprehension** 🔊 **Cause and Effect** T 🔊 **Summarize** 🔊 **Decodable Text:** *Crow's Plan; Brent Skunk Sings* **Science Link:** Captions Using Directions
Leveled Readers • Fluency Practice • Independent Reading • Lessons and Leveled Practice	**Leveled Readers** *Max the Pet Show Star* *The Best Job for Scooter* *Daisy Divine, Dancing Dog* *Max Is a Star!*	**Leveled Readers** *Earthworms* *Busy Bees* *Butterflies!* *The Amazing Earthworm*	**Leveled Readers** *Bird Race* *Turtle's Small Pond* *Possum's Bare Tail* *A Race to the Mountain*
Word Work Vocabulary High-Frequency Words Spelling	🔊 **Dictionary Entry Words** T 🔊 **High-Frequency Words:** T *board, listen, told* The Vowel + *r* Sounds T	🔊 **Using a Thesaurus** T 🔊 **High-Frequency Words:** T *between, care, weigh* Words That End with *nd, ng,* or *nk* T	🔊 **Parts of a Dictionary Entry** T 🔊 **High-Frequency Words:** T *ago, field, half, war* More Long *o* Words T
Writing and Oral Language Writing Grammar Listening/Speaking/ Viewing	✏️ **Writing an Invitation** Writing Times T Words for Nouns T Giving a Talk	✏️ **Writing a Poem** Using *I* and *me* T Singular Possessive Nouns T Discussing a Factual Topic	✏️ **A News Article** Adding Details Plural Possessive Nouns T Giving Clear Directions
Cross-Curricular Activities	Responding: Health, Listening and Speaking, Internet Classroom Management Activities	Responding: Math, Art, Internet Classroom Management Activities	Responding: Science, Social Studies, Internet Classroom Management Activities

T Skill tested on Theme Skills Test and/or Integrated Theme Test

Target Skills

Phonics
Comprehension
Vocabulary
Fluency

Monitoring Student Progress	Focus on Genre

Monitoring Student Progress

Check Your Progress
Little Grunt and the Big Egg
Fantasy

Mighty Dinosaurs
Nonfiction

pp. T244–T300

 Phonics Skills Review T

Guiding Comprehension

Theme Connections

 Comprehension Skills Review T

Question T

Taking Tests: Vocabulary Items

Connecting Leveled Readers

Vocabulary Skills Review T

High-Frequency Word Review T

Spelling Skills Review T

✏ **Writing Skills Review** T
Grammar Skills Review T

Cross-Curricular Activities

Classroom Management Activities

Focus on Genre

Biography
pp. T300–T365

Review: *r*-Controlled Vowel Sounds

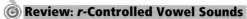 **Review: Word Endings, *-tion*, *-ture***

Guiding Comprehension

Understanding Biographies

Evaluate

Decodable Text: *Where Do I Start?*

Using Text Features

Leveled Readers

Florence Griffith-Joyner
Mae Jemison
Theodore Roosevelt
Florence Griffith-Joyner

Abbreviations

High-Frequency Word Review

The Vowel + *r* Sounds in *for* and *before*

✏ **Write a Biography**
Dates and Time-Order Words

Nouns and Pronouns Together

Making Introductions

Responding: Internet

Classroom Management Activities

Combination Classroom

See the **Combination Classroom Planning Guide** for lesson planning and management support.

Writing Process ▶

Reading-Writing Workshop: Research Report
• Student Writing Model
• Writing Process Instruction
• Writing Traits Focus

Additional Theme Resources

• Theme Big Book Text
• Leveled Theme Paperback Lessons
• Reteaching Lessons
• Challenge/Extension Activities
• Word Wall Cards
• Activity Masters

 **Technology**

Education Place®
www.eduplace.com

Log on to Education Place for more activities relating to *Amazing Animals*.

Lesson Planner CD-ROM
Customize your planning for *Amazing Animals* with the Lesson Planner CD-ROM.

Management Routines

Ongoing Informal Assessment

Valuable information about children's progress can be gathered routinely through ongoing informal assessment. The information you obtain by observing children at work and evaluating the work they produce will allow you to assess children's skill mastery and plan the pace and nature of instruction to meet individual needs.

Observing Children As They Work

There are many opportunities to observe children as they work independently and in cooperative groups.

- Note children's behavior during fluency checks, story retellings, conferences, and group discussions.
- Record your observations using observation checklists or anecdotal records. (Refer to the **Teacher's Assessment Handbook** and **Teacher's Resource Blackline Masters** for helpful assessment checklists and planning guidelines.)

Evaluating Children's Work Samples

Collecting and evaluating children's work samples over the course of the year will give you tangible evidence of their progress. Include samples of written, oral (via tape recordings), and creative work. Review children's work samples periodically, and adjust subsequent instruction.

Managing Informal Assessment

Use these general tips to help manage informal assessment. Specific, skill-related suggestions can be found throughout the **Teacher's Edition** in the Monitoring Student Progress boxes.

Tips for Managing Informal Assessment

- Set goals for what you will assess.
- Plan how often to make notes about each child.
- Add only one new informal assessment method at a time.
- Let children's needs guide your decisions. Not all children need the same types of assessment every time.
- Decide how you will make notes or record observations.
- Record observations while they are still fresh in your mind.

Instructional Routines

Self-Assessment

As children learn to set goals for their own learning, they begin to see how they can improve their work themselves.

- Encourage children to reflect on their reading and writing. Guide them to ask questions such as: *What did I like best about this story (my writing) and why? What was the best part of the activity?*

- Help children learn to evaluate their work. Again, use questions: *What did I do when I came to a word I didn't know? Does the story make sense? Did I use descriptive words in my writing?*

- Refer to features in the Teacher's Edition and Practice Book to help children assess their work. Self-assessment questions are provided after each reading selection and as part of each Reading-Writing Workshop.

- Refer to the **Teacher's Assessment Handbook** for additional ideas.

Monitoring Student Progress

End-of-Selection Assessment

Selection Test Use the test on pages 119–120 in the **Teacher's Resource Blackline Masters** to assess selection comprehension and vocabulary.

Student Self-Assessment Have children assess their reading with questions such as

- How did making predictions as I read help me understand the story?

- What parts of the story were difficult for me? Why?

- What did I like best about this story? Why?

Word Play

Use word games to help children practice vocabulary, spelling, and phonics skills and improve their reasoning and memory while they work cooperatively.

Word Matches Children place cards face down randomly. They take turns revealing two card faces to find a matching pair, for example, two copies of the same word, two words with the same spelling patterns, or a word and its meaning.

Word Hunts Children search Anthologies and other texts to find words that exemplify a target skill such as a spelling pattern or phonic element.

Word Sorts Children sort words into categories that are meaning or skill based. Suggest that children sort words in more than one way, coming up with new categories and explaining how the words are alike.

officer

teacher

firefighter

Gloria

bat

ant

Cross-Curricular Activities

Independent Activities

Assign these activities at any time during the theme while you work with small groups.

Independent Activities

- Challenge/Extension Activities, Theme Resources, pp. R11, R13, R15, R17, R19, R21, R23, R25, R27, R29, R31

- **Classroom Management Handbook,** Activity Masters CM4-1–CM4-12

- **Challenge Handbook,** Activity Masters CH4-1–CH4-6

- Theme 4 **Assignment Cards** pp. 1–12, **Teacher's Resource Blackline Masters,** pp. 63–68

- Classroom Management Activities, pp. T28–T29, T114–T115, T184–T185

Look for more activities in the Classroom Management Kit.

Art Center
Thumbprint Animals

🧍 Singles	🕐 30 minutes
Objective	Make animals out of thumbprints.
Materials	Paper, washable ink pad, markers

Making thumbprint animals is fun!

- Press your thumb onto a stamp pad and then onto a piece of paper.

- Put thumbprints close together to make heads and bodies. Use markers to add details such as eyes, ears, mouths, legs, tails, or wings to your animals.

- Display your thumbprint animals in the classroom.

Math Center
Animal Sizes

🧍 Singles	🕐 30 minutes
Objective	Order animals by size.
Materials	Encyclopedia or animal books, drawing paper, colored pencils

Think about the animals in this theme. How big or small are they?

- Divide your paper into three sections.

- Pick five animals of different sizes. If you need to, find this information in an encyclopedia.

- In the first section, draw the animals in any order. Write their names.

- In the second section, draw pictures of those animals from smallest to largest. Write *Smallest to Largest*.

- In the third section, draw pictures of the animals from largest to smallest. Write *Largest to Smallest*.

Consider copying and laminating these activities for use in centers.

Writing Center

Animal Booklet

Groups	🕐 40 minutes
Objective	Make an animal ABC book.
Materials	Animal books, dictionary, drawing paper, stapler, pencil, markers

is for *Aardvark!* Make an animal BC book for a young friend.

Write each letter of the alphabet and the words "is for _____" on separate sheets of paper.

Think of an animal for each letter. Write the animal name on the blank line. Check an animal book or dictionary for the correct spelling. Write a silly sentence about each animal.

Draw a picture of each animal.

Staple the pages together.

Share your animal ABC book.

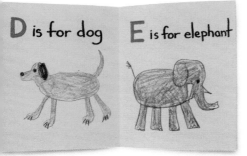

Science Center

Animal Research

Pairs	🕐 30 minutes
Objective	Find out about where animals live.
Materials	Encyclopedia or Internet, index cards, pencils

Animals live in different places, called habitats.

- Pick a habitat where animals live: the forest, ocean, rain forest, plains, or the desert.
- Look this place up in an encyclopedia or on the Internet. Read about the animals that live there.
- Write important facts and information about five animals.
- Share your information.

Music Center

Animal Songs

Groups	🕐 20 minutes
Objective	Sing animal songs.
Materials	Song lyrics

Do you remember *Old MacDonald* and *B-I-N-G-O?* Sing animal songs.

- Choose an animal song from the list below.
- Have each person in the group sing a different verse. Sing some verses together.
- See if you can sing all the songs on the list and more!

Animal Songs
Baby Beluga
B-I-N-G-O
Down by the Bay
The Farmer in the Dell
Old MacDonald

Planning for Assessment

During instruction in Theme 4 . . .

1 SCREENING AND DIAGNOSIS

Screening • Baseline Group Test

Diagnosis • Leveled Reading Passages Assessment Kit
• Phonics/Decoding Screening Test
• Lexia Quick Phonics Assessment CD-ROM

2 MONITORING PROGRESS

Ongoing Informal Assessment	• Guiding Comprehension questions • Literature Discussion groups • Comprehension Checks • Fluency Practice	• Monitoring Student Progress boxes • Writing Samples • Observation Checklists • Skill lesson applications
End-of-Theme Review and Test Preparation	• **Monitoring Student Progress** emphasizes use of comparing and contrasting critical thinking skills, teaches test-taking strategies as preparation for formal assessments, and reviews tested theme skills and reading strategies. • **Assessing Student Progress** provides suggestions for administering formal assessments, identifies areas of difficulty, and lists program resources for differentiating instruction.	
Formal Assessment	• Selection Tests • Integrated Theme Tests • Theme Skills Tests • Fluency Assessment • Reading-Writing Workshop	

3 MANAGING AND REPORTING

Technology Record each child's performance on the **Learner Profile®** CD-ROM.

National Test Correlation
Documenting Adequate Yearly Progress

SKILLS for *Amazing Animals*	ITBS	Terra Nova (CTBS)	CAT	SAT	MAT
Phonics					
• *r*-Controlled Vowel Sounds *ar*	O	O	O	O	O
• Vowel Pairs *oa, ow*		O	O	O	O
• Words with *nd, nt, mp, ng, nk*	O	O	O	O	O
High-Frequency Words					
• High-Frequency Words	O	O	O	O	O
Comprehension Strategies and Skills					
• Strategies: Question, Summarize, Monitor/Clarify*		O	O		O
• Skills: Text Organization, Cause and Effect, Drawing Conclusions, Compare/Contrast*, Fantasy/Realism*, Fact and Opinion*, Problem Solving*	O	O	O	O	O
Vocabulary/Dictionary					
• Dictionary Entry Words, Parts of a Dictionary Entry					
• Using a Thesaurus	O	O	O	O	O
Information and Study Skills					
• Using a Glossary					
• Using Directions*			O		
Spelling					
• The Vowel + *r* Sounds in *car*	O	O	O	O	O
• More Long *o* Words	O	O	O	O	O
• Words That End with *nd, ng,* or *nk*		O	O	O	O
Grammar					
• Words for Nouns			O		
• Nouns: Singular Possessive and Plural Possessive				O	O
Writing					
• Formats: Writing an Invitation, a Poem, a News Article		O			O
• Writing Times of Day					
• Using *I* and *Me*		O	O	O	O
• Reading-Writing Workshop: Research Report					

*These skills are taught, but not tested, in this theme.

KEY

ITBS Iowa Tests of Basic Skills

Terra Nova (CTBS) Comprehensive Tests of Basic Skills

CAT California Achievement Tests

SAT Stanford Achievement Tests

MAT Metropolitan Achievement Tests

Theme 4

Amazing Animals

The Animal Song

Alligator, hedgehog, anteater, bear,
Rattlesnake, buffalo, anaconda, hare.

Mud turtle, whale, glowworm, bat,
Salamander, snail, and Maltese cat.

Polecat, dog, wild otter, rat,
Pelican, hog, dodo, and bat.

Anonymous

10   11

Introducing the Theme: Discussion Options

Read aloud the theme title and poem on Anthology page 11. Explain that "The Animal Song" is a poem written by an unknown author. Point out that the poet develops a pattern of rhythm and rhyme using only animal names. Ask:

1 What might you read about in a theme called *Amazing Animals?*
(animals that look amazing or do amazing things)

2 Name some amazing things that animals can really do.
(Sample responses: Penguins "fly" underwater; seeing-eye dogs help blind people; kangaroos carry their young in pouches.)

3 Think of some famous storybook animals. What makes them amazing?
(Responses will vary but should include details and information related to storybook animals.)

Amazing Animals

with Joseph Bruchac

Hello My Friends,

Isn't it fun to watch animals? Sometimes they do things that amaze us. Here's a poem about my dog Toni, who found some new friends in our backyard pond. What's amazing about that? You'll see!

Frog Dog

Our poodle likes
to play with frogs,
she doesn't like to swim.

The frogs leap
right on out to her,
as if to invite her in.

She waits beside
our garden pond
for hours every day.

We shake our heads
and wonder why
those frogs behave that way.

She barks and barks
when they're not there
as if she wants to say,
"Come on you guys,
I'm waiting,
this puppy's here to play."

12

13

Building Theme Connections

Read aloud Anthology page 12. Tell children that Joseph Bruchac wrote *The Great Ball Game,* a selection that they will read later in this theme. (See Teacher's Edition page T202 for more information about Joseph Bruchac.)

Ask volunteers to read aloud Anthology pages 13–14. Use the following questions to prompt discussion about the author's letter and poem.

1 What is so amazing about Toni, Joseph Bruchac's poodle?
(She likes to play with frogs.)

2 Joseph Bruchac wrote a poem to tell about his amazing dog. What makes a poem a good choice for telling about Toni?
(Sample responses: Rhyming words make the story fun to read; the lines sound playful like Toni and the frogs.)

3 How do you think Toni and the frogs play together?
(Answers will vary.)

Home Connection

Send home the theme letter for *Amazing Animals* to introduce the theme and suggest home activities. (See the **Teacher's Resource Blackline Masters.**)

For other suggestions relating to *Amazing Animals,* see **Home/Community Connections.**

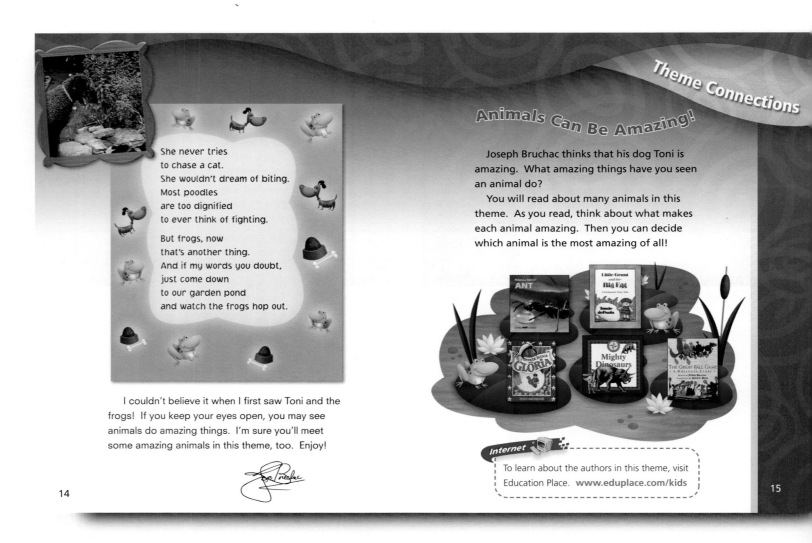

She never tries
to chase a cat.
She wouldn't dream of biting.
Most poodles
are too dignified
to ever think of fighting.

But frogs, now
that's another thing.
And if my words you doubt,
just come down
to our garden pond
and watch the frogs hop out.

I couldn't believe it when I first saw Toni and the frogs! If you keep your eyes open, you may see animals do amazing things. I'm sure you'll meet some amazing animals in this theme, too. Enjoy!

14

Animals Can Be Amazing!

Joseph Bruchac thinks that his dog Toni is amazing. What amazing things have you seen an animal do?

You will read about many animals in this theme. As you read, think about what makes each animal amazing. Then you can decide which animal is the most amazing of all!

Internet To learn about the authors in this theme, visit Education Place. **www.eduplace.com/kids**

15

Building Theme Connections, continued

Have volunteers read aloud Anthology page 15.

- Have children discuss how Toni and the frogs act. Then ask what amazing things children have seen different animals do.
- Brainstorm with children a list of animals and the amazing things they can do. Post the list so children can refer to it while working on this theme.

Read aloud the Theme Big Book *From Caterpillar to Butterfly*.
(See also pages R2–R3 for the text.)

- Discuss with children what amazing things happen to the caterpillar.
- Elicit from children that they also grow and change. Talk about the things they can do now that they could not do when they were younger and smaller.

Making Selection Connections

Use the Anthology to introduce the Selection Connections. Allow children time to look ahead at each selection in this theme to predict what they might learn about amazing animals.

- Have students complete **Practice Book** page 1.
- Preview the **Graphic Organizer** on **Practice Book** page 2. Read aloud the directions, column heads, and selection titles. Explain to children that they will add to the chart after reading each story in *Amazing Animals*.

Classroom Management

Assign the independent cross-curricular activities on Teacher's Edition pages T12–T13 while you give differentiated instruction to small groups. For additional independent activities related to specific selections, see the Teacher's Edition pages listed below.

- Week 1: pages T28–T29
- Week 2: pages T114–T115
- Week 3: pages T184–T185

Monitoring Student Progress

Monitoring Progress

Throughout the theme, monitor children's progress by using the following program features in the Teacher's Edition:

- Guiding Comprehension questions
- Literature discussion groups
- Skill lesson applications
- Monitoring Student Progress boxes

Wrapping Up and Reviewing the Theme

Use **Monitoring Student Progress** on pages T244–T297 to review theme skills, connect and compare theme literature, and prepare children for the Integrated Theme Test and the Theme Skills Test, as well as for standardized tests measuring adequate yearly progress.

Practice Book page 1

Launching the Theme
Selection Connections

Name _____

Amazing Animals

Name some animals that you think are amazing.
Then list words that describe these animals. Sample answers shown.

Animal	Describing Words
cat	clever

Write a description that tells about your favorite amazing animal.
Use one of your describing words in the title. (5 points)

Cats Are Clever

Practice Book page 2

Launching the Theme
Selection Connections

Name _____

Amazing Animals

Fill in the chart as you read the stories. Sample answers shown.

	What animals appear in this theme?	What amazing things do these animals do?
Officer Buckle and Gloria	a police dog named Gloria (1 point)	Gloria does funny tricks on stage. (1)
Ant	many types of ants (1)	Ants build ant bridges and grow their own food. (1)
The Great Ball Game	birds, a bear, a bat (1)	The birds and the animals play a ball game; the bat helps the animals win the game. (1)

Lesson Overview

Literature

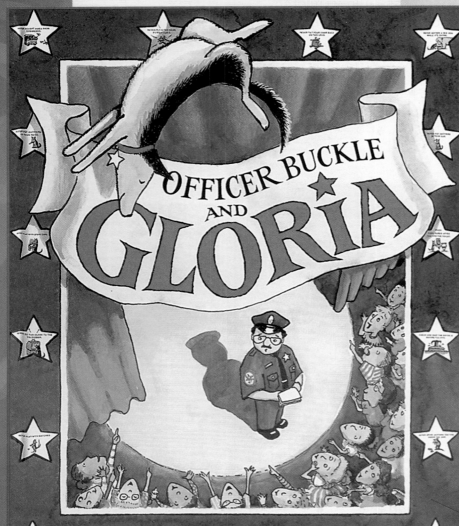

OFFICER BUCKLE AND GLORIA

PEGGY RATHMANN

Selection Summary

Napville Elementary School's students always ignore Officer Buckle's safety tips, until a police dog named Gloria accompanies him when he gives safety speeches.

1 Decodable Text

Phonics Library

- *A Park for Parkdale*
- *Arthur's Book*

2 Background and Vocabulary

Get Set to Read

Background and Vocabulary

Officer Buckle and Gloria

Read to find the meanings of these words.

Glossary
attention
audience
officers
safety

Safety Officers

Police **officers** who visit schools to talk about **safety** are sometimes called safety officers. In the story you're going to read next, an officer and his partner give safety speeches at an elementary school. Like the **audience** in this story, you should always pay close **attention** to a safety officer's speech. He or she will explain many ways to avoid accidents and to stay safe.

3 Main Selection

Officer Buckle and Gloria
Genre: Fantasy

4 Social Studies Link

Social Studies Link

The Story of Owney

from *Postal Pack for Elementary School Students, National Postal Museum and Smithsonian Institution*

Skill: How to Read a Map
- Look for a **key**, or **legend**, that shows what the symbols or colors on the map mean.
- Use the **compass rose** to find the directions of north, south, east, and west.
- Read the **labels** to find cities, states, countries, or other places the map shows.

More than one hundred years ago, a little dog wandered into a post office and made himself at home among the mailbags. He loved traveling with the mail. Once, when a mailbag accidentally fell off a cart, Owney stayed with the bag to protect it until the postal clerks came back to fetch it.

Owney became a famous dog. He jumped onto mail trains whenever he liked. The clerks loved having him along because he was a good luck charm. There was never a railroad accident when Owney was aboard. Wherever he went, postal clerks made a dog tag for him, so others would know where he had traveled. The National Postal Museum has more than one thousand Owney tags that show all the places Owney visited.

These are just some of the cities Owney visited.

Owney loved to ride in the mail cars.

Instructional Support

Planning and Practice

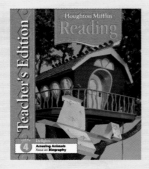

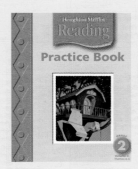

- Planning and Classroom Management
- Reading and skill instruction
- Materials for reaching all learners

Teacher's Resource Blackline Masters

- Newsletters
- Selection Summaries
- Assignment Cards
- Observation Checklists
- Selection Tests

- Independent practice for skills

- Decodable Text, Books 34, 37–39

Instruction Transparencies/Masters and Strategy Posters

- Charts/ Transparencies
- Strategy Posters
- Blackline Masters

Reaching All Learners

Coordinated lessons, activities, and projects for additional reading instruction

For
- Classroom Teacher
- Extended Day
- Pull Out
- Resource Teacher
- Reading Specialist

Technology

Audio Selection

Officer Buckle and Gloria

Get Set for Reading CD-ROM
- Background building
- Vocabulary support
- Selection Summary in English and Spanish

Accelerated Reader®
- Practice quiz for the selection

www.eduplace.com

Log on to Education Place® for more activities related to the selection, including vocabulary support—
  e • Glossary
  e • WordGame

Leveled Books for Reaching All Learners

Leveled Readers and Leveled Practice

- Independent reading for building fluency
- Topic, comprehension strategy, and vocabulary linked to main selection
- Lessons in Teacher's Edition, pages T90–T93
- Leveled practice for every book

Technology

Leveled Readers
Audio available

Book Adventure®
- Practice quizzes for the Leveled Theme Paperbacks
www.bookadventure.org

● BELOW LEVEL

Max the Pet Show Star
by Michele Perreault
illustrated by Richard Hoit

● Below Level Practice

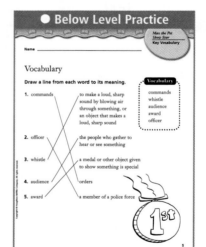

● Below Level Practice

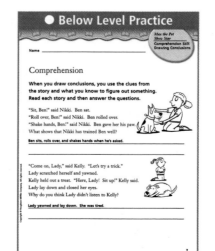

▲ ON LEVEL

The Best Job for Scooter
by Ryan Fadus   illustrated by Barry Gott

▲ On Level Practice

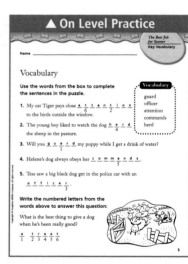

▲ On Level Practice

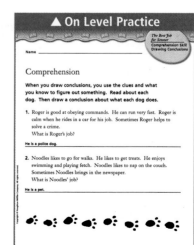

■ ABOVE LEVEL

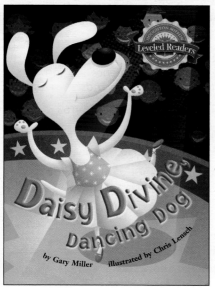

Daisy Divine, Dancing Dog
by Gary Miller   illustrated by Chris Lensch

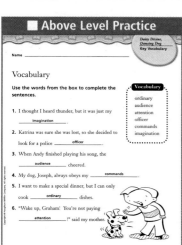

■ Above Level Practice

Daisy Divine, Dancing Dog
Key Vocabulary

Name _____

Vocabulary

Use the words from the box to complete the sentences.

Vocabulary
ordinary
audience
attention
officer
commands
imagination

1. I thought I heard thunder, but it was just my _____ imagination.

2. Katrina was sure she was lost, so she decided to look for a police _____ officer.

3. When Andy finished playing his song, the _____ audience cheered.

4. My dog, Joseph, always obeys my _____ commands.

5. I want to make a special dinner, but I can only cook _____ ordinary dishes.

6. "Wake up, Graham! You're not paying _____ attention!" said my mother.

5

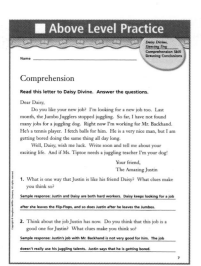

■ Above Level Practice

Daisy Divine, Dancing Dog
Comprehension Skill
Drawing Conclusions

Name _____

Comprehension

Read this letter to Daisy Divine. Answer the questions.

Dear Daisy,

Do you like your new job? I'm looking for a new job too. Last month, the Jumbo Jugglers stopped juggling. So far, I have not found many jobs for a juggling dog. Right now I'm working for Mr. Backhand. He's a tennis player. I fetch balls for him. He is a very nice man, but I am getting bored doing the same thing all day long.

Well, Daisy, wish me luck. Write soon and tell me about your exciting life. And if Ms. Tiptoe needs a juggling teacher I'm your dog!

Your friend,
The Amazing Justin

1. What is one way that Justin is like his friend Daisy? What clues make you think so?

Sample response: Justin and Daisy are both hard workers. Daisy keeps looking for a job after she leaves the Flip-Flops, and so does Justin after he leaves the Jumbos.

2. Think about the job Justin has now. Do you think that this job is a good one for Justin? What clues make you think so?

Sample response: Justin's job with Mr. Backhand is not very good for him. The job doesn't really use his juggling talents. Justin says that he is getting bored.

7

◆ LANGUAGE SUPPORT

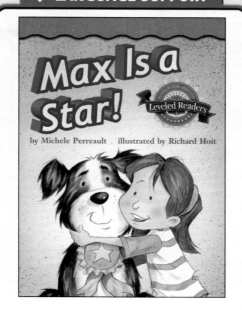

Max Is a Star!
by Michele Perreault   illustrated by Richard Hoit

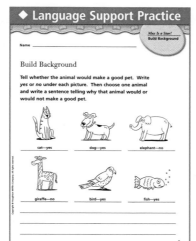

◆ Language Support Practice

Max Is a Star!
Build Background

Name _____

Build Background

Tell whether the animal would make a good pet. Write yes or no under each picture. Then choose one animal and write a sentence telling why that animal would or would not make a good pet.

cat—yes   dog—yes   elephant—no

giraffe—no   bird—yes   fish—yes

_____
_____
_____

5

◆ Language Support Practice

Max Is a Star!
Key Vocabulary

Name _____

Vocabulary

Use the words in the box to fill in the award.

Vocabulary
juggle
jump
officer
pet show
star
whistle

AWARD

Cute Cat can:
☑ _____ whistle
☑ _____ jump
☑ _____ juggle

Cute Cat is the _____ star of the _____ pet show !

Signed _____ Officer _____ Jim.

6

Leveled Theme Paperbacks

- Extended independent reading in theme-related paperbacks
- Lessons in Teacher's Edition, pages R4–R9

Sandy Goes to the Vet
by Becky Cheston
illustrated by Kathryn Mitter

Houghton Mifflin

Below Level

RAPTORS!
Written by Lisa McCourt
Illustrated by Monika Popowitz

On Level

RUSSELL E. ERICKSON
A Toad for Tuesday

Above Level

Daily Lesson Plans

 Technology

Lesson Planner CD-ROM allows you to customize the chart below to develop your own lesson plans.

T Skill tested on Theme Skills Test and/or Integrated Theme Test

DAILY LESSON PLANS

WEEK 1

	80–90 minutes	**DAY 1**	**DAY 2** 
Reading **Phonics** **Comprehension**	 **Leveled Readers** • Fluency Practice • Independent Reading	**Daily Routines,** T30–T31 Phonics and Language Activities **Listening Comprehension,** T32–T33 *Xero and Officer Mike: Police Partners* **Phonics,** T34–T35 r-Controlled Vowel *ar* **T** r-Controlled Vowels *or, ore* **T** **Reading Decodable Text,** T37–T39 *A Park for Parkdale* 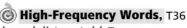**Leveled Readers** *Max the Pet Show Star* *The Best Job for Scooter* *Daisy Divine, Dancing Dog* *Max Is a Star!* Lessons and Leveled Practice, T90–T93	**Daily Routines,** T42–T43 Phonics and Language Activities Building Background, T44 **Key Vocabulary,** T45 accident audience officer attention commands safety **Reading the Selection,** T46–T63 **Comprehension Strategy,** T46 Monitor/Clarify **Comprehension Skill,** T46, T52 Drawing Conclusions **T** **Leveled Readers** *Max the Pet Show Star* *The Best Job for Scooter* *Daisy Divine, Dancing Dog* *Max Is a Star!* Lessons and Leveled Practice, T90–T93
Word Work **Vocabulary** **High-Frequency Words** **Spelling**	20–30 minutes	**Vocabulary,** T31 Using Guide Words **High-Frequency Words,** T36 *board, listen, told* **T** **Spelling,** T40 The Vowel + *r* Sounds in *car* **T**	**Vocabulary,** T43 Dramatize Action Words **High-Frequency Words,** T42 Word Wall **Spelling,** T64 Review, Practice: The Vowel + *r* Sounds in *car*
Writing and Oral Language **Writing** **Grammar** **Listening/Speaking/Viewing**	20–30 minutes	**Writing,** T31 Daily Writing Prompt **Grammar,** T41 Words for Nouns **T** **Daily Language Practice** 1. Sam green drives a bright red carr. (Sam Green drives a bright red car.) **Listening/Speaking/Viewing,** T32–T33 Teacher Read Aloud	**Writing,** T65 An Invitation **Grammar,** T64 Practice: Words for Nouns **T** **Daily Language Practice** 2. I see three dog at the parck. (I see three dogs at the park.) **Listening/Speaking/Viewing,** T56, T63 Stop and Think, Wrapping Up

 A Park for Parkdale
by Patty Moynahan
Illustrated by Nathanie Thornburgh

Parkdale is a very nice town. It has houses and farms and stores. It has a market that sells nearly everything. It is a fine town, except for one thing. Parkdale has no park.

T24   **THEME 4: Amazing Animals**

Target Skills of the Week

Phonics	*r*-Controlled Vowels *ar, or, ore*
Comprehension	Drawing Conclusions; Monitor/Clarify
Vocabulary	High-Frequency Words; Dictionary Entry Words
Fluency	Decodable Text; Leveled Readers

DAY 3

Daily Routines, T66–T67
Phonics and Language Activities

Rereading the Selection, T46–T63

Comprehension Check, T68
Responding, T68

Comprehension Skill, T70–T71
Drawing Conclusions **T**

Reading for Understanding, T72
Visual Literacy: Illustrator's Craft
Genre Lesson: Fantasy

Leveled Readers
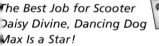
Max the Pet Show Star
The Best Job for Scooter
Daisy Divine, Dancing Dog
Max Is a Star!

Lessons and Leveled Practice, T90–T93

Vocabulary, T67
Word-Learning Strategies

High-Frequency Words, T66
Word Wall

Spelling, T73
Vocabulary Connection: The Vowel + *r* Sounds in *car* **T**

Writing, T68
Write a Thank-You Letter

Grammar, T73
Activity: Words for Nouns **T**

Daily Language Practice
3. A tree in my yared has five peaches on them.
(A tree in my yard has five peaches on it.)

Listening/Speaking/Viewing, T68
Responding

DAY 4

Daily Routines, T74–T75
Phonics and Language Activities

Reading the Social Studies Link, T76–T77

Comprehension: How to Read a Map, T76

Phonics Review, T79
Common Syllables, *-tion, -ture*

Reading Decodable Text, T80–T81
Arthur's Book

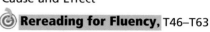
Arthur's Book
by Patty Meynaker
Illustrated by John Manders

Leveled Readers

Max the Pet Show Star
The Best Job for Scooter
Daisy Divine, Dancing Dog
Max Is a Star!

Lessons and Leveled Practice, T90–T93

Vocabulary, T78
Dictionary Entry Words **T**

High-Frequency Words, T74
Word Wall

Spelling, T82
Game, Proofreading:
The Vowel + *r* Sounds in *car* **T**

Writing, T83
Writing Times of Day **T**

Grammar, T82
Practice: Words for Nouns **T**

Daily Language Practice
4. Ten mans pick corn at the ferm.
(Ten men pick corn at the farm.)

Listening/Speaking/Viewing, T76
Discuss the Link

DAY 5

Daily Routines, T84–T85
Phonics and Language Activities

Comprehension: Rereading for Understanding, T86
Fantasy and Realism
Cause and Effect

Rereading for Fluency, T46–T63

Cross-Curricular Responding Activities, T69

Information and Study Skill, T87
Interviewing

Leveled Readers
Max the Pet Show Star
The Best Job for Scooter
Daisy Divine, Dancing Dog
Max Is a Star!

Lessons and Leveled Practice, T90–T93

Vocabulary, T85
Vocabulary Expansion

High-Frequency Words, T84
Word Wall

Spelling, T88
Test: The Vowel + *r* Sounds in *car* **T**

Writing, T85
Daily Writing Prompt

Grammar, T88
Improving Writing

Daily Language Practice
5. Them like to play in a baren.
(They like to play in a barn.)

Listening/Speaking/Viewing, T89
Giving a Talk

Managing Flexible Groups

Leveled Instruction and Leveled Practice

	DAY 1	DAY 2
WHOLE CLASS	• Daily Routines (TE pp. T30–T31) • Teacher Read Aloud (TE pp. T32–T33) • Phonics lesson (TE pp. T34–T35) • High-Frequency Words lesson (TE p. T36)	• Daily Routines (TE pp. T42–T43) • Get Set to Read, Strategy and Skill, Purpose Setting (TE pp. T44–T47) ***After Reading at Small Group Time*** • Wrapping Up (TE p. T63)
SMALL GROUPS		
Extra Support	**TEACHER-LED** • Read Phonics Library: *A Park for Parkdale.* (TE pp. T37–T39) • Selected I Love Reading Books: 34, 36–39	**TEACHER-LED** • Read Main Selection. (TE pp. T46–T63) **Partner or Individual Reading** • Read with audio CD of Main Selection. • **Fluency Practice** Reread Phonics Library: *A Park for Parkdale* (TE pp. T37–T39) OR selected I Love Reading Books: 34, 36–39.
On Level	**TEACHER-LED** • Reread Transparency 4–2 aloud. (TE p. T36) • Read Phonics Library: *A Park for Parkdale.* (TE pp. T37–T39)	**TEACHER-LED** • Read Main Selection. (TE pp. T46–T63) • Begin Leveled Reader: On Level (TE p. T91) OR book from Bibliography. (TE pp. T6–T7) • **Fluency Practice** Reread Phonics Library: *A Park for Parkdale.* (TE pp. T37–T39) ✔
Challenge	**Partner or Individual Reading** • Read Phonics Library: *A Park for Parkdale.* (TE pp. T37–T39)	**Partner or Individual Reading** • Read Main Selection. (TE pp. T46–T63) • **Fluency Practice** Reread Phonics Library: *A Park for Parkdale.* (TE pp. T37–T39)
English Language Learners	**TEACHER-LED** • Read Phonics Library: *A Park for Parkdale.* (TE pp. T37–T39) • Selected I Love Reading Books: 34, 36–39	**TEACHER-LED** • Selected I Love Reading Books: 34, 36–39 • **Fluency Practice** Reread Phonics Library: *A Park for Parkdale.* (TE pp. T37–T39) ✔ **Partner or Individual Reading** • Read with audio CD of Main Selection.

Independent Activities

• Get Set for Reading CD-ROM OR audio CD of Anthology selection.
• Journals: selection notes, questions.
• Complete, review **Practice Book** (pp. 3–7, 11–13) and **Leveled Reader Practice Blackline Masters.** (TE pp. T90–T93)
• Assignment Cards. (**Teacher's Resource Blackline Masters** pp. 63–64)

✔ Opportunity to informally assess oral reading rate.

• Daily Routines (TE pp. T66–T67)	• Daily Routines (TE pp. T74–T75)	• Daily Routines (TE pp. T84–T85)
After Reading at Small Group Time	• Link (TE pp. T76–T77)	• Comprehension Review lesson (TE p. T86)
• Responding (TE p. T68)	• Phonics Review (TE pp. T79)	• Information and Study Skill (TE p. T87)
• Comprehension lesson (TE pp. T70–T71)		• Responding: select from activities (TE p. T69)
• Rereading for Understanding (TE p. T72)		

TEACHER-LED

• Read aloud from Main Selection to answer Guiding Comprehension. (TE pp. T46–T63)
• Begin Leveled Reader: Below Level (TE p. T90) OR book from Bibliography. (TE pp. T6–T7)

Partner or Individual Reading

• **Fluency Practice** Selected I Love Reading Books: 34, 36–39

Partner or Individual Reading

• Reread Main Selection. (TE pp. T46–T63)
• Complete Leveled Reader: On Level (TE p. T91) OR book from Bibliography. (TE pp. T6–T7)
• **Fluency Practice** Selected I Love Reading Books: 34, 36–39

TEACHER-LED

• Read aloud from Main Selection to answer Guiding Comprehension. (TE pp. T46–T63) ✔
• Begin Leveled Reader: Above Level (TE p. T92) OR book from Bibliography. (TE pp. T6–T7)

Partner or Individual Reading

• Complete Leveled Reader: Above Level (TE p. T92) OR book from Bibliography. (TE pp. T6–T7)

TEACHER-LED

• Reread Main Selection. (TE pp. T46–T63)

Partner or Individual Reading

• Selected I Love Reading Books: 34, 36–39

TEACHER-LED

• Read Phonics Library: *Arthur's Book.* (TE pp. T80–T81)
• Complete Leveled Reader: Below Level (TE p. T90) OR book from Bibliography. (TE pp. T6–T7)
• **Fluency Practice** Reread Phonics Library: *Arthur's Book* (TE pp. T80–T81) OR Leveled Reader: Below Level. (TE p. T90) ✔

TEACHER-LED

• Read aloud from Main Selection to answer Guiding Comprehension. (TE pp. T46–T63)
• Read Phonics Library: *Arthur's Book.* (TE pp. T80–T81)
• **Fluency Practice** Reread Link (TE pp. T76–T77) OR Leveled Reader: On Level. (TE p. T91) ✔

Partner or Individual Reading

• Read Phonics Library: *Arthur's Book.* (TE pp. T80–T81)
• **Fluency Practice** Reread Main Selection and Link (TE pp. T46–T63, T76–T77) AND Phonics Library: *Arthur's Book.* (TE pp. T80–T81)

TEACHER-LED

• Continue Main Selection. (TE pp. T46–T63)
• Begin Leveled Reader: Language Support (TE p. T93) OR On My Way Practice Reader. (TE pp. R4–R5)

Partner or Individual Reading

• **Fluency Practice** Read Phonics Library: *Arthur's Book.* (TE pp. T80–T81)

TEACHER-LED

• Reread Phonics Library: *Arthur's Book.* (TE pp. T80–T81)
• Read the On My Way Practice Reader. (TE pp. R4–R5)
• **Fluency Practice** Reread Phonics Library (TE pp. T37–T39, T80–T81) OR On My Way Practice Reader. (TE pp. R4–R5) ✔

Partner or Individual Reading

• Reread Link. (TE pp. T76–T77)
• Begin Theme Paperback: On Level (TE pp. R6–R7) OR book from Bibliography. (TE pp. T6–T7)
• **Fluency Practice** Reread Main Selection (TE pp. T46–T63) OR Leveled Reader: On Level. (TE p. T91)

TEACHER-LED

• **Fluency Practice** Reread Link (TE pp. T76–T77) OR Leveled Reader: Above Level. (TE p. T92) ✔

Partner or Individual Reading

• Begin Theme Paperback: Above Level (TE pp. R8–R9) OR book from Bibliography. (TE pp. T6–T7)

TEACHER-LED

• Reread Link. (TE pp. T76–T77)
• Complete Leveled Reader: Language Support (TE p. T93) OR On My Way Practice Reader. (TE pp. R4–R5)
• **Fluency Practice** Reread Phonics Library (TE pp. T37–T39, T80–T81). ✔

• Reread familiar selections.
• Read trade book from Leveled Bibliography. (TE pp. T6–T7)
• Responding activities. (TE pp. T68–T69)
• Activities related to *Officer Buckle and Gloria* at Education Place: www.eduplace.com

Turn the page for more independent activities.

FLEXIBLE GROUPS

Officer Buckle and Gloria

Managing Flexible Groups **T27**

Classroom Management

Independent Activities

Assign these activities while you work with small groups.

Differentiated Instruction for Small Groups

- **Handbook for English Language Learners,** pp. 124–133

- **Extra Support Handbook,** pp. 120–129

Additional Independent Activities

- Daily Routines, pp. T30, T42, T66, T74, T84

- Challenge/Extension Activities, pp. R11, R13, R21, R27

- **Classroom Management Handbook,** Activity Masters CM4-1–CM4-4

- **Challenge Handbook,** Activity Masters CH4-1–CH4-2

Look for more activities in the Classroom Management Kit.

Writing Center

You're Invited

👤 Singles	🕐 30 minutes
Objective	Write an invitation.
Materials	Writing paper, pencil, crayons or markers

Officer Buckle gets invitations to speak about safety. Write an invitation asking Officer Buckle and Gloria to come to your school. Follow the form shown below.

Math Center

Guessing Jars

👥 Pairs	🕐 30 minutes
Objective	Estimate and verify large numbers
Materials	Slips of paper, pencil, clear jar, over 25 marbles or small objects

Officer Buckle has jelly beans and dog treats in jars. Make your own jar full of objects.

- Count out over 25 of the same object. Put them in rows of ten for easy counting.

- Write down the exact number of objects on a slip of paper.

- Put the objects in the jar.

- Have classmates guess how many objects are in the jar. Check your slip of paper for the answer!

Consider copying and laminating these activities for use in centers.

Science Center

Animal Match

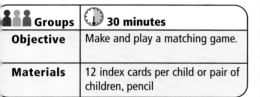 Groups	🕐 30 minutes
Objective	Make and play a matching game.
Materials	12 index cards per child or pair of children, pencil

Gloria is a grown dog. A baby dog is called a puppy.

Make a list of six animals. Find out what their babies are called.

Write the name of each animal and baby on a separate card.

Mix up all twelve cards and place them face-down.

Take turns turning over pairs of cards. Try to match parents with babies. If you make a match, keep the cards. If not, turn the cards back over.

Take turns playing until all the matches are made. The player with the most matches wins.

Technology Center

Safety Tip Research

👥 Pairs	🕐 30 minutes
Objective	Find out about safety tips.
Materials	Computer with Internet access, writing paper, pencil

Read Officer Buckle's safety tips. Learn more about safety.

- Log on to the Internet. Use a search engine that your teacher says is okay.
- Type in *safety tips, child safety,* or *safety.*
- Read the screen. Click on sites that look interesting. Write down interesting facts and tips.
- Make a poster to share your tips. Tell how you got your information.

Health Center

Safety Stars

👤 Singles	🕐 45 minutes
Objective	Make and label paper stars.
Materials	Colored paper, pencils, scissors, markers

Make your own safety stars like the ones in *Officer Buckle and Gloria.*

- Cut out four or five paper stars.
- Write a safety tip on each star.
- Draw a picture to go with each safety tip. The pictures can be funny or serious.
- Hang your stars in your classroom.

Keep wet hands away from outlets.

Day at a Glance
pp. T30–T41

Reading Instruction

Teacher Read Aloud

Phonics Instruction
r-Controlled Vowel *ar*
r-Controlled Vowels *or, ore*

Reading Decodable Text
A Park for Parkdale

. . . .

Leveled Readers, *T90–T93*
- ● *Max the Pet Show Star*
- ▲ *The Best Job for Scooter*
- ■ *Daisy Divine, Dancing Dog*
- ◆ *Max Is a Star!*

Word Work

Vocabulary Review

High-Frequency Words

Spelling: The Vowel + *r* Sounds
in *car*

Writing & Oral Language

Writing Activity

Grammar: Words for Nouns

Listening/Speaking/Viewing

Daily Routines

Daily Message

Phonics Review Point to each word as you read aloud the Daily Message.

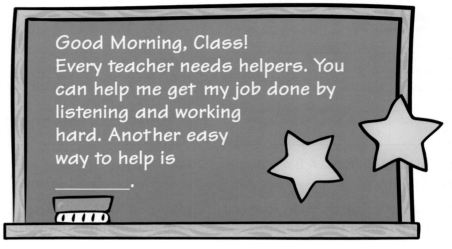

Good Morning, Class!
Every teacher needs helpers. You can help me get my job done by listening and working hard. Another easy way to help is

_____.

Have children
- read the Daily Message, discuss it, and ask volunteers to complete the last sentence;
- find and read aloud words with *ee, ea*. (*teacher, needs, easy*)

Word Wall

High-Frequency Word Review Briefly review these previously taught high-frequency words. Post the words on the Word Wall. Have children practice reading, chanting, spelling, and writing them.

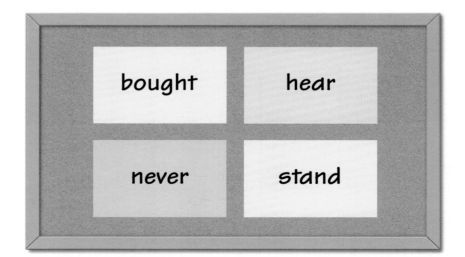

bought   hear

never   stand

Blackline Masters for these word cards appear on p. R35.

Vocabulary

Using Guide Words Review with children that guide words help them find a word in the dictionary.

Write a word from the Anthology glossary. Ask children to use the glossary guide words to find on which page the word appears. Have children stand up when they find the word. Have children identify the guide words on the page where the word appears. Repeat with other words.

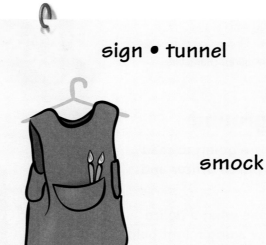

sign • tunnel

smock

Daily Writing Prompt

Have children choose a topic to write about, or have them use the prompt below.

Write an amazing animal poem. Write the letters of its name down on the left side of your paper. Use the letter on each line to begin a sentence or phrase that tells why animals are amazing.

Daily Language Practice

Grammar Skill: Words for Nouns
Spelling Skill: The Vowel + *r* Sounds in *car*

Display **Transparency 4–1.** Ask children to rewrite Sentence 1 correctly. Then model how to write it, and have children check their work.

Transparency 4–1
Daily Language Practice

Day 1

1. Sam green drives a bright red carr.

Sam **Green** drives a bright red **car**.

Day 3
3. A tree in my yared has five peaches on them.

A tree in my **yard** has five peaches on **it**.

Day 4
4. Ten mans pick corn at the ferm.

Ten **men** pick corn at the **farm**.

Day 5
5. Them like to play in a baren.

They like to play in a **barn**.

TRANSPARENCY 4–1
TEACHER'S EDITION PAGES T31, T43, T67, T75, AND T85

Listening Comprehension

Building Background

Tell children that you are going to read aloud a story about a police officer and his dog.

- Have children describe what a police officer does and how a dog might help a police officer.

Fluency Modeling

Explain that as you read aloud, you will be modeling fluent oral reading. Ask children to listen carefully to your phrasing and expression, or tone of voice and emphasis.

COMPREHENSION SKILL

Drawing Conclusions

Explain that

- authors don't always explain everything in a story,
- readers can use story clues to figure out things that are not directly stated.

Purpose Setting Read the story aloud, asking children to think about conclusions they can draw as they listen. Then use the Guiding Comprehension questions to assess children's understanding. Reread the story for clarification as needed.

Teacher Read Aloud

Aero and Officer Mike: Police Partners
by Joan Plummer Russell

❶ It is very early in the morning. Everyone in the house is still asleep. A large black-and-tan German shepherd is lying on the floor by Officer Mike's bed. The alarm rings. Officer Mike reaches down to pet his dog, Aero. Aero is a police dog, also known as a K-9 officer.

Officer Mike and Aero are partners. They work together. They practice together. They play together. They live with Officer Mike's wife and daughter, a cat named Tarzan, and a Chihuahua named Zeus.

Aero, with his powerful nose, can do many things Officer Mike cannot. He can sniff and find lost children. He can sniff and find lost things.

Police dogs are very strong and well trained. They have to be ready to go anywhere they are needed. They can be very fierce when they are helping to catch criminals. They can run faster than any human being. But when police dogs are not working, they are gentle pets that like to have their tummies scratched.

Officer Mike and Aero start their patrol by driving slowly up and down the streets to see if everyone is safe. If a burglar alarm goes off at someone's house, a dispatcher calls Officer Mike on his radio and sends him to that address.

Officer Mike and Aero check all around the house to make sure there has not been a break-in. Sometimes it's a false alarm. They also may be called to a store if a robbery is taking place, or to help control large crowds and keep everyone safe. Whenever an officer answers a call, a second officer is always sent as backup.

Nurses and teachers often write to the chief of police to ask if Aero can visit children in their hospital or their school. Aero likes children and is always gentle with them. He is even gentler when visiting a sick child. He lies down, staying very still and quiet so the child won't be afraid of him.

When Officer Mike and Aero visit schools, Aero rests on the floor beside Officer Mike. Together they demonstrate the different commands Aero will obey. The children ask many questions. Why is there a police badge on Aero's collar? How high can Aero jump? How fast can Aero run?

Officer Mike carefully answers the questions. Aero's **❷** badge shows everyone he is a working police dog. He can jump over an eight-foot wall when he is chasing a criminal. He can run very fast, about forty miles an hour. Even the fastest person can run only about twenty-four miles an hour.

At the end of a twelve-hour work shift, there is always a final job to be done at the police station. After talking with his friends on the force, Officer Mike sits down and writes a report for the police chief about the whole day or night. Aero lies down by Officer Mike's chair. Maybe he's dreaming about his next meal or hoping Officer Mike will change into sweatpants so they can take a long run by the lake.

After the report is written, Officer Mike and Aero go home together and have a meal with Officer Mike's wife and daughter and Tarzan and Zeus.

When Officer Mike takes a shower, Aero follows him into the bathroom and stays by the tub. Aero is always there to protect his partner. When Officer Mike goes to bed, Aero will plop down on the floor near the bed, lay his head on his paws, and with a sigh go to sleep near his best friend. Neither of them knows what surprises tomorrow's patrol will bring, but they are well prepared. They both love being police officers.

CRITICAL THINKING

Guiding Comprehension

❶ DRAWING CONCLUSIONS How does Officer Mike feel about Aero? What makes you think so? (He likes him. He pets Aero in the morning, they work together, they practice together, and they play together.)

❷ DRAWING CONCLUSIONS What makes Aero a good working police dog? (Sample answers: Aero is big, obeys commands, runs fast, and jumps high. He is strong and well trained to help a police officer with his job.)

Discussion Options

Personal Response Ask children to tell whether or not they would like Aero to visit their classroom and why.

⭐ **Connecting/Comparing** Ask children to tell how Aero is an amazing animal.

English Language Learners

Supporting Comprehension

Write a word web with *Aero* in the central circle. Ask students to tell about Aero, in words or by using gestures and pantomime. Ask students questions like What is Aero? (a dog) What is Aero's job? (He is a police dog, or a K-9 officer.) What can Aero do? (He can sniff, run fast, find lost children, and catch criminals.) How high can Aero jump? (over eight feet) Help students with the vocabulary they need to fill in the word web.

OBJECTIVES

- Identify *ar* as spelling the /är/ sound.
- Read and write words with *ar*.

Target Skill Trace

Teach	p. T34
Reteach	p. R10
Review	pp. T161, T262
See	*Handbook for English Language Learners,* p. 125; *Extra Support Handbook,* pp. 120, 126

Materials

- Sound/Spelling Card *artist*
- Blending Routines Card 1

Practice Book page 3

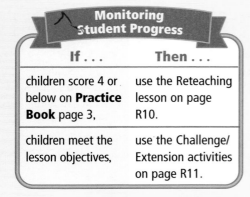

Officer Buckle and Gloria
Phonics Skill *r*-Controlled
Vowel *ar*

Name _____

Missing Letters

Finish each sentence by choosing a letter or letters from each of the stars below. Print those letters on the line to make a word that makes sense in the sentence.

1. Gloria likes to run in the p____ar_k____. (1 point)
2. Gloria b____ar_ks____ every time she sees another dog. (1)
3. Gloria does her p____ar_t____ to teach safety tips. (1)
4. When the children st____ar_t____ to laugh, Gloria is happy. (1)
5. Gloria is not afraid of the d____ar_k____ even when she is all alone. (1)
6. Gloria is one of the st____ar_s____ at school. (1)

Monitoring Student Progress

If . . .	Then . . .
children score 4 or below on **Practice Book** page 3,	use the Reteaching lesson on page R10.
children meet the lesson objectives,	use the Challenge/ Extension activities on page R11.

 TARGET SKILL

PHONICS: *r*-Controlled Vowel *ar*

❶ Phonemic Awareness Warm-Up

Model how to blend phonemes. Say /k/ /är/ /d/. Have children repeat the sounds, blend them, and say the word. (*card*) Repeat with *star* and *smart.*

❷ Teach Phonics

Connect sounds to letters. Write and say *card,* underlining *ar.* Then display the **Sound/Spelling Card.**

- Explain that *a* followed by *r* usually stands for /är/, as in *artist.* Have children blend the sounds to read *card.*

- Write *smart, farm,* and *chart.* Have a child underline the vowel plus *r* as the class says /är/. Help children blend each word.

Model how to decode longer words with *ar*. Write *market* and sound it out. Remind children that every syllable must have a vowel sound.

- Underline *ar.* Explain that these two letters stay together and stand for /är/. Divide *market* into syllables: *mar/ket.*

- Use **Blending Routine 1** to help children blend each syllable and read the word. Repeat with *harvest, barnyard,* and *department.*

har/vest   barn/yard   de/part/ment

❸ Guided Practice

Check understanding. Write *large, spark, partner, harder* and *sharpen.* Have children read each word. Then have them write *march, dark, scar, artist,* and *target.* Display the correctly spelled words. Have children correct any mistakes.

❹ Apply

Assign Practice Book page 3.

PHONICS: *r*-Controlled Vowels *or, ore*

❶ Phonemic Awareness Warm-Up

Model how to blend phonemes. Say /t/ /ôr/ /n/. Have children repeat the sounds, blend them, and say the word. (torn) Repeat with *north* and *store*.

❷ Teach Phonics

Connect sounds to letters. Write *torn* and *more*, underlining *or* and *ore* as you say /ôr/. Display the **Sound/Spelling Card.**

or
ore

- Explain that *o* followed by *r* or *re* usually stands for /ôr/, as in *orange*. Point out these spelling patterns on the card. Help children read *torn* and *more*.

- Write *north, store, porch,* and *snore*. Underline *or* and *ore*. Have children read each word.

Model decoding longer words with *or* and *ore*. Write *orbit* and sound it out using **Blending Routine 1.**

- Underline *or*. Explain that these two letters usually stay together in a syllable.

- Divide *orbit* into syllables: *or/bit*. Help children sound out each syllable and read the word. Repeat with *shortest, ignore,* and *tornado*.

short/est   ig/nore   t or/na/do

❸ Guided Practice

Check understanding. Write *storm, horse, chores, forget,* and *important.* Have children read each word. Then have them write *born, shore, explore,* and *report.* Guide them by pointing to the appropriate vowel spelling pattern on the **Sound/Spelling Card.** Display the words. Have children correct their work.

❹ Apply

Assign Practice Book page 4.

OBJECTIVES

- Identify *or* and *ore* as spelling the /ôr/ sound.
- Read and write words with *or* and *ore.*

Target Skill Trace

Teach	p. T35
Reteach	p. R12
Review	pp. T161, T271
See	*Handbook for English Language Learners,* p. 125; *Extra Support Handbook,* pp. 121, 126–127

Materials

- **Sound/Spelling Card** *orange*
- **Blending Routines Card 1**

Practice Book page 4

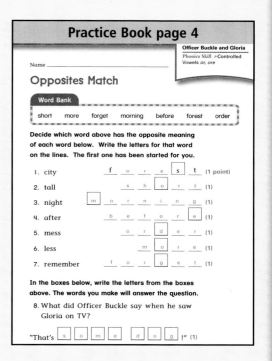

Officer Buckle and Gloria
Phonics Skill *r*-Controlled
Vowels *or, ore*

Name _____

Opposites Match

Word Bank

| short | more | forget | morning | before | forest | order |

Decide which word above has the opposite meaning of each word below. Write the letters for that word on the lines. The first one has been started for you.

1. city   f o r e [s] [t]   (1 point)
2. tall   s h [o] r t   (1)
3. night   [m] o r n i n g [ ]   (1)
4. after   b e f o r [e]   (1)
5. mess   o r d e r   (1)
6. less   m o r e   (1)
7. remember   f o r g e t   (1)

In the boxes below, write the letters from the boxes above. The words you make will answer the question.

8. What did Officer Buckle say when he saw Gloria on TV?

"That's [s] [o] m e [ ] d o g !" (1)

Monitoring Student Progress

If . . .	Then . . .
children score 6 or below on **Practice Book** page 4,	use the Reteaching lesson on page R12.
children meet the lesson objectives,	use the Challenge/ Extension activities on page R13.

OBJECTIVE

● Recognize new high-frequency words:
board   *told*
listen

Target Skill Trace

Teach	p. 36
Reteach	p. R20
Review	p. T42
See	*Handbook for English Language Learners*, pp. 127, 129; *Extra Support Handbook*, p. 124

Materials

● index cards, one high-frequency word per card or Word Wall Cards from page R35.

Transparency 4–2

High-Frequency Words

The teacher wrote safety rules on the <u>board</u>.

We will <u>listen</u> for the fire drill bells.

Officer Ruiz <u>told</u> us about calling 9-1-1.

Mr. Hyde <u>told</u> us to stay in our classrooms.

That <u>board</u> has a nail in it.

Did you <u>listen</u> to the warning?

TRANSPARENCY 4–2
TEACHER'S EDITION PAGE T36

ANNOTATED VERSION

AMAZING ANIMALS Officer Buckle and Gloria
High-Frequency Words

Monitoring Student Progress

If . . .	Then . . .
children score 4 or below on **Practice Book** page 5,	use the Reteaching lesson on page R20.
children are ready for more challenging material,	use the Challenge/ Extension activities on page R21.

HIGH-FREQUENCY WORDS

❶ Teach

Introduce the high-frequency words. Display **Transparency 4–2.**

● Point out the high-frequency word in each of the first three sentences on the transparency. Say the word, and have children repeat it. Read the sentences together.

● Then have volunteers read the underlined word in the remaining sentences. Have children read the sentences together.

● Discuss the two meanings of the word *board*.

❷ Guided Practice

Have children choose a word for each sentence. Write:

1. *The principal* <u>(told)</u> *us who won the school safety award.*

2. *You must* <u>(listen)</u> *carefully to the safety rules.*

3. *Be careful when you hammer a nail into a* <u>(board)</u>.

● Have children tell which high-frequency word belongs in each sentence. Write the word in the sentence and read it together.

● Post the new words on the Word Wall. Have children write a sentence for each high-frequency word.

❸ Apply

Assign Practice Book page 5.

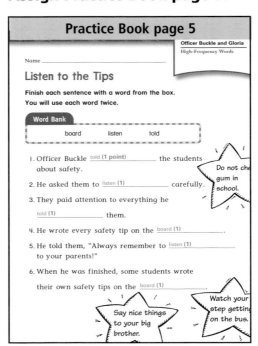

Practice Book page 5

Officer Buckle and Gloria
High-Frequency Words

Name _____

Listen to the Tips

Finish each sentence with a word from the box.
You will use each word twice.

Word Bank

board   listen   told

1. Officer Buckle <u>told (1 point)</u> the students about safety.

2. He asked them to <u>listen (1)</u> carefully.

3. They paid attention to everything he <u>told (1)</u> them.

4. He wrote every safety tip on the <u>board (1)</u>.

5. He told them, "Always remember to <u>listen (1)</u> to your parents!"

6. When he was finished, some students wrote their own safety tips on the <u>board (1)</u>.

Do not che gum in school.

Watch your step getting on the bus.

Say nice things to your big brother.

Phonics Library

HOUGHTON MIFFLIN
Reading

Amazing Animals

A Park for Parkdale

by Patty Moynahan
illustrated by Bethann Thornburgh

Parkdale is a very nice town. It has houses and farms and stores. It has a market that sells nearly everything. It is a fine town, except for one thing. Parkdale has no park.

1

1

At the town meeting, Bart Horn stood up. "I have something important to say this morning," he told the town board. "We feel that a town named Parkdale needs a park."

Doctor Short nodded. So did Miss Martin.

2

"Pardon me," said Cora Barkway, "but how will we pay for this park? We will need land. We will need someone to tend to this park."

The people began to think. Then Bart had an idea.

3

3

Word Key

Decodable words with *ar, or, ore* _____

High-Frequency Words _____

TARGET SKILL **PHONICS LIBRARY**

Reading Decodable Text

OBJECTIVES

- Apply the Phonics/Decoding Strategy to decode words in context.
- Recognize high-frequency words in context.
- Reread to build fluency.

Have children preview *A Park for Parkdale*. Ask them to predict how Parkdale got its park.

Model the Phonics/Decoding Strategy. Review the strategy. Then point to *Parkdale* in the story title.

Think Aloud *I see a long word in the title. It has a shorter word I know,* park. *The next part has the* a-consonant-e *pattern, so it probably has a long vowel sound and a silent* e. *I blend the sounds to say /dāl/. When I put the parts together, I read* Parkdale. *That's probably the name of a place.*

Apply the Phonics/Decoding Strategy. Have children read *A Park for Parkdale* with partners. Remind them to use the Phonics/Decoding Strategy.

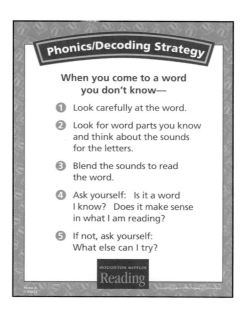

Phonics/Decoding Strategy

When you come to a word you don't know—

1. Look carefully at the word.
2. Look for word parts you know and think about the sounds for the letters.
3. Blend the sounds to read the word.
4. Ask yourself: Is it a word I know? Does it make sense in what I am reading?
5. If not, ask yourself: What else can I try?

HOUGHTON MIFFLIN
Reading

Reading Decodable Text T37

Prompts for Decoding

Support children as they read.
Use prompts such as these to help children with words such as *important* (page 2):

- Scan the word. Do you see any word parts you know?
- This word has three parts, or syllables. Sound out the parts and say the word.
- Read the sentence. Does the word make sense?

Oral Language

Discuss the story. Ask children to answer the questions in complete sentences.

- What does Bart say the town needs? (The town needs a park.)
- Who does Bart tell about his plan? (He tells the town board.) What does the word *board* mean here? (*Board* means a group of people who are in charge of something.)
- Who helps make the new park? (Many people in the town help make the park.)
- Why is the mayor of Parkdale proud? (He is proud that so many people worked together to help make a nice, new park.)

"Listen!" said Bart. "We will work together to make this park."
The people liked this smart plan.
"We'll start right now!" said Bart. "I know a good spot for our park."

4

Bart led everyone to an old, weedy lot. "Let's make a park!" he shouted.
Doctor Short and others cleaned up trash. Miss Martin planted a garden. More and more people came to help.

5

4

On March first, Parkdale Park opened. People ate and played and had fun. The mayor made a speech.

He said, "We are proud. See what can happen when everyone helps out!"

6

Parkdale is a very nice town. It has houses and farms and stores and a market.

And now it has a park!

7

 Build Fluency

Model fluent reading.

- Read aloud page 1. Have children read aloud the same page.

- Have children look at page 2. Have them point to the words a character speaks. Remind them that those words are enclosed by quotation marks.

- Have a volunteer tell who is speaking. Model reading the words with expression, then have children repeat.

- Repeat with the remaining pages.

Have children practice fluent reading.
Have groups of three reread the story as a Readers' Theater.

- Have one child read the narrator's words, another child read Bart's words, and the third child read the words spoken by other characters.

- Have children switch parts twice. Encourage them to read smoothly and with good expression.

Home Connection

Hand out the take-home version of *A Park for Parkdale*. Ask children to reread the story with their families. (See the **Phonics Library Blackline Masters**.)

OBJECTIVE

- Write spelling words with the vowel + *r* sound in *car.*

SPELLING WORDS

Basic

car	barn
smart	hard
arm	party
park*	farm
yard	are *†
part	warm†

Review	**Challenge**
start*	department*
far	carpet

* Forms of these words appear in the literature.
† These words are exceptions to the principle.

REACHING ALL LEARNERS

Extra Support/ Intervention

Basic Word List Use only Basic Words 1–5, words with daggers, and the Review Words with children who have difficulty with this spelling principle.

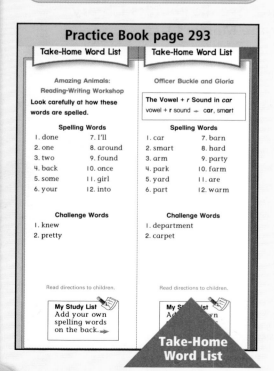

Practice Book page 293

Take-Home Word List	Take-Home Word List
Amazing Animals: Reading-Writing Workshop	Officer Buckle and Gloria
Look carefully at how these words are spelled.	**The Vowel + *r* Sound in *car*** vowel + r sound → car, smart
Spelling Words	**Spelling Words**
1. done 7. I'll	1. car 7. barn
2. one 8. around	2. smart 8. hard
3. two 9. found	3. arm 9. party
4. back 10. once	4. park 10. farm
5. some 11. girl	5. yard 11. are
6. your 12. into	6. part 12. warm
Challenge Words	**Challenge Words**
1. knew	1. department
2. pretty	2. carpet
Read directions to children.	Read directions to children.
My Study List Add your own spelling words on the back.→	**My Study List** Add your own

Take-Home Word List

SPELLING: The Vowel + *r* Sounds in *car*

❶ Teach the Principle

Pretest Say each sentence. Have children write only the underlined word.

Basic Words

1. Our **car** had a flat tire.
2. My dog is very **smart**.
3. I broke my **arm**.
4. We play ball in the **park**.
5. Trees grow in my **yard**.
6. A leaf is **part** of a tree.
7. The cow is in the **barn**.
8. That old bun is **hard**.
9. Taj came to my **party**.
10. Sheep live on a **farm**.
11. They **are** sleeping.
12. The sun is **warm**.

Challenge Words

13. We visited the police **department**.
14. The floor is covered with a **carpet**.

Teach Write *car* and *smart,* underlining *ar.*

- Say each word and have children repeat it.
- Explain that the letter *a* in each word is followed by *r*, so the letters are pronounced as /är/.
- Have children repeat /är/. Remind them that /är/ is spelled *ar.*

Write *are* and *warm.* Say these words and have children repeat them.

- Point out that *warm* has the *ar* spelling pronounced /ôr/.
- Explain that *are* is pronounced /är/ but has the *a*-consonant-e pattern.

❷ Practice

Write *arm, park, yard, part, barn, hard, party,* and *farm.*

- Say each word and have children repeat it.
- Write *ar* on the board. Choose children to add letters to this spelling pattern to spell one of the Basic Words. Repeat until all the Basic Words have been spelled.

❸ Apply

Practice/Homework Assign **Practice Book** page 293, the Take-Home Word List.

GRAMMAR: Words for Nouns

OBJECTIVES
- Identify pronouns.
- Learn academic language: *noun, pronoun.*

❶ Teach

Read aloud the first two sentences on Transparency 4–3.

- Point out the name *Officer Buckle* in the first sentence.
- Explain that in the second sentence, the name *Officer Buckle* is replaced by the pronoun *He.*

Go over these points.

- A noun names a person, place, or thing.
- A pronoun is a word that can take the place of a noun.

❷ Practice

Check children's understanding. Ask children to read aloud each remaining pair of sentences on **Transparency 4–3.** For each pair, have children identify the pronoun in the second sentence and tell which noun it replaces in the first sentence.

❸ Apply

Have each child write two sentences. Tell children to underline the noun in each sentence that can be replaced with a pronoun. Pairs can then exchange papers and rewrite the sentences using pronouns in place of the underlined nouns.

Officer Buckle tells us safety tips.

He tells us safety tips.

The letters were funny.

They were funny.

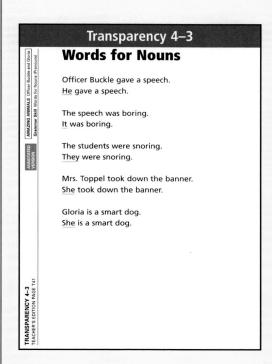

Transparency 4–3

Words for Nouns

Officer Buckle gave a speech.
He gave a speech.

The speech was boring.
It was boring.

The students were snoring.
They were snoring.

Mrs. Toppel took down the banner.
She took down the banner.

Gloria is a smart dog.
She is a smart dog.

AMAZING ANIMALS Officer Buckle and Gloria
Grammar Skill Words for Nouns (Pronouns)

ANNOTATED VERSION

TRANSPARENCY 4–3
TEACHER'S EDITION PAGE T41

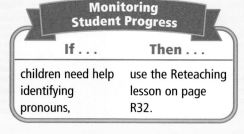

Monitoring Student Progress

If . . .	Then . . .
children need help identifying pronouns,	use the Reteaching lesson on page R32.

Day at a Glance

pp. T42–T65

Reading Instruction

Background and Vocabulary

Reading the Anthology
Officer Buckle and Gloria

• •

Leveled Readers, *T90–T93*
- ● *Max the Pet Show Star*
- ▲ *The Best Job for Scooter*
- ■ *Daisy Divine, Dancing Dog*
- ◆ *Max Is a Star!*

Word Work

Vocabulary Review
Word Wall
Spelling Practice

Writing & Oral Language

Writing: An Invitation
Grammar Practice
Listening/Speaking/Viewing

Daily Routines

Daily Message

Phonics Review Point to each word as you read aloud the Daily Message.

Hello, Boys and Girls!
Did you ever see a smart dog in school? Did you ever know a dog to be a TV star? You will meet one in the next story we read.

Have children
- read the Daily Message aloud and discuss the questions;
- find words with the *r*-controlled vowel *ar*; (*smart, star*)
- read the words aloud and then circle them.

Word Wall

High-Frequency Word Review Briefly review these high-frequency words that were introduced on Day 1. Display the words and have children practice recognizing, chanting, spelling, and writing them.

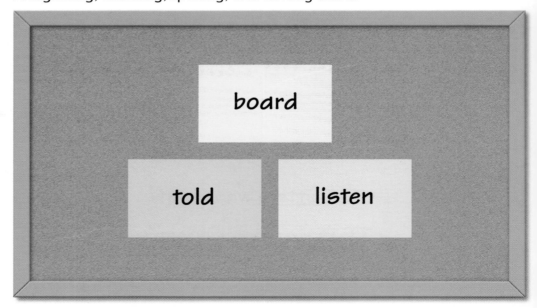

board

told   listen

Blackline Masters for these word cards appear on p. R35.

Vocabulary

Dramatize Action Words Write these and other action words, including those in the selection. Say a word and have children act it out. Then have children choose a word to illustrate.

stare   snore
applaud   listen
frown

frown

Daily Writing Prompt

Have children revise work they are currently writing, or have them use this prompt to begin a new writing activity.

> You listened to a story about Aero, the police dog. If Aero could talk, what do you think he might say about his work and his family? Do you think he likes keeping people safe?

Daily Language Practice

Grammar Skill: Words for Nouns
Spelling Skill: The Vowel + *r* Sounds in *car*

Display **Transparency 4–1.** Ask children to rewrite Sentence 2 correctly. Then model how to write it, and have children check their work.

Transparency 4–1
Daily Language Practice

Proofread each sentence. Correct any errors.

Day 1
1. Sam green drives a bright red carr.

Day 2
2. I see three dog at the parck.

I see three **dogs** at the **park**.

A tree in my yard has five peaches on it.

Day 4
4. Ten mans pick corn at the ferm.

Ten **men** pick corn at the **farm**.

Day 5
5. Them like to play in a baren.

They like to play in a **barn**.

TRANSPARENCY 4–1
TEACHER'S EDITION PAGES T31, T43, T67, T75, AND T85

Building Background

Key Concept:
Learning Safety Rules

Ask children to name some of your school safety rules. Then use "Safety Officers" on Anthology page 16 to introduce Key Vocabulary.

- Have individuals read the paragraph on Anthology page 16 and the rules on the chalkboard on page 17 aloud.
- Have children brainstorm a third Bicycle and In-Line Skating Safety rule.

Get Set to Read

Background and Vocabulary

Safety Officers

Officer Buckle and Gloria

PEGGY RATHMANN

Read to find the meanings of these words.

e ◦ Glossary

attention
audience
officers
safety

Police **officers** who visit schools to talk about **safety** are sometimes called safety officers. In story you're going to read next, an officer and partner give safety speeches at an elementary school. Like the **audience** in this story, you should always pay close **attention** to a safety officer's speech. He or she will explain many w to avoid accidents and to stay safe.

16

English Language Learners

Language Development

Beginning/Preproduction Have children make a group bulletin board of useful school and classroom safety tips. Have them illustrate and label each tip.

Early Production and Speech Emergence Have pairs of children brainstorm and act out school safety tips, for example, *Always walk on the right side of the stairs.* Record children's ideas.

Intermediate and Advanced Fluency Have pairs of children orally present school and classroom safety tips. Have children support their presentations with posters, charts, and classroom objects.

Bicycle and In-line Skating Safety

1. Always wear a helmet.

2. Obey traffic signals.

3.

17

Introducing Vocabulary

Key Vocabulary

These words support the Key Concept and appear in the selection.

accident something you did not want or expect to happen

attention looking and listening with care

audience a group that listens or watches

commands orders that are given to someone

officer a person who helps enforce the law

safety having to do with freedom from danger

e • Glossary
e • WordGame

See Vocabulary notes on pages T48, T50, T51, T53, and T57.

Use Transparency 4–4.

- Read aloud the first sentence on the transparency.

- Model how to figure out what *safety officer* means, based on context clues.

- Ask children to use context clues to figure out the meaning of each Key Vocabulary word in the remaining sentences. Have children explain how they figured out each meaning.

- Ask children to look for these words as they read and to use them as they discuss the selection.

Practice/Homework Assign **Practice Book** page 6.

Transparency 4–4

Safety-Related Words

Officer Eric

Mrs. Warwick chose Eric to be a safety officer for her second-grade class. This means that Eric will learn about safety rules and teach them to the class. He will also look for ways to prevent any kind of accident in the classroom.

Eric gave his first safety speech today. "Everyone please pay attention," he said to his classmates in the audience. "Matches can start fires. Do not play with matches that you find."

Then Eric helped the class learn what to do in case of a fire. He gave commands to his classmates. "Get away from the fire. A fire can spread very quickly!" he said. "Then call 9-1-1. Tell a grown-up about the fire."

Practice Book page 6

Officer Buckle and Gloria
Key Vocabulary

Name _____

Safety Officer Words

Meanings
a. a group of people who watch and listen   c. something you don't want to happen
b. a person who helps others follow the law   d. freedom from danger
	e. looking and listening with care
	f. orders

Write the meaning from the box to match each word below.

1. accident _something you don't want to happen_ **(1 point)**

2. attention _looking and listening with care_ (1)

3. audience _a group of people who watch and listen_ (1)

4. commands _orders_ (1)

5. officer _a person who helps others follow the law_ (1)

6. safety _freedom from danger_ (1)

Get Set to Read
(Anthology p. 17)

COMPREHENSION STRATEGY
Monitor/Clarify

Teacher Modeling Read aloud the book's title and author on Anthology page 19. Ask someone to read aloud the strategy focus. Then have children read pages 21–22 silently. Model Monitor/Clarify.

Think Aloud *I don't understand why the children don't listen to Officer Buckle's safety tips. I'll reread to make sure I didn't miss something. No, the story doesn't answer my question yet, so I'll keep reading ahead to find out.*

✔ **Test Prep** Many questions on reading tests ask children to draw conclusions. Tell children that, for these questions, they should monitor and clarify their understanding of the passage to help them form and support their conclusions.

COMPREHENSION SKILL
Drawing Conclusions

Introducing the Graphic Organizer.
Tell children that they can use a Drawing Conclusions Chart to understand story events not fully explained by the author.

- Display **Transparency 4–5.** Have someone read aloud Anthology pages 22–23.

- Model how to find clues to support the sentence in the first box. Write these on the transparency.

- Have children fill in the clues on **Practice Book** page 7. Ask them to complete the chart as they read.

THEME 4: Amazing Animals
(Anthology p. 18)

T46

FACT FILE

- Peggy Rathmann was born in St. Paul, Minnesota.
- The first time she tried to write a children's book, the book was 150 pages long!
- *Officer Buckle and Gloria* won the Caldecott Medal in 1996.
- Officer Buckle's safety tips are ideas Ms. Rathmann collected from her nieces, nephew, and other children. She gave them each twenty-five dollars for any safety tip she used in the book.

Other books by Peggy Rathmann:
Ruby the Copycat
Good Night, Gorilla

Meet the Author and Illustrator
Peggy Rathmann

Internet To find out how Peggy Rathmann's dog is a lot like Gloria, take a look at Education Place.
www.eduplace.com/kids

18

Transparency 4–5
Drawing Conclusions Chart

AMAZING ANIMALS Officer Buckle and Gloria
Graphic Organizer Drawing Conclusions Chart

What I Think	My Clues
Officer Buckle's speeches are boring. (pages 22–23)	Nobody ever listens.
	The kids look like they're asleep.
	People keep having accidents.
Gloria makes the speeches more interesting. (pages 26–31)	The children sit up and stare.
	Gloria does tricks.
	The children clap and cheer.
Officer Buckle doesn't know Gloria is doing tricks. (pages 27, 40, 43, 44)	Gloria sits at attention when he looks at her.
	She always does her tricks behind his back.
	He's surprised to see Gloria on TV.
Officer Buckle and Gloria work best together. (pages 22, 45, 48, 50)	His speeches are boring without Gloria.
	Gloria falls asleep without him.
	His best tip is "Always stick with your buddy!"

TRANSPARENCY 4–5
TEACHER'S EDITION PAGES T46 AND T70

Practice Book page 7

Name _____

Officer Buckle and Gloria
Graphic Organizer Drawing Conclusions

Drawing Conclusions Chart

As you read the story, use this chart to help you keep track of what happens.

What I Think	My Clues
Officer Buckle's speeches are boring. (pages 22–23)	Nobody ever listens. **(1 Point)**
	The kids look like they're asleep. **(1)**
	People keep having accidents. **(1)**
Gloria makes the speeches more interesting. (pages 26–31)	The children sit up and stare. **(1)**
	Gloria does tricks. **(1)**
	The children clap and cheer. **(1)**
Officer Buckle doesn't know Gloria is doing tricks. (pages 27, 40, 43, 44)	Gloria sits at attention when he looks at her. **(1)**
	She always does her tricks behind his back. **(1)**
	He's surprised to see Gloria on TV. **(1)**
Officer Buckle and Gloria work best together. (pages 22, 45, 48, 50)	His speeches are boring without Gloria. **(1)**
	Gloria falls asleep without him. **(1)**
	His best tip is "Always stick with your buddy!" **(1)**

Selection 1

OFFICER BUCKLE
AND
GLORIA

PEGGY RATHMANN

19

Strategy Focus

Officer Buckle's safety speeches are more exciting than he'd planned. As you read the story, **monitor** how well you understand what happens in it.

Purpose Setting

- Have children study the title and cover illustration, and then compare the expressions of the police officer and the children. Ask them to make predictions about Officer Buckle and his dog, Gloria.

- Ask children to turn to Responding on Anthology page 52. Read the questions aloud. Encourage children to find answers to these questions as they read *Officer Buckle and Gloria*.

Journal ▶ Children can use their journals to write and revise their predictions. They can also record their reactions to the story.

Extra Support/Intervention

Preview pages 20–37.

pages 21–23 Describe Officer Buckle. Are the children paying attention to him?

pages 24–25 How do you think Officer Buckle and his dog, Gloria, feel about each other?

pages 26–31 Why do you think the children are paying attention now? Does Officer Buckle know what Gloria is doing?

pages 32–37 Do people like Gloria? How can you tell?

Preview pages 38–50.

pages 38–41 Find the TV cameras. What is happening?

pages 42–45 Why do you think Officer Buckle and Gloria look unhappy on these pages? Why aren't the children paying attention?

pages 46–47 Describe the accidents you see in this picture.

pages 48–50 Why do you think Officer Buckle and Gloria are happy again?

Reading the Selection
(Anthology p. 19)

T47

Officer Buckle knew <u>more</u> safety tips than anyone else in Napville.

Every time he thought of a new one, he thumbtacked it to his bulletin <u>board</u>.

Safety Tip #77

NEVER stand on a SWIVEL CHAIR. **2**

20

21

CRITICAL THINKING

Guiding Comprehension

1 **NOTING DETAILS** What are some of the safety tips on Officer Buckle's bulletin board? (Accept any tip that appears in the illustration on Anthology page 21.)

2 **DRAWING CONCLUSIONS** How do you think Officer Buckle came up with Safety Tip #77? (It looks like he stood on his chair and fell off. He probably decided to make a safety tip so no one else would have the same accident.)

Vocabulary

officer a person who helps enforce the law

safety having to do with freedom from danger

Word Key

Decodable words with *ar, or, ore* _____

High-Frequency Words _____

Vocabulary Words _____

THEME 4: Amazing Animals
(Anthology pp. 20–21)

Officer Buckle shared his safety tips with the students at Napville School. Nobody ever <u>listened</u>. **3** Sometimes, there was <u>snoring</u>.

22

Afterward, it was business as usual. **4**

Mrs. Toppel, the principal, took down the welcome banner.

"NEVER stand on a SWIVEL CHAIR," said Officer Buckle, but Mrs. Toppel didn't hear him.

5

23

CRITICAL THINKING

Guiding Comprehension

3 **CAUSE AND EFFECT** What happens when Officer Buckle shares his safety tips with the children? (No one listens.)

4 **MAKING INFERENCES** What do you think the author means by saying *it was business as usual?* (The author might mean that people at the school do not change their habits and keep doing unsafe things even after hearing the safety tips.)

5 **PREDICTING OUTCOMES** Look at the accidents on page 23. What safety tips could have prevented them from happening? (Never carry too many books at once; always tie your shoes; always clean up wet spills.)

REACHING ALL LEARNERS

English Language Learners

Words with Double Meanings

- Explain that *tip* in this story means *useful information,* but it can also mean *the farthest point or end of something* and *to knock something over.* Have children find tips on classroom objects such as pencils and crayons. Then have them pantomime tipping something over.

Reading the Selection
(Anthology pp. 22–23)

Then one day, Napville's police department bought a police dog named <u>Gloria</u>.

When it was time for Officer Buckle to give the safety speech at the school, Gloria went along.

24

"Children, this is Gloria," announced Officer Buckle. "Gloria obeys my commands. Gloria, SIT!" And Gloria sat.

25

 READING STRATEGY

Phonics/Decoding

Base Words and Ending -ed

Teacher/Student Modeling Write *named* and *announced* on the board. Remind children that the *-ed* ending can be pronounced as /d/ or /t/. Have children blend each word sound by sound. Have them read the word in the sentences on Anthology pages 24 and 25. Ask which sound the *-ed* makes each time. For more practice, do the same with *tied* on page 26 and *checked* on page 27.

Vocabulary

commands orders that are given to someone

 English Language Learners

Commands

Tell children that a command is a sentence that often begins with an action word and has no spoken subject. Have children think of commands they might hear at school. Record children's ideas. Examples are: *Line up. Push in your chairs. Go to recess.*

THEME 4: Amazing Animals
(Anthology pp. 24–25)

Officer Buckle gave Safety Tip Number One:
"KEEP your SHOELACES tied!"
The children sat up and stared. **6**

26

Officer Buckle checked to see if Gloria was
sitting at attention. She was. **7**

27

x

CRITICAL THINKING

Guiding Comprehension

6 **DRAWING CONCLUSIONS** What are the children staring
at? Why? (They are staring at Gloria because she is acting
just like Officer Buckle.)

7 **DRAWING CONCLUSIONS** Do you think Officer Buckle
noticed the unusual thing that Gloria did? How do you
know? (He probably didn't notice because he only looks at
Gloria when she's acting like a regular dog.)

Vocabulary

attention looking and listening with
care

 Extra Support/Intervention

Strategy Modeling: Monitor/Clarify

Use this example to model the strategy.

*I remember that the children were bored with Officer
Buckle's safety tips at the beginning of the story. So why
is it that they sit up and stare on this page? I'll ask
myself:* What is different this time? *I notice that Officer
Buckle has Gloria with him on this page, but he didn't
have her with him before. The kids are staring because
Gloria is doing something amazing.*

y

z

Reading the Selection
(Anthology pp. 26–27)

a

T51

b

c

d

e

DAY **2**

READ & COMPREHEND

Officer Buckle and Gloria

"Safety Tip Number Two," said Officer Buckle.
"ALWAYS wipe up spills BEFORE someone SLIPS
AND FALLS!"
The children's eyes popped.

28

Officer Buckle checked on Gloria again.
"Good dog," he said.
Officer Buckle thought of a safety tip he had
discovered that <u>morning</u>.

29

Comprehension Preview

Drawing Conclusions

Teach

Model how to draw a conclusion about something the author
doesn't fully explain. Say *The author doesn't explain why the
children's eyes popped. The safety tip is not the reason; it's not
amazing or unusual. Gloria standing on her head is amazing. I
think that's why the children's eyes popped.*

Practice/Apply

List a selection of page numbers and an example of what's
happening on each page. Have children give a *why* for each
entry and explain how they drew their conclusion.

Target Skill Trace	
Preview, Teach	pp. T32, T46, T52, T70
Reteach	p. R26
Review	p. T262; Theme 1, p. T156; Theme 2, p. T230; Theme 5, p. T80

What's Happening	Why
(p. 26) Children stared.	Gloria is imitating Officer Buckle.
(p. 45) The audience fell asleep.	Gloria is alone and does nothing funny.
(p. 48) Officer Buckle smiled.	The note says he was missed yesterday.

Officer Buckle grinned. He said the rest of the tips with *plenty* of expression.

The children clapped their hands and cheered. Some of them laughed until they cried.

Officer Buckle was surprised. He had never noticed how funny safety tips could be.

After *this* safety speech, there wasn't a single accident.

"NEVER leave a THUMBTACK where you might SIT on it!"

The audience roared.

30

COMPREHENSION STRATEGY

Monitor/Clarify

Teacher/Student Modeling Point out that the author doesn't tell the reader why the children roar and cheer on Anthology pages 30–31. Help children model how to figure this out by using Monitor/Clarify. Say *Let's reread these pages and look at the pictures for clues about why the children cheer. Is Officer Buckle's safety tip amazing? Is Gloria's behavior in the illustrations amazing? Why do you think the audience cheers?*

Vocabulary

audience a group that listens or watches

accident something you did not want or expect to happen

 English Language Learners

Verbs That Tell About the Past

Reread pages 30 and 31 and ask children to mime the action verbs *roared, grinned, clapped, cheered, laughed, cried*. Then have children read these pages aloud with you, individually or chorally. As they read, listen for correct pronunciation of the past tense ending. (/t/; /d/)

Every letter had a drawing of Gloria on it.

Officer Buckle thought the drawings showed a lot **10** of imagination.

9

The next day, an <u>enormous</u> envelope arrived at the police station. It was stuffed with thank-you letters from the students at Napville School. **8**

32

33

CRITICAL THINKING
Guiding Comprehension

8 NOTING DETAILS Why is the envelope that arrived at the station so enormous? (because it held so many thank-you letters)

9 FANTASY AND REALISM What funny things does Gloria do that real dogs can't do? (She stands on her head, imitates Officer Buckle, and behaves like a person.)

10 MAKING INFERENCES Why does Officer Buckle think the children's drawings show a lot of imagination? (The drawings show Gloria doing tricks. Officer Buckle doesn't know that Gloria does tricks.)

THEME 4: Amazing Animals
(Anthology pp. 32–33)

His favorite letter was written on a star-shaped piece of paper. It said:

You and Gloria make a good team.

Your friend,
Claire

P.S. I always wear a crash helmet. (Safety Tip #7)

34

Officer Buckle was thumbtacking Claire's letter to his bulletin board when the phones started ringing. Grade schools, high schools, and day-care centers were calling about the safety speech.

"Officer Buckle," they said, "our students want to hear your safety tips! And please, bring along that police dog."

35

READING STRATEGY

Phonics/Decoding

Consonant Clusters

Teacher/Student Modeling Write *speech*. Underline *sp*. Remind children that the sounds of the two consonants *sp* are usually blended when pronouncing a word that contains them. Have children blend *speech,* sound by sound. Next, write *children* and *please*. Underline the consonant clusters. Have children look carefully for parts they know, think about the sounds for the letters, and blend the sounds.

REACHING ALL LEARNERS

Extra Support/Intervention

Selection Review

Before children join in Stop and Think, have them

- check the accuracy of their **predictions,**
- model the reading **strategies** they used,
- add to **Practice Book** page 7,
- **summarize** the important parts of the story up to this point.

Officer Buckle <u>told</u> his safety tips to 313 schools. Everywhere he and Gloria went, children sat up and listened.

After every speech, Officer Buckle took Gloria out <u>for</u> ice cream.
Officer Buckle loved having a buddy.

36

37

Stop and Think

Critical Thinking Questions

1. **DRAWING CONCLUSIONS** Do you think Officer Buckle suspects that Gloria is an amazing animal? (No; he doesn't notice what she is doing when he is making speeches.)

2. **MAKING INFERENCES** How does Officer Buckle feel about Gloria? How does the author/illustrator show this? (He loves Gloria. The author says Officer Buckle loves having a buddy; Officer Buckle takes Gloria out for ice cream.)

Strategies in Action

Have individuals model **Monitor/Clarify** and other strategies they used. Make sure children **Summarize** the story so far.

Discussion Options

Bring the entire class together to do either of these activities.

Review Predictions/Purpose Have children review and revise their predictions and make new ones if necessary.

Share Group Discussions Have children share their responses for Assignment Card 3.

THEME 4: Amazing Animals
(Anthology pp. 36–37)

ASSIGNMENT CARD 3

Literature Discussion

- Why do the children sit up and listen everywhere Officer Buckle and Gloria go?

- Does Officer Buckle know how amazing Gloria is? Explain your answer.

- Would you tell Officer Buckle what Gloria does during his safety tips talk? Why or why not?

Theme 4: Amazing Animals

Teacher's Resource BLM page 64

Monitoring Student Progress

If . . .	Then . . .
children have successfully completed the Extra Support activities on pages T47 and T55,	have them read the rest of the story cooperatively or independently.

Then one day, a television news team videotaped  **11**
Officer Buckle in the state-college auditorium.

38

39

CRITICAL THINKING
Guiding Comprehension

11 **MAKING INFERENCES** Why do you think a television news team decides to tape Officer Buckle and Gloria? (They probably have heard of Gloria's amazing tricks and want to put her on television.)

12 **NOTING DETAILS** How does the author/illustrator show that Officer Buckle and Gloria are very popular? (She draws them in a huge auditorium with lots of people watching.)

Vocabulary

auditorium a public building where an audience sits

When he finished Safety Tip Number Ninety-nine,
DO NOT GO SWIMMING DURING ELECTRICAL
STORMS!, the students jumped to their feet and
applauded.

40

41

CRITICAL THINKING

Guiding Comprehension

13 **SEQUENCE OF EVENTS** When do the children jump to their feet? (after Officer Buckle finishes Safety Tip Number Ninety-nine)

14 **DRAWING CONCLUSIONS** What is Gloria doing in the illustration? Why? (She is pretending to be electrocuted because Officer Buckle is giving a tip about electrical storms.)

15 **MAKING INFERENCES** Why do you think Officer Buckle is bowing? (He probably thinks the audience is cheering for him, although they are really cheering for Gloria.)

THEME 4: Amazing Animals
(Anthology pp. 40–41)

That night, Officer Buckle watched himself on the 10 o'clock news. **16** **17**

42

43

CRITICAL THINKING

Guiding Comprehension

16 **MAKING INFERENCES** How do you think Officer Buckle feels about what he sees on television? Explain. (He's probably shocked; his expression is surprised.)

17 **MAKING INFERENCES** Why do you think Gloria looks worried? (Officer Buckle can see for the first time on television what she has been doing, and she may be worried about how he will react.)

Extra Support/Intervention

Strategy Modeling: Monitor/Clarify

Use this example to model the strategy.

I wonder why Officer Buckle looks so surprised when he watches himself on the news. I'll look more closely at the illustration. Why is the TV behind him? Oh, I see, it's a mirror reflecting the TV, and he's surprised because it's the first time he sees Gloria doing funny tricks on stage.

ASSIGNMENT CARD 4

Picture Clues

Character Sketch

Look at page 43 of the story.

The picture has many clues about what kind of person Officer Buckle is. Look closely at the picture.

Make notes about what these things tell you about Officer Buckle. Read your notes to your class.

Theme 4: Amazing Animals

Teacher's Resource BLM page 64

Reading the Selection
(Anthology pp. 42–43)

T59

The next day, the principal of Napville School telephoned the police station.

"Good morning, Officer Buckle! It's time for our safety speech!"

Officer Buckle frowned.

"I'm not giving any more speeches! Nobody looks at me, anyway!"

"Oh," said Mrs. Toppel. "Well! How about Gloria? Could she come?"

44

Someone else from the police station gave Gloria a ride to the school.

Gloria sat onstage looking lonely. Then she fell asleep. So did the audience. **18**

After Gloria left, Napville School had its biggest accident ever....

45

READING STRATEGY

Phonics/Decoding

Contractions

Teacher/Student Modeling Write *it's* on the board. Remind children that a contraction is a short way of writing one or more words; the apostrophe means a letter has been left out of *it is*. Have children look carefully at the word and think about the sounds for the letters. Have them blend the sounds to read the word. Repeat with *I'm*. Then have them find these words on page 44 and read the sentences containing them.

English Language Learners

Nouns and Verbs

Ask children to model what Officer Buckle is doing on page 44. Ask *Do you see his frown? Why do you think he is frowning?* Make sure children understand that *frown* is both a noun and a verb. Model how to use *frown* as both a noun and a verb in sentences, and have children try it. Repeat with other words in the story that are both nouns and verbs: *videotape, thumbtack.*

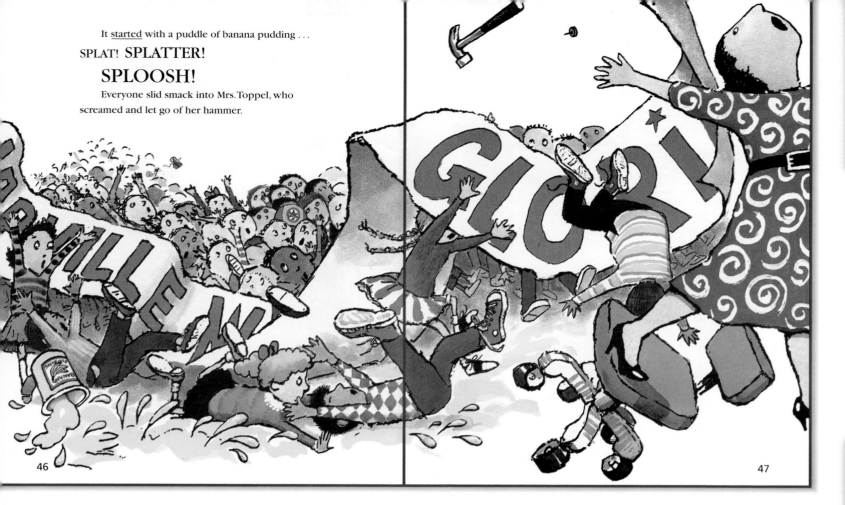

It <u>started</u> with a puddle of banana pudding . . .

SPLAT! **SPLATTER!**

SPLOOSH!

Everyone slid smack into Mrs. Toppel, who screamed and let go of her hammer.

46

47

CRITICAL THINKING

Guiding Comprehension

 18 CAUSE AND EFFECT On page 45, why does the audience fall asleep when Gloria appears at Napville School alone?
(The audience falls asleep because Gloria falls asleep.)

COMPREHENSION STRATEGY

Monitor/Clarify

Student Modeling Have children model how they used Monitor/Clarify as they were reading. If they need help, ask *If you were not sure why such a big accident occurred, how could you find out what happened in the story?*

English Language Learners

Supporting Comprehension

Ask children to find the biggest printed word on page 46. (sploosh) Ask *Why do you think the illustrator made this word so big? What other words on this page are big words?* (splat, splatter) Call attention to the exclamation points, explaining that these words make the reader think of big noises and big accidents.

Reading the Selection
(Anthology pp. 46–47)

T61

The next morning, a pile of letters arrived at the police station.

Every letter had a drawing of the accident. **19**

Officer Buckle was shocked.

At the bottom of the pile was a note written on a paper <u>star</u>.

Officer Buckle smiled. **20**

The note said:

Gloria missed you yesterday!
Your friend,
Claire
P.S. Don't worry,
I was wearing
my helmet!
(Safety Tip #7)

48

Gloria gave Officer Buckle a big kiss on the nose.
Officer Buckle gave Gloria a nice pat on the back.
Then, Officer Buckle thought of his best safety tip yet....

49

CRITICAL THINKING
Guiding Comprehension

19 **DRAWING CONCLUSIONS** Why is Officer Buckle shocked to see the letters? (They show the big accident at school.)

20 **MAKING INFERENCES** Why do you think the letter at the bottom of the pile makes Officer Buckle smile? (It says that Gloria misses him and also shows that the child who wrote the letter has learned from Officer Buckle's safety tips.)

21 **DRAWING CONCLUSIONS** What do you think makes Officer Buckle think of his last safety tip on page 50? (He realizes that he and Gloria are buddies and work best when they are together.)

REACHING ALL LEARNERS
Extra Support/Intervention

Selection Review

Before Wrapping Up, have children

- check the accuracy of their **predictions,**
- model the reading **strategies** they used,
- review and complete **Practice Book** page 45,
- **summarize** the entire story.

On Level	Challenge

Have small groups discuss the story, using their own questions and questions from Think About the Selection on Anthology page 52.

THEME 4: Amazing Animals
(Anthology pp. 48–49)

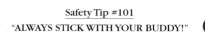

Safety Tip #101
"ALWAYS STICK WITH YOUR BUDDY!" **21**

50

Wrapping Up

Critical Thinking Questions

1. **MAKING INFERENCES** How do you think Gloria feels about Officer Buckle? (She likes him very much and enjoys being his buddy.)

2. **PREDICTING OUTCOMES** Do you think Officer Buckle will change his mind and start giving more safety speeches again? Explain. (Sample response: Yes, he realizes that his speeches are important and Gloria can't amaze audiences without him.)

Strategies in Action

Have individuals model **Monitor/Clarify** and other strategies they used. Have children **Summarize** the story.

Discussion Options

Bring the entire class together to do either of these activities.

Review Predictions/Purpose Discuss the accuracy of children's predictions.

Share Group Discussions Have children share their literature discussions and their reactions to the story.

Monitoring Student Progress

If . . .	Then . . .
children have difficulty summarizing the story,	work with them to recall events that happened in the beginning, middle, and end of the story.

Reading the Selection
(Anthology pp. 50–51) **T63**

Challenge

Word Practice

Have children write safety tips to follow when visiting a store, company, or public office. Ask them to include Challenge Words in their tips.

Practice Book page 8

Officer Buckle and Gloria
Spelling: The Vowel + r
Sounds in car

Name _____

Words with *ar*

► You hear the vowel + r sound in **car** and **start**. This sound is spelled **ar**.
► The word **warm** does not follow this pattern.

Write the Spelling Words that have the same vowel sound as **cart**. Order of answers may vary.

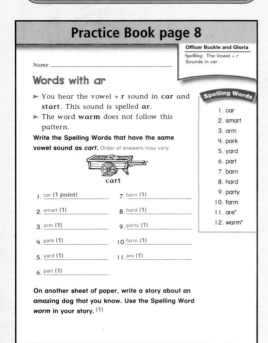

cart

Spelling Words
1. car
2. smart
3. arm
4. park
5. yard
6. part
7. barn
8. hard
9. party
10. farm
11. are*
12. warm*

1. car **(1 point)**   7. barn **(1)**

2. smart **(1)**   8. hard **(1)**

3. arm **(1)**   9. party **(1)**

4. park **(1)**   10. farm **(1)**

5. yard **(1)**   11. are **(1)**

6. part **(1)**

On another sheet of paper, write a story about an amazing dog that you know. Use the Spelling Word **warm** in your story. **(1)**

Practice Book page 9

Officer Buckle and Gloria
Grammar Skill: Words for
Nouns (Pronouns)

Name _____

Pronoun Show

► A **noun** names a person, a place, or a thing.
► A **pronoun** is a word that can take the place of a noun.

Rewrite each sentence. Replace the word or words in dark print with the pronouns *she, he, it,* or *they.*

1. **Gloria** likes to go to school.

   She likes to go to school. **(1 point)**

2. The **children** cheer when Gloria arrives.

   They cheer when Gloria arrives. **(1)**

3. You can hear **the cheer** outside the school.

   You can hear it outside the school. **(1)**

4. When **Officer Buckle** starts to talk, the children are quiet.

   When he starts to talk, the children are quiet. **(1)**

5. **Officer Buckle and Gloria** put on a great show.

   They put on a great show. **(1)**

PRACTICE

SPELLING: The Vowel + *r* Sounds in *car*

Review the Principle Use *yard* and *barn* to remind children that when *a* is followed by *r* it has neither the short nor long vowel sound, but is pronounced as /är/. Review that *are* is pronounced /är/ but has the *a*-consonant-*e* spelling pattern. *Warm* has the *ar* spelling but is pronouced /ôr/.

Write the Basic Words and say two of them. Have a child tell which comes first in alphabetical order. Have everyone spell that word together. Continue in this way to spell all the words.

Practice/Homework Assign **Practice Book** page 8.

PRACTICE

GRAMMAR: Words for Nouns

Review the Skill Have volunteers read aloud the information about nouns and pronouns at the top of **Practice Book** page 9.

Practice/Homework Assign **Practice Book** page 9.

> A noun names a person, place, or thing.

> The pronouns <u>he</u>, <u>she</u>, <u>it</u>, and <u>they</u> can take the place of a noun.

> Example: Don rides a bike to school.
> <u>He</u> rides a bike to school.

> Example: Kara and Jim wait for the bus.
> <u>They</u> wait for the bus.

WRITING: An Invitation

- Identify the format and elements of an effective invitation.
- Write an invitation.
- Learn academic language: *invitation*.

❶ Teach

Discuss the characteristics of an invitation. Explain that an invitation is a spoken or written request that asks someone to go somewhere or do something. List and discuss what is usually included in an invitation:

- the name of who is invited;
- what the event is;
- the date, time, and location of the event;
- who the invitation is from.

Display and discuss the invitation on Transparency 4–6.

- Explain that an invitation such as this might have been sent from the principal of Napville School to the children at Parkdale School.
- Have volunteers read aloud the information on the invitation.
- Ask children to identify each part of the invitation, based on the items you listed.

Display and discuss the guidelines on Transparency 4–7.

❷ Practice/Apply

Assign Practice Book page 10. Have children use this page to plan and organize their own invitations. Have them fold paper to create the invitations and then decorate them.

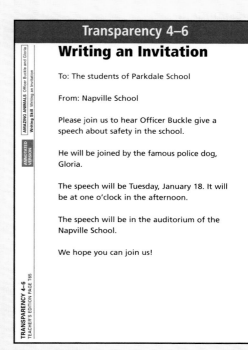

Transparency 4–6

Writing an Invitation

To: The students of Parkdale School

From: Napville School

Please join us to hear Officer Buckle give a speech about safety in the school.

He will be joined by the famous police dog, Gloria.

The speech will be Tuesday, January 18. It will be at one o'clock in the afternoon.

The speech will be in the auditorium of the Napville School.

We hope you can join us!

TRANSPARENCY 4–6
TEACHER'S EDITION PAGE T65
AMAZING ANIMALS *Officer Buckle and Gloria*
Writing Skill Writing an Invitation
ANNOTATED VERSION

Transparency 4–7

Guidelines for Writing an Invitation

- Tell who is being invited.
- Tell what the invitation is for.
- Include important information, such as the date, the time, and the place.
- Tell who is doing the inviting.

TRANSPARENCY 4–7
TEACHER'S EDITION PAGE T65
AMAZING ANIMALS *Officer Buckle and Gloria*
Writing Guidelines An Invitation
ANNOTATED VERSION

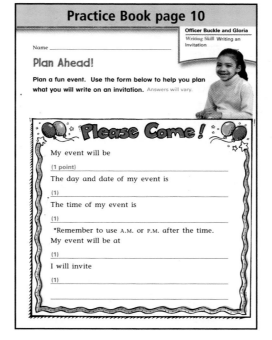

Practice Book page 10

Officer Buckle and Gloria
Writing Skill Writing an Invitation

Name _____

Plan Ahead!

Plan a fun event. Use the form below to help you plan what you will write on an invitation. Answers will vary.

Please Come!

My event will be _____
(1 point)
The day and date of my event is _____
(1)
The time of my event is _____
(1)
*Remember to use A.M. or P.M. after the time.
My event will be at _____
(1)
I will invite _____
(1)

Day at a Glance

pp. T66–T73

Reading Instruction

Responding

Comprehension Instruction
  Drawing Conclusions

Rereading for Understanding

• • • • • • • • • • • • • • • • • • •

Leveled Readers, *T90–T93*

● *Max the Pet Show Star*
▲ *The Best Job for Scooter*
■ *Daisy Divine, Dancing Dog*
◆ *Max Is a Star!*

Word Work

Vocabulary Review

Word Wall

Spelling Practice

Writing & Oral Language

Writing Activity

Grammar Practice

Listening/Speaking/Viewing

Daily Routines

Daily Message

Phonics Review Point to each word as you read aloud the Daily Message.

Good Morning, Boys and Girls,

Don't forget to tie your shoelaces. Look both ways before you cross the street. Don't run around a corner. Be more _____.

Have children

• read the Daily Message and discuss it, and ask volunteers to complete the last sentence;
• find and read aloud words with *r*-controlled vowels *or, ore.* (*Morning, forget, before, corner, more*)

Word Wall

Speed Drill Have children review and practice these and other previously taught high-frequency words. Also have them practice reading a few decodable words that feature new phonics skills.

• Have children take turns holding up a card for partners to read.
• Have individuals read the cards to you quickly.

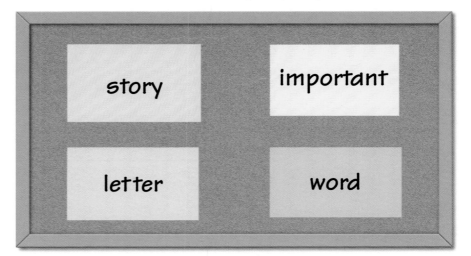

story

important

letter

word

Blackline Masters for these word cards appear on pp. R35, R36.

Vocabulary

Word-Learning Strategies

Write these words from the selection.
Have children fold a piece of paper into six
boxes and illustrate each word. Suggest that
they use a dictionary if needed.
Have children exchange papers and label each
picture with the word it illustrates.

snoring   scream
buddy   splatter
single   enormous

Daily Writing Prompt

Have children revise work they are currently
writing, or have them use this prompt to
begin a new writing activity.

Choose a picture of
Gloria in the story.
Look carefully at what
she is doing and at
the expression on her
face. Write what
Gloria is thinking.
Explain why she is
thinking that.

Daily Language Practice

Grammar Skill: Words for Nouns
Spelling Skill: The Vowel + *r* Sounds in *car*

Display **Transparency 4–1.** Ask children to
rewrite Sentence 3 correctly. Then model how to
write it, and have children check their work.

Transparency 4–1
Daily Language Practice

Proofread each sentence. Correct any errors.

Day 1
1. Sam green drives a bright red carr.

   Sam **Green** drives a bright red **car.**

Day 2

Day 3
   3. A tree in my yared has five peaches on them.

   A tree in my **yard** has five peaches on **it.**

4. Ten mans pick corn at the ferm.

   Ten men pick corn at the **farm.**

Day 5
   5. Them like to play in a baren.

   They like to play in a **barn.**

AMAZING ANIMALS Officer Buckle and Gloria
Grammar Skill Words for Nouns (Pronouns)
Spelling Skill The Vowel + r Sound in car

TRANSPARENCY 4–1
TEACHER'S EDITION PAGES T31, T43, T6...

Responding

Comprehension Check

Have children reread or finish reading the selection. Then assign **Practice Book** page 11 to assess children's comprehension of the selection.

Think About the Selection

Have children discuss or write answers. Sample answers are provided; accept reasonable responses.

1. **MAKING JUDGMENTS** Children may mention any two of these: Never stand on a swivel chair; keep your shoelaces tied; always wipe up spills before someone slips and falls; never leave a thumbtack where you might sit on it; do not go swimming during electrical storms.

2. **EVALUATING** Children may say that the pictures add humor. They tell part of the story because the text alone does not tell what Gloria is doing.

3. **DRAWING CONCLUSIONS** Officer Buckle probably felt embarrassed that the real attraction was Gloria, not his speeches.

4. **MAKING INFERENCES** The story teaches that a good friendship can come from working together and is more important than one's pride.

5. **Connecting/Comparing**
   Children may say that Gloria is amazing because she understands what Officer Buckle says and acts out his safety tips.

THEME 4: Amazing Animals
(Anthology p. 52)

T68

Responding

Think About the Selection

1. Choose two safety tips from the story. Explain why they are important.

2. How do Peggy Rathmann's illustrations make this story funny?

3. How do you think Officer Buckle felt when he saw himself on the 10 o'clock news?

4. What does this story teach about teamwork and friendship?

5. **Connecting/Comparing** In what ways is Gloria an amazing animal?

Expressing

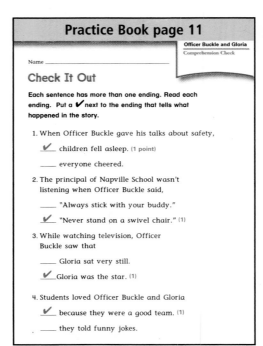

Write a Thank-You Letter

The students at Napville School sent letters to Officer Buckle and Gloria. Write your own thank-you letter. Tell Officer Buckle and Gloria what you thought of their speeches. Tell what you learned about safety.

Tips

- To get started, look at the letters in the story.
- Be sure to include the date, greeting, closing, and your name.

52

Practice Book page 11

Name _____

Officer Buckle and Gloria
Comprehension Check

Check It Out

Each sentence has more than one ending. Read each ending. Put a ✔ next to the ending that tells what happened in the story.

1. When Officer Buckle gave his talks about safety,

    ✔ children fell asleep. (1 point)

    ___ everyone cheered.

2. The principal of Napville School wasn't listening when Officer Buckle said,

    ___ "Always stick with your buddy."

    ✔ "Never stand on a swivel chair." (1)

3. While watching television, Officer Buckle saw that

    ___ Gloria sat very still.

    ✔ Gloria was the star. (1)

4. Students loved Officer Buckle and Gloria

    ✔ because they were a good team. (1)

    ___ they told funny jokes.

Practice Book page 2

Name _____

Launching the Theme
Selection Connections

Amazing Animals

Fill in the chart as you read the stories. Sample answers shown.

	What animals appear in this theme?	What amazing things do these animals do?
Officer Buckle and Gloria	a police dog named Gloria (1 point)	Gloria does funny tricks on stage. (1)
Ant	many types of ants (1)	Ants build ant bridges and grow their own food. (1)
The Great Ball Game	birds, a bear, a bat (1)	The birds and the animals play a ball game; the bat helps the animals win the game. (1)

Make a School Safety Poster

Identify places in your school where safety tips would help. Make a poster showing one of these tips. Be sure to explain why students should follow it.

Present a Safety Tip

Work with a partner. Think of a safety tip that your class should follow. Have one partner act out the safety tip while the other explains it. Can you make your presentation as exciting as Officer Buckle and Gloria's?

> **Tips**
>
> - Brainstorm a list of possible safety tips.
> - Look at the class as you present your safety tip.

Complete a Web Crossword Puzzle

What started with a puddle of banana pudding? Test what you've learned from the story by completing the crossword puzzle on Education Place.

www.eduplace.com/kids

53

Additional Responses

Personal Response Invite volunteers to share their personal responses to *Officer Buckle and Gloria* orally in small groups.

 Journal ▶ Ask children to write in their journals about a safety tip from the story that they will be sure to use, and why.

Selection Connections Remind children to add to **Practice Book** page 2.

Writing Support

Have children make notes of several ideas for a thank-you letter before they start writing. Suggest that they cut their paper into an interesting shape.

Supporting Comprehension

Beginning/Preproduction Have children go back and find their favorite part of the story. Help them explain why they like that part.

Early Production and Speech Emergence Ask children to choose part of the story and describe it to a partner. The partner should ask questions.

Intermediate and Advanced Fluency Have small groups play "Telephone" to retell the story. Each child says one sentence in turn until the retelling is completed.

End-of-Selection Assessment

Selection Test Use the test on pages 119–120 in the **Teacher's Resource Blackline Masters** to assess selection comprehension and vocabulary.

Student Self-Assessment Have children assess their reading with questions such as

- How did making predictions as I read help me understand the story?
- What parts of the story were difficult for me? Why?
- What did I like best about this story? Why?

Responding
(Anthology p. 53)

T69

OBJECTIVES

- Give information from the story and illustrations to support conclusions.
- Learn academic language: *conclusions*.

Target Skill Trace

Preview, Teach	pp. T32, T46, T52, T70
Reteach	p. R26
Review	p. T262; Theme 1, p. T156; Theme 2, p. T230; Theme 5, p. T80
See	*Extra Support Handbook*, pp. 122–123, 128–129

Transparency 4–5

Drawing Conclusions Chart

What I Think	My Clues
Officer Buckle's speeches are boring. (pages 22–23)	Nobody ever listens.
	The kids look like they're asleep.
	People keep having accidents.
Gloria makes the speeches more interesting. (pages 26–31)	The children sit up and stare.
	Gloria does tricks.
	The children clap and cheer.
Officer Buckle doesn't know Gloria is doing tricks. (pages 27, 40, 43, 44)	Gloria sits at attention when he looks at her.
	She always does her tricks behind his back.
	He's surprised to see Gloria on TV.
Officer Buckle and Gloria work best together. (pages 22, 45, 48, 50)	His speeches are boring without Gloria.
	Gloria falls asleep without him.
	His best tip is "Always stick with your buddy!"

TRANSPARENCY 4–5
TEACHER'S EDITION PAGES T46 AND T70

AMAZING ANIMALS Officer Buckle and Gloria
Graphic Organizer: Drawing Conclusions Chart

ANNOTATED VERSION

Practice Book page 7

Officer Buckle and Gloria
Graphic Organizer: Drawing Conclusions

Name _____

Drawing Conclusions Chart

As you read the story, use this chart to help you keep track of what happens.

What I Think	My Clues
Officer Buckle's speeches are boring. (pages 22-23)	Nobody ever listens. (1 Point)
	The kids look like they're asleep. (1)
	People keep having accidents. (1)
Gloria makes the speeches more interesting. (pages 26-31)	The children sit up and stare. (1)
	Gloria does tricks. (1)
	The children clap and cheer. (1)
Officer Buckle doesn't know Gloria is doing tricks. (pages 27, 40, 43, 44)	Gloria sits at attention when he looks at her. (1)
	She always does her tricks behind his back. (1)
	He's surprised to see Gloria on TV. (1)
Officer Buckle and Gloria work best together. (pages 22, 45, 48, 50)	His speeches are boring without Gloria. (1)
	Gloria falls asleep without him. (1)
	His best tip is "Always stick with your buddy!" (1)

COMPREHENSION: Drawing Conclusions

TARGET SKILL

❶ Teach

Display the Graphic Organizer on Transparency 4–5. Have children use the Drawing Conclusions Chart on **Practice Book** page 7 to review what they have learned about *Officer Buckle and Gloria*.

- Have children read what they listed under My Clues for each conclusion. Record these on the transparency.
- Have them read parts of the text and describe illustrations to support their conclusions.

Modeling Point out that although the author never actually says that Officer Buckle gives boring speeches, the point is made in other ways.

Think Aloud *I know from the story that people don't listen when Officer Buckle shares safety tips. In the picture on page 22, I can see children ignoring Officer Buckle's advice. The text says that even the principal doesn't hear him. From these clues, I conclude that Officer Buckle's speeches must be boring.*

❷ Guided Practice

Discuss a conclusion. Write the conclusion shown under What I Think. Have children identify story clues showing that Officer Buckle and Gloria like each other. List them under the heading My Clues. Have children discuss how the clues support the conclusion.

What I Think

Officer Buckle and Gloria care about one another.

My Clues

(p. 37) Officer Buckle takes Gloria out for ice cream.

(p. 48) Officer Buckle smiles when he reads the note that says Gloria missed you yesterday.

(p. 49) Gloria gives Officer Buckle a big kiss on the nose.

❸ Apply

Assign Practice Book pages 12–13. Have children apply this skill as they read their Leveled Readers for this week. You may also select books from the Leveled Bibliography for this theme (pages T6–T7).

✔️ **Test Prep** Explain that many questions on reading tests ask children to draw conclusions. Tell children that for these types of questions, they should look for clues and details in the passage that can help them form and support their conclusions.

Leveled Readers and Leveled Practice

Children at all levels apply the comprehension skill as they read their Leveled Readers. See lessons on pages T90–T91.

● BELOW LEVEL ▲ ON LEVEL ■ ABOVE LEVEL ◆ LANGUAGE SUPPORT

Reading Traits

Teaching children how to draw conclusions is one way of encouraging them to "read between the lines" of a story. This comprehension skill supports the reading trait **Developing Interpretations**.

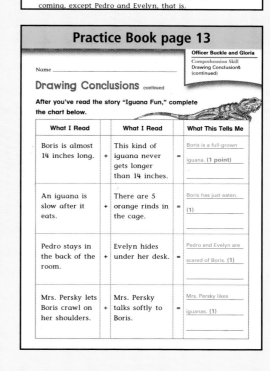

Practice Book page 12

Officer Buckle and Gloria
Comprehension Skill
Drawing Conclusions

Name _____

Drawing Conclusions

Read the story below. Then complete the chart on page 13.

Iguana Fun

Mrs. Persky's class was studying reptiles. So Ada's father brought his pet iguana Boris to school. When Ada's father walked into the classroom, Pedro ran to the back of the room. He stayed there the whole time.

Ada introduced her father and Boris to the class. Boris was dark green and had yellow eyes. Her father took Boris out of his cage. That made Evelyn hide under her desk. Ada said Boris was a nice iguana, but Evelyn would not move.

Ada's father said that Boris was almost fourteen inches long. He explained that this kind of iguana never gets longer than fourteen inches. Ada's father told the children not to worry about Boris. He said that iguanas move slowly after they have eaten. The children counted five orange rinds in the cage.

Mrs. Persky asked if she could hold Boris. Boris wrapped himself around her shoulders. Mrs. Persky talked softly to Boris. Some of the children petted Boris. Everyone thanked Ada's father for coming, except Pedro and Evelyn, that is.

Practice Book page 13

Officer Buckle and Gloria
Comprehension Skill
Drawing Conclusions
(continued)

Name _____

Drawing Conclusions continued

After you've read the story "Iguana Fun," complete the chart below.

What I Read		What I Read		What This Tells Me
Boris is almost 14 inches long.	+	This kind of iguana never gets longer than 14 inches.	=	Boris is a full-grown iguana. (1 point)
An iguana is slow after it eats.	+	There are 5 orange rinds in the cage.	=	Boris has just eaten. (1)
Pedro stays in the back of the room.	+	Evelyn hides under her desk.	=	Pedro and Evelyn are scared of Boris. (1)
Mrs. Persky lets Boris crawl on her shoulders.	+	Mrs. Persky talks softly to Boris.	=	Mrs. Persky likes iguanas. (1)

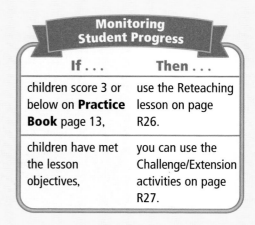

Monitoring Student Progress

If . . .	Then . . .
children score 3 or below on **Practice Book** page 13,	use the Reteaching lesson on page R26.
children have met the lesson objectives,	you can use the Challenge/Extension activities on page R27.

REREADING FOR UNDERSTANDING

Visual Literacy: Illustrator's Craft

Teach Tell children that the illustrations are an important part of many stories because they

- provide information not given in the text,
- show funny situations.

Have children turn to Anthology page 26. Point out that Gloria is standing behind Officer Buckle, imitating him. Since this information does not appear in the text, the reader has to look at the picture to know what Gloria is doing. The illustration supplies humor by showing what the words do not tell.

Practice/Apply Have children look at Anthology page 28 and tell what information can be found only in the pictures. (Gloria is standing on her head, acting out Officer Buckle's safety tip.) Have children tell why the pictures are funny. (A dog standing on her head is funny; it is funny that Officer Buckle does not know what Gloria is doing.)

Genre Lesson: Fantasy

Teach Explain that fantasy stories may have make-believe

- characters
- events
- settings

Have someone read aloud Anthology page 26. Point out the fantasy elements that appear in this illustration. (A dog, such as Gloria, probably cannot really understand enough to act out safety tips.)

Practice/Apply Have children search Anthology pages 27–31 for other examples of fantasy elements. (Possible answers: page 28: Gloria standing on her head; page 30: Gloria jumping into the air while acting out a safety tip; page 31: Gloria pretending to faint.)

SPELLING: The Vowel + *r* Sounds in *car*

Vocabulary Connection Write the Basic Words.

car	park	barn	farm
smart	yard	hard	are
arm	part	party	warm

Antonyms Dictate the following words and have children write the Basic Word with the opposite meaning.

- cool (warm)
- whole (part)
- soft (hard)
- easy (hard)

Have children use each Basic Word in an oral sentence.

Practice/Homework Assign **Practice Book** page 14.

Practice Book page 14

Officer Buckle and Gloria
Spelling The Vowel + *r*
Sounds in *car*

Name _____

Spelling Spree

Rhyme Time Finish the sentences. Write Spelling Words to rhyme with the words in dark print.

1. Gloria will **bark** at the __park (1 point)__ .
2. The **card** says that it is not __hard (1)__ to like Gloria.
3. Officer Buckle says to **start** being __smart (1)__ about safety.
4. Stand **far** from a moving __car (1)__ .
5. Would you like to be a **star** like Officer Buckle and Gloria __are (1)__ ?

Unscramble the Letters Unscramble each group of letters to make a Spelling Word. Write the words on the lines.

6. n r b a __barn (1)__
7. m r a __arm (1)__
8. y r t a p __party (1)__
9. a f m r __farm (1)__
10. a y d r __yard (1)__

Spelling Words
1. car
2. smart
3. arm
4. park
5. yard
6. part
7. barn
8. hard
9. party
10. farm
11. are*
12. warm*

GRAMMAR: Words for Nouns

Pronouns Have children tell which pronoun can take the place of the underlined noun in each sentence.

<u>The children</u> watched Gloria. (They)

<u>Gloria</u> jumped high in the air. (She)

<u>Officer Buckle</u> likes his buddy. (He)

Officer Buckle read <u>the letter</u>. (it)

DAY 4
week 1

Day at a Glance
pp. T74–T83

Reading Instruction

Social Studies Link
Phonics Review
Reading Decodable Text
Arthur's Book

• • • • • • • • • • • • • • • • • • • •

Leveled Readers, *T90–T93*
- ● *Max the Pet Show Star*
- ▲ *The Best Job for Scooter*
- ■ *Daisy Divine, Dancing Dog*
- ◆ *Max Is a Star!*

Word Work

Vocabulary Instruction
Dictionary Entry Words
Word Wall
Spelling Practice

Writing & Oral Language

Improving Writing
Grammar Practice
Listening/Speaking/Viewing

Daily Routines

Daily Message

Strategy Review Remind children of the Phonics/Decoding Strategy. Guide them in applying it to selected words in today's message.

Animals do some pretty amazing things. Did you ever see funny home videos with animals and children? Who makes you laugh more, the children or the animals?

Read aloud the entire Daily Message with children, pointing to each word as you read. Ask children to read the message aloud. Then have volunteers answer the questions, and discuss their responses.

Word Wall

High Frequency Word Review Review the high-frequency words from this week's Word Wall.

- Have children choose a word from the Word Wall and then use it to write a question that begins with *who, what, when,* or *where*.
- Have children trade papers with a partner who will use the same word to write an answer to the question.

Q: When do you like to underline{listen} to stories?

A: I like to underline{listen} to stories at bedtime.

Vocabulary

Key Vocabulary Review Ask children to write a sentence for two key vocabulary words or use sentences from the Glossary.

- Have them cut each sentence into word cards and put the cards in an envelope.
- Have partners trade envelopes and arrange the word cards to make each sentence. Then have them read the sentences to each other.

(A large audience sat in the theater.)

Daily Writing Prompt

Have children revise work they are currently writing, or have them use this prompt to begin a new writing activity.

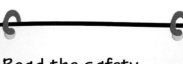

Read the safety tips that Officer Buckle puts on the bulletin board in his office. Choose one tip and write about what happened to someone who didn't follow it.

Daily Language Practice

Grammar Skill: Words for Nouns
Spelling Skill: The Vowel + *r* Sounds in *car*

Display **Transparency 4–1.** Ask children to rewrite Sentence 4 correctly. Then model how to write it, and have children check their work.

Transparency 4–1

Daily Language Practice

Proofread each sentence. Correct any errors.

Day 1
1. Sam green drives a bright red carr.
Sam **Green** drives a bright red **car**.

Day 2
2. I see three dog at the parck.
I see three **dogs** at the **park**.

Day 4
4. Ten mans pick corn at the ferm.
Ten **men** pick corn at the **farm**.

5. Them like to play in a baren.
They like to play in a **barn**.

The Story of Owney

Skill: How to Read a Map

- Look for a **key**, or **legend**, that shows what the symbols or colors on the map mean.

- Use the **compass rose** to find the directions of north, south, east, and west.

- Read the **labels** to find cities, states, countries, or other places the map shows.

from *Postal Pack for Elementary School Students*, National Postal Museum and Smithsonian Institution

More than one hundred years ago, a little dog wandered into a post office and made himself at home among the mailbags. He loved traveling with the mail. Once, when a mailbag accidentally fell off a cart, Owney stayed with the bag to protect it until the postal clerks came back to fetch it.

These are just some of the cities Owney visited.

Owney became a famous dog. He jumped onto mail trains whenever he liked. The clerks loved having him along because he was a good luck charm. There was never a railroad accident when Owney was aboard. Wherever he went, postal clerks made a dog tag for him, so others would know where he had traveled. The National Postal Museum has more than one thousand Owney tags that show all the places Owney visited.

Owney loved to ride in the mail cars.

54

55

Social Studies Link

Skill: How to Read a Map

- **Introduce** the link by reading aloud the article's title and source. Explain that "The Story of Owney" is an article about a real-life dog that lived more than one hundred years ago and loved to travel by train. Point out that the map shows places the dog visited in his travels. Have children read pages 54–55.

- **Discuss** the Skill Lesson, How to Read a Map, on Anthology page 54.

- **Model** Discuss map features. Have volunteers locate the map key and compass rose. Ask children to identify the names of cities Owney visited. Then work with children to identify and label the names of places with which they are familiar.

- **Assign** volunteers to locate the compass rose and map key on classroom maps, and describe the function of these features.

English Language Learners

Language Development

Before children discuss the compass rose, ask them to point out where their families come from on a world map. Prompt children to use direction words, such as *north, south, east,* and *west* to describe the journey they or their families made to the United States.

THEME 4: Amazing Animals
(Anthology pp. 54–55)

Wrapping Up

Critical Thinking Questions

Have children locate map features on classroom maps and discuss their functions. Then ask children to read aloud parts of the text that support each answer.

1. **MAKING JUDGMENTS** What do you think was the most amazing part of Owney's journey? (Sample response: Owney traveled thousands of miles and visited many parts of the country.)

2. **NOTING DETAILS** Why did clerks on mail trains like having Owney around? (There was never an accident with Owney aboard.)

3. **MAIN IDEA** Why do you think the map was included in the article? (Sample response: to show where Owney traveled.)

4. **COMPARE AND CONTRAST** How is "The Story of Owney" like *Officer Buckle and Gloria*? different? (Both are about dogs that like adventure. The article is about a real dog who visited real places, but the story is about a make-believe dog and make-believe adventures.)

REACHING ALL LEARNERS

Challenge

Design a Stamp

Ask children to design a postal stamp that honors Owney. Have children display their designs on a classroom bulletin board.

READ & COMPREHEND

Officer Buckle and Gloria

OBJECTIVES

- Identify entry words in a dictionary.
- Learn academic language: *dictionary entry word, guide words, definition, sample sentence.*

Target Skill Trace

Teach	p. T78
Review	p. T272
See	*Handbook for English Language Learners,* p. 131

Materials

- children's dictionaries

VOCABULARY: Dictionary Entry Words

❶ Teach

Introduce dictionary entry words. Write and read aloud *Mrs. Toppel, the principal, took down the welcome <u>banner</u>.* Tell children that if they aren't able to figure out the meaning of *banner* in this sentence, they can look it up in a dictionary.

Display Transparency 4–8.

- Point out that *banner* is an entry word and that all entry words on a dictionary page are listed in alphabetical order.
- Explain that an entry word is followed by one or more definitions. Have children read the two definitions for *banner.*
- Explain that sometimes a sentence using the word is also given. Have a volunteer read the sample sentence.

Model how to find an entry word. Point out the guide words on **Transparency 4–8.** Remind children that these words are the first and last words on the page. Model how to find *envelope.* Then have children read its definition and sample sentence.

Think Aloud *I look at the guide words* enter *and* even. *Will* envelope *be on this page? Yes, it will be because* envelope *comes between* enter *and* even *in alphabetical order.* Envelope *must come after* enter *because its third letter,* v, *comes after the* t *in* enter.

❷ Guided Practice

Have partners take turns finding entry words. Distribute dictionaries. List entry words. Have children work together to find each word, read its definition, and use the word in a sentence.

❸ Apply

Assign Practice Book page 15.

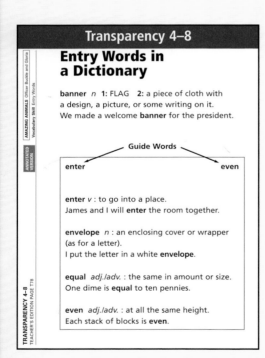

Transparency 4–8

Entry Words in a Dictionary

banner *n* **1:** FLAG **2:** a piece of cloth with a design, a picture, or some writing on it. We made a welcome **banner** for the president.

Guide Words

enter — even

enter *v* : to go into a place. James and I will **enter** the room together.

envelope *n* : an enclosing cover or wrapper (as for a letter). I put the letter in a white **envelope**.

equal *adj./adv.* : the same in amount or size. One dime is **equal** to ten pennies.

even *adj./adv.* : at all the same height. Each stack of blocks is **even**.

TRANSPARENCY 4–8
TEACHER'S EDITION PAGE T78

AMAZING ANIMALS Officer Buckle and Gloria
Vocabulary Skill Entry Words
ANNOTATED VERSION

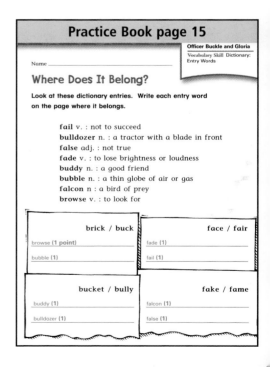

Practice Book page 15

Officer Buckle and Gloria
Vocabulary Skill Dictionary:
Entry Words

Name _____

Where Does It Belong?

Look at these dictionary entries. Write each entry word on the page where it belongs.

fail v. : not to succeed
bulldozer n. : a tractor with a blade in front
false adj. : not true
fade v. : to lose brightness or loudness
buddy n. : a good friend
bubble n. : a thin globe of air or gas
falcon n : a bird of prey
browse v. : to look for

brick / buck	face / fair
browse (1 point)	fade (1)
bubble (1)	fail (1)

bucket / bully	fake / fame
buddy (1)	falcon (1)
bulldozer (1)	false (1)

Monitoring Student Progress

If . . .	Then . . .
children score 6 or below on **Practice Book** page 15,	have partners work together to correct the items they missed.

PHONICS: Common Syllables *-tion, -ture*

1 Review

Review the pattern. Use *station, attention,* and *capture* to explain the following concepts. Then have children read the words.

- The endings *-tion* and *-ture* form separate syllables at the end of words.

- Both *-tion* and *-ture* have a "softened vowel sound" which is neither long nor short.

2 Guided Practice

Assign Practice Book page 16. Also have children make Word Ladders.

Word Ladders

Get ready to play.

- Write *nature, action, future, section, fraction, contraction, departure, fracture, pasture, protection, attraction,* and *adventure*.

- Give partners twelve strips of colored paper, and have them copy the listed words, one word per strip.

- Tell children to glue the strips with words ending in *-ture* on paper to form the rungs of a ladder. Have them make a ladder for words ending in *-tion* on another paper.

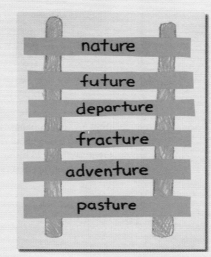

Play the game.

- Partners each choose a different word ladder. They alternate reading the words and using that word in an oral sentence.

- Have children score a point for each word read correctly and another point for using it in a sentence that makes sense.

OBJECTIVES

- Read and write words with *-tion* and *-ture*.

Review Skill Trace

Teach	Theme 3, p. T259
Reteach	Theme 3, p. R24
▸ Review	p. T79; Theme 3, p. T365
See	*Handbook for English Language Learners,* p. 129

Materials

- 12 1- by 6-inch strips of colored construction paper per pair of children
- glue and markers

Practice Book page 16

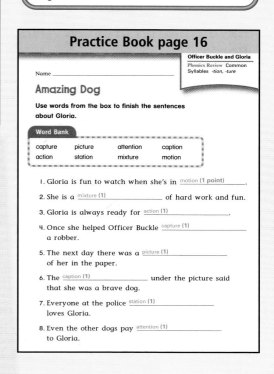

Name _____

Amazing Dog

Use words from the box to finish the sentences about Gloria.

Word Bank

capture	picture	attention	caption
action	station	mixture	motion

1. Gloria is fun to watch when she's in _motion (1 point)_ .
2. She is a _mixture (1)_ of hard work and fun.
3. Gloria is always ready for _action (1)_ .
4. Once she helped Officer Buckle _capture (1)_ a robber.
5. The next day there was a _picture (1)_ of her in the paper.
6. The _caption (1)_ under the picture said that she was a brave dog.
7. Everyone at the police _station (1)_ loves Gloria.
8. Even the other dogs pay _attention (1)_ to Gloria.

PHONICS LIBRARY

Reading Decodable Text

OBJECTIVES

- Apply the Phonics/Decoding Strategy to decode words in context.
- Reread to build fluency.

Have children preview *Arthur's Book*.

Have children model the Phonics/ Decoding Strategy. Ask children how they figure out new words. Use the poster to review the steps of the Phonics/Decoding Strategy.

Apply the Phonics/Decoding Strategy. Have children read the story independently. If necessary, use prompts such as these for *mixture* (page 10):

- Find the word *m-i-x-t-u-r-e* in the last sentence.

- What word part that you know do you see at the end of this word? Say it.

- Read the first syllable. Blend the syllables to read the word.

- Try the word in the sentence. Does it make sense?

HOUGHTON MIFFLIN
Reading
Phonics Library

Amazing Animals

Arthur's Book
by Patty Moynahan
illustrated by John Manders

Arthur wanted to write his own book. He had stacks and stacks of nice white paper. He had three new pens. He had lots of time for writing. Just one thing was missing.

9

Arthur needed an idea. He started thinking and thinking.
"I'll tell a tale about a frightful sea creature," he told himself. "It could be a mixture of fact and fiction."

10

Arthur looked out the window. He saw his cat chasing his dog.
"How will this sea creature act?" he asked. "That's the question."
Arthur kept thinking and thinking.

11

10   1

Word Key

Decodable words with *-tion, -ture* _____

Review High-Frequency Words _____

Outside, his dog jumped up a tree. Arthur did not see.

"My brain is starting to hurt," said Arthur. "How hard can it be to get an idea?"

12

Then Arthur looked back outside. He saw his cat run up the tree. He saw his dog in the tree. It was very funny.

"Sea <u>creatures</u> do not do funny things like that!" Arthur said. "I need a new idea."

13

Arthur felt that it might be helpful to look at books. He picked up a book from the fiction <u>section</u> of his shelf. Just then, his dog and cat raced by. They made him drop his book. That got his <u>attention</u>.

14

"That's it!" he yelled. He had an idea. "My story will be about a cat that chases a dog. I know about that!" he said.

Then he went back to his desk and started to write.

15

Oral Language

Discuss the story. Ask children to answer in complete sentences.

- Where does Arthur get an idea for his book? (Arthur gets an idea from watching his dog and cat.)

- What funny things do Arthur's cat and dog do? (The cat chases the dog. The dog jumps up a tree.)

- Why does Arthur think it is better to write about a dog and cat than about a sea creature? (He knows what a dog and cat can do.)

Build Fluency

Model fluent reading.

- Read aloud page 12. Tell children to notice how you read Arthur's question. Have children read aloud the same text.

- Have partners alternate modeling how to read pages in the story. Have one child read a page and the other reread it. Encourage children to read with expression to show Arthur's feelings.

 **Home Connection**
Hand out the take-home version of *Arthur's Book.* Ask children to reread the story with their families. (See the **Phonics Library Blackline Masters.**)

Reading Decodable Text T81

Practice Book page 17

Name _____

Officer Buckle and Gloria
Spelling The Vowel + r
Sound in car

Proofreading and Writing

Proofreading Read the list of safety rules below. Circle the Spelling Words that are not spelled correctly.

Spelling Words

1. car
2. smart
3. arm
4. park
5. yard
6. part
7. barn
8. hard
9. party
10. farm
11. are*
12. warm*

1. Before you cross the street, look to see if a (care) is coming. **(1 point)**
2. In the (pak) look out for people on bicycles. **(1)**
3. Never touch a (wharm) iron. **(1)**
4. Never swallow (harrd) candy whole. **(1)**
5. Don't give the small (purt) of a toy to your baby sister. **(1)**
6. Always be (smahrt) and safe! **(1)**

Write each word you circled. Spell the word correctly.

1. car **(1)** _____   4. hard **(1)** _____
2. park **(1)** _____   5. part **(1)** _____
3. warm **(1)** _____   6. smart **(1)** _____

Write Your Own Safety Rules On another sheet of paper, write five safety rules you think are important. Use Spelling Words from the list. Responses will vary. **(2)**

SPELLING: The Vowel + *r* Sounds in *car*

Collect the Biscuit Divide children into groups of three. Give each group a Basic Word list and twelve cards shaped like dog biscuits.

- Each child chooses four Basic Words and writes a clue for each word on a biscuit. The clue might be a definition, a rhyming word, or the word's initial or final sound.

- Children mix up the biscuits and place them face-down.

- Each player selects a biscuit, reads the clue, guesses the word, and spells it aloud.

- If the child guesses incorrectly or misspells the word, the biscuit is placed face-down again. If correct, the child keeps the biscuit.

- The child who collects the most biscuits wins.

Practice/Homework Assign **Practice Book** page 17 for proofreading and writing practice.

Practice Book page 18

Name _____

Officer Buckle and Gloria
Grammar Skill Words for
Nouns (Pronouns)

Pronoun Smart

Replace the underlined words with *she, he, it,* or *they.* Write the new sentences on the lines.

1. On Saturday, Officer Buckle takes Gloria to the park.

   On Saturday, he takes Gloria to the park. **(1 point)**

   _____

2. Officer Buckle throws a ball for Gloria to catch.

   Officer Buckle throws it for Gloria to catch. **(1)**

3. Gloria runs after the big blue ball.

   She runs after the big blue ball. **(1)**

4. Officer Buckle and Gloria have a fun time together.

   They have a fun time together. **(1)**

5. Then Gloria takes a nap under a tree.

   Then she takes a nap under a tree. **(1)**

GRAMMAR: Words for Nouns

Practice/Homework Assign **Practice Book** page 18.

Officer Buckle throws a ball for Gloria to catch.
He throws a ball for Gloria to catch.

IMPROVING WRITING: Writing Times of Day

OBJECTIVE

• Use correct punctuation in writing the time of day.

❶ Teach

Writing Traits: Conventions Explain to children that using correct punctuation makes their writing easier to read.

Model different ways to write the time of an event. Display Transparency 4–9.

• Read aloud the first sentence on the transparency. Remind children that an invitation should show the time of the event.

• Point out the numeral 7 followed by a colon, and the *P.M.* in capital letters with periods. Explain that *P.M.* refers to afternoon and evening.

• Write *9:00 A.M.* Tell children that *A.M.* refers to morning.

• Read aloud the second sentence. Point out the words *o'clock* and explain that this is a shortened form of the words *of the clock*. An apostrophe is used for the missing letters.

❷ Practice

Complete Transparency 4–9.

• Have volunteers read the remaining sentences.

• Have them tell which words express the time and which punctuation mark or marks are used to write the time.

❸ Apply

Assign Practice Book page 19. Then have children reread their invitations to check that they wrote the time correctly. You might also suggest that children write a schedule for their activities today. Ask them to include the times when they expect to do the activities.

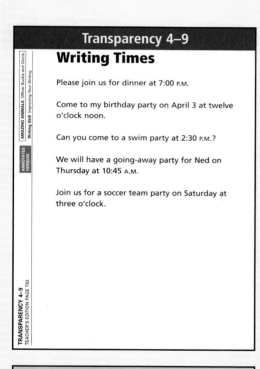

Transparency 4–9

Writing Times

Please join us for dinner at 7:00 P.M.

Come to my birthday party on April 3 at twelve o'clock noon.

Can you come to a swim party at 2:30 P.M.?

We will have a going-away party for Ned on Thursday at 10:45 A.M.

Join us for a soccer team party on Saturday at three o'clock.

AMAZING ANIMALS *Officer Buckle and Gloria*
Writing Skill Improving Your Writing

ANNOTATED VERSION

TRANSPARENCY 4–9
TEACHER'S EDITION PAGE T83

Practice Book page 19

Officer Buckle and Gloria
Writing Skill Writing Times

Name _____

What Time Is It?

Read the paragraph below that tells what a day for a police officer and his dog, Spike, might be like. Then write the times that they did each thing in the schedule below. Remember to include A.M. or P.M. after the time.

At eight o'clock in the morning, the two go for a walk. At nine o'clock in the morning, they drive to Woodview Elementary School. They finish their safety talk at eleven o'clock. At twelve o'clock they stop in the park for lunch. Spike finds other dogs to play with. At one-thirty in the afternoon, they go to Smith Elementary School. Then at three o'clock they help children get safely on the school bus.

Schedule	
8:00 A.M. **(1 point)** ____	Go for walk
9:00 A.M. **(1)** ____	Go to Woodview Elementary School
11:00 A.M. **(1)** ____	Finish safety talk
12:00 P.M. **(1)** ____	Lunch in park
1:30 P.M. **(1)** ____	Go to Smith Elementary School
3:00 P.M. **(1)** ____	Help children get on school bus

Day at a Glance
pp. T84–T89

Reading Instruction

Rereading for Understanding and Fluency

Study Skill: Interviewing

• •

Leveled Readers, *T90–T93*
- ● *Max the Pet Show Star*
- ▲ *The Best Job for Scooter*
- ■ *Daisy Divine, Dancing Dog*
- ◆ *Max Is a Star!*

Word Work

Vocabulary Expansion

Word Wall

Spelling Test: The Vowel + *r* Sounds in *car*

Writing & Oral Language

Writing Activity

Grammar: Improving Writing

Listening/Speaking/Viewing: Giving a Talk

Daily Routines

Daily Message

Strategy Review Remind children of the Phonics/Decoding Strategy. Guide them in applying it to selected words in today's message.

> Do you like to perform on the stage? Maybe you like to dance, recite poems, or act in plays. Would you rather be a polite listener in the audience?

Ask children to read aloud the entire Daily Message. Point to each word as they read. Then have volunteers answer the questions, and discuss their responses.

Word Wall

Cumulative Review Review previously taught high-frequency words by playing a word search game. Duplicate and distribute **Activity Master 4–1** on page R40. Have children find and circle the high-frequency words shown on the dog shape.

Vocabulary

Vocabulary Expansion Brainstorm with children words associated with writing letters.

- Suggest that partners page through other sources to add to the list.
- Write children's responses on a chart that is similar to the one shown.

<u>Words About Writing Letters</u>
paper
stamp
pen
envelope
address
message

Daily Writing Prompt

Have children revise work they are currently writing, or have them use this prompt to begin a new writing activity.

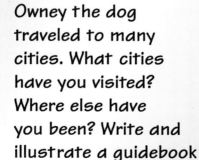

Owney the dog traveled to many cities. What cities have you visited? Where else have you been? Write and illustrate a guidebook of your favorite place. Tell what you liked best and why.

Daily Language Practice

Grammar Skill: Words for Nouns
Spelling Skill: The Vowel + *r* Sounds in *car*

Display **Transparency 4–1.** Ask children to rewrite Sentence 5 correctly. Then model how to write it, and have children check their work.

Transparency 4–1
Daily Language Practice

AMAZING ANIMALS *Officer Buckle and Gloria*
Grammar Skill Words for Nouns (Pronouns)
Spelling Skill The Vowel + r Sound in *car*

ANNOTATED VERSION

Proofread each sentence. Correct any errors.

Day 1
1. Sam green drives a bright red carr.

   Sam **Green** drives a bright red **car**.

Day 2
2. I see three dog at the parck.

   I see three **dogs** at the **park**.

Day 3
3. A tree in my yared has five peaches on them.

   A tree in my **yard** has five peaches on **it**.

Day 5
5. Them like to play in a baren.

   They like to play in a **barn**.

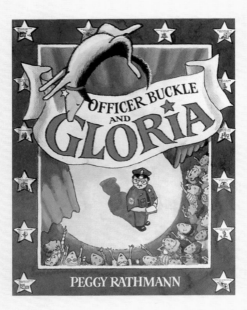

REVIEW

COMPREHENSION: Rereading for Understanding

Fantasy and Realism

Review Explain that an author may choose to combine fantasy and realism in the same story in order to entertain the reader. Remind children that

- fantasy is make-believe,
- a story can have both fantastic and realistic details.

Have children look at the illustrations on Anthology pages 36–37 and identify fantastic and realistic details. Record these details on a Fantasy and Realism Chart. (Fantasy: A dog signs autographs. Realism: A dog will eat ice cream.)

Practice/Apply Have children skim the story to find details to add to the Fantasy and Realism Chart.

Cause and Effect

Review Explain that a cause is why something happens or happened. An effect is what happened. Use a Cause and Effect Chart to review story events.

- List something that happens in the story in the first column, under Effect.
- Have children find and describe why it happened. Record that information in the second column, under Cause. (Effect: Children slid into Mrs. Toppel. Cause: They slipped on a puddle of pudding.)

Practice/Apply Have children find and record other cause-and-effect relationships in the story.

PRACTICE

REREADING FOR FLUENCY

Rereading the Selection Have children choose part of the story to reread orally in small groups, or suggest that they reread Anthology pages 46–50. If children are not reading with feeling and expression, model for them.

STUDY SKILL: Interviewing

OBJECTIVES
- Interview to gather information.
- Follow tips for interviewing.
- Learn academic language: *interview*.

❶ Teach

Explain that interviewing is a good way to gather information. Tell children the following:

- An interview is a conversation with someone who might have information to share.

- One person asks questions and the other person answers them.

Share these tips for conducting a good interview.

⭐ Decide what you want to know.

⭐ Write your questions. Use the question words, *Who? What? Where? When? Why? How?*

⭐ Ask questions clearly and politely.

⭐ Take notes to help you remember what the person said.

⭐ If you don't understand something, ask more questions.

❷ Practice/Apply

Have partners complete the assignable activity below.
First, brainstorm interview questions. Then discuss the results.

Give a Good Interview

- Choose who you will pretend to be from *Officer Buckle and Gloria*.

- Find out which character your partner will be.

- Write three interview questions to ask the character your partner is playing.

- Interview your partner. Write what he or she says.

- Take turns. Now answer your partner's questions.

Information and Study Skills T87

OBJECTIVES

- Write spelling words with the vowel + *r* sounds in *car*.
- Proofread sentences for the correct use of pronouns to improve writing.

SPELLING: The Vowel + *r* Sounds in *car*

Test

Say each underlined word, read the sentence, and then repeat the word. Have children write only the underlined word.

Basic Words

1. Our **car** had a flat tire.
2. My dog is very **smart**.
3. I broke my **arm**.
4. We play ball in the **park**.
5. Trees grow in my **yard**.
6. A leaf is **part** of a tree.
7. The cow is in the **barn**.
8. That old bun is **hard**.
9. Taj came to my **party**.
10. Sheep live on a **farm**.
11. They **are** sleeping.
12. The sun is **warm**.

Challenge Words

13. We visited the police **department**.
14. The floor is covered with a **carpet**.

Transparency 4–10

AMAZING ANIMALS Officer Buckle and Gloria
Grammar Skill Improving Your Writing

ANNOTATED VERSION

Writing Clearly with Pronouns

Mrs. Toppel called Officer Buckle.

_____She_____ called Officer Buckle.

The students want to hear the safety tips.

_____They_____ want to hear the safety tips.

The crash helmet was in the drawing.

_____It_____ was in the drawing.

The safety tips are important.

_____They_____ are important.

Gloria looked lonely.

_____She_____ looked lonely.

Officer Buckle was happy again.

_____He_____ was happy again.

TRANSPARENCY 4–10
TEACHER'S EDITION PAGE T88

GRAMMAR: Improving Writing

Writing Clearly with Pronouns

Teach Demonstrate how to write clearly with pronouns. Read aloud the first pair of sentences on **Transparency 4–10.**

- Ask what pronoun can take the place of the first noun.
- Write this word on the line in the second sentence.
- Have children read both sentences aloud to make sure the second sentence makes sense.
- Repeat with the other pairs of sentences.

Have children check that they have used pronouns correctly in a sample of their own writing.

Practice/Apply Assign **Practice Book** page 20.

Practice Book page 20

Officer Buckle and Gloria
Grammar Skill Words for Nouns (pronouns)

Name _____

Pronoun News

Read the article from the school newspaper. Find places where a noun can be replaced with a pronoun. Draw a circle around the nouns that can be replaced.

Today Officer Buckle and Gloria came to our school. Officer Buckle is a safety officer and Gloria is a dog. Officer Buckle gave a safety talk. The safety talk was an important lesson for children. While Officer Buckle was talking, Gloria acted out the tips. Gloria is the funniest dog the students have ever seen. Don't miss their next visit! Students should circle four nouns that could be replaced with a pronoun. Their answers may vary.

Rewrite the article. Replace each noun you drew a circle around with a pronoun. Then read the article you have written to see if it makes sense.

Responses will vary. Student should replace at least four of the

nouns with pronouns. Students' completed article should make

sense. (4 points)

LISTENING & SPEAKING: Giving a Talk

❶ Teach

Explain that you speak to a group when you give a talk.
An organized talk includes

- a main idea that tells what your talk is about,
- lots of supporting details,
- facial expressions or body movements that help with understanding.

Share these tips for giving a talk.

⭐ Choose a topic that you know something about.

⭐ Plan what you will say. Write notes on index cards.

⭐ Practice out loud.

⭐ Speak loudly enough to be heard.

⭐ Look at the audience when you speak.

❷ Practice/Apply

Prepare children to give a talk. Have them write a main idea and supporting details on index cards. Allow them time to practice speaking to a small group or to the class.

OBJECTIVES

- Identify the characteristics of a talk.
- Plan and give a talk.
- Learn academic language: *talk*.

Materials

- index cards

English Language Learners

Present a Safety Tip

Work with children to list safety tips useful at school. Help them figure out tips based on their school surroundings and what might happen if there were no safety rules. Teach important vocabulary. Ask children to make a safety poster.

Talking About Safety

- Plan a talk about school or home safety.
- Write notes about what you will say.
- Draw a picture to go with your talk.
- Practice it aloud.
- Give your talk.

Safety is for everyone. Don't run in the halls.

LEVELED READERS

WEEK 1

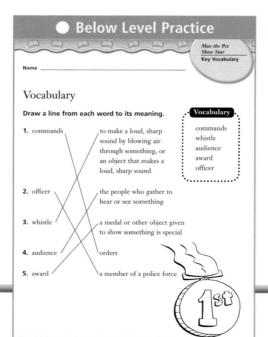

Max the Pet Show Star

Summary *Katie and her dog, Max, are going to be in a Police Pet Show. Katie is sure that Max will be the star, because he can perform many tricks. Max, however, has other plans, and shows off his talents in a way that surprises Katie.*

Vocabulary

Introduce the Key Vocabulary and ask children to complete the BLM.

commands* orders given to someone, *p. 5*

whistle to make a loud, sharp sound by blowing air through something, or an object that makes a loud, sharp sound, *p. 6*

audience* a group that listens or watches, *p. 10*

award a medal or other object given to show something is special, *p. 12*

officer* a person who helps enforce the law, *p. 12*

*Forms of these words are Anthology Key Vocabulary words.

● BELOW LEVEL

Building Background and Vocabulary

Explain to children that this story is about what happens when Katie enters her dog, Max, in the Police Pet Show. Discuss how pets sometimes don't follow orders when they are interested in something else. Use some of the language of the book and key vocabulary as you guide children through the text.

Comprehension Skill: Drawing Conclusions

Have children read the Strategy Focus on the book flap. Remind children to use the strategy and to use story clues and personal knowledge to draw conclusions as they read the book. (See the Leveled Readers Teacher's Guide for **Vocabulary and Comprehension Practice Masters.**)

Responding

Have partners discuss how to answer the questions on the inside back cover.

Think About What You Have Read Sample answers:

1. She thinks he is special and will be the star of the show.
2. He watches the rabbit.
3. Responses will vary.

Making Connections Responses will vary.

Building Fluency

Model Read aloud pages 4–5 and discuss the presence of quotation marks with *Katie said* and the absence of them with *Katie knew*.

Practice Ask children to find and read aloud a sentence in quotation marks.

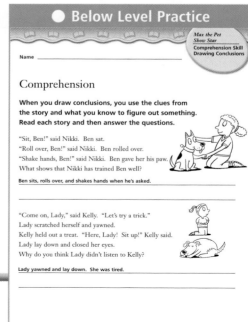

● Below Level Practice

Name _____

Vocabulary

Draw a line from each word to its meaning.

Vocabulary
commands
whistle
audience
award
officer

1. commands — to make a loud, sharp sound by blowing air through something, or an object that makes a loud, sharp sound

2. officer — the people who gather to hear or see something

3. whistle — a medal or other object given to show something is special

4. audience — orders

5. award — a member of a police force

● Below Level Practice

Name _____

Comprehension

When you draw conclusions, you use the clues from the story and what you know to figure out something. Read each story and then answer the questions.

"Sit, Ben!" said Nikki. Ben sat.
"Roll over, Ben!" said Nikki. Ben rolled over.
"Shake hands, Ben!" said Nikki. Ben gave her his paw.
What shows that Nikki has trained Ben well?

Ben sits, rolls over, and shakes hands when he's asked.

_____

"Come on, Lady," said Kelly. "Let's try a trick."
Lady scratched herself and yawned.
Kelly held out a treat. "Here, Lady! Sit up!" Kelly said.
Lady lay down and closed her eyes.
Why do you think Lady didn't listen to Kelly?

Lady yawned and lay down. She was tired.

_____

The Best Job for Scooter

Summary The Halls have puppies to give away. Only one puppy—Scooter—is left. The Halls have to find a home for Scooter, so they try to find a job that he can do. Scooter tries out lots of different jobs, but he doesn't seem to be good at any of them. Finally, when a boy named Bart and his mother show up, they find a perfect job for Scooter.

Vocabulary

Introduce the Key Vocabulary and ask children to complete the BLM.

guard to watch over, *p. 4*

officer* a person who helps enforce the law, *p. 7*

attention* looking and listening with care, *p. 8*

commands* orders given to someone, *p. 8*

herd to gather or keep animals in a group, *p. 11*

*Forms of these words are Anthology Key Vocabulary words.

▲ ON LEVEL

Building Background and Vocabulary

Explain that this story is about a dog that is looking for the right job. Ask children to tell what they know about different jobs that dogs can do. Use some of the language of the book and key vocabulary as you guide children through the text.

Comprehension Skill: Drawing Conclusions

Have children read the Strategy Focus on the book flap. Remind children to use the strategy and to use story clues and personal knowledge to draw conclusions as they read the book. (See the Leveled Readers Teacher's Guide for **Vocabulary and Comprehension Practice Masters.**)

Responding

Have partners discuss how to answer the questions on the inside back cover.

Think About What You Have Read Sample answers:

1. He doesn't want to guard the store. He falls asleep.

2. Possible response: I thought he would be a good police dog because he liked to ride in the police car.

3. Scooter doesn't care for herding. He likes to play and swim.

4. Possible response: Scooter will be a good pet because he can do all the things he likes to do.

Making Connections Responses will vary.

Building Fluency

Model Read aloud page 5. Emphasize the last sentence.

Practice Ask small groups to read aloud the rest of the selection. Have them note the different ways Scooter's return is repeated and phrased.

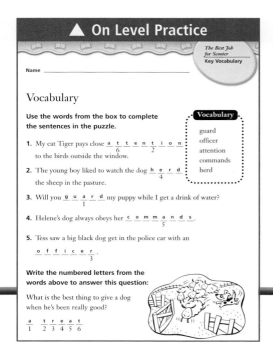

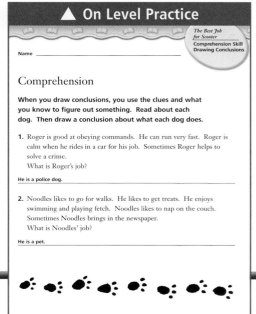

Daisy Divine, Dancing Dog

Summary *Daisy is an average dog by day, but at night, she performs in a circus as Daisy Divine, Dancing Dog. When the circus closes, she has to find a new job. Just when she is about to give up, she finds the perfect job as a dance teacher.*

Vocabulary

Introduce the Key Vocabulary and ask children to complete the BLM.

ordinary average; not unusual, *p. 2*

audience* a group that listens or watches, *p. 4*

attention* looking and listening with care, *p. 4*

officer* a person who helps enforce the law, *p. 8*

commands* orders given to someone, *p. 8*

imagination the creative part of the mind, *p. 13*

*Forms of these words are Anthology Key Vocabulary words.

■ ABOVE LEVEL

Building Background and Vocabulary

Explain to children that this story is about a dog with special talents. Ask children to tell what special talents some dogs have. Have they ever heard of a dog that dances? Use some of the language of the book and key vocabulary as you guide children through the text.

Comprehension Skill: Drawing Conclusions

Have children read the Strategy Focus on the book flap. Remind children to use the strategy and to use story clues and personal knowledge to draw conclusions as they read the book. (See the Leveled Readers Teacher's Guide for **Vocabulary and Comprehension Practice Masters**.)

Responding

Have partners discuss how to answer the questions on the inside back cover.

Think About What You Have Read Sample answers:

1. The circus closes down, and Daisy has to look for a new home.
2. She lives with a police officer, but she misses dancing. She lives with a family, but the children are mean. She tries a quiet life, but she is bored.
3. Daisy finally finds a job as a dance teacher at Tiptoe School of Dance.
4. Responses will vary.

Making Connections Responses will vary.

Building Fluency

Model Read aloud page 5, including the text within the illustration to show how to read such text as part of the story.

Practice Ask pairs of students to read the text on pages 7, 9, 11, and 15, practicing reading illustration text as part of the story.

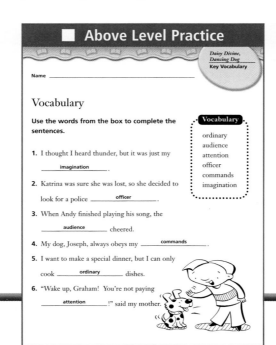

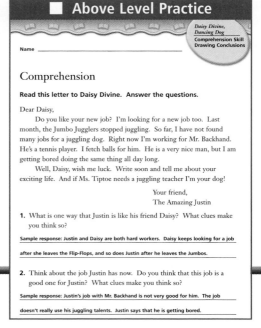

Max Is a Star!

Summary *Katie is sure her dog, Max, will be the star of the Police Pet Show, but Max does not perform like a star on stage. Later, he finds a boy's missing rabbit and becomes a star in his own way.*

Vocabulary

Introduce the Key Vocabulary and ask children to complete the BLM.

pet show a display or competition to show pets, *p. 2*

star an important person, *p. 4*

whistle to make a musical sound by blowing through your teeth or lips, *p. 6*

juggle to keep one or more objects, such as balls, in the air by tossing and catching them, *p. 6*

jump to move through the air by using the leg muscles, *p. 6*

officer* a person who helps enforce the law, *p. 12*

*Forms of these words are Anthology Key Vocabulary words.

◆ LANGUAGE SUPPORT

Building Background and Vocabulary

Take a survey of class pets and chart the results on the board. Those children without pets can name their favorite type of pet. Then distribute the **Build Background Practice Master.** Read the directions aloud, model how to follow them, and have children complete the page in pairs.

Comprehension Skill: Drawing Conclusions

Have children read the Strategy Focus on the book flap. Remind children to use the strategy and to draw conclusions as they read the book. (See the Leveled Readers Teacher's Guide for **Build Background, Vocabulary,** and **Graphic Organizer Masters.**)

Responding

Have partners discuss how to answer the questions on the inside back cover.

Think About What You Have Read Sample answers:

1. They are looking for the boy's rabbit.
2. He finds the lost rabbit and brings it back.
3. Answers will vary.

Making Connections Answers will vary.

Building Fluency

Model Read aloud pages 11–12 as children follow along in their books. Remind them that a comma tells a reader to pause briefly before continuing.

Practice Have small groups take the roles of the boy, Katie, the police officer, and the narrator, and act out the scene. Suggest that students rehearse several times before performing for the class.

Reading-Writing Workshop

Research Report

In the Reading-Writing Workshop for Theme 4, *Amazing Animals,* children read Celsey's research report on Anthology pages 56–57. Then they follow the five steps of the writing process to write a research report.

Meet the Author

Celsey B.
Grade: two
State: Georgia
Hobbies: horseback riding, swimming, and skating
What she'd like to be when she grows up: a horseback rider who jumps or a dentist

---

Theme Skill Trace

Writing
- Writing Times of Day, T83
- Using *I* and *me*, T165
- Adding Details, T233

Grammar
- Writing Clearly with Pronouns, T88
- Proofreading for Apostrophes, T170
- Proofreading for Apostrophes, T238

Spelling
- The Vowel + *r* Sound in *car*, T40
- Words That End with *nd, ng,* or *nk*, T126
- More Long *o* Words, T196

Pacing the Workshop

Here is a suggestion for how you might pace the workshop within one week or on five separate days across the theme.

DAY 1 PREWRITING

Children
- read the student model, Anthology 56–57
- choose a topic, T98
- organize their report, T99
- find and evaluate information, T100

Spelling Frequently Misspelled Words, T103; *Practice Book,* 293

DAY 2 DRAFTING

Children
- write research questions and facts about their topic, T101
- draft their research report, T101

Spelling *Practice Book,* 23

Focus on Writing Traits: Research Report

This workshop for this theme focuses on the traits of ideas and organization. However, children should think about all the writing traits during the writing process.

IDEAS Children will do their best research if they are motivated. Consider these points to keep children motivated.

- Children need a topic that interests them. Are they enthusiastic about the topic they chose?

- They need a topic that is a manageable size. Can they narrow their topic?

- They need help finding sources. Can the school librarian, an older student, or a parent volunteer help you guide children to the right sources for their topic?

ORGANIZATION Encourage children to use the questions in their K-W-L charts (see page T99) to help group, or categorize, the facts they have collected.

- Point to a specific question, and ask, *Which facts answer this question?*

- Point to specific facts, and ask, *Which question does this fact answer?*

- If a fact doesn't fit a question, discuss deleting the fact. If several facts don't fit, discuss adding a new question to the K-W-L chart.

Tips for Teaching the Writing Traits

- Teach one trait at a time.

- Discuss examples of the traits in the literature children are reading.

- Encourage children to talk about the traits during a writing conference.

- Encourage children to revise their writing for one trait at a time.

DAY 3 REVISING

Children

- evaluate their research report, T102

- revise their report, T102

- have a writing conference, T102

- improve their writing by using exact nouns, T102

Spelling *Practice Book,* 24

DAY 4 PROOFREADING

Children

- proofread their research report, T102

- correct frequently misspelled words in their report, T103

Spelling *Practice Book,* 25

DAY 5 PUBLISHING

Children

- publish their research report, T103

- reflect on their writing experience, T103

Spelling Assessment, T103

Research Report

Discussing the Guidelines

Display **Transparency RWW4–1,** and discuss with children what makes a great research report.

- Remember to introduce all the writing traits as children work through the writing process: ideas, organization, voice, word choice, sentence fluency, conventions, and presentation.

Discussing the Model

Have children read the Student Writing Model on Anthology pages 56–57.

- Discuss with children what the writer did to make her writing interesting to read.
- Use the Reading As a Writer questions on the next page.

Student Writing Model

A Research Report

A research report tells facts about a topic in the writer's own words. Use this student's writing as a model when you write a research report of your own.

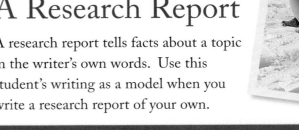

> The **title** tells what the report is about.

> A **research report** gives **facts** from other sources.

> Writers give the facts in their **own words**.

The Harp Seal

My favorite animal is the harp seal. I've found out a lot about the harp seal that I would like to share with you.

A real harp seal has beautiful gray fur and lives in the cold water in the North Atlantic Ocean. Harp seals are happiest when they are in the water. Their flippers really help them swim quickly. When harp seals are on the icy land, they have to wiggle their bodies so they can move. Their front flippers have claws that help them hold on to the ice and rocks. Mostly they just stay in the water.

When harp seals are in the water they eat shrimp and squid. They also eat big fish. The seals have to be very careful in the water. That's

56

Transparency RWW4–1

What Makes a Great Research Report?

A **research report** tells facts about a topic in the writer's own words.

When you write a research report, remember to do these things.

- Choose a topic that interests you.
- Find enough interesting facts about the topic.
- Take notes on the facts you find.
- Organize the facts in an order that makes sense.
- Share the facts in your own words.
- Write a good ending.

AMAZING ANIMALS
Reading-Writing Workshop: Research Report
ANNOTATED VERSION

TRANSPARENCY RWW 4–1
TEACHER'S EDITION PAGE T96

THEME 4: Amazing Animals
(Anthology p. 56)

when the polar bears, sharks, and killer whales could swim up and hurt them. Another interesting thing about harp seals is that they don't have ears! They hear sounds through their heads, instead.

The harp seal is very cute, even though it's pretty big. It grows to be six feet long. Someday I would like to see one in person.

A good **ending** wraps up the report.

Meet the Author

Celsey B.
Grade: two
State: Georgia
Hobbies: horseback riding, swimming, and skating
What she'd like to be when she grows up: a horseback rider who jumps or a dentist

57

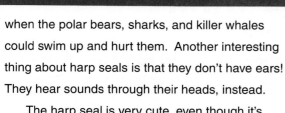

Reading As a Writer

1. **What is the research report about?** (harp seals)

2. **What makes the opening sentence interesting?** (The writer tells you the topic of the report and gives a personal opinion.)

3. **What facts does Celsey tell about how harp seals move?** (Their flippers help them swim quickly; on the icy land, they wiggle their bodies; their front flippers have claws that help them hold on to the ice and rocks.)

4. **What other facts does Celsey tell about harp seals?** (Sample answer: They eat shrimp, squid, and big fish. They hear sounds through their heads. A harp seal has gray fur and lives in the North Atlantic Ocean.)

5. **What makes this report enjoyable?** (the writer's interest in the topic, her use of colorful words to describe the seal, and facts that are interesting)

Choosing a Topic

1 **Tell children that they are going to write their own research report.** Have children list at least three ideas for a topic they could write about. If children have difficulty thinking of ideas, use the following prompts.

- There are unusual animals that live in the desert, jungle, and forest. Which of these animals are you curious about?

- Animals live in zoos. Which zoo animal would you like to write about?

- Special places and people are good topics for research reports. What person or place would you like to know more about?

2 **Have children answer these questions** as they choose a topic, either in a writing journal or on a sheet of paper.

- Is this topic really interesting to you?

- What do you already know about this topic?

- Where can you find facts about this topic?

- Who will read your report on this topic?

3 **Have children discuss their ideas with a partner** and decide which topic would be the best one to write about. Discuss the writing trait of ideas, and then review the tips below.

Writing Traits

IDEAS Remind children that the topic they choose should be focused on a specific person, animal, place, or thing.

- Explain that the topic *Birds* is too general. There is too much information about birds to write a good report.

- It would be easier to write a report on a specific kind of bird, such as a parrot or woodpecker.

Tips for Getting Started with a Topic

- Talk with a partner about your topic. Is it too big? If so, what part of the topic could you write about?

- Tell your partner what you already know about the topic. What questions do you have? What questions does your partner have?

- Brainstorm where to find information on your topic.

Organizing and Planning

Writing Traits

ORGANIZATION A K-W-L chart will help children decide which facts to include in their report. Explain the following about these charts.

- Children should write what they know about the topic (K).

- They should write questions about what they want to learn (W).

- They should answer these questions by doing research and taking notes about the topic. (L)

1 **Display Transparency RWW4–2.**

- Explain that before writing her report on harp seals, Celsey might have started a K-W-L chart.

- Use the Student Writing Model on Anthology pages 56–57, and model starting to fill in the chart.

K	W	L
What I Know	What I Want to Learn	What I Learned
Harp seals live in the water.	Where do they live?	
They can swim.	What do they look like?	
Harp seals eat fish.	How do they move on land?	
	How do they move in the water?	

2 **Distribute copies of Transparency RWW4–2.**

- Have children fill in the first two boxes of their K-W-L Chart.

- Tell children that they can choose another topic if the one they have chosen no longer interests them.

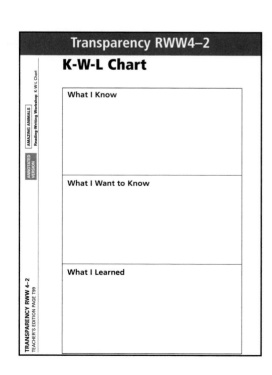

Transparency RWW4–2

K-W-L Chart

What I Know

What I Want to Know

What I Learned

TRANSPARENCY RWW 4–2
TEACHER'S EDITION PAGE T99

AMAZING ANIMALS   Reading-Writing Workshop K-W-L Chart

ANNOTATED VERSION

Finding and Evaluating Information

1 **Explain that a source is a place to find information about a topic.**

- Some sources, such as the Internet, magazines, or newspapers, are better for finding current information that might change.
- Some sources, such as an encyclopedia or nonfiction book, might be better for in-depth information.

2 **Discuss choosing sources.** Show the chart below on the board. Fill in the first column. Brainstorm with children which sources would be best for each topic.

Sources for Different Topics

Topic	Where to Look
Toucans	nonfiction bird books, encyclopedia, Internet
Latest Toy Crazes	newspapers, maga-zines, Internet
Sports Scores	newspapers, Internet

3 **Explain taking notes.** Tell children that they will need to take notes to remember the information they read. Explain that they should do the following when taking notes.

- They should write words and phrases that help them remember important information.
- They should use their own words. They should not copy the information.

4 **Have children research their topic and take notes.**

- Help children find age-appropriate sources for their topic.
- Have them research their topic, taking notes in the What I Learned box on their K-W-L Chart.

Using Facts

1 **Help children organize their facts.** Tell children that they can organize the facts they wrote down on their K-W-L chart.

- They can number the facts in the order that they want to use them.
- They can then write the facts as sentences for their report.

2 **Model how to turn notes into complete sentences.** On the board, display the questions and the facts shown on the pink note card below.

- Have children read the facts. Point out that the facts are not written as complete sentences.
- Then model how to write these facts as complete sentences. Use the sentences shown on the blue paper below.

Q: How do harp seals move on land?
A: wiggle bodies on icy land
A: front flippers with claws
A: hold on to ice and rocks

Harp seals wiggle their bodies over icy land. They use the claws on their front flippers to hold on to ice and rocks.

3 **Have children draft their research reports,** using their K-W-L charts.

- Tell children to write complete sentences.
- Remind children to use their own words and to put the facts in an order that makes sense.
- Encourage them to use questions and exclamations as well as statements.
- Remind children to write an ending that wraps up the report. This might be a sentence that tells how they feel about the topic or a few sentences that summarize what they have learned.

Practice Book page 21

Reading-Writing Workshop
Revising Your Research Report

Name _____

Revising Your Research Report

Decide how to make your paper better. Put a check beside the sentences that describe your research report.

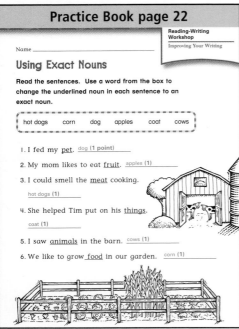

Superstar

☐ My report tells many interesting facts.

☐ I wrote my facts in a clear order.

☐ I wrote the facts in my own words.

☐ I used exact nouns.

☐ My report has a good ending.

☐ I used different kinds of sentences. There are not many mistakes.

Rising Star

☐ I need to include more facts about my topic.

☐ I wrote my facts in a mixed-up order.

☐ I did not write the facts in my own words.

☐ I need to use more exact nouns.

☐ My report is missing an ending.

☐ Most of my sentences are short and some are not complete. There are many mistakes.

Practice Book page 22

Reading-Writing Workshop
Improving Your Writing

Name _____

Using Exact Nouns

Read the sentences. Use a word from the box to change the underlined noun in each sentence to an exact noun.

| hot dogs | corn | dog | apples | coat | cows |

1. I fed my pet. _dog (1 point)_

2. My mom likes to eat fruit. _apples (1)_

3. I could smell the meat cooking. _hot dogs (1)_

4. She helped Tim put on his things. _coat (1)_

5. I saw animals in the barn. _cows (1)_

6. We like to grow food in our garden. _corn (1)_

Transparency RWW4–3

Using Exact Nouns

I like to eat food.
I like to eat chicken soup.

1. I like to play games.

2. Don has a pet.

3. Tanya lives in a building.

4. The person teaches us about writing.

5. Justin passes that place on the way to school.

6. Jeanine likes sports.

7. I keep things in this box.

8. She takes care of animals.

TRANSPARENCY RWW 4–3
TEACHER'S EDITION PAGE T102

Revising

Have children use **Practice Book** page 21 to help them evaluate and then revise their research report. Children should also discuss their drafts in a writing conference with one or more classmates. (Distribute the Conference Master R44. Discuss the sample thoughts and questions before children have their conferences.) Remind children to keep in mind their listeners' comments and questions when they revise.

Improving Writing: Using Exact Nouns

Explain to children that good writers use words that tell exactly what they mean so that their writing is clear and interesting. Review the following.

- A noun is the name of a person, place, or thing: *building, water.*

- An exact noun gives the most information and detail: *barn, pond.*

Display **Transparency RWW4–3.** Read the pair of sentences at the top.

- Have a volunteer underline the sentence that gives the most exact information about what someone likes to eat. (*I like to eat chicken soup.*)

- Have volunteers read each remaining sentence. Have children suggest an exact noun for each underlined word.

Assign **Practice Book** page 22. Then have children look at their research report to change any general nouns to more exact nouns.

Proofreading

Have children proofread their papers to correct capitalization, punctuation, spelling, and usage. You may want to have children use the Word Wall or **Practice Book** page 292 to help them check their spelling. Children can use the proofreading checklist on **Practice Book** page 311.

Frequently Misspelled Words

Write the Spelling Words on the board, or distribute the list on **Practice Book** page 293. Say the words and have children repeat them. Help children identify the part of the word likely to be misspelled.

Spelling Pretest/Test

Basic Words

1. Have you **done** any fishing?
2. Stephanie caught **one** fish.
3. The **two** sisters were excited.
4. Ken sat in the **back** of the boat.
5. They took **some** bait, too.
6. Put the bait on **your** hook.
7. **I'll** try to catch some fish, too.
8. Look **around** for more bait.
9. We **found** worms in the box.
10. **Once** I caught a huge fish.
11. Which **girl** told the story?
12. She put the fish **into** the basket.

Challenge Words

13. I **knew** we would all enjoy fishing.
14. The sunset was very **pretty**.

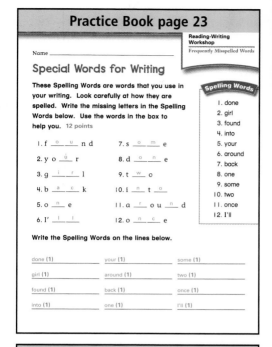

Practice Book page 23

Name _____

Reading-Writing Workshop
Frequently Misspelled Words

Special Words for Writing

These Spelling Words are words that you use in your writing. Look carefully at how they are spelled. Write the missing letters in the Spelling Words below. Use the words in the box to help you. **12 points**

Spelling Words
1. done
2. girl
3. found
4. into
5. your
6. around
7. back
8. one
9. some
10. two
11. once
12. I'll

1. f o u n d
2. y o u r
3. g i r l
4. b a c k
5. o n e
6. I' l l
7. s o m e
8. d o n e
9. t w o
10. i n t o
11. a r o u n d
12. o n c e

Write the Spelling Words on the lines below.

done (1)   your (1)   some (1)
girl (1)   around (1)   two (1)
found (1)   back (1)   once (1)
into (1)   one (1)   I'll (1)

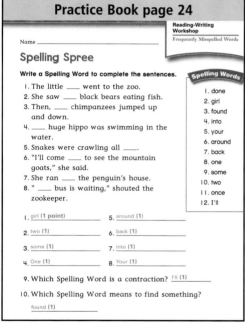

Practice Book page 24

Name _____

Reading-Writing Workshop
Frequently Misspelled Words

Spelling Spree

Write a Spelling Word to complete the sentences.

Spelling Words
1. done
2. girl
3. found
4. into
5. your
6. around
7. back
8. one
9. some
10. two
11. once
12. I'll

1. The little ____ went to the zoo.
2. She saw ____ black bears eating fish.
3. Then, ____ chimpanzees jumped up and down.
4. ____ huge hippo was swimming in the water.
5. Snakes were crawling all ____.
6. "I'll come ____ to see the mountain goats," she said.
7. She ran ____ the penguin's house.
8. " ____ bus is waiting," shouted the zookeeper.

1. girl (1 point)   5. around (1)
2. two (1)   6. back (1)
3. some (1)   7. into (1)
4. One (1)   8. Your (1)

9. Which Spelling Word is a contraction? I'll (1)
10. Which Spelling Word means to find something? found (1)

Practice Book page 293

Take-Home Word List	Take-Home Word List
Amazing Animals: Reading-Writing Workshop	Officer Buckle and Gloria
Look carefully at how these words are spelled.	The Vowel + r Sound in *car*
	vowel + r sound → car, smart
Spelling Words	**Spelling Words**
1. done 7. I'll	1. car 7. barn
2. one 8. around	2. smart 8. hard
3. two 9. found	3. arm 9. party
4. back 10. once	4. park 10. farm
5. some 11. girl	5. yard 11. are
6. your 12. into	6. part 12. warm
Challenge Words	**Challenge Words**
1. knew	1. department
2. pretty	2. carpet
Read directions to children.	Read directions to children.
My Study List Add your own spelling words on the back.	**My Study List** Add your own spelling words on the back.

Take-Home Word List

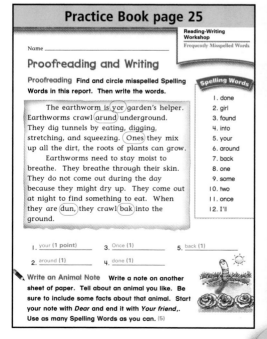

Practice Book page 25

Name _____

Reading-Writing Workshop
Frequently Misspelled Words

Proofreading and Writing

Proofreading Find and circle misspelled Spelling Words in this report. Then write the words.

Spelling Words
1. done
2. girl
3. found
4. into
5. your
6. around
7. back
8. one
9. some
10. two
11. once
12. I'll

The earthworm is yor garden's helper. Earthworms crawl arund underground. They dig tunnels by eating, digging, stretching, and squeezing. Ones they mix up all the dirt, the roots of plants can grow.

Earthworms need to stay moist to breathe. They breathe through their skin. They do not come out during the day because they might dry up. They come out at night to find something to eat. When they are dun, they crawl bak into the ground.

1. your (1 point)   3. Once (1)   5. back (1)
2. around (1)   4. done (1)

Write an Animal Note Write a note on another sheet of paper. Tell about an animal you like. Be sure to include some facts about that animal. Start your note with *Dear* and end it with *Your friend*. Use as many Spelling Words as you can. (5)

READING-WRITING WORKSHOP

Publishing

Have children publish their research report.

- Discuss the Ideas for Sharing box below.
- Then ask children to decide how they will publish their writing.
- Tell them to make a neat final copy of their research report. Remind them to use good penmanship or careful typing on a computer and to be sure that they have fixed all mistakes.

Portfolio Opportunity

Save children's final copy of their research report as an example of the development of their writing skills.

Ideas for Sharing

Write It.
- Post your report on your school's Internet site.
- Put all reports in a class book.

Say It
- Read your report aloud to classmates.
- Use a tape recorder to record your report so others can listen to it.

Show It
- Create a visual display for your report. Draw or cut pictures from magazines to show facts in your report. Write captions.

Tips for Creating a Visual Display

- Draw or find pictures, maps, or other visuals that show facts in your report.
- Make your visuals large enough for your audience to see.
- Add helpful labels. Use nice lettering.
- Put your visuals on poster board. Display your report next to it.

Monitoring Student Progress

Student Self-Assessment

- What part of your research report do you like best?
- Did you use enough facts in your research report?
- Did you write the facts in your research report in your own words?
- Are there any parts of your research report you would change?

Evaluating

Have children discuss responses to the Student Self-Assessment questions.

Evaluate children's writing, using the Writing Traits Scoring Rubric. The rubric is based on the criteria in this workshop and reflects the criteria children used in Revising Your Research Report on **Practice Book** page 21.

Research Report

Writing Traits Scoring Rubric

4

IDEAS	The report is focused on an interesting topic. The writer told many facts about a specific topic.
ORGANIZATION	Facts are written in an order that makes sense. The ending wraps up the report.
VOICE	The writer always used his or her own words.
WORD CHOICE	The writer used exact nouns.
SENTENCE FLUENCY	The writing flows well. Sentence length and structure vary.
CONVENTIONS	There are few errors in grammar, capitalization, spelling, or usage.
PRESENTATION	The final copy is neat and legible.

3

IDEAS	The report is focused on a topic. More facts are needed in some places.
ORGANIZATION	Some facts may be out of order. The ending may not wrap up the report.
VOICE	The writer mostly used his or her own words.
WORD CHOICE	The writer used some general rather than exact nouns.
SENTENCE FLUENCY	The report would benefit from greater sentence variety.
CONVENTIONS	There are some mistakes, but they do not affect understanding.
PRESENTATION	The final copy is messy in a few places but still legible.

2

IDEAS	The report may not be clearly focused on a single topic. Many additional facts are needed.
ORGANIZATION	Many facts may be out of order. The report ends abruptly.
VOICE	The writer often did not use his or her own words.
WORD CHOICE	The writer chose words that were sometimes unclear.
SENTENCE FLUENCY	The report lacks sentence variety.
CONVENTIONS	Mistakes sometimes make the report hard to understand.
PRESENTATION	The final copy is messy. It may be illegible in a few places.

1

IDEAS	The report does not have a focus. There are almost no facts and no research may have been done.
ORGANIZATION	Facts are disorganized, unclear, or presented as a list.
VOICE	The writer copied many sentences from a source instead of using his or her own words.
WORD CHOICE	The writer chose words that were often confusing.
SENTENCE FLUENCY	Sentences are unclear, incomplete, or repetitive.
CONVENTIONS	Many mistakes make the report hard to understand.
PRESENTATION	The final copy is messy. It may be illegible in many places.

READING-WRITING WORKSHOP

Lesson Overview

Literature

Rebecca Stefoff

ANT

Selection Summary

This photographic nonfiction book examines the physical characteristics, life cycle, and natural habitat of various types of ants.

1 ## Decodable Text

Phonics Library

- *Hank's Pandas*
- *Marta's Larks*

2 ## Background and Vocabulary

3 ## Main Selection

Ant
Genre: Nonfiction

4 ## Music Link

Instructional Support

Planning and Practice

- Planning and Classroom Management
- Reading and skill instruction
- Materials for reaching all learners

- Newsletters
- Selection Summaries
- Assignment Cards
- Observation Checklists
- Selection Tests

- Independent practice for skills

- Decodable Text, Books 40–44

- Charts/ Transparencies
- Strategy Posters
- Blackline Masters

Reaching All Learners

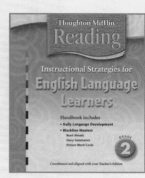

Coordinated lessons, activities, and projects for additional reading instruction

For
- Classroom Teacher
- Extended Day
- Pull Out
- Resource Teacher
- Reading Specialist

Technology

Audio Selection
Ant

Get Set for Reading CD-ROM
- Background building
- Vocabulary support
- Selection Summary in English and Spanish

Accelerated Reader®
- Practice quiz for the selection

www.eduplace.com
Log on to Education Place® for more activities related to the selection, including vocabulary support—
e • Glossary
e • WordGame

Leveled Books for Reaching All Learners

Leveled Readers and Leveled Practice

- Independent reading for building fluency

- Topic, comprehension strategy, and vocabulary linked to main selection

- Lessons in Teacher's Edition, pages T172–T175

- Leveled practice for every book

Technology

Leveled Readers
Audio available

Book Adventure®

- Practice quizzes for the Leveled Theme Paperbacks
  www.bookadventure.org

● BELOW LEVEL

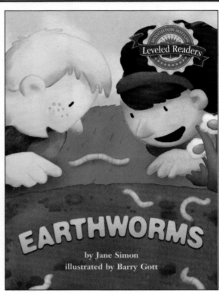

EARTHWORMS
by Jane Simon
illustrated by Barry Gott

● Below Level Practice

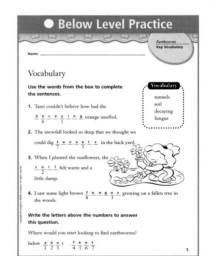

▲ ON LEVEL

Busy Bees
by Margaretha Takmar

▲ On Level Practice

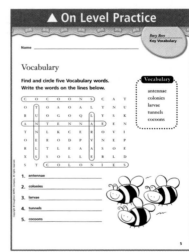

● Below Level Practice

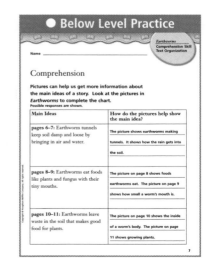

▲ On Level Practice

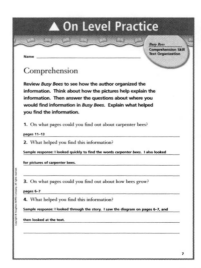

■ ABOVE LEVEL

Butterflies!
by Josie Strummer

HOUGHTON MIFFLIN Leveled Readers

◆ LANGUAGE SUPPORT

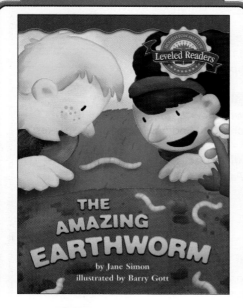

Leveled Readers

THE AMAZING EARTHWORM
by Jane Simon
illustrated by Barry Gott

Leveled Theme Paperbacks

- Extended independent reading in theme-related paperbacks
- Lessons in Teacher's Edition, pages R4–R9

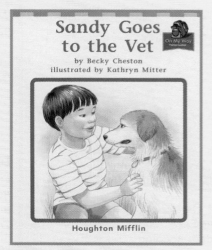

Sandy Goes to the Vet
by Becky Cheston
illustrated by Kathryn Mitter

Houghton Mifflin

Below Level

■ Above Level Practice

Name _____

Butterflies!
Key Vocabulary

Vocabulary

Draw a line from each word to its meaning.

| Vocabulary |
| antennae |
| coiled |
| larva |
| chrysalis |
| enemies |
| poisonous |

1. enemies — a pair of thin organs on the heads of insects that can be used to touch and smell

2. coiled — things that mean to do harm to others

3. chrysalis — newly hatched insects that have no wings and look like worms

4. antennae — something, often chemical, that can harm or kill

5. poisonous — gathered or wound into a ring

6. larva — a firm case, like a cocoon, that protects a growing insect until it is fully grown

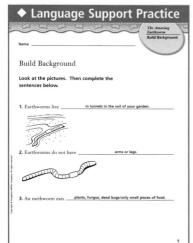

5

◆ Language Support Practice

Name _____

The Amazing Earthworm
Build Background

Build Background

Look at the pictures. Then complete the sentences below.

1. Earthworms live _____ in tunnels in the soil of your garden.

2. Earthworms do not have _____ arms or legs.

3. An earthworm eats _____ plants, fungus, dead bugs/only small pieces of food.

5

■ Above Level Practice

Name _____

Butterflies!
Comprehension Skill
Text Organization

Comprehension

Authors use pictures, headings, captions, and text to help them organize information. Review *Butterflies!* to see how the author organized the information. Then answer the questions and tell how you found the information.

1. On what page could you find out about how butterflies use their markings to help them blend in with their surroundings?

page 11

2. How did you find this information?

Sample response: I looked quickly at the headings, and found *How Butterflies Survive.*

Then I looked at the pictures in that section and saw the one on page 11. Then I read the words.

3. On what page could you find out about how a butterfly eats?

page 4

4. How did you find this information?

Sample response: I saw the heading *A Butterfly's Body* and looked there. I saw the picture of a butterfly drinking nectar. Then I read the words.

7

◆ Language Support Practice

The Amazing Earthworm
Key Vocabulary

Name _____

Vocabulary

Use the words in the box to label the pictures.

| Vocabulary |
| earthworms |
| garden |
| grow |
| soil |
| tunnels |
| waste |

earthworms / tunnels

grow / soil

garden / waste

6

RAPTORS!
Written by Lisa McCourt
Illustrated by Monica Popovici
troll

On Level

RUSSELL E. ERICKSON
A Toad for Tuesday
"A small-scale Wind in the Willows ... adventure and charm."—ALA Booklist

Above Level

Daily Lesson Plans

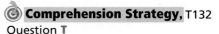
 WEEK 2 **DAILY LESSON PLANS**

T Skill tested on Theme Skills Test and/or Integrated Theme Test

---

80–90 minutes

Reading
Phonics
Comprehension

Leveled Readers
- Fluency Practice
- Independent Reading

20–30 minutes

Word Work
Vocabulary
High-Frequency Words
Spelling

20–30 minutes

Writing and Oral Language
Writing
Grammar
Listening/Speaking/Viewing

DAY 1

Daily Routines, T116–T117
Phonics and Language Activities

Listening Comprehension,
T118–T119
An Octopus Is Amazing

Phonics, T120–T121
Words with *nd, nt, mp, ng, nk* **T**
Base Words and Endings in Nouns (*-s, -es, -ies*) **T**

Reading Decodable Text, T123–T125
Hank's Pandas

....

Leveled Readers
Earthworms
Busy Bees
Butterflies!
The Amazing Earthworm

Lessons and Leveled Practice, T172–T175

Vocabulary, T117
Anagram Animals

High-Frequency Words, T122
between, care, weigh **T**

Spelling, T126
Words That End with *nd, ng,* or *nk* **T**

Writing, T117
Daily Writing Prompt

Grammar, T127
Singular Possessive Nouns **T**

Daily Language Practice
1. Will you sind me a picture of your house.
(Will you send me a picture of your house?)

Listening/Speaking/Viewing, T118–T119
Teacher Read Aloud

DAY 2

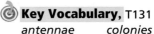

Daily Routines, T128–T129
Phonics and Language Activities

Building Background, T130

Key Vocabulary, T131
antennae   colonies   larvae
cocoons   fungus   tunnels

Reading the Selection, T132–T145

Comprehension Strategy, T132
Question **T**

Comprehension Skill, T132, T140
Text Organization **T**

....

Leveled Readers
Earthworms
Busy Bees
Butterflies!
The Amazing Earthworm

Lessons and Leveled Practice, T172–T175

Vocabulary, T129
Using a Dictionary

High-Frequency Words, T128
Word Wall

Spelling, T146
Review, Practice: Words That End with *nd, ng,* or *nk* **T**

Writing, T147
A Poem

Grammar, T146
Practice: Singular Possessive Nouns **T**

Daily Language Practice
2. We will seeing three song in the school play.
(We will sing three songs in the school play.)

Listening/Speaking/Viewing, T137, T145
Stop and Think, Wrapping Up

Target Skills of the Week

Phonics	Words with *nd, nt, mp, ng, nk;* Base Words and Endings in Nouns *(-s, -es, -ies)*
Comprehension	Text Organization; Question
Vocabulary	High-Frequency Words; Using a Thesaurus
Fluency	Decodable text; Leveled Readers

DAY 3

Daily Routines, T148–T149
Phonics and Language Activities

Rereading the Selection, T132–T145

Comprehension Check, T150
Responding, T150

Comprehension Skill, T152–T153
Text Organization **T**

Rereading for Understanding, T154
Visual Literacy: Descriptive Photographs

Leveled Readers
Earthworms
Busy Bees
Butterflies!
The Amazing Earthworm

Lessons and Leveled Practice, T172–T175

Vocabulary, T149
Relationships

High-Frequency Words, T148
Word Wall

Spelling, T155
Vocabulary Connection: Words That End with *nd, ng,* or *nk* **T**

Writing, T150
Write a Report

Grammar, T155
Activity: Singular Possessive Nouns **T**

Daily Language Practice
3. May i thank you for this gift?
(May I thank you for this gift?)

Listening/Speaking/Viewing, T150
Responding

DAY 4

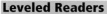

Daily Routines, T156–T157
Phonics and Language Activities

Reading the Music Link, T158–T159

Comprehension: How to Read Song Lyrics, T158

Phonics Review, T161
r-Controlled Vowels *ar, or, ore*

Reading Decodable Text, T162–T163
Marta's Larks

Leveled Readers
Earthworms
Busy Bees
Butterflies!
The Amazing Earthworm

Lessons and Leveled Practice, T172–T175

Vocabulary, T160
Using a Thesaurus **T**

High-Frequency Words, T156
Word Wall

Spelling, T164
Game, Proofreading: Words That End with *nd, ng,* or *nk* **T**

Writing, T165
Using *I* and *me* **T**

Grammar, T164
Practice: Singular Possessive Nouns **T**

Daily Language Practice
4. Will you breeng a bag of peachs when you come to the beach. (Will you bring a bag of peaches when you come to the beach?)

Listening/Speaking/Viewing, T158
Discuss the Link

DAY 5

Daily Routines, T166–T167
Phonics and Language Activities

Comprehension: Rereading for Understanding, T168
Cause and Effect
Fact and Opinion

Rereading for Fluency, T132–T145

Cross-Curricular Responding Activities, T151

Information and Study Skill, T169
Using a Glossary **T**

Leveled Readers
Earthworms
Busy Bees
Butterflies
The Amazing Earthworm

Lessons and Leveled Practice, T172–T175

Vocabulary, T167
Vocabulary Expansion

High-Frequency Words, T166
Word Wall

Spelling, T170
Test: Words That End with *nd, ng,* or *nk* **T**

Writing, T167
Daily Writing Prompt

Grammar, T170
Improving Writing

Daily Language Practice
5. I hold Janes haend when we dance.
(I hold Jane's hand when we dance.)

Listening/Speaking/Viewing, T171
Discussing a Factual Topic

Managing Flexible Groups

Leveled Instruction and Leveled Practice

	DAY 1	**DAY 2**
WHOLE CLASS	• Daily Routines (TE pp. T116–T117) • Teacher Read Aloud (TE pp. T118–T119) • Phonics lesson (TE pp. T120–T121) • High-Frequency Words lesson (TE p. T122)	• Daily Routines (TE pp. T128–T129) • Get Set to Read, Strategy and Skill, Purpose Setting (TE pp. T130–T133) *After Reading at Small Group Time* • Wrapping Up (TE p. T145)
SMALL GROUPS		
Extra Support	**TEACHER-LED** • Read Phonics Library: *Hank's Pandas.* (TE pp. T123–T125) • Selected I Love Reading Books: 40–44	**TEACHER-LED** • Read Main Selection. (TE pp. T132–T145) **Partner or Individual Reading** • Read with audio CD of Main Selection. • **Fluency Practice** Reread Phonics Library: *Hank's Pandas.* (TE pp. T123–T125) OR selected I Love Reading Books: 40–44.
On Level	**TEACHER-LED** • Reread Transparency 4–12 aloud. (TE p. T122) • Read Phonics Library: *Hank's Pandas.* (TE pp. T123–T125)	**TEACHER-LED** • Read Main Selection. (TE pp. T132–T145) • Begin Leveled Reader: On Level (TE p. T173) OR book from Bibliography. (TE pp. T6–T7) • **Fluency Practice** Reread Phonics Library: *Hank's Pandas.* (TE pp. T123–T125) ✔
Challenge	**Partner or Individual Reading** • Read Phonics Library: *Hank's Pandas.* (TE pp. T123–T125) • **Fluency Practice** Reread Little Big Book for this theme.	**Partner or Individual Reading** • Read Main Selection. (TE pp. T132–T145) • **Fluency Practice** Reread Phonics Library: *Hank's Pandas.* (TE pp. T123–T125)
English Language Learners	**TEACHER-LED** • Read Phonics Library: *Hank's Pandas.* (TE pp. T123–T125) • Selected I Love Reading Books: 40–44	**TEACHER-LED** • Selected I Love Reading Books: 40–44 • **Fluency Practice** Reread Phonics Library: *Hank's Pandas.* (TE pp. T123–T125) ✔ **Partner or Individual Reading** • Read with audio CD of Main Selection.

Independent Activities

- Get Set for Reading CD-ROM OR audio CD of Anthology selection.
- Journals: selection notes, questions.
- Complete, review **Practice Book** (pp. 26–30, 34–36) and **Leveled Reader Practice Blackline Masters.** (TE pp. T172–T175)
- Assignment Cards. (**Teacher's Resource Blackline Masters** pp. 64–65)

✔ Opportunity to informally assess oral reading rate.

DAY 3

Daily Routines (TE pp. T148–T149)

After Reading at Small Group Time

Responding (TE p. T150)

Comprehension lesson (TE pp. T152–T153)

Rereading for Understanding (TE p. T154)

TEACHER-LED

Read aloud from Main Selection to answer Guiding Comprehension. (TE pp. T132–T145)

Begin Leveled Reader: Below Level (TE p. T172) OR book from Bibliography. (TE pp. T6–T7)

Partner or Individual Reading

Fluency Practice Selected I Love Reading Books: 40–44

Partner or Individual Reading

Reread Main Selection. (TE pp. T132–T145)

Complete Leveled Reader: On Level (TE p. T173) OR book from Bibliography. (TE pp. T6–T7)

Fluency Practice Selected I Love Reading Books: 40–44

TEACHER-LED

Read aloud from Main Selection to answer Guiding Comprehension. (TE pp. T132–T145) ✔

Begin Leveled Reader: Above Level (TE p. T174) OR book from Bibliography. (TE pp. T6–T7)

Partner or Individual Reading

Complete Leveled Reader: Above Level (TE p. T174) OR book from Bibliography. (TE pp. T6–T7)

TEACHER-LED

Reread Main Selection. (TE pp. T132–T145)

Partner or Individual Reading

Selected I Love Reading Books: 40–44

DAY 4

- Daily Routines (TE pp. T156–T157)
- Link (TE pp. T158–T159)
- Phonics Review (TE p. T161)

TEACHER-LED

- Read Phonics Library: *Marta's Larks*. (TE pp. T162–T163)
- Complete Leveled Reader: Below Level (TE p. T172) OR book from Bibliography. (TE pp. T6–T7)
- **Fluency Practice** Reread Phonics Library: *Marta's Larks* (TE pp. T162–T163) OR Leveled Reader: Below Level. (TE p. T172) ✔

TEACHER-LED

- Read aloud from Main Selection to answer Guiding Comprehension. (TE pp. T132–T145)
- Read Phonics Library: *Marta's Larks*. (TE pp. T162–T163)
- **Fluency Practice** Reread Link (TE pp. T158–T159) OR Leveled Reader: On Level. (TE p. T173) ✔

Partner or Individual Reading

- Read Phonics Library: *Marta's Larks*. (TE pp. T162–T163)
- **Fluency Practice** Reread Main Selection and Link (TE pp. T132–T145, T158–T159) AND Phonics Library: *Marta's Larks*. (TE pp. T162–T163)

TEACHER-LED

- Continue Main Selection. (TE pp. T132–T145)
- Begin Leveled Reader: Language Support (TE p. T175) OR On My Way Practice Reader. (TE pp. R4–R5)

Partner or Individual Reading

- **Fluency Practice** Read Phonics Library: *Marta's Larks*. (TE pp. T162–T163)

DAY 5

- Daily Routines (TE pp. T166–T167)
- Comprehension Review lesson (TE p. T168)
- Information and Study Skill (TE p. T169)
- Responding: select from activities (TE p. T151)

TEACHER-LED

- Reread Phonics Library: *Marta's Larks*. (TE pp. T162–T163)
- Read the On My Way Practice Reader. (TE pp. R4–R5)
- **Fluency Practice** Reread Phonics Library (TE pp. T123–T125, T162–T163) OR On My Way Practice Reader. (TE pp. R4–R5) ✔

Partner or Individual Reading

- Reread Link. (TE pp. T158–T159)
- Continue Theme Paperback: On Level (TE pp. R6–R7) OR book from Bibliography. (TE pp. T6–T7)
- **Fluency Practice** Reread Main Selection (TE pp. T132–T145) OR Leveled Reader: On Level. (TE p. T173)

TEACHER-LED

- **Fluency Practice** Reread Link (TE pp. T158–T159) OR Leveled Reader: Above Level. (TE p. T174) ✔

Partner or Individual Reading

- Continue Theme Paperback: Above Level (TE pp. R8–R9) OR book from Bibliography. (TE pp. T6–T7)

TEACHER-LED

- Reread Link. (TE pp. T158–T159)
- Complete Leveled Reader: Language Support (TE p. T175) OR On My Way Practice Reader. (TE pp. R4–R5)
- **Fluency Practice** Reread Phonics Library (TE pp. T123–T125, T162–T163). ✔

- Reread familiar selections.
- Read trade book from Leveled Bibliography. (TE pp. T6–T7)
- Responding activities. (TE pp. T150–T151)
- Activities related to *Ant* at Education Place: www.eduplace.com

Turn the page for more independent activities.

Classroom Management

Independent Activities

Assign these activities while you work with small groups.

Differentiated Instruction for Small Groups

- **Handbook for English Language Learners,** pp. 134–143

- **Extra Support Handbook,** pp. 130–139

Independent Activities

- Daily Routines, pp. T116, T128, T148, T156, T166

- Challenge/Extension Activities, pp. R15, R17, R23, R29

- **Classroom Management Handbook,** Activity Masters CM4-5–CM4-8

- **Challenge Handbook,** Activity Masters CH4-3–CH4-4

Look for more activities in the Classroom Management Kit.

Science Center

Human Antennae

Pairs	⏱ **30 minutes**
Objective	Identify objects by touch.
Materials	Small classroom objects, a bag

Ants identify things with their antennae. Can your fingers identify objects, too?

- Collect eight small objects and put them in a bag. Don't let anyone see!

- Tell a classmate to close his or her eyes. Give him or her an object from the bag.

- Ask your classmate to guess what the object is by touching it, not by looking at it.

- Repeat until all your objects have been guessed. Then guess what is in your classmate's bag.

Social Studies Center

Cooperation

Groups	⏱ **30 minutes**
Objective	Make a chart.
Materials	Writing paper, pencil

Ants cooperate and work together. Do people cooperate, too? Cooperate with classmates to do this project.

- Divide a sheet of paper into two columns, *Ants* and *People*.

- In the first column, write ways that ants cooperate. In the second column, write ways that people cooperate.

- Compare the ways ants and people cooperate.

- Talk about your ideas with a classmate.

Do Ants and People Cooperate in the Same Ways?

Ants	People
1) Ants feed their babies and each other.	1) People feed their babies.
2)	2)
3)	3)
4)	4)
5)	5)

Consider copying and laminating these activities for use in centers.

Art Center

Ant Sculptures

🧍 Singles	🕐 30 minutes
Objective	Make a model of an ant.
Materials	Modeling clay, pipe cleaners, index card, pencil

Make a clay model of an ant.

Use modeling clay and pipe cleaners to make a model of an ant. Use a photograph from *Ant* to help you.

Write a fact that you learned about ants on an index card.

Display your ant model and writing in the classroom.

Poetry Center

Insect Poetry

🧍🧍 Pairs	🕐 30 minutes
Objective	Write a counting poem.
Materials	Encyclopedias, books about insects, drawing paper, pencils

Write a counting poem about insects.

- Make a list of ten insects. Use science books and encyclopedias if you need help.
- Write a poem with ten lines. Begin each line with a number and the name of an insect. For example, *One ladybug sat on a leaf*.
- Use a different insect for each line.
- Draw a picture to go with your poem.
- Share your poem.

Math Center

Ant Maze

🧍 Singles	🕐 30 minutes
Objective	Make a maze.
Materials	Drawing paper, pencil, ruler

- Draw an ant maze.
- Draw a large shape with straight or round edges. Leave an opening along the top and label it *Enter*.
- Draw a winding or zigzag path from *Enter* to the bottom of the paper. Label the end point *Home*.
- Fill in your maze with lots of turns and dead ends.
- Use a ruler to measure the number of inches the ant would travel to get through the maze. Write this distance below the maze.
- Ask a classmate to follow the maze.

Activities for Classroom Management

Day at a Glance
pp. T116–T127

Reading Instruction

Teacher Read Aloud

Phonics Instruction
Words with *nd, nt, mp, ng, nk*
Base Words and Endings *-s, -es, -ies* (in Nouns)

Reading Decodable Text
Hank's Pandas

. . . .

Leveled Readers, T172–T175
- ● *Earthworms*
- ▲ *Busy Bees*
- ■ *Butterflies!*
- ◆ *The Amazing Earthworm*

Word Work

Vocabulary Review

High-Frequency Words

Spelling: Words That End with *nd, ng,* or *nk*

Writing & Oral Language

Writing Activity

Grammar: Singular Possessive Nouns

Listening/Speaking/Viewing

Daily Routines

Daily Message

Phonics Review Point to each word as you read aloud the Daily Message.

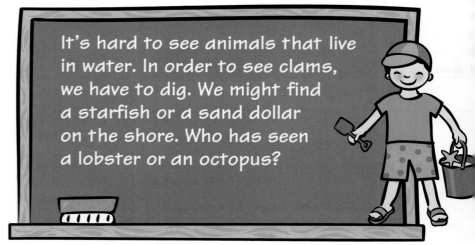

> It's hard to see animals that live in water. In order to see clams, we have to dig. We might find a starfish or a sand dollar on the shore. Who has seen a lobster or an octopus?

Have children
- read the Daily Message aloud, and then discuss the question;
- find words with *ar, or, ore; (hard, order, starfish, dollar, shore)*
- read the words aloud and then circle them.

Word Wall

High-Frequency Word Review Briefly review these high-frequency words that were previously taught in Grade 1. Post the words on the Word Wall. Have children practice reading, chanting, spelling, and writing them.

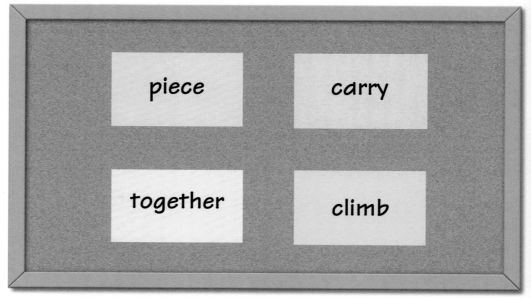

piece   carry

together   climb

Blackline Masters for these word cards appear on p. R36.

Vocabulary

Mixed-Up Animals Write the scrambled words below. Have children rearrange the letters of each word to identify and write an animal name. You may want to have pairs of children give each other animal anagrams to solve.

odg	gorf
noli	rabe
seroh	bribta
grite	netkti

lion

Daily Writing Prompt

Have children choose a topic to write about, or have them use the prompt below.

> Write an ad for an animal shelter. Tell about an animal that needs a home. Describe the animal. Give facts you think will persuade the reader to adopt the animal as a pet.

Daily Language Practice

Grammar Skill: Singular Possessive Nouns
Spelling Skill: Words That End with *nd, ng,* or *nk*

Display **Transparency 4–11.** Ask children to rewrite Sentence 1 correctly. Then model how to write it, and have children check their work.

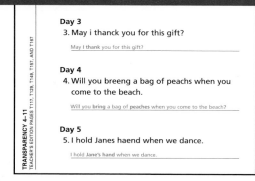

Transparency 4–11
Daily Language Practice

Day 1

1. Will you sind me a picture of your house.

   Will you **send** me a picture of your house?

Day 3
3. May i thank you for this gift?

   May **I** **thank** you for this gift?

Day 4
4. Will you breeng a bag of peachs when you come to the beach.

   Will you **bring** a bag of **peaches** when you come to the beach?

Day 5
5. I hold Janes haend when we dance.

   I hold **Jane's** **hand** when we dance.

TRANSPARENCY 4–11
TEACHER'S EDITION PAGES T117, T129, T148, T157, AND T167

Listening Comprehension

OBJECTIVE

- Listen to identify examples of text organization.

Building Background

Tell children that you are going to read aloud a selection about an octopus.

- Display a picture of an octopus.
- Ask children to share what they know about octopuses.

Fluency Modeling

Explain that as you read aloud, you will be modeling fluent oral reading. Ask children to listen carefully to your phrasing and expression or tone of voice and emphasis.

COMPREHENSION SKILL

Text Organization

Explain that authors of nonfiction works organize information

- by main ideas and details that support the ideas,
- to help readers better understand what the author has to say.

Purpose Setting Read the selection aloud, asking children to pay attention to main ideas as they listen. Then use the Guiding Comprehension questions to assess children's understanding. Reread the selection for clarification as needed.

Teacher Read Aloud

An Octopus Is Amazing

by Patricia Lauber

An octopus is an animal that lives in the sea. It has a soft, bag-shaped body and eight rubbery arms.

There are many kinds of octopus. The best-known is the common octopus. This octopus—like most others—lives alone. Its den is just big enough for its body. An octopus can squeeze into a small space because it has no backbone. In fact, it has no bones at all.

1 An octopus can change color in a flash. Usually the octopus matches its surroundings and is hard to see. If **2** it climbs into an empty shell, it turns pink and gray. If it crawls among rocks and seaweeds, it may turn brown and gray and green. Changing color helps an octopus hide or escape from enemies. Its color may also show how an octopus is feeling. An angry octopus turns dark red. A frightened one turns pale. An octopus has a big appetite. The common octopus likes crabs, lobsters, and clams best. Sometimes an octopus waits in its den until a crab or lobster passes by. Then it reaches out an arm and grabs its prey.

Each arm is lined with suckers. They work like little rubber suction cups. The octopus holds its catch with these suckers and examines it. Then the octopus carries the food toward its mouth, which is on the underside of its body. Inside its mouth is a hard, curved beak. The octopus uses this beak to crack the shell of its prey.

An octopus may leave its den and hunt for food. The octopus may crawl along, using its suckers to hold on to rocks and pull itself forward. Or it may move quickly, by shooting water out of its body through a tube called a siphon. With each spurt, the octopus jets through the sea.

Sometimes other animals try to eat an octopus. If a big fish attacks, the octopus changes colors and jets off. The octopus no longer looks like the animal the fish was going to attack. And so the fish is fooled.

An octopus can also give off an ink-black liquid through its siphon. The ink forms a blob that has the shape and smell of an octopus. The enemy attacks the blob, and the octopus escapes.

An octopus is truly amazing.

CRITICAL THINKING
Guiding Comprehension

1 **TEXT ORGANIZATION** What is one main idea about the octopus that the author writes about? (Sample answer: why an octopus changes color)

2 **TEXT ORGANIZATION** What details did you learn about an octopus changing color? (An octopus turns pink and gray near or in sea shells; it turns brown, gray and green near or around seaweed and rocks; it uses color to hide and escape from enemies; it turns color to show its feelings.)

3 **TEXT ORGANIZATION** What details did you learn about how an octopus protects itself? (Sample answers: the octopus can change colors and jet off; the octopus can give off an ink-black liquid that makes a blob that has the shape and smell of the octopus.)

Discussion Options

Personal Response Ask children if they think the author did a good job of explaining why an octopus is an amazing animal and to give reasons.

⭐ **Connecting/Comparing** Have children tell why this selection about an octopus belongs in this theme.

English Language Learners

Supporting Comprehension

Start a word web for *octopus.* Invite children to give main ideas about the octopus, such as appearance, catching food, and avoiding enemies. Then discuss details that can go under each idea as part of the web.

Teacher Read Aloud **T119**

OBJECTIVE

• Read and write words with *nd, nt, mp, ng, nk*.

Target Skill Trace

Teach	p. T120
Reteach	p. R14
Review	pp. T229, T279
See	*Handbook for English Language Learners*, p. 149; *Extra Support Handbook*, pp. 130, 136

Materials

• Blending Routines Card 1

Practice Book page 26

Name _____

Ant
Phonics Skill Words with *nd, nt, mp, ng, nk*

Letter Changes

Change the dark letter in each word to make a new word. Each word should end with the letters *nd, nt, mp, ng,* or *nk*. The clues will help you.

1. kin**d**	not queen	king (1 point)
2. ca**m**e	place for tents	camp (1)
3. thin**g**	you do this with your brain	think (1)
4. **p**anes	piece of clothing	pants (1)
5. chi**m**e	small ape	chimp (1)
6. si**ng**	something to wash dishes in	sink (1)
7. la**ne**	not water	land (1)

On the lines below write 3 sentences. Use one of the new words you made in each sentence.

8. Answers will vary. (3)

_____
_____
_____

Monitoring Student Progress

If . . .	Then . . .
children score 7 or below on **Practice Book** page 26,	use the Reteaching lesson on page R14.
children meet the lesson objectives,	use the Challenge/Extension activities on page R15.

 TARGET SKILL

PHONICS: Words with *nd, nt, mp, ng, nk*

❶ Phonemic Awareness Warm-Up

Model how to identify phonemes. Say *dump*, /mp/. Have children repeat /mp/. Then have them raise their hands if they hear /mp/ when you say *jump, late, sink,* and *stamp*. Repeat, using the final consonant sounds in *ba**nd**, be**nt**, pi**nk**,* and *si**ng***.

❷ Teach Phonics

Connect sounds to letters. Write *dump*. Underline *mp* and blend the sounds, /mp/.

• Explain that these consonants often stay together in words and that the sounds of the letters blend closely together. Have children blend the sounds to read the word. Repeat with *band* and *sent* for /nd/ and /nt/.

• Write *king*, underline *ng*, and say /ng/. Have children read the word. Repeat with *pink* and /nk/.

Model how to decode longer words. Write *dampen* and underline *mp*.

• Count the vowels and point out that there are two syllables. Remind children that *mp* stays together in a syllable. Divide the word after *mp*. Use **Blending Routine 1** to help children sound it out.

• Repeat with *clanging*. Underline each *ng*. Explain that *ng* stands for one sound and stays together in a syllable.

• Write, *du**mp**ling, mome**nt**, longest,* and *ha**nd**shake*. Help children divide each word into syllables and read the word.

dump/ling   mo/ment

❸ Guided Practice

Check understanding. Write *stamp, spend, string, thankful, absent*. Have children read each word. Have them write *camp, bent, skunk, swing,* and *bending*. Display the words. Have children correct any mistakes.

❹ Apply

Assign Practice Book page 26.

PHONICS: Base Words and Endings in Nouns (-s, -es, -ies)

❶ Teach Phonics

Connect sounds to letters. Write -s, -e̶ ~~Josh~~ ~~Arg.~~

- Remind children that some base wor̶ ~~RS~~ ~~fd~~
  Explain that -es or -ies contain a vo̶ ~~Quintin~~
  syllable to the base word.

- Write *lunches*. Underline the bas̶
  Cover the base word and sound̶
  syllables to read *lunches*. Have

- Repeat with *puppy* and *pupp̶*
  before an ending is added.

- Write the words shown. F̶
  decode the words.

P26

bike	bikes
beach	beaches
bunny	bunnies

- Explain that when -s, -es, or -ies is added to a naming word, it changes the meaning from one to more than one. Randomly point to each word. Have a child read it and use the word in a sentence.

❷ Guided Practice

Check understanding. Write *rings, benches, guppies, inches,* and *cities.* Have children sound out the base word and ending to read each word. Have children write *hands, foxes, penny,* and *pennies.* Remind them that *y* changes to *i* before the ending is added. Display the words and have children correct any mistakes.

❸ Apply

Assign Practice Book 27.

OBJECTIVE

- Read and write words with -s, -es, and -ies endings.

Target Skill Trace

Teach	p. T121
Reteach	p. R16
Review	pp. T142, T295
See	*Handbook for English Language Learners,* p. 135; *Extra Support Handbook,* pp. 131, 137

Monitoring Student Progress

If . . .	Then . . .
children score 8 or below on **Practice Book** page 27,	use the Reteaching Lesson on page R16.
children meet the lesson objectives,	use the Challenge/ Extension activities on page R17.

OBJECTIVE

- Recognize new high-frequency words:
  between   weigh
  care

Target Skill Trace

Teach	p. T122
Reteach	p. R22
Review	p. T128
See	*Handbook for English Language Learners*, pp. 137, 139; *Extra Support Handbook*, p. 134

Materials

- punchout high-frequency words for *Ant*
- index cards, one high-frequency word per card or Word Wall Cards from pp. R36–R37

Transparency 4–12

High-Frequency Words

There is a park <u>between</u> my house and the school.

The mother cat takes <u>care</u> of her kittens.

Elephants <u>weigh</u> more than most other animals.

TRANSPARENCY 4–12
TEACHER'S EDITION PAGE T122

AMAZING ANIMALS *Ant*
High-Frequency Words

ANNOTATED
VERSION

Monitoring Student Progress

If . . .	Then . . .
children score 4 or below on **Practice Book** page 28,	use the Reteaching lesson on page R22.
children are ready for more challenging material,	use the Challenge/ Extension activities on page R23.

HIGH-FREQUENCY WORDS

❶ Teach

Introduce the high-frequency words. Display **Transparency 4–12.** Ask children to read the first sentence to themselves.

- Point to the word *between*. Say it, and have children repeat it.
- Together, have children read the sentence. Repeat with the other sentences and underlined words. Discuss word meanings.

❷ Guided Practice

Have children write a sentence for each of the words.

- Call on children to read one of their sentences, saying "blank" where the high-frequency word belongs. Write the sentence with a line for the missing word and read it together.
- Have children hold up the punchout high-frequency word that completes the sentence. Write the correct word in the sentence and read it together.
- Post the new words on the Word Wall.

❸ Apply

Assign Practice Book page 28.

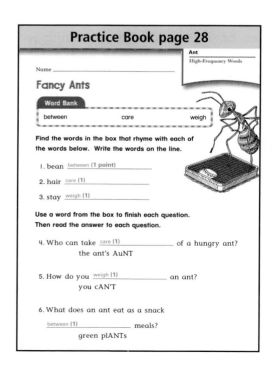

Practice Book page 28

Ant
High-Frequency Words

Name _____

Fancy Ants

Word Bank		
between	care	weigh

Find the words in the box that rhyme with each of the words below. Write the words on the line.

1. bean   between (1 point) _____
2. hair   care (1) _____
3. stay   weigh (1) _____

Use a word from the box to finish each question. Then read the answer to each question.

4. Who can take   care (1) _____ of a hungry ant?
    the ant's AuNT

5. How do you   weigh (1) _____ an ant?
    you cAN'T

6. What does an ant eat as a snack
    between (1) _____ meals?
    green plANTs

Hank's Pandas
by Linda Dunlap
illustrated by Teri Sloat

My big brother is named <u>Hank</u>. He takes <u>care</u> of <u>pandas</u> at Animal Park. Hank <u>tells</u> me <u>stories</u> about his work. If I <u>want</u>, he <u>takes</u> me to see his pandas.

17

17

Hank begins his work day by feeding the pandas. Zoo pandas eat <u>foods</u> that wild pandas eat. They <u>chomp</u> on <u>plants</u>.

18

Then Hank might <u>weigh</u> the new baby. It is so small! Hank can hold it in his arms.

19

18

19

Word Key

Decodable words with *nd, nt, mp, ng, nk;* endings *-s, -es, -ies* _____

High-Frequency Words _____

Reading Decodable Text

PHONICS LIBRARY

OBJECTIVES

- Apply the Phonics/Decoding Strategy to decode words in context.
- Recognize high-frequency words in context.
- Reread to build fluency.

Have children preview *Hank's Pandas*. Ask them to predict what they might learn about pandas.

Model the Phonics/Decoding Strategy. Review the strategy. Then model how to read each word in the story title.

Think Aloud *The first word ends with* nk. *The sound of these letters is /nk/. The vowel sound is short, and the last sound is /s/. I blend the sounds to say* Hank's. *The next word has the vowel-consonant-consonant-vowel pattern* a-n-d-a, *so I'll divide the word between the* n *and* d. *The first syllable is /păn/. Oh, I know that word. It's* Pandas. *I see a picture of these animals too.*

Apply the Phonics/Decoding Strategy. Have children read *Hank's Pandas* with partners. Remind them to use the Phonics/Decoding Strategy.

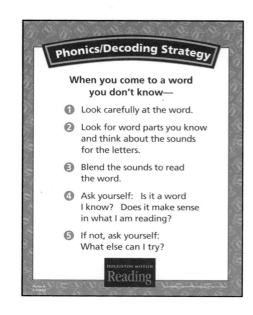

Phonics/Decoding Strategy

When you come to a word you don't know—

❶ Look carefully at the word.

❷ Look for word parts you know and think about the sounds for the letters.

❸ Blend the sounds to read the word.

❹ Ask yourself: Is it a word I know? Does it make sense in what I am reading?

❺ If not, ask yourself: What else can I try?

Reading Decodable Text **T123**

Prompts for Decoding

Support children as they read. Use prompts such as these:

- Look at the word *c-h-o-m-p* on page 18.
- How do you say *ch*? How do you say *mp*?
- Will the vowel sound be long or short? Say it.
- Blend the sounds to read the word. Now read the sentence. Does the word make sense?

Oral Language

Discuss the story. Ask children to answer the questions in complete sentences.

- What is Hank's job? (Hank takes care of the pandas at Animal Park.)
- What are some of Hank's chores? (He feeds the pandas and weighs the baby panda.)
- How does Hank learn about the pandas? (He learns by watching them.)

Between his <u>chores</u>, Hank just watches the pandas. He likes to <u>think</u> and learn about pandas. Hank tells me what he <u>sees</u>.

20

Mom and her baby <u>drink</u> <u>pond</u> water. Dad sits close by.

21

20

2

Pandas have nice fur. They groom it every day. Their light parts look as clean as snow.

22

Mom cleans baby panda. Dad lends a hand. Then they go to sleep.

Hank and I go away quietly. We will be back to see the pandas soon.

23

22   23

Build Fluency

Model fluent reading.

- Model how to group words in phrases in order to read sentences smoothly. Read aloud page 17. Phrasing can vary, but you may want to use the following: *My big brother / is named Hank. / He takes care of pandas / at Animal Park. / Hank tells me stories / about his work. / If I want, / he takes me / to see his pandas.*

- Have children read aloud the same page, modeling your phrasing.

Have children practice fluent reading. Have partners reread the story aloud.

- Tell children to alternate pages, modeling how to group words into phrases.

- Encourage children to read smoothly and with good expression and phrasing.

Home Connection

Hand out the take-home version of *Hank's Pandas*. Ask children to reread the story with their families. (See the **Phonics Library Blackline Masters.**)

Reading Decodable Text   **T125**

OBJECTIVE

- Write spelling words ending with *nd*, *ng*, or *nk*.

SPELLING WORDS

Basic

king	think*
thank	bring*
hand	bang
sing	end
send	thing*

Review	**Challenge**
and*	grand
long*	young*

* *Forms of these words appear in the literature.*

Extra Support/ Intervention

Basic Word List Use only Basic Words 1–5 and the Review Words with children who have difficulty with this spelling principle.

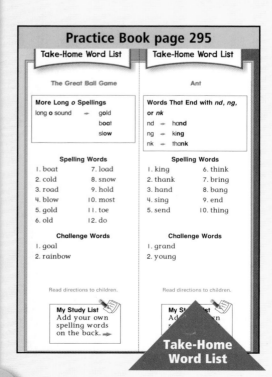

Practice Book page 295

Take-Home Word List

The Great Ball Game

More Long *o* Spellings

long o sound	➞	gold
		boat
		slow

Spelling Words

1. boat		7. load	
2. cold		8. snow	
3. road		9. hold	
4. blow		10. most	
5. gold		11. toe	
6. old		12. do	

Challenge Words

1. goal
2. rainbow

Read directions to children.

My Study List
Add your own spelling words on the back. ➞

Take-Home Word List

Ant

Words That End with *nd*, *ng*, or *nk*

nd	➞	hand
ng	➞	king
nk	➞	thank

Spelling Words

1. king		6. think	
2. thank		7. bring	
3. hand		8. bang	
4. sing		9. end	
5. send		10. thing	

Challenge Words

1. grand
2. young

Read directions to children.

My Study List
Add your own spelling words

Take-Home Word List

SPELLING: Words That End with *nd*, *ng*, or *nk*

❶ Teach the Principle

Pretest Say each sentence. Have children write only the underlined word.

Basic Words

1. A **king** wears a crown.
2. Will you **thank** her today?
3. Hold my **hand**.
4. I like to hear you **sing**.
5. We will **send** a note.
6. I **think** you are nice.
7. Did you **bring** the ball?
8. I heard a loud **bang**.
9. It is the **end** of the day.
10. What is that **thing**?

Challenge Words

11. The queen lives in a **grand** palace.
12. The boy is too **young** to be king.

Teach Write *hand, king, thank* at the top of three columns.

- Say each word and have children repeat it.
- Underline the final consonant pair and say the sounds those consonants spell.
- Point out that /n/ and /d/ are blended to say /nd/ and that these sounds are spelled *nd*.
- Tell children that, although the sound for *n* is different in words that end with *ng* or *nk*, the /ng/ sound is usually spelled *ng* and the /nk/ sound is usually spelled *nk*.

❷ Practice

Write *sing, send, think, bring, bang, end,* and *thing*.

- Choose children to underline the final consonant pair in each word, pronounce it, and say the word. Add each word to the appropriate column.
- Spell the words in each column together.

❸ Apply

Practice/Homework Assign **Practice Book** page 295, the Take-Home Word List.

GRAMMAR: Singular Possessive Nouns

OBJECTIVES
- Identify singular possessive nouns.
- Learn academic language: *possessive noun, singular noun.*

❶ Teach

Read aloud the first pair of sentences on Transparency 4–13.

- Explain that the shorter sentence uses a naming word that shows possession, or ownership.
- Point out that an apostrophe and *s* have been added to the name *Tim* to make it a possessive noun.

Go over these points.

- A possessive noun is a noun that shows ownership.
- To form the possessive of a singular noun, add an apostrophe and *s.*

❷ Practice

Check children's understanding. Ask children to read aloud each remaining sentence pair on **Transparency 4–13,** identifying the possessive noun in the second sentence. Then have children identify the possessive nouns in sentences 1–8, telling what each one shows ownership of.

❸ Apply

Have each child write a sentence using a singular possessive noun. Pairs can exchange papers, identify the possessive noun in the sentence, and tell what it shows ownership of.

Transparency 4–13

Singular Possessive Nouns

This is the book of Tim.
This is Tim's book.

The feathers of the bird were red.
The bird's feathers were red.

Is that the hat of your mother?
Is that your mother's hat?

1. That is my dog's bone.
2. Where is Jimmy's coat?
3. The bird's nest is made of sticks and straw.
4. The campfire's heat warmed our toes.
5. My family's friend will visit us.
6. Do you have the baby's bottle?
7. The barn's roof is made of tin.
8. Each child's name is on the board.

AMAZING ANIMALS Art
Grammar Skill Singular Possessive Nouns

ANNOTATED VERSION

TRANSPARENCY 4–13
TEACHER'S EDITION PAGE T127

Monitoring Student Progress

If . . .	Then . . .
children need help identifying singular possessive nouns,	use the Reteaching lesson on page R33.

Day at a Glance
pp. T128–T147

Reading Instruction

Background and Vocabulary
Reading the Anthology
  Ant
• • • • • • • • • • • • • • • • • • • •
Leveled Readers, *T172–T175*
  ● *Earthworms*
  ▲ *Busy Bees*
  ■ *Butterflies!*
  ◆ *The Amazing Earthworm*

Word Work

Vocabulary Review
Word Wall
Spelling Practice

Writing & Oral Language

Writing: A Poem
Grammar Practice
Listening/Speaking/Viewing

Daily Routines

Daily Message

Phonics Review Point to each word as you read aloud the Daily Message.

Let's pretend!
Pretend we're busy bees that drink from a flower. Pretend we're busy ants who chomp on a leaf or dig in the sand.
Pretend we're _____.

Have children
• read the Daily Message, discuss it, and ask volunteers to complete the last sentence;
• find and read aloud words with *nd, nk, nt, mp.* (*pretend, drink, ants, chomp, sand*)

Word Wall

High-Frequency Word Review Briefly review these high-frequency words that were introduced on Day 1. Display the words and have children practice recognizing, chanting, spelling, and writing them.

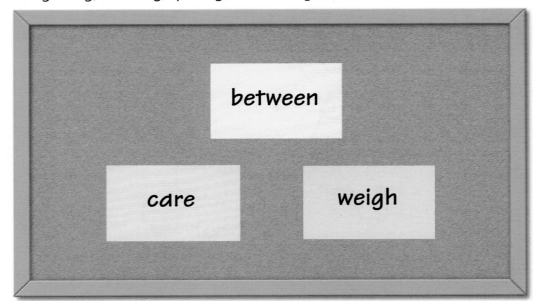

between

care

weigh

Blackline Masters for these word cards appear on pp. R36, R37.

Vocabulary

Using a Dictionary Review with children that guide words at the top of a dictionary page help them find an entry word on the page.

- Distribute **Activity Master 4–2** on page R41.
- Have children use the guide words to write the entry words from the box on the correct page.

amaze • bridge

anthill
big
branch

Daily Writing Prompt

Have children revise work they are currently writing, or have them use this prompt to begin a new writing activity.

Have you seen fish in an aquarium or a large fish tank? Maybe you have visited a shop with a large aquarium. Maybe you have a small one at home. Write a paragraph describing the aquariums and fish you have seen.

Daily Language Practice

Grammar Skill: Singular Possessive Nouns
Spelling Skill: Words That End with *nd*, *ng*, or *nk*

Display **Transparency 4–11.** Ask children to rewrite Sentence 2 correctly. Then model how to write it, and have children check their work.

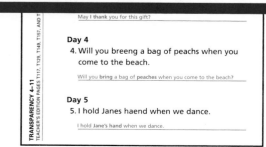

Transparency 4–11
Daily Language Practice

Proofread each sentence. Correct any errors.

Day 1
1. Will you sind me a picture of your house.

Day 2
2. We will seeng three song in the school play.

We will **sing** three **songs** in the school play.

May **I thank** you for this gift?

Day 4
4. Will you breeng a bag of peachs when you come to the beach.

Will you **bring** a bag of **peaches** when you come to the beach?

Day 5
5. I hold Janes haend when we dance.

I hold **Jane's hand** when we dance.

Building Background

Key Concept:
Ants as Amazing and Interesting Insects

Ask children what they know about ants. Then use "Fun Facts About Ants" on Anthology pages 58–59 to build additional background and introduce Key Vocabulary.

- Have individuals read aloud the paragraph on page 58 and the captions on pages 58–59.

- Help children identify the words in red by using context clues, then have them find examples in the illustration.

Get Set to Read

Background and Vocabulary

Rebecca Stefoff
ANT

LIVING THINGS

Ant

Read to find the meanings of these words.

e • Glossary

antennae
cocoons
colonies
fungus
larvae
tunnels

58

Fun Facts About Ants

Have you ever looked closely at an ant? In the next selection, you'll learn some fun facts about ants from all around the world.

Ants usually live under the ground in groups called **colonies**. Colonies of ants build **tunnels** and store food.

Ants guide themselves inside their tunnels by using the two long **antennae** on their heads.

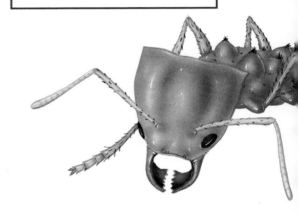

REACHING ALL LEARNERS

English Language Learners

Language Development

Beginning/Preproduction Have children draw and label a diagram of an ant. Preview the Key Vocabulary word *antennae*, and provide other terms such as *legs, head, mouth, eyes,* and *body.*

Early Production and Speech Emergence Have children refer to Anthology pages 59 and 71 and find *eggs, larvae, cocoons,* and *ants.* Then have them create a chart depicting the life stages of an ant.

Intermediate and Advanced Fluency Have small groups use a variety of resources, such as dictionaries, encyclopedias, and the Internet, to research a particular type of ant. Have children brainstorm questions, such as *What do these ants eat? Where do they live?* Have them present their findings to the class.

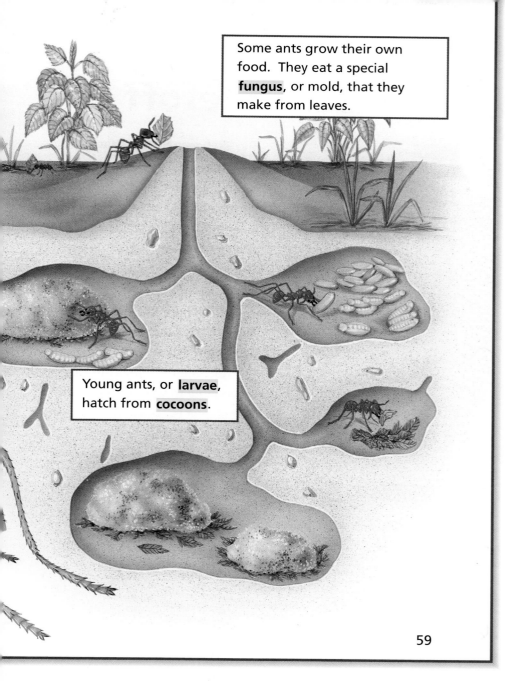

Some ants grow their own food. They eat a special **fungus**, or mold, that they make from leaves.

Young ants, or **larvae**, hatch from **cocoons**.

59

Introducing Vocabulary

Key Vocabulary
These words support the Key Concept and appear in the selection.

antennae a pair of long, thin feelers on the head of an insect

cocoons coverings of silky thread in which larvae live as they grow

colonies groups of insects of the same kind that live together

fungus one of a large group of plants, such as mushrooms and mold, that do not have leaves or flowers

larvae the worm-like forms of very young ants or other insects

tunnels long holes under the ground

e • Glossary
e • WordGame

See Vocabulary notes on pages T135, T136, T138, T139, and T141.

Use Transparency 4–14.

- Read aloud the first sentence on the transparency.

- Model how to use context clues to determine the meaning of *colonies*.

- Ask children to use context clues to figure out the meaning of each Key Vocabulary word in the remaining sentences. Have them explain how they figured out each meaning.

- Ask children to look for these words as they read and to use them as they discuss the selection.

Practice/Homework Assign **Practice Book** page 29.

Transparency 4–14
Ant-Related Words

1. We discovered three insect <u>colonies</u> in the old tree trunk.

2. The groundhogs dug <u>tunnels</u> to connect their underground homes.

3. Each insect uses its two long <u>antennae</u> to feel and smell.

4. Butterfly <u>larvae</u> look like fuzzy worms.

5. <u>Cocoons</u> are like warm blankets that larvae wrap themselves in.

6. The wet weather caused a slimy <u>fungus</u> to grow on the rocks.

Practice Book page 29

Ant
Key Vocabulary

Name _____

How Are They Alike?

Read the questions. Use words from the box to write sentences that answer the questions. The first one has been done for you.
Answers will vary. Sample answers are provided.

Vocabulary
antennae
larvae
fungus
cocoons
colonies
tunnels

1. Where do ants, prairie dogs, and termites live in groups?

They live in colonies.

2. What underground place do ants, cars, and gophers travel through?

They travel through tunnels. **(1 point)**

3. What do ants, moths, and other insects have on their heads?

They have antennae on their heads. **(1)**

4. What are mushrooms, molds, and mildew that grow in damp places?

They are each a kind of fungus. **(1)**

5. What do silkworms, ants, and butterflies live in as they change and grow?

They live in cocoons. **(1)**

6. What are young butterflies, ants, or moths called?

They are called larvae. **(1)**

Introducing Vocabulary
(Anthology p. 59) **T131**

COMPREHENSION STRATEGY
Question

Teacher Modeling Have children read aloud the book's title, author, and the Strategy Focus on Anthology page 61. Have children turn to and read page 63. Model how to ask a question that will help children understand the selection better.

Think Aloud *I've learned from the second paragraph on this page that if you see one ant, there will probably be more ants nearby. I'll ask others this question to check their understanding:* Do ants usually travel alone or in groups?

Test Prep Tell children that looking at the way the text is organized will help them find important details in the test passage. They can scan the title, the byline, the headings, and the captions.

COMPREHENSION SKILL
Text Organization

Introduce the Graphic Organizer. Tell children they can use a Text Organization Chart to help them keep track of the main ideas and details in the selection.

- Display **Transparency 4–15.** Have children read Anthology pages 64–65 silently.
- Model how to use details from the text, photographs, and captions to fill in details about anthills. Have children do the same on **Practice Book** page 30.
- Have children add to the chart as they read.

THEME 4: Amazing Animals
(Anthology p. 60)

T132

Meet the Author
Rebecca Stefoff

Other books by Rebecca Stefoff:
Octopus
Owl
Butterfly

Rebecca Stefoff's favorite things to do are traveling and watching animals. She enjoys birdwatching and has traveled all over the world. She has gone scuba diving to observe moray eels, barracuda, and brightly colored coral fish.

When at home in Oregon, she watches the crabs, seals, and shore birds that live nearby.

Ms. Stefoff thinks ants are interesting to watch because they live almost everywhere. "Wherever you go, they're there," she says.

Did you know that one of Rebecca Stefoff's favorite animals is the slug? Find out more about this author by visiting Education Place.

www.eduplace.com/kids

60

Transparency 4–15
Text Organization Chart

Main Idea	Details
Ants make anthills. (pages 64–65)	Ants carry dirt out of tunnels.
	Some anthills are in sidewalk cracks.
	Some anthills are huge.
Ants have antennae. (pages 66–67)	Antennae are like noses and fingers.
	Antennae tell the ant what is going on.
	Ants talk by rubbing their antennae together.
Ants work together. (pages 68–69)	Ants pass food to each other.
	Ants carry things together.
	Ants make a bridge together.
Some ants are called leafcutter ants. (pages 72–73)	Leafcutter ants live in Costa Rica.
	They carry pieces of leaves over their heads.
	They chew the leaves into paste and eat the fungus that grows on it.

Practice Book page 30
Text Organization Chart

As you read the story, use this chart to help you keep track of what you learn about ants.

Main Idea	Details
Ants make anthills. (pages 64–65)	Ants carry dirt out of tunnels. **(1 point)**
	Some anthills are in sidewalk cracks. **(1)**
	Some anthills are huge. **(1)**
Ants have antennae. (pages 66–67)	Antennae are like noses and fingers. **(1)**
	Antennae tell the ant what is going on. **(1)**
	Ants talk by rubbing their antennae together. **(1)**
Ants work together. (pages 68-69)	Ants pass food to each other. **(1)**
	Ants carry things together. **(1)**
	Ants make a bridge together. **(1)**
Some ants are called leafcutter ants. (pages 72-73)	Leafcutter ants live in Costa Rica. **(1)**
	They carry pieces of leaves over their heads. **(1)**
	They chew the leaves into paste and eat the fungus that grows on it. **(1)**

Rebecca Stefoff

ANT

Strategy Focus

As you read this nonfiction selection, think of **questions** to ask your classmates about the amazing world of ants.

61

Purpose Setting

- Have children read the title of the selection and look at the photograph. Ask them what kinds of questions they have about ants. Have children read to find answers to their questions.

- Ask children to turn to Responding on Anthology page 84. Read the questions aloud. Encourage children to find answers to these questions as they read *Ant*.

Journal ▶ Children can use their journals to record their questions and answers to their questions as they read. They can also record interesting details about ants.

Extra Support/Intervention

Preview pages 62–69.

pages 62–63 Do these look like ants you've seen before?

pages 64–65 Do any of these anthills look like ones you've seen before?

pages 66–67 These stalks on the ants' heads are called *antennae.* Can you see the two ants "talking" by rubbing their antennae?

pages 68–69 What can you tell about ants from the pictures on these pages?

Preview pages 70–83.

pages 70–71 Where do these ants live? What are the worm-like things in the photograph?

pages 72–75 What different things do you see the ants doing with leaves?

pages 76–77 Why do you think these ants are called *farmer ants?*

pages 78–83 How do the ants work together on these pages?

Reading the Selection
(Anthology p. 61)

black ant, Costa Rica

Ants.
They're everywhere. You can see
ants in almost any part of the world.
But you hardly ever see just
one <u>ant</u>. If you see an ant, you
will probably find <u>lots</u> of other
ants nearby.

62   63

CRITICAL THINKING
Guiding Comprehension

1 **TEXT ORGANIZATION** What does the caption tell you
about the ant in the picture? (The caption tells the kind of
ant, a black ant, and where it is from, Costa Rica.)

English Language Learners

Language Development

Have children look through the photographs and name
what they see. Write what they say on the board, and
introduce new vocabulary as needed. Have them draw,
label, and name *ant, anthill, leaves,* and *caterpillar* before
reading the selection.

Word Key

Decodable words with *nd, nt, mp, ng, nk;*
endings *-s, -es, -ies* _____

High-Frequency Words _____

Vocabulary Words _____

THEME 4: Amazing Animals
(Anthology pp. 62–63)

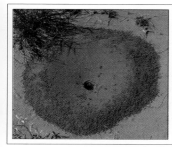

anthill, Australia

Ants live <u>and</u> work together in busy, <u>crowded</u> <u>groups</u> called colonies. Most <u>colonies</u> are in <u>tunnels</u> under the <u>ground</u>. The ants carry dirt out of the tunnels to make a pile. We call these <u>piles</u> anthills.

anthill in sidewalk

When you see an anthill in a sidewalk crack, you know there is a city of ants under the sidewalk.

64

Some anthills are huge and filled with tunnels. An ant colony has lived under this tree for years. Each year the ants dig new tunnels and make the anthill a little bigger.

anthill, East Africa

❷

65

CRITICAL THINKING

Guiding Comprehension

❷ **TEXT ORGANIZATION** How does the author give examples of the ability of ants to live in different parts of the world? (by showing three examples of places where ants can live, and writing the names of those places in captions)

READING STRATEGY

Phonics/Decoding

Vowel Pairs *ow* and *ou*

Teacher/Student Modeling Write *crowded*. Underline *ow* and say /ou/. Have children blend each syllable and then the word. Repeat with *ground*. Have children find *crowded* and *ground* on page 64. Ask how many syllables each word has. Then point out the word *group*. Remind children that *ou* can also make the /o͞o/ sound.

Vocabulary

colonies groups of insects of the same kind that live together.

tunnels long holes under the ground

ASSIGNMENT CARD 6

Hear! Hear! Listen to Me!

Kinds of Antennae

Think about an ant's antennae. Write what you know about them.

Then think of other kinds of antennae that you know about. Write about another kind of antenna.

Are the two kinds of antennae alike in any way? Tell how.

Theme 4: Amazing Animals

Teacher's Resource BLM page 65

Reading the Selection
(Anthology pp. 64–65)

The antennae tell the ant what is going on around it. They help it find food and then find its way back to its colony.

These two ants are "talking" by rubbing their antennae together. The big ant is the queen. She is the mother of all the ants in the colony. The little ant is a worker. Workers take care of the queen's eggs and bring food to the colony.

Every ant has two long, waving stalks on its head. These are its antennae. They are like a nose and fingers all in one.

66

67

CRITICAL THINKING
Guiding Comprehension

3 **TOPIC/MAIN IDEA/DETAILS** Name two details that the author gives about antennae on page 67. (Antennae help an ant find food; ants can talk using their antennae.)

COMPREHENSION STRATEGY
Question

Teacher/Student Modeling Have children ask any questions about ants that they now know the answer to, for example, *How do ants use their antennae?*

REACHING ALL LEARNERS   **Extra Support/Intervention**

Review pages 62–69.

Before children join in Stop and Think, have them

- check their **predictions** and revise if necessary,
- model the reading **strategies** they used,
- review and add to **Practice Book** page 30,
- **summarize** the main ideas of the selection.

red ants transferring food

Ants do all kinds of things together. They pass pieces of food to one another. Sometimes they even carry each other around.

Some jobs are too big for one ant. That's when ants team up. A bunch of little ants working together can carry a big dead bug. It will make a fine meal for the colony.

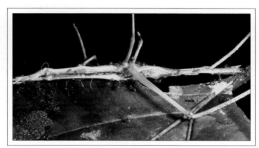

ants carrying dead stick insect, Brazil

ant bridge, Panama

Ants take a shortcut between tree branches. Some of them hold one another's legs to make a bridge. Others can walk across the bridge to the new branch.

68

69

Stop and Think

Critical Thinking Questions

- **COMPARE AND CONTRAST** Name at least two ways in which ants and people are alike. (Sample response: Both live in groups and work together to do jobs.)

- **FACT AND OPINION** Would you agree with the idea that ants are amazing? Which details support your opinion? (Sample response: Yes, because they talk with their antennae and work together in unusual ways.)

Strategies in Action

Have individuals model **Question** and other strategies they used. Make sure children **Summarize** the story so far.

Discussion Options

Bring the entire class together to do either of these activities:

Review Predictions/Purpose Discuss the accuracy of children's predictions and have them make new ones.

Share Group Discussions Have children share their answers for Assignment Card 7 and the results of their literature discussions.

Monitoring Student Progress

If . . .	Then . . .
children have successfully completed the Extra Support activities on pages T133 and T136,	have them read the rest of the story cooperatively or independently.

Reading the Selection
(Anthology pp. 68–69)

T137

Deep in the log, the queen's eggs are turning into larvae. When the larvae hatch from their cocoons, they look like little worms. Later the larvae will turn into ants and pour out of the log.

Carpenter ants live in wood. A pile of yellow sawdust on a log means that carpenter ants are busy inside, chewing new tunnels.

4 **5**

70

71

CRITICAL THINKING

Guiding Comprehension

4 **MAKING INFERENCES** Why are the ants shown on page 70 called *carpenter ants?* (because they make tunnels in wood, and carpenters work with wood)

5 **MAKING GENERALIZATIONS** How could you tell whether there are carpenter ants in a log? (There would be a pile of sawdust on the log if there were.)

Vocabulary

larvae the worm-like forms of very young ants or other insects

cocoons coverings of silky thread in which larvae live as they grow

THEME 4: Amazing Animals
(Anthology pp. 70–71)

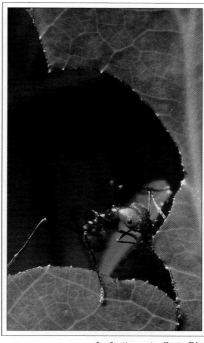

leafcutter ants, Costa Rica

Leafcutter ants live in Central and South America. Some people call them parasol ants. Do you know why?

72

The ants chew off pieces of <u>leaves</u> and carry them back to their tunnels. They march with the leaves held over their heads like little <u>sunshades</u>, or <u>parasols</u>.

 The ants don't eat the leaves. They chew them into a paste. A yellow fungus grows on the paste, and the ants eat the <u>fungus</u>.

73

CRITICAL THINKING

Guiding Comprehension

6 **CAUSE AND EFFECT** How do ants cause fungus to grow in their tunnels? (They bring leaves back to their tunnels and chew them into a paste on which the fungus grows.)

COMPREHENSION STRATEGY

Question

Teacher/Student Modeling Have children ask a classmate a question about the selection, based on what they have learned so far. If necessary, allow children to look for facts in the selection, and remind them that they should know the answer to their question before they ask it.

Vocabulary

parasol an umbrella used for protection from the sun

fungus one of a large groups of plants, such as mushrooms and mold, that do not have leaves or flowers

English Language Learners

Vocabulary and Language Development

Have children look at the pictures of leafcutter, or *parasol* ants on pages 72 and 73. Explain that a *parasol* is an umbrella used to protect people from the sun. Discuss why these ants are called *parasol ants.* Then have children describe other forms of sun protection they have seen people use or wear. Have them draw and label a scene involving different kinds of sun protection.

Reading the Selection
(Anthology pp. 72–73) **T139**

DAY **2**

READ & COMPREHEND

Ant

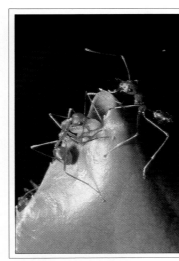
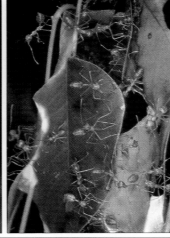

weaver ants with larva   *white larval thread binds leaves*

Weaver ants live in <u>trees</u> in southern Asia and on Pacific islands. They make <u>nests</u> by fastening leaves together with sticky silk thread. The thread comes from the young ants, or larvae. Older ants hold the larvae that spin the thread.

Teams of ants join together into <u>chains</u> to <u>bend</u> the big, stiff leaves.

74

nest making, Australia

75

Comprehension Preview

⊙ Text Organization

TARGET SKILL

Teach

Write *Weaver ants make nests,* and have children read it. Explain that children should look at the photographs, captions, and text on Anthology pages 74–75 to find details that support, or tell more about, this main idea.

Practice/Apply

Have children name details to add to a chart, next to the main idea.

Target Skill Trace	
Preview, Teach	pp. T118, T132, T140, T152
Reteach	p. R28
Review	p. T280

Main Idea	Details
Weaver ants make nests.	make nests in trees
	use sticky thread to fasten leaves
	teams bend big, stiff leaves

THEME 4: Amazing Animals
(Anthology pp. 74–75)

farmer ants with aphids, New York

76

ants "milking" caterpillar

Some ants eat juices that come from inside other insects. They take care of these <u>insects</u> and "milk" them for their juice, like a farmer milks a herd of <u>cows</u>. **7**

    The little green <u>bugs</u> are <u>plant</u> eaters called <u>aphids</u>. The ants <u>tending</u> them are called farmer ants.

77

Guiding Comprehension

7 MAKING INFERENCES Why do you think the author uses the example *like a farmer milks a herd of cows?* (to compare the ants' behavior to something familiar)

READING STRATEGY

Phonics/Decoding

Vowel Pair *ea*

Teacher/Student Modeling Write *eat*. Underline *ea*. Remind children that *ea* usually stands for the long e sound. Have them blend the word, sound by sound. Then write *leaves* and *teams* from Anthology page 74. Have children read each word and tell which letters spell the long e sound. Write *thread*. Point out that in this word, *ea* stands for the short e sound. Have children blend the sounds in *thread*.

Vocabulary

aphids tiny insects that suck juices from plants

ASSIGNMENT CARD 8

What's for Dinner?

What Ants Eat

What do ants eat? How do they get their food?

Look back at the story. Make a list of three ways ants get their food.

Can you add to your list? Look for books or magazines in your classroom that tell more about ants and their food.

Theme 4: Amazing Animals

Teacher's Resource BLM page 66

Reading the Selection
(Anthology pp. 76–77) **T141**

Army ants live in tropical jungles. They march from place to place, eating plants and insects as they go. They climb right over logs and rocks and even houses.

A colony of army ants on the march covers the ground like a moving, munching carpet. Some colonies are as wide as a street and as long as a city block.

army ants, Costa Rica

78

79

READING STRATEGY

Phonics/Decoding

Base Words and Endings *-s, -es, -ies*

Teacher/Student Modeling Write *plants*. Cover the ending. Have children sound out the base word. Cover the base word and have them sound out the ending. Have them slowly blend the base word and ending. Write *insects, houses, colonies*. Have children look for parts they know and blend each word sound by sound. Ask what the base word is for *colonies*. Then have them read the words in sentences on page 78.

Extra Support/Intervention

Strategy Modeling: Question

Use this example to model the strategy.

After reading, I understand why these ants are called army ants. *It's because they march from place to place together like an army of soldiers. Because I know the answer, a good question is* Why are these tropical ants called army ants?

THEME 4: Amazing Animals
(Anthology pp. 78–79)

A lot of little ants working together can beat one big black beetle. When it comes to teamwork, ants are experts. **8**

Can you pick up your mother and carry her over your head? You could if you were an ant. Ants are very strong. They can carry things that weigh a lot more than they do. It takes only two ants to lift this fat caterpillar. **9**

CRITICAL THINKING
Guiding Comprehension

8 **NOTING DETAILS** Describe some examples of teamwork among ants. (building tunnels, finding food, building nests, carrying things)

9 **MAKING INFERENCES** Why do you think the author asks readers whether they can pick up their mother? (to help readers understand how strong ants are)

English Language Learners

Idioms

After reading page 80, pause to discuss the phrase "When it comes to…" Explain that this phrase is often used to give an example of something outstanding or significant. Provide examples such as *When it comes to friends, she's the best,* or *When it comes to food, pizza is my favorite.* Have children complete original sentences beginning with *When it comes to….*

Reading the Selection
(Anthology pp. 80–81) **T143**

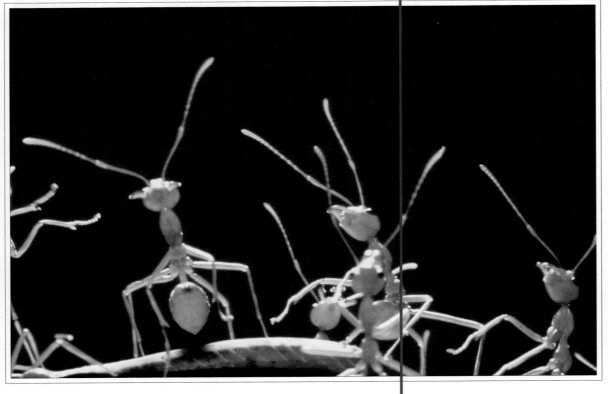

Ants live in colonies that are like <u>cities</u>. They help one another, and they work together **11** on big jobs.

I <u>think</u> ants are a lot like us. **10**
Do you? **12**

CRITICAL THINKING
Guiding Comprehension

10 **AUTHOR'S VIEWPOINT** What does the author think about ants? (She probably likes ants, since she wrote a book about them, and she thinks they are a lot like us.)

11 **FACT AND OPINION** What details on page 83 are facts that can be proved? (Ants live in colonies and work together.)

12 **FACT AND OPINION** What details on page 83 are opinions? Why? (Saying ant colonies are like cities and ants are like people are opinions because someone might find facts and reasons to disagree.)

REACHING ALL LEARNERS
Extra Support/Intervention

Selection Review
Before Wrapping Up, have children

- check the accuracy of their **predictions,**
- model the reading **strategies** they used,
- review and complete **Practice Book** page 30,
- **summarize** the entire story.

On Level	Challenge

Have small groups discuss the story, using their own questions and questions from Think About the Selection on Anthology page 84.

THEME 4: Amazing Animals
T144 (Anthology pp. 82–83)

Wrapping Up

Critical Thinking Questions

1. **AUTHOR'S VIEWPOINT** Why do you think the writer tells about different kinds of ants? (to show that there are more than just a few kinds of ants; to show how interesting the study of ants can be)

2. **MAKING JUDGMENTS** Would you recommend the book to someone? Why or why not? (Children should provide specific reasons to support their responses.)

Strategies in Action

Have individuals discuss the strategies they found most useful. Make sure children **Summarize** the main ideas of *Ants*.

Discussion Options

Bring the entire class together to do either of these activities:

Review Predictions/Purpose Discuss reasons why children's predictions were or were not accurate.

Share Group Discussions Have children share answers from their literature discussions.

Monitoring Student Progress

If . . .	Then . . .
children have difficulty identifying main ideas,	review features such as photos, captions, and sections that help them focus on a main idea.

Reading the Selection   **T145**

Challenge

Word Practice

Have children write tongue twisters using the Challenge Words. (Example: *Your young yellow yak yells.*) Have children exchange tongue twisters and read them aloud.

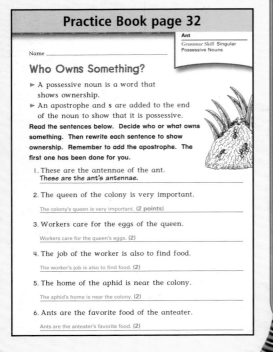

Practice Book page 31

Name _____

Ant
Spelling Skills Words That End with *nd, ng, or nk*

Words That End with *nd*, *ng*, or *nk*

► You hear the sounds of **n** and **d** in words that end with the consonants **nd**.

► You may not hear the sound of **n** in words that end with the consonants **ng** or **nk**.

Order of answers for each category may vary.

Write the Spelling Words that end with *nd*.

pond

hand (1 **point**)   end (1)

send (1)   and (1)

Write the Spelling Words that end with *ng*.

ring

king (1)   bang (1)

sing (1)   thing (1)

bring (1)   long (1)

Write the Spelling Words that end with *nk*.

skunk

thank (1)   think (1)

Spelling Words

1. king
2. thank
3. hand
4. sing
5. send
6. think
7. bring
8. bang
9. end
10. thing
11. and
12. long

SPELLING: Words That End with *nd*, *ng*, or *nk*

Review the Principle Write and say *send*, *sing*, and *think*. Underline the *nd*, *ng*, and *nk* as you remind children that the /nd/ sounds are usually spelled *nd*, the /ng/ sound is usually spelled *ng*, and the /nk/ sound is usually spelled *nk*.

Write the remaining Basic Words. Say /nd/, /ng/, or /nk/. Have children take turns pointing to Basic Words with that sound or sounds. Have the whole class spell each word aloud.

Practice/Homework Assign **Practice Book** page 31.

GRAMMAR: Singular Possessive Nouns

Review the Skill Have volunteers read aloud the information about possessive nouns at the top of **Practice Book** page 32.

Practice/Homework Assign **Practice Book** page 32.

Practice Book page 32

Name _____

Ant
Grammar Skill Singular Possessive Nouns

Who Owns Something?

► A possessive noun is a word that shows ownership.

► An apostrophe and **s** are added to the end of the noun to show that it is possessive.

Read the sentences below. Decide who or what owns something. Then rewrite each sentence to show ownership. Remember to add the apostrophe. The first one has been done for you.

1. These are the antennae of the ant.
   These are the ant's antennae.

2. The queen of the colony is very important.
   The colony's queen is very important. (2 **points**)

3. Workers care for the eggs of the queen.
   Workers care for the queen's eggs. (2)

4. The job of the worker is also to find food.
   The worker's job is also to find food. (2)

5. The home of the aphid is near the colony.
   The aphid's home is near the colony. (2)

6. Ants are the favorite food of the anteater.
   Ants are the anteater's favorite food. (2)

A possessive noun is a word that shows ownership.

An apostrophe and *s* are added to the end of the noun to show that it is possessive.

WRITING: A Poem

OBJECTIVES

- Identify the elements of a poem.
- Write a poem.
- Learn academic language: *verse, rhythm, rhyming words, lyrics, poem*

❶ Teach

Discuss the characteristics of a poem. Have children turn to "The Ants Go Marching," on Anthology pages 86–87. Explain that the words, or lyrics, of a song are one type of poem.

- Tell children that a poem often has rhyming words, or words that sound alike, at the end of lines. Have a child name the rhyming words in verse 1. (one, fun)

- Explain that a poem usually has a rhythm, or a set number of repeated beats or syllables.

- Read aloud the first verse and chorus of the song, clapping out the rhythm. Have children read and clap it with you.

- Have volunteers read the remaining verses of the song.

- Lead the class in clapping the rhythm. Then have children identify the rhyming words in each verse.

Display and discuss the guidelines on Transparency 4–16.

❷ Practice/Apply

Assign Practice Book page 33. Have children use this page to record topics and rhyming words for a poem. Then have them write a short poem of four to eight lines. Have volunteers read aloud their poems.

Portfolio Opportunity

Save children's completed poems as examples of their writing development.

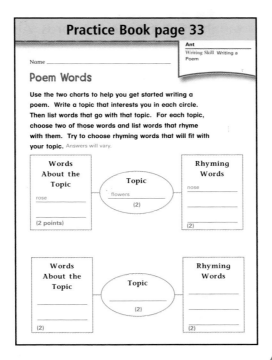

Practice Book page 33

Ant
Writing Skill Writing a Poem

Name _____

Poem Words

Use the two charts to help you get started writing a poem. Write a topic that interests you in each circle. Then list words that go with that topic. For each topic, choose two of those words and list words that rhyme with them. Try to choose rhyming words that will fit with your topic. Answers will vary.

Words About the Topic
rose
(2 points)

Topic
flowers
(2)

Rhyming Words
nose
(2)

Words About the Topic
(2)

Topic
(2)

Rhyming Words
(2)

Transparency 4–16

Guidelines for Writing a Poem

AMAZING ANIMALS *Ant*
Writing Guidelines: A Poem

ANNOTATED
VERSION

- List topics to write about. Circle the one you like best.

- Think of what you want to say about your topic. Write your ideas.

- Think about how you will write your poem. Remember that each line of your poem can be a sentence or a part of a sentence.

- Decide whether or not your poem will rhyme. If so, make a list of rhyming words you might use.

- Write your first line. Try repeating the same rhythm or pattern of beats in other lines.

TRANSPARENCY 4–16
TEACHER'S EDITION PAGE T147

DAY 3
week 2

Day at a Glance
pp. T148–T155

Reading Instruction

Responding
Comprehension Instruction
Text Organization
Rereading for Understanding
• • • • • • • • • • • • • • • •
Leveled Readers, *T172–T175*
- ● *Earthworms*
- ▲ *Busy Bees*
- ■ *Butterflies!*
- ◆ *The Amazing Earthworm*

Word Work

Vocabulary Review
Word Wall
Spelling Practice

Writing & Oral Language

Writing Activity
Grammar Practice
Listening/Speaking/Viewing

Daily Routines

Daily Message

Phonics Review Point to each word as you read aloud the Daily Message.

Let's go on a picnic. We'll pack knives, forks, and dishes. We'll also bring sandwiches, chips, tomatoes, and drinks. Everyone likes a picnic, even the flies.

Have children
- read the Daily Message aloud;
- find plural nouns; (*knives, forks, dishes, sandwiches, chips, tomatoes, drinks, flies*)
- read the words aloud and then circle them.

Word Wall

Speed Drill Have children review and practice these and other previously taught high-frequency words. Also have them practice reading a few decod able words that feature the new phonics skills.
- Have children take turns holding up a card for partners to read.
- Have individuals read the words to you quickly.

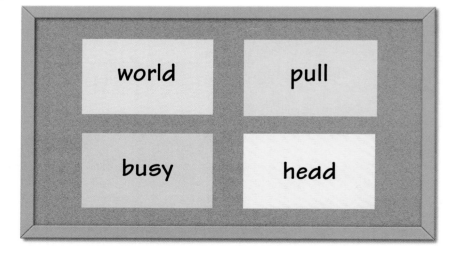

world   pull

busy   head

Blackline Masters for these word cards appear on p. R37.

Vocabulary

Relationships Discuss how *ant* is related to *tunnel*. Then have children name and illustrate other animals and their homes or the places they build. Have children share their work. List their responses.

Animal	Place
ant	tunnel
bear	den
woodchuck	burrow
beaver	dam
bird	nest
spider	web

beehive

Daily Writing Prompt

Have children revise work they are currently writing, or have them use this prompt to begin a new writing activity.

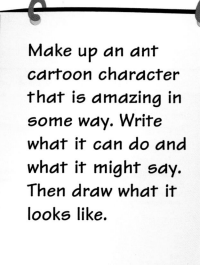

Make up an ant cartoon character that is amazing in some way. Write what it can do and what it might say. Then draw what it looks like.

Daily Language Practice

Grammar Skill: Singular Possessive Nouns
Spelling Skill: Words That End with *nd, ng,* or *nk*

Display **Transparency 4–11.** Ask children to rewrite Sentence 3 correctly. Then model how to write it, and have children check their work.

Transparency 4–11

Daily Language Practice

Proofread each sentence. Correct any errors.

Day 1
1. Will you sind me a picture of your house.

Will you **send** me a picture of your house?

Day 2

Day 3
3. May i thank you for this gift?

May **I thank** you for this gift?

4. Will you breeng a bag of peaches when you come to the beach.

Will you **bring** a bag of **peaches** when you come to the beach?

Day 5
5. I hold Janes haend when we dance.

I hold **Jane's hand** when we dance.

AMAZING ANIMALS Ant
Grammar Skill Singular Possessive Nouns
Spelling Skill Words That End with nd, ng, or nk

TRANSPARENCY 4–11
TEACHER'S EDITION PAGES T117, T129

Responding

Comprehension Check

Have children reread or finish reading the selection. Then assign **Practice Book** page 34 to assess children's comprehension of the selection.

Think About the Selection

Have children discuss or write answers. Sample answers are provided; accept reasonable responses.

1. NOTING DETAILS Possible answer: It's amazing that ants can be found almost everywhere and that some ants grow fungus for food.

2. MAKING INFERENCES The questions are: *Do you know why? Can you pick up your mother and carry her over your head?* and *Do you?* The author asks questions to make the reader think about what the answers might be before reading them.

3. COMPARE/CONTRAST Both ant colonies and cities can be found in many places. Ant colonies and cities are made up of individuals living and working together.

4. NOTING DETAILS Ants work in teams to build tunnels, gather food, make bridges, grow fungus for food, make nests, and lift heavy things.

5. Connecting/Comparing
Officer Buckle and Gloria is a story about a policeman and a dog. It has characters, a setting, and a beginning, middle, and end. *Ant* gives information about ants. It has a topic, main ideas, and details.

THEME 4: Amazing Animals
(Anthology p. 84)

Responding

Think About the Selection

1. Which facts about ants did you find most amazing?

2. Find three questions the author asks the reader. Why does she ask questions instead of just telling facts?

3. How are ant colonies like cities? Give examples from the selection.

4. In what ways do ants work in teams?

5. **Connecting/Comparing** *Ant* is a nonfiction selection. *Officer Buckle and Gloria* is fiction. Compare the two.

Informing

Write a Report

Choose a type of ant described in the selection. In your own words, write a report that tells facts about the ant that you chose.

Tips
- Use complete sentences.
- Your report should be one or two paragraphs long.

84

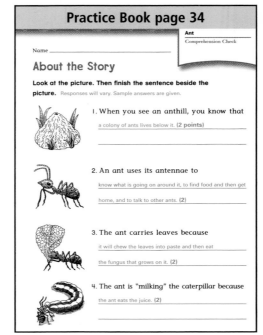

Practice Book page 34

Name _____

About the Story

Look at the picture. Then finish the sentence beside the picture. Responses will vary. Sample answers are given.

1. When you see an anthill, you know that
a colony of ants lives below it. **(2 points)**

2. An ant uses its antennae to
know what is going on around it, to find food and then get
home, and to talk to other ants. **(2)**

3. The ant carries leaves because
it will chew the leaves into paste and then eat
the fungus that grows on it. **(2)**

4. The ant is "milking" the caterpillar because
the ant eats the juice. **(2)**

Practice Book page 2

Name _____

Amazing Animals

Fill in the chart as you read the stories. Sample answers shown.

	What animals appear in this theme?	What amazing things do these animals do?
Officer Buckle and Gloria	a police dog named Gloria **(1 point)**	Gloria does funny tricks on stage. **(1)**
Ant	many types of ants **(1)**	Ants build ant bridges and grow their own food. **(1)**
The Great Ball Game	birds, a bear, a bat **(1)**	The birds and the animals play a ball game; the bat helps the animals win the game. **(1)**

Math

Count Legs

Ants have six legs. If there are five ants on a leaf, how many legs are there in all? Use numbers from the problem to write a multiplication sentence.

Bonus If three more ants climb onto the leaf, how many legs are there in all?

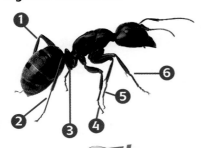

Art

Make Ant Prints

Here's a fun way to decorate a card or plain book cover. Press the eraser end of a pencil into black paint. Print ant bodies on paper. Then draw in the details with a fine-tip black pen. If you want to make red ants, use red paint!

Internet

Solve a Web Maze

Help an ant find its way through a Web maze and back to its colony. Print a maze from Education Place, and then fill it in.

www.eduplace.com/kids

85

Additional Responses

Personal Response Invite volunteers to share their personal responses to *Ant* orally in small groups.

Journal ▶ Ask children to write in their journals about something particularly memorable they learned about ants.

Selection Connections Remind children to add to **Practice Book** page 2.

REACHING ALL LEARNERS

Extra Support/ Intervention	English Language Learners

Writing Support

After children select a topic, have them find one or two facts in a book, encyclopedia, or on the Internet. Once they have their information, they can put each fact into a paragraph.

Supporting Comprehension

Beginning/Preproduction Have children draw ant and human cities. Help them discuss how they are the same and different.

Early Production and Speech Emergence Make a Venn diagram labeled Ant Colonies, Both, and Cities. Have children give you information about each category, and place it in the appropriate circle.

Intermediate and Advanced Fluency As you work on the Venn diagram, call on children to write the information.

Monitoring Student Progress

End-of-Selection Assessment

Selection Test Use the test on pages 121–122 in the **Teacher's Resource Blackline Masters** to assess selection comprehension and vocabulary.

Student Self-Assessment Have children assess their reading with questions such as

● Which ideas were easy to understand? Why?

● Which strategy could I use to help me with the difficult parts?

● What new words did I learn while reading this selection?

Responding
(Anthology p. 85)   **T151**

OBJECTIVES

- Identify and use captions, photos, and text to understand main ideas.
- Learn academic language: *caption, text*.

Target Skill Trace

Preview, Teach	pp. T118, T132, T140, T152
Reteach	p. R28
Review	p. T280
See	*Extra Support Handbook,* pp. 132–133, 138–139

Transparency 4–15

Text Organization Chart

Main Idea	Details
Ants make anthills. (pages 64–65)	Ants carry dirt out of tunnels.
	Some anthills are in sidewalk cracks.
	Some anthills are huge.
Ants have antennae. (pages 66–67)	Antennae are like noses and fingers.
	Antennae tell the ant what is going on.
	Ants talk by rubbing their antennae together.
Ants work together. (pages 68–69)	Ants pass food to each other.
	Ants carry things together.
	Ants make a bridge together.
Some ants are called leafcutter ants. (pages 72–73)	Leafcutter ants live in Costa Rica.
	They carry pieces of leaves over their heads.
	They chew the leaves into paste and
	eat the fungus that grows on it.

AMAZING ANIMALS Ant
Graphic Organizer Text Organization

ANNOTATED VERSION

TRANSPARENCY 4–15
TEACHER'S EDITION PAGES T132 AND T152

Practice Book page 30

Ant
Graphic Organizer Text Organization

Name _____

Text Organization Chart

As you read the story, use this chart to help you keep track of what you learn about ants.

Main Idea	Details
Ants make anthills. (pages 64–65)	Ants carry dirt out of tunnels. **(1 point)**
	Some anthills are in sidewalk cracks. **(1)**
	Some anthills are huge. **(1)**
Ants have antennae. (pages 66–67)	Antennae are like noses and fingers. **(1)**
	Antennae tell the ant what is going on. **(1)**
	Ants talk by rubbing their antennae together. **(1)**
Ants work together. (pages 68-69)	Ants pass food to each other. **(1)**
	Ants carry things together. **(1)**
	Ants make a bridge together. **(1)**
Some ants are called leafcutter ants. (pages 72-73)	Leafcutter ants live in Costa Rica. **(1)**
	They carry pieces of leaves over their heads. **(1)**
	They chew the leaves into paste and
	eat the fungus that grows on it. **(1)**

INSTRUCTION

TARGET SKILL COMPREHENSION: Text Organization

❶ Teach

Display the Graphic Organizer on Transparency 4–15. Use the Text Organization Chart to review what children recorded and what they learned about ants.

- Have children read the details they listed in the first box.
- Have them read aloud or discuss photos, captions, and text that support their notes.

Children can refer to the selection and to **Practice Book** page 30.

Modeling Model how to use text organization to look in the selection for information about ants.

Think Aloud *I want to find information about leafcutter ants. I see a picture of an ant chewing a leaf on page 72. The caption tells me that the leafcutter ants shown are from Costa Rica, so I'll write* Leafcutter ants are from Costa Rica. *I see two more pictures on the next page. By reading the words and looking at the pictures on that page, I learn that these ants chew pieces of leaves to make a paste. This is another detail that I can write down.*

Have children explain how the captions, text, and picture clues supplied them with additional information about ants.

❷ Guided Practice

Have children work in small groups to review their Text Organization Charts.

- Have groups compare their charts and add information as necessary.
- Have children refer to text features, such as photographs or captions, that support their ideas.

❸ Apply

Assign Practice Book pages 35–36. Have children apply this skill as they read their Leveled Readers for this week. You may also select books from the Leveled Bibliography for this theme (pages T6–T7).

Test Prep Tell children that using text organization and text features such as the title, headings, and captions will help them find information to answer test questions.

Leveled Readers and Leveled Practice

Children at all levels apply the comprehension skill as they read their Leveled Readers. See lessons on pages T172–T175.

● BELOW LEVEL   ▲ ON LEVEL   ■ ABOVE LEVEL   ◆ LANGUAGE SUPPORT

Reading Traits

Teaching children how to recognize text organization is one way of encouraging them to "read the lines" of a selection. This comprehension skill supports the reading trait **Decoding Conventions**.

Practice Book page 35

Name _____

Ant
Comprehension Skill Text Organization

Text Organization

Read the article below. Then complete the chart on page 36.

Amazing Beetles

Beetles may be the kings of insects. Beetles have lived on Earth longer than any other insect. There are more beetles than any other kind of insect.

Almost 400,000 kinds of beetles live on Earth. You need a magnifying glass to see the smallest beetle. The biggest beetles live in the jungle. They are six inches long. That's longer than your hand! Some beetles have shiny green bodies. Some are plain and brown. You may have held one kind of beetle in your hand — the ladybug.

People do many things with beetles. People with gardens buy boxes of ladybugs. Ladybugs are good for gardens. They eat insects that hurt plants. Some people make jewelry from fancy green beetles. Other people keep beetles for pets. In some parts of the world, beetles are food. People eat the beetles.

If all the living creatures in the world were standing in a line, every fourth creature would be a beetle. That is a lot of beetles! This is why the beetle is called the king of insects.

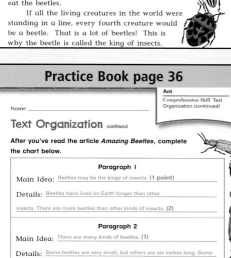

Practice Book page 36

Name _____

Ant
Comprehension Skill Text Organization (continued)

Text Organization continued

After you've read the article *Amazing Beetles*, complete the chart below.

Paragraph 1
Main Idea: Beetles may be the kings of insects. **(1 point)**
Details: Beetles have lived on Earth longer than other insects. There are more beetles than other kinds of insects. **(2)**

Paragraph 2
Main Idea: There are many kinds of beetles. **(1)**
Details: Some beetles are very small, but others are six inches long. Some are shiny and green, but others are plain and brown. Ladybugs are beetles. **(3)**

Paragraph 3
Main Idea: People do many things with beetles. **(1)**
Details: People put them in gardens. People make jewelry from them. People keep them as pets. People eat them. **(4)**

Paragraph 4
Main Idea: Every fourth creature on Earth is a beetle. **(1)**
Details: This is why the beetle is called the king of insects. **(1)**

Monitoring Student Progress

If . . .	Then . . .
children score 10 or below on **Practice Book** page 36,	use the Reteaching lesson on page R28.
children have met the lesson objectives,	you can use the Challenge/Extension activities on page R29.

Rebecca Stefoff
ANT

LIVING THINGS

REREADING FOR UNDERSTANDING

Visual Literacy: Descriptive Photographs

Teach Tell children that descriptive photographs

- provide information that may not be in the text,
- can help readers better understand facts that are explained in the text.

Have children look at Anthology page 71. Write *Larvae look like little worms.* Point out that this is the only information the text gives about what the larvae look like. By looking at the photograph, however, readers can see that ant larvae are smooth and tan, and about the size of a grain of rice.

Practice/Apply Ask children to find examples of other photographs in the selection that give more information about a topic than is presented in the text.

Larvae look like little worms.

SPELLING: Words That End with *nd, ng,* or *nk*

Vocabulary Connection Write the Basic Words.

king	send	bang	sing
thank	think	end	thing
hand	bring		

Word Building Write the word beginnings shown below. Ask children to add *nd, ng,* and *nk* to each beginning. Have them write and read the new words. Discuss word meanings as needed.

- ba (band, bang, bank)
- ha (hand, hang, Hank)
- ki (kind, king, kink)
- ri (rind, ring, rink)
- sa (sand, sang, sank)
- wi (wind, wing, wink)

Have children use each Basic Word in an oral sentence.

Practice/Homework Assign **Practice Book** page 36.

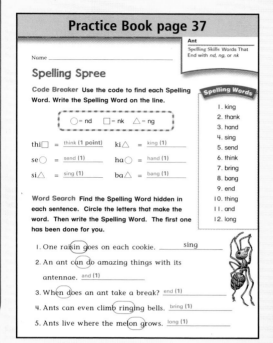

Practice Book page 37

Ant
Spelling Skills Words That
End with *nd, ng,* or *nk*

Name _____

Spelling Spree

Code Breaker Use the code to find each Spelling Word. Write the Spelling Word on the line.

◯ = nd   ☐ = nk   △ = ng

thi☐ = think **(1 point)**   ki△ = king **(1)**
se◯ = send **(1)**   ha◯ = hand **(1)**
si△ = sing **(1)**   ba△ = bang **(1)**

Word Search Find the Spelling Word hidden in each sentence. Circle the letters that make the word. Then write the Spelling Word. The first one has been done for you.

1. One raisin goes on each cookie. _____ sing
2. An ant can do amazing things with its antennae. and **(1)**
3. When does an ant take a break? end **(1)**
4. Ants can even climb ringing bells. bring **(1)**
5. Ants live where the melon grows. long **(1)**

Spelling Words
1. king
2. thank
3. hand
4. sing
5. send
6. think
7. bring
8. bang
9. end
10. thing
11. and
12. long

GRAMMAR: Singular Possessive Nouns

Whose Is This? Have children play a naming game using singular possessive nouns.

- Pick up an item, such as a pencil, from a child's desk and ask *Whose pencil is this?* Have children respond, for example, *It is Maria's pencil.*

- Have children take turns asking *Whose is this?*

This is Maria's pencil.

Day at a Glance
pp. T156–T165

Reading Instruction

Music Link

Phonics Review

Reading Decodable Text
Marta's Larks

• •

Leveled Readers, *T172–T175*

- ● *Earthworms*
- ▲ *Busy Bees*
- ■ *Butterflies!*
- ◆ *The Amazing Earthworm*

Word Work

Vocabulary Instruction
Using a Thesaurus

Word Wall

Spelling Practice

Writing & Oral Language

Improving Writing

Grammar Practice

Listening/Speaking/Viewing

Daily Routines

Daily Message

Strategy Review Remind children of the Phonics/Decoding Strategy. Guide them in applying it to selected words in today's message.

> In the library, look for a nonfiction book about animals. You will learn lots of information, and you will see colorful photographs. Read about some animals such as _____.

Read aloud the entire Daily Message with children, pointing to each word as you read. Ask children to read the message aloud. Then have volunteers complete the last sentence, and discuss their responses.

Word Wall

Missing Word Review the high-frequency words from this week's Word Wall.

- Have each child write five sentences, each using one Word Wall word. Ask them to replace the word with a write-on line.
- Have children trade papers and complete each sentence by writing the missing word.
- Have children illustrate one of the sentences.

The _____ spider is spinning a web.

Vocabulary

Key Vocabulary Review Briefly review the words *antennae, cocoons, colonies, larvae,* and *tunnels.*

Have children illustrate one of the words and write a clue to identify it.

Ask partners to trade papers and solve the clues. Suggest that they reread the text of *Ant* and use the Glossary as necessary.

Daily Writing Prompt

Have children revise work they are currently writing, or have them use this prompt to begin a new writing activity.

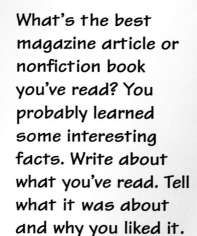

What's the best magazine article or nonfiction book you've read? You probably learned some interesting facts. Write about what you've read. Tell what it was about and why you liked it.

Daily Language Practice

Grammar Skill: Singular Possessive Nouns
Spelling Skill: Words That End with *nd, ng,* or *nk*

Display **Transparency 4–11.** Ask children to rewrite Sentence 4 correctly. Then model how to write it, and have children check their work.

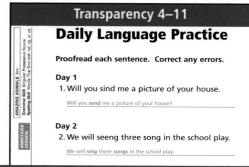

Transparency 4–11

Daily Language Practice

Proofread each sentence. Correct any errors.

Day 1
1. Will you sind me a picture of your house.

Will you **send** me a picture of your house?

Day 2
2. We will seeing three song in the school play.

We will **sing** three **songs** in the school play.

Day 4

4. Will you breeng a bag of peachs when you come to the beach.

Will you **bring** a bag of **peaches** when you come to the beach?

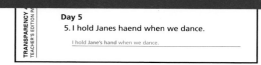

Day 5
5. I hold Janes haend when we dance.

I hold **Jane's hand** when we dance.

The Ants Go Marching
Traditional Children's Song

Skill: How to Read Song Lyrics

❶ Skim the **lyrics**, or words of the song, before singing.

❷ Sing the first **verse** and then the **chorus**.

❸ Repeat for the remaining verses.

1. The ants go march-ing one by one, Hur - rah,— Hur - rah.— The ants go march-ing one by one, Hur - rah,— Hur - rah.— The ants go march-ing one by one; The lit-tle one stops to have some fun, and they all go march - ing down in - to the ground to get out of the rain. Boom! Boom! Boom!

86

2. The ants go marching two by two,
    Hurrah, Hurrah. *(repeat)*
   The ants go marching two by two;
    The little one stops to tie his shoe.

   Chorus:
   And they all go marching down into the ground
   to get out of the rain. Boom! Boom! Boom!

3. The ants go marching three by three;
    Hurrah, Hurrah. *(repeat)*
   The ants go marching three by three;
    The little one stops to climb a tree.
    Chorus

4. The ants go marching four by four;
    Hurrah, Hurrah. *(repeat)*
   The ants go marching four by four;
    The little one stops to shut the door.
    Chorus

5. The ants go marching five by five;
    Hurrah, Hurrah. *(repeat)*
   The ants go marching five by five;
    The little one stops to take a dive.
    Chorus

87

Music Link

Skill: How to Read Song Lyrics

- **Introduce** Read aloud the song's title. Explain that "The Ants Go Marching" is a traditional song that children might sing as they march or parade around the room or playground. Ask children to name other songs to which they could march.

- **Discuss** the Skill Lesson, How to Read Song Lyrics, on Anthology page 86.

- **Model** skimming the lyrics. Together, skim pages 86–87. Emphasize that skimming the lyrics will help children fit the words with the music when they begin to sing. Read aloud Verses 2–5, including the chorus. As you read, have children listen and clap the rhythm.

- **Assign** Have children sing the entire song along with you.

REACHING ALL LEARNERS

English Language Learners

Sing a Song

As children listen, play or sing the song once. Then help them read and sound out the lyrics. Sing the song again. Encourage children to join in when they feel ready.

THEME 4: Amazing Animals
(Anthology pp. 86–87)

Wrapping Up

Critical Thinking Questions

Ask children to read aloud parts of the text that support each answer.

1. **NOTING DETAILS** What changes in each verse in the song? (The number of ants in the marching group increases by one. The little ant does something different each time.)

2. **MAKING GENERALIZATIONS** If the ants went marching six by six, what might the little one stop to do? Why? (Sample response: pick up sticks; because the activity always rhymes with the number of ants marching)

3. **COMPARE AND CONTRAST** Based on what you read in *Ant,* is it possible the song was written about weaver ants? If not, why? (No; because weaver ants live in trees, but the ants in the song go underground.)

REACHING ALL LEARNERS **On Level**   **Challenge**

Write a Verse

Explain that some versions of "The Ants Go Marching" have ten verses. Ask children to write their own versions of Verses 6–10, following the rhyming format of the original song. For example, in the case of "nine by nine," the little ant might stop to "draw a line." Have children share their new verses with the class.

VOCABULARY: Using a Thesaurus

❶ Teach

Display a children's thesaurus.

- Explain that a thesaurus is a book that lists synonyms, or words with nearly the same meanings, in alphabetical order.

- Write and read *Ants are <u>little</u>.* Point out that a thesaurus would list other more exact words for *little* such as *small, tiny,* or *wee.*

Model how to use a thesaurus. Ask children where in the thesaurus they would find the word *little.* (in the middle) Turn to the page in the *L* section that lists *little.*

Think Aloud *Next to the entry word* little, *I find its meaning: not big. The synonyms* small *and* tiny *are listed. I know that ants are very little, so the exact word I'm looking for is* tiny. *If I replace the word* little *with* tiny, *the sentence will describe ants more exactly.*

❷ Guided Practice

Provide a thesaurus to each group of children. Write *The cake tastes <u>good</u>. My horse can <u>run</u> as fast as yours. I want to <u>make</u> a birdhouse. My neighbor is a <u>nice</u> person.*

- Have children use the thesaurus to find more exact words to replace the underlined words.

❸ Apply

Assign Practice Book page 38.

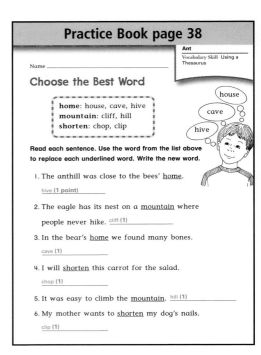

Practice Book page 38

Ant
Vocabulary Skill: Using a Thesaurus

Name ___

Choose the Best Word

> **home:** house, cave, hive
> **mountain:** cliff, hill
> **shorten:** chop, clip

Read each sentence. Use the word from the list above to replace each underlined word. Write the new word.

1. The anthill was close to the bees' <u>home</u>.
   hive **(1 point)**
2. The eagle has its nest on a <u>mountain</u> where people never hike. cliff **(1)**
3. In the bear's <u>home</u> we found many bones.
   cave **(1)**
4. I will <u>shorten</u> this carrot for the salad.
   chop **(1)**
5. It was easy to climb the <u>mountain</u>. hill **(1)**
6. My mother wants to <u>shorten</u> my dog's nails.
   clip **(1)**

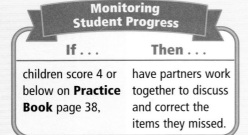

Monitoring Student Progress

If . . .	Then . . .
children score 4 or below on **Practice Book** page 38,	have partners work together to discuss and correct the items they missed.

T160 **THEME 4: Amazing Animals**

PHONICS: *r*-Controlled Vowels *ar, or, ore*

❶ Review

Review the pattern. Use the words *shark, thorn, store, morning,* and *harmful* and the **Sound/Spelling Cards** *artist* and *orange* to explain these concepts:

- When *r* follows a vowel, it can change the vowel sound.
- The letters *ar* stand for /är/ in *artist*.
- The letters *or* and *ore* stand for /ôr/ in *orange*.

❷ Guided Practice/Apply

Assign Practice Book page 39. Also have children play Concentration.

Concentration

Get ready to play.

- Write *scarf, porch, score, north, large, marching, seashore, hardly, adore,* and *shortcut*. Have children copy each word on a square of paper.
- Pair children. Have them combine their word cards and place them face-down in rows.

Play the game.

- Partners alternate turning over and reading two words. If the words match and are read correctly, the child keeps the cards.
- If the cards do not match or the words are read incorrectly, the cards are returned face-down.
- The child with the most matching words read correctly wins.

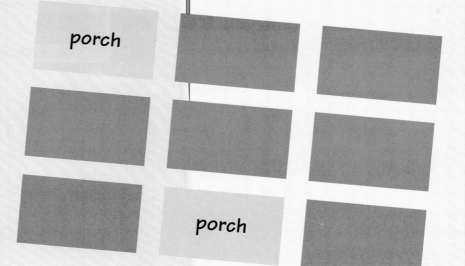

OBJECTIVE

- Read and write words with *ar, or,* and *ore.*

Review Skill Trace

Teach	pp. T34–T35
Reteach	pp. R10, R12
▶ Review	pp. T161, T263, T271
See	*Handbook for English Language Learners,* p. 139

Materials

- **Sound/Spelling Cards** *artist* and *orange*
- squares of paper to make word cards

Practice Book page 39

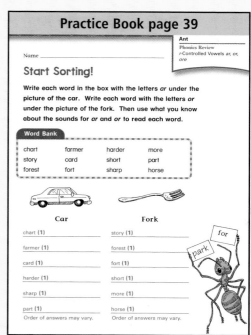

Name _____

Ant
Phonics Review
r-Controlled Vowels *ar, or, ore*

Start Sorting!

Write each word in the box with the letters *ar* under the picture of the car. Write each word with the letters *or* under the picture of the fork. Then use what you know about the sounds for *ar* and *or* to read each word.

Word Bank

chart	farmer	harder	more
story	card	short	part
forest	fort	sharp	horse

Car

chart **(1)**

farmer **(1)**

card **(1)**

harder **(1)**

sharp **(1)**

part **(1)**

Order of answers may vary.

Fork

story **(1)**

forest **(1)**

fort **(1)**

short **(1)**

more **(1)**

horse **(1)**

Order of answers may vary.

PHONICS LIBRARY

Reading Decodable Text

OBJECTIVES

- Apply the Phonics/Decoding Strategy to decode words in context.
- Reread to build fluency.

Have children preview *Marta's Larks*.

Have children model the Phonics/ Decoding Strategy. Have a volunteer read the story title and tell how to figure out each word. Ask children to tell how they can figure out other new words

Apply the Phonics/Decoding Strategy. Have children read the story independently. If necessary, use prompts such as these for *chores* (page 25) and *hardly* (page 28):

- Find the word *c-h-o-r-e-s*. What is the vowel sound? With what sound does the word begin? end? Blend the sounds to read the word.

- Find the word *h-a-r-d-l-y*. Break this word into syllables. Say each syllable and blend the syllables together to read the word.

Marta's Larks
by Linda Dunlap
Illustrated by Christiane Beauregard

Marta was born on a farm. She has chores every day. The chore she likes best is feeding larks. Larks are birds that sing a lot. Marta likes to hear them each day.

25

2

In March, Marta works in her garden. She sees larks try teamwork to turn a leaf. "What is under that leaf?" Marta thinks.

26

Marta picks up the leaf. A fat bug looks back at her! "Wow! Those larks are smart!" exclaims Marta. "I will start watching larks at work."

27

26   2

Word Key

Decodable words with *ar, or, ore* _____

Marta sees larks working <u>hard</u> finding food. Even little larks eat lots of bugs. Larks swoop and <u>dart</u> in the sky. <u>Hardly</u> any bugs get away!

28

Marta sees larks working hard making nests. Larks pull bits of <u>bark</u> from <u>large</u> trees. They take blades of grass from the <u>yard</u>. Larks find <u>torn yarn</u>. They carry these things to a safe place. Then larks turn bark, grass, and yarn into nests!

29

8   29

Marta likes watching larks at work. And larks feel safe when Marta is close. Marta would never <u>harm</u> her larks!

30

Marta is a <u>part</u> of her larks' life. Larks perch on her <u>arms</u>. Others eat seeds from her hands. Marta is glad to have larks for friends.

31

0   31

PHONICS LIBRARY

Oral Language

Discuss the story. Ask children to answer in complete sentences.

- How does Marta make the larks her friends? (Marta feeds the larks every day, never harms them, makes them feel safe, and lets them perch on her arms and eat from her hands.)

- What does Marta learn about larks? (Marta learns that larks sing a lot, are smart, eat lots of bugs, and make nests in safe places.)

- How do larks make nests? (Larks use bits of tree bark, grass, and yarn.)

Build Fluency

Model fluent reading.

- Read aloud page 25.

- Write *Marta was born / on a farm. / She has chores / every day. The chore she likes best / is feeding larks.* Explain that this is one way of grouping words for smooth reading. Have children read the sentences with you.

- Have volunteers show how to group the remaining sentences into phrases. Have the class repeat the phrasing.

Have children practice fluent reading. Have partners each reread another story page aloud. Encourage them to group words into phrases for smooth reading.

 Home Connection
Hand out the take-home version of *Marta's Larks*. Ask children to reread the story with their families. (See the **Phonics Library Blackline Masters**.)

Reading Decodable Text T163

SPELLING: Words That End with *nd*, *ng*, or *nk*

Ant Additions Have partners each draw an ant with no legs and together make a card for each Basic and Review Word.

- Have partners place the word cards face-down in a stack.
- Player A chooses a card and gives Player B clues about the word that include the word's ending sound or sounds.
- Player B tries to guess the word and spell it correctly.
- Players take turns giving clues, guessing the word, and spelling it.
- If correct, a player adds a leg to his or her ant. The first player to add all six legs to his or her ant wins.

Practice/Homework Assign **Practice Book** page 40 for proofreading and writing practice.

Practice Book page 40

Name _____

Ant
Spelling Skills Words That
End with nd, ng, or nk

Proofreading and Writing

Proofreading Circle four Spelling Words that are incorrect. Then write each word correctly.

Spelling Words

April 4 Today I watched six ants carry a grasshopper. They must be very strong. What a (ting) to do. That would be like six men carrying an elephant!

April 8 I put my (hande) on a fire-ant nest by accident. The stings really hurt, but my dad helped. He put honey on them!

April 9 Today I read about the queen ant. I wonder if there is a king. I don't (thenk) so.

April 12 I visited the nature museum today. A man there who studies ants showed me around. Tomorrow I will write to (thaink) him for the great visit.

1. king
2. thank
3. hand
4. sing
5. send
6. think
7. bring
8. bang
9. end
10. thing
11. and
12. long

1. thing (1 point)   3. think (1)
2. hand (1)   4. thank (1)

Write a Report Read more about ants. Write a short report on a separate piece of paper. Use the Spelling Words.
Responses will vary. (4 points)

GRAMMAR: Singular Possessive Nouns

Practice/Homework Assign **Practice Book** page 41.

Practice Book page 41

Name _____

Ant
Grammar Skill Singular
Possessive Nouns

Who Owns What?

Read each group of words below.

Word Bank

queen's eggs   colony's tunnel
worker's leaf   tree's roots

Choose a phrase from the Word Bank that gives the meaning of the two pictures. Write it on the line.

+ = worker's leaf (2 points)

+ = queen's eggs (2)

Now write two sentences. Use one of the phrases at the top of the page in each of your sentences.

Sentences will vary. (2)

The ant's eggs are on the leaf.

IMPROVING WRITING:
Using *I* and *me*

OBJECTIVE

● Use *I* and *me* correctly.

❶ Teach

Writing Traits: Conventions Tell children that when they name themselves in writing, they often use the words *I* and *me*. Explain that there are rules for when to use *I* and *me*. Following these rules will make their writing correct and clear.

Model how to use *I* and *me* correctly in sentences.

● Write *Ed and I rode our bikes to school.*

● Tell children that when they write about another person and themselves, it is correct to name themselves last. Explain that *I,* not *me,* is used in the naming part of the sentence.

● Write *My mom drove Ed and me* to school. Explain that *me* is used in the action part of the sentence.

❷ Practice

Have children model using *I* and *me* correctly. Display **Transparency 4–17.**

● Have volunteers take turns reading the sentences aloud, filling in the blank spaces with a friend's name and either *I* or *me*.

● Remind children to use *I* in the naming part of the sentence and *me* in the action part and to say *I* or *me* after naming their friend.

● Then have children say sentences of their own that show the correct use of *I* and *me*.

❸ Apply

Assign Practice Book page 42. Have children read previous writing samples and correct any errors in the use of *I* and *me*.

Transparency 4–17
Using *I* and *me*

1. _____ and ___I___ went to the store.

2. She gave the book to _____ and ___me___.

3. On Tuesday, _____ and ___I___ play soccer.

4. Can _____ and ___I___ paint a picture together?

5. Would you like to go to the game with _____ and ___me___?

6. Yesterday _____ and ___I___ helped the teacher.

7. Sam asked _____ and ___me___ to come to his party.

8. Tran walked home with _____ and ___me___.

9. _____ and ___I___ like to help with cooking.

10. Tomorrow _____ and ___I___ will clean the room.

AMAZING ANIMALS Ant
Writing Skill Improving Your Writing
ANNOTATED VERSION
TRANSPARENCY 4–17
TEACHER'S EDITION PAGE T147

Practice Book page 42

Ant
Writing Skill Using *I* and *me*

Name _____

I or Me?

Read the letter below. The word *I* or the word *me* belongs in each blank space. Rewrite the letter using the words *I* and *me* correctly.

Dear Jamie,
    Yesterday my dad and ____ went to the nature museum. There was a giant ant farm there. Dad and ____ watched the ants for almost an hour. Then the museum guide took Dad and ____ on a tour around the museum. We had so much fun. If we go again, would you like to go with Dad and ____?
                    Your friend,
                    Brett

Dear Jamie, _____

Yesterday my dad and I **(1 point)** went to the nature museum. There was a giant

ant farm there. Dad and I **(1)** watched the ants for almost an hour. Then the

museum guide took Dad and me **(1)** on a tour around the museum. We had so

much fun. If we go again, would you like to go with Dad and me **(1)**?

                    Your friend,

                    Brett

Day at a Glance
pp. T166–T171

Reading Instruction

Rereading for Understanding and Fluency

Study Skill: Using a Glossary

Leveled Readers, *T172–T175*

- ● *Earthworms*
- ▲ *Busy Bees*
- ■ *Butterflies!*
- ◆ *The Amazing Earthworm*

Word Work

Vocabulary Expansion

Word Wall

Spelling Test: Words That End with *nd, ng,* or *nk*

Writing & Oral Language

Writing Activity

Grammar: Improving Writing

Listening/Speaking/Viewing: Discussing a Factual Topic

Daily Routines

Daily Message

Strategy Review Remind children of the Phonics/Decoding Strategy. Guide them in applying it to selected words in today's message.

> We might not hear ants, moths, or other insects in the garden, but we know they have been hard at work. Ants can leave behind _____.

Ask children to read aloud the entire Daily Message. Point to each word as they read. Then have volunteers complete the last sentence, and discuss their responses.

Word Wall

Cumulative Review Review previously taught high-frequency words by adding endings to make new words.

Have children

- choose any five punchout word cards;
- add word endings *-ed, -ing,* or *-es* to each one and write the new word on a separate paper;
- make as many new words from five high-frequency words as they can.

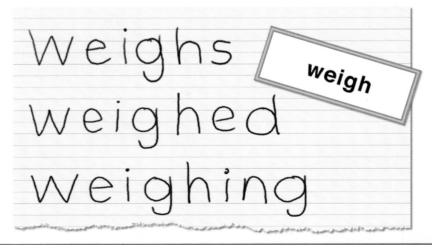

Vocabulary

Vocabulary Expansion Write the word *queen*. Ask children what they learned about an ant queen. (The queen is the mother of all the ants in the colony.) Ask what they know about human queens. (They are the leaders of their countries.) Explain that there are many kinds of leaders.

Ask children to name other kinds of leaders, including those in their community and in the animal kingdom.

Add their suggestions to the list.

king	queen
president	teacher
director	chief
principal	pack leader

Daily Writing Prompt

Have children revise work they are currently writing, or have them use this prompt to begin a new writing activity.

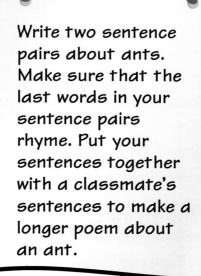

Write two sentence pairs about ants. Make sure that the last words in your sentence pairs rhyme. Put your sentences together with a classmate's sentences to make a longer poem about an ant.

Daily Language Practice

Grammar Skill: Singular Possessive Nouns
Spelling Skill: Words That End with *nd, ng,* or *nk*

Display **Transparency 4–11**. Ask children to rewrite Sentence 5 correctly. Then model how to write it, and have children check their work.

Transparency 4–11

Daily Language Practice

Proofread each sentence. Correct any errors.

Day 1
1. Will you sind me a picture of your house.

   Will you **send** me a picture of your house?

Day 2
2. We will seeng three song in the school play.

   We will **sing** three **songs** in the school play.

Day 3
3. May i thank you for this gift?

   May **I thank** you for this gift?

Day 5
5. I hold Janes haend when we dance.

   I hold **Jane's hand** when we dance.

Review Skill Trace	
Teach	Theme 4, pp. T220–T221
	Theme 2, pp. T144–T145
Reteach	Theme 4, p. R30
	Theme 2, p. R30
▶ **Review**	Theme 4, p. T168
	Theme 1, pp. T76, T224; Theme 3, p. T236

COMPREHENSION: Rereading for Understanding

Cause and Effect

Review Tell children that *Ant* is a nonfiction selection that explains ant behavior. Have children look for cause-and-effect relationships in *Ant*.

- Write several statements describing effects (What Happens) in the left-hand column of a Cause-Effect Chart. (Example: Piles, called anthills, are formed outside of tunnel entrances.)

- Have children review the selection to find a cause (Why It Happens) for each statement. Record this information in the right-hand column of the chart. (Example: Ants carry dirt out of tunnels.)

Practice/Apply Have children skim the selection to find information to add to the Why It Happens column of the Cause/Effect Chart.

Fact and Opinion

Review Remind children that a fact is a statement that can be proved, while an opinion states something that a person believes or feels. Read aloud from Anthology page 81: *Ants are very strong.* Ask *Can this statement be proved? How might you prove it?*

Lead children to see that the statement is a fact, since photographs on pages 81 and 73 show ants performing tasks that require great strength. Next, say *I think ants are interesting.* Explain that this statement is an opinion, since it states a feeling or belief that cannot be proved to be true.

Practice/Apply Have children write at least three facts and a personal opinion about ants.

REREADING FOR FLUENCY

Rereading the Selection Have children choose part of the story to reread orally in small groups, or suggest that they reread Anthology pages 66–68. If children are not reading with feeling and expression, model for them.

STUDY SKILL:
Using a Glossary

❶ Teach

Discuss reasons for using a glossary.

- Explain that when seeing an unfamiliar word in books, children should check the glossary for the definition.
- Define a glossary as a list of words and their definitions found at the back of a book.

Display and discuss the glossary page on Transparency 4–18. Point to the different features, and ask:

- How are the words are listed? (alphabetical order)
- How does the sample sentence help you to understand the definition? (It makes the meaning and use of the word clearer.)
- Which word means "likely to break or fall apart"? (*rickety*)
- What is a pennant? Where might you find one? (a long flag, shaped like a triangle; a basketball game)

❷ Practice/Apply

Have pairs of children complete the assignable activity below.

OBJECTIVES

- Use information from a glossary.
- Learn academic language: *glossary.*

Materials

- children's Anthology glossaries

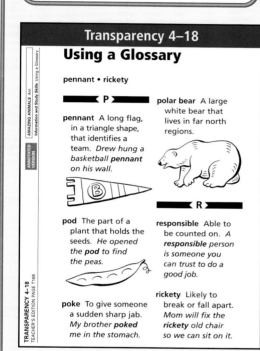

Transparency 4–18

Using a Glossary

pennant • rickety

◀ P ▶

pennant A long flag, in a triangle shape, that identifies a team. *Drew hung a basketball pennant on his wall.*

pod The part of a plant that holds the seeds. *He opened the pod to find the peas.*

poke To give someone a sudden sharp jab. *My brother poked me in the stomach.*

polar bear A large white bear that lives in far north regions.

◀ R ▶

responsible Able to be counted on. *A responsible person is someone you can trust to do a good job.*

rickety Likely to break or fall apart. *Mom will fix the rickety old chair so we can sit on it.*

Out of the Glossary

- Use your glossary to find two words that have the same beginning letter as <u>pennant</u>.
- Tell your partner the words and what they mean.
- Take turns choosing a word in the glossary, and then asking your partner to find it and tell what it means. Draw a picture to go with one of the definitions.

fungus

Information and Study Skills   **T169**

DAY 5

SPELLING & GRAMMAR

WEEK 2

OBJECTIVES

- Write spelling words ending with *nd, ng,* or *nk.*
- Proofread sentences for the correct use of apostrophes to improve writing.

Transparency 4–19

Proofreading for Apostrophes

1. The tree's leaves turned red and gold.

2. This pillow feels as soft as a kitten's fur.

3. My dog's tail wags when I come home.

4. Kate's jokes are always funny.

5. This is the winter's first snow.

6. Mr. Smith's apples are ready to be picked.

7. Can you see Rick's house from here?

8. The duck's beak was bright orange.

9. Today's weather is cold and windy.

10. Our soccer team's game was called off.

TRANSPARENCY 4–19
TEACHER'S EDITION PAGE T170

AMAZING ANIMALS Ant
Grammar Skill Improving Your Writing

ANNOTATED VERSION

Practice Book page 43

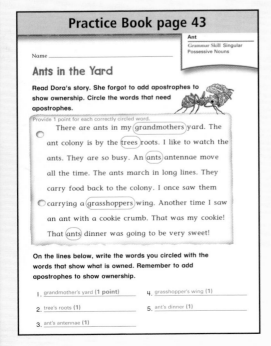

Ant
Grammar Skill Singular
Possessive Nouns

Name _____

Ants in the Yard

Read Dora's story. She forgot to add apostrophes to show ownership. Circle the words that need apostrophes.

Provide 1 point for each correctly circled word.

There are ants in my (grandmothers) yard. The ant colony is by the (trees) roots. I like to watch the ants. They are so busy. An (ants) antennae move all the time. The ants march in long lines. They carry food back to the colony. I once saw them carrying a (grasshoppers) wing. Another time I saw an ant with a cookie crumb. That was my cookie! That (ants) dinner was going to be very sweet!

On the lines below, write the words you circled with the words that show what is owned. Remember to add apostrophes to show ownership.

1. grandmother's yard **(1 point)**   4. grasshopper's wing (1)

2. tree's roots (1)   5. ant's dinner (1)

3. ant's antennae (1)

TEST

SPELLING: Words That End with *nd, ng,* or *nk*

Test

Say each underlined word, read the sentence, and then repeat the word. Have children write only the underlined word.

Basic Words

1. A **king** wears a crown.
2. Will you **thank** her today?
3. Hold my **hand**.
4. I like to hear you **sing**.
5. We will **send** a note.
6. I **think** you are nice.
7. Did you **bring** the ball?
8. I heard a loud **bang**.
9. It is the **end** of the day.
10. What is that **thing**?

Challenge Words

11. The queen lives in a **grand** palace.
12. The boy is too **young** to be king.

INSTRUCTION

GRAMMAR: Improving Writing

Proofreading for Apostrophes

Teach Demonstrate how to proofread for apostrophes in singular possessive nouns. Read aloud the first sentence on **Transparency 4–19.**

- Point out that the word *trees* should have an apostrophe to show ownership of the leaves.
- Add the apostrophe to change *trees* to *tree's.*
- Repeat with the other sentences.

Have children proofread a sample of their own writing for apostrophes in singular possessive nouns.

Practice/Apply Assign **Practice Book** page 43.

THEME 4: Amazing Animals

LISTENING & SPEAKING: Discussing a Factual Topic

❶ Teach

Review discussions.

- Define a discussion as a talk about one topic meant to answer a question or solve a problem.
- Explain that it is important to listen for facts and details.

Brainstorm tips for having a group discussion.

⭐ Stick to the topic.

⭐ Speak clearly.

⭐ Take turns. Let others speak without interrupting them.

⭐ Look at and listen to the person speaking.

⭐ Think about what each person says. Be sure to ask questions!

❷ Practice/Apply

Have children break into groups. Assign the topics *army ants, leafcutter ants, carpenter ants,* and *weaver ants* to research and discuss.

Have groups of children complete the activity. After they have practiced their discussion, have groups present it to the class.

OBJECTIVES

- Learn rules for a group discussion.
- Have a factual discussion in a group.
- Listen to a factual discussion.

Materials

- encyclopedia, science texts, science CD-ROMs, or other reference sources

REACHING ALL LEARNERS

English Language Learners

Factual Discussion

Have children list key words or phrases they might use in discussing their topic. Help them add pertinent facts and ideas that they have learned from their own culture.

Factual Group Discussion

- Look up your topic. Find the facts you need.
- Practice having a group discussion. Tell the group the facts you found.
- Hold a group discussion in front the class.
- Which part of the discussion went well? What can you do better next time?

Where do they live?
What do they eat?
What do they look like?
How do they work together?
What interesting facts did you learn?

Leveled Readers

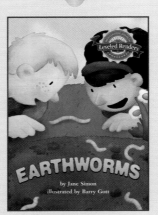

EARTHWORMS
by Jane Simon
illustrated by Barry Gott

Earthworms

Summary *Earthworms help make gardens grow. They help bring air and water into the earth. The waste they leave behind helps make rich food for plants. Even though we don't see them at work, these wiggly creatures are always busy underground.*

Vocabulary

Introduce the Key Vocabulary and ask children to complete the BLM.

tunnels* long holes under the ground, *p. 5*

soil earth that is good for growing plants, *p. 6*

decaying rotting, *p. 8*

fungus* one of a large group of plants, such as mushrooms and mold, that do not have leaves or flowers, *p. 8*

*Forms of these words are Anthology Key Vocabulary words.

● BELOW LEVEL

Building Background and Vocabulary

Explain to children that this story is about earthworms and how they help plants to grow. Lead a discussion about what they think earthworms do, and why. Use some of the language of the book and key vocabulary as you guide children through the text.

🅖 Comprehension Skill: Text Organization

Have children read the Strategy Focus on the book flap. Remind children to use the strategy and to think about the ways text is organized as they read the book. (See the Leveled Readers Teacher's Guide for **Vocabulary and Comprehension Practice Masters.**)

Responding

Have partners discuss how to answer the questions on the inside back cover.

Think About What You Have Read Sample answers:

1. The tunnels bring air and water into the soil. That is good for plants.
2. They eat pieces of plants and decaying animals and fungus. It becomes waste that is full of rich food for plants.
3. Possible response: Earthworms are small but very important for growing plants.

Making Connections Responses will vary.

🅖 Building Fluency

Model Read aloud the text on page 2, asking students how they know the sentence is a question (question mark appears, voice lifts at the end of the sentence).

Practice Ask children to find the other page in the text which contains a question (page 10), and have them read it aloud.

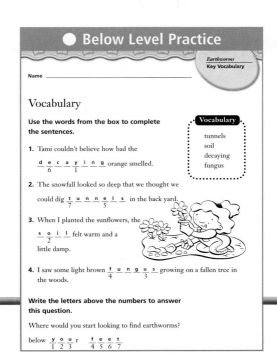

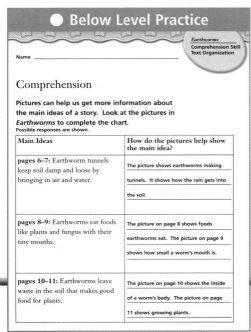

Busy Bees

Summary *Different types of bees lead different lives. While they are quite different, the many types of bees are alike in some ways; they spread pollen that helps plants make seeds, and many produce honey.*

Vocabulary

Introduce the Key Vocabulary and ask children to complete the BLM.

antennae* a pair of long, thin feelers on the head of an insect, *p. 2*

colonies* groups of insects of the same kind that live together, *p. 3*

larvae* the worm-like forms of very young insects, *p. 6*

tunnels* long holes under the ground, *p. 11*

cocoons* coverings of silky thread that larvae live in as they change and grow, *p. 13*

*Forms of these words are Anthology Key Vocabulary words.

▲ ON LEVEL

Building Background and Vocabulary

Explain that this story is about bees. Ask children to tell what they know about bees. Use some of the language of the book and key vocabulary as you guide children through the text.

Ⓒ Comprehension Skill: Text Organization

Have children read the Strategy Focus on the book flap. Remind children to use the strategy and to think about the ways text is organized as they read the book. (See the Leveled Readers Teacher's Guide for **Vocabulary and Comprehension Practice Masters.**)

Responding

Have partners discuss how to answer the questions on the inside back cover.

Think About What You Have Read Sample answers:

1. Honeybees, bumblebees, carpenter bees, and leaf-cutting bees

2. They make honey from it. They also mix it with pollen to make bee bread.

3. First a queen bee lays an egg. The egg hatches into larva. The larva turns into pupa. The pupa turns into a honeybee.

4. Both bees have six pairs of legs, wings, and antennae. Carpenter bees live alone and make their nests in wood or plant stems. Honeybees live in colonies of thousands of bees. The colonies are in hives.

Making Connections Responses will vary.

Ⓒ Building Fluency

Model Read aloud pages 2–3. Demonstrate how and when to read the captions along with the text.

Practice Have partners read the selection aloud, one child reading the text, the other reading the captions.

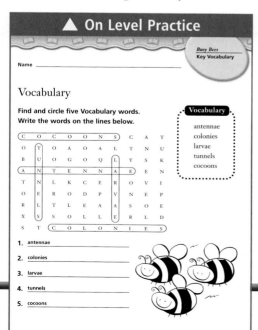

▲ On Level Practice

Busy Bees
Key Vocabulary

Name _____

Vocabulary

Find and circle five Vocabulary words. Write the words on the lines below.

Vocabulary
antennae
colonies
larvae
tunnels
cocoons

C	O	C	O	O	N	S	C	A	T
O	T	O	A	O	A	L	T	N	U
B	U	O	G	O	Q	L	Y	S	K
A	N	T	E	N	N	A	E	E	N
T	N	L	K	C	E	R	O	V	I
O	E	R	O	D	P	V	N	E	P
R	L	T	L	E	A	A	S	O	E
X	S	S	O	L	L	E	R	L	D
S	T	C	O	L	O	N	I	E	S

1. antennae
2. colonies
3. larvae
4. tunnels
5. cocoons

▲ On Level Practice

Busy Bees
Comprehension Skill
Text Organization

Name _____

Comprehension

Review *Busy Bees* to see how the author organized the information. Think about how the pictures help explain the information. Then answer the questions about where you would find information in *Busy Bees.* Explain what helped you find the information.

1. On what pages could you find out about carpenter bees?

pages 11–13

2. What helped you find this information?

Sample response: I looked quickly to find the words *carpenter bees.* I also looked

for pictures of carpenter bees.

3. On what pages could you find out about how bees grow?

pages 6–7

4. What helped you find this information?

Sample response: I looked through the story. I saw the diagram on pages 6–7, and

then looked at the text.

Leveled Readers

Butterflies!

Summary *There are more than 20,000 kinds of butterflies, but their body parts are all the same, and they all go through four stages of life. Butterflies help flowers produce seeds.*

Vocabulary

Introduce the Key Vocabulary and ask children to complete the BLM.

antennae* a pair of long, thin feelers on the head of an insect, *p. 3*

coiled gathered or wound into a ring, *p. 4*

larva* the worm-like form of a very young insect, *p. 7*

chrysalis a firm case, like a cocoon, that protects a growing insect until it is fully grown, *p. 7*

enemies creatures that mean to do harm to others, *p. 9*

poisonous something, often chemical, that can harm or kill, *p. 12*

*Forms of these words are Anthology Key Vocabulary words.

■ ABOVE LEVEL

Building Background and Vocabulary

Explain to children that this story is about butterflies. Lead a discussion about whether they think butterflies are insects. Use some of the language of the book and key vocabulary as you guide children through the text.

Comprehension Skill: Text Organization

Have children read the Strategy Focus on the book flap. Remind children to use the strategy and to think about the ways text is organized as they read the book. (See the Leveled Readers Teacher's Guide for **Vocabulary and Comprehension Practice Masters.**)

Responding

Have partners discuss how to answer the questions on the inside back cover.

Think About What You Have Read   Sample answers:

1. Butterflies are like other insects because they have three pairs of legs and their bodies have three parts. Butterflies are different because their feeding tubes are coiled when not in use.

2. There are four stages: egg, larva, chrysalis, and adult.

3. A butterfly's markings and coloring can help it to scare other animals away.

4. Possible response: Some butterflies fly over 2,000 miles to spend winter in a warmer place.

Making Connections   Responses will vary.

Building Fluency

Model   Read aloud page 3. Point out the presence of the heading (*A Butterfly's Body*) and show how to read it aloud.

Practice   Ask two volunteers to read the selection to the class, one child reading the body of the text, the other reading the headings.

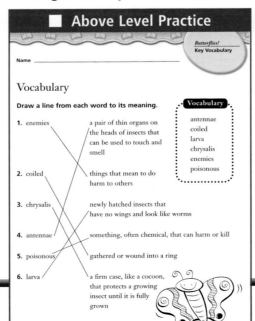

■ Above Level Practice

Name _____

Vocabulary

Draw a line from each word to its meaning.

Vocabulary: antennae, coiled, larva, chrysalis, enemies, poisonous

1. enemies — a pair of thin organs on the heads of insects that can be used to touch and smell
2. coiled — things that mean to do harm to others
3. chrysalis — newly hatched insects that have no wings and look like worms
4. antennae — something, often chemical, that can harm or kill
5. poisonous — gathered or wound into a ring
6. larva — a firm case, like a cocoon, that protects a growing insect until it is fully grown

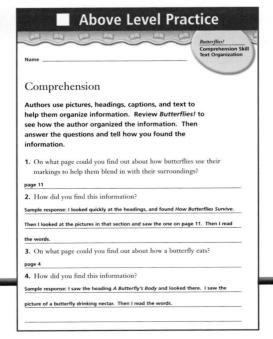

■ Above Level Practice

Name _____

Comprehension

Authors use pictures, headings, captions, and text to help them organize information. Review *Butterflies!* to see how the author organized the information. Then answer the questions and tell how you found the information.

1. On what page could you find out about how butterflies use their markings to help them blend in with their surroundings?
   page 11
2. How did you find this information?
   Sample response: I looked quickly at the headings, and found *How Butterflies Survive*. Then I looked at the pictures in that section and saw the one on page 11. Then I read the words.
3. On what page could you find out about how a butterfly eats?
   page 4
4. How did you find this information?
   Sample response: I saw the heading *A Butterfly's Body* and looked there. I saw the picture of a butterfly drinking nectar. Then I read the words.

Leveled Readers

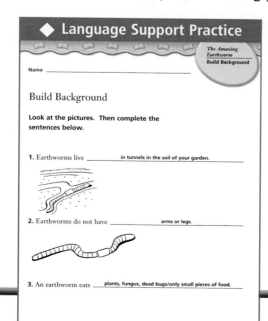

The Amazing Earthworm

Summary As they eat, earthworms make tunnels that help bring air and moisture into the soil. Their waste provides essential nutrients for plants. Earthworms help gardens grow.

Vocabulary

Introduce the Key Vocabulary and ask children to complete the BLM.

earthworms common worms that live in the soil, *p. 2*

garden a piece of land used for growing flowers, vegetables, or fruit, *p. 2*

grow to become larger, *p. 3*

soil the loose top layer of the earth's surface in which plant life can grow, *p. 5*

tunnels* long holes under the ground, *p. 5*

waste material eliminated from the body after food has been digested, *p. 10*

*Forms of these words are Anthology Key Vocabulary words.

◆ LANGUAGE SUPPORT

Building Background and Vocabulary

Ask children to share what they know about earthworms. During the discussion, write on the board any Key Vocabulary words mentioned. Distribute the **Build Background Practice Master,** discuss the illustrations, and have children complete the master in pairs.

Comprehension Skill: Text Organization

Have children read the Strategy Focus on the book flap. Remind children to use the strategy and to keep track of what they learn as they read the book. (See the Leveled Readers Teacher's Guide for **Build Background, Vocabulary,** and **Graphic Organizer Masters.**)

Responding

Have partners discuss how to answer the questions on the inside back cover.

Think About What You Have Read Sample answers:

1. Earthworms live in tunnels underground, in the soil.

2. Earthworm tunnels allow water and air to go into the soil. Earthworms' waste is good for the soil.

3. Answers will vary, but should indicate that children understand that earthworms are good for gardens.

Making Connections Answers will vary.

Building Fluency

Model Read aloud pages 4–5 as children follow along in their books. Explain that reading with expression makes material more interesting to listen to. Demonstrate reading with and without expression.

Practice Lead an echo reading of the same text. Read aloud each sentence and have children repeat, imitating your pronunciation and tone.

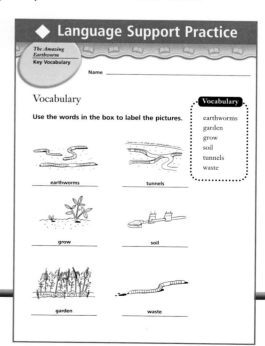

Lesson Overview

Literature

THE GREAT BALL GAME
◄ A MUSKOGEE STORY ►

RETOLD BY JOSEPH BRUCHAC
ILLUSTRATED BY SUSAN L. ROTH

Selection Summary

In this Muskogee legend, Bat plays an important part in a game between the Birds and the Animals.

1 Decodable Text

Phonics Library

- *Crow's Plan*
- *Brent Skunk Sings*

2 Background and Vocabulary

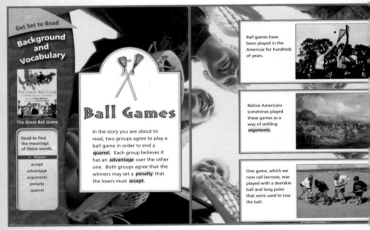

3 Main Selection

The Great Ball Game
Genre: Folktale

4 Science Link

Instructional Support

Planning and Practice

Practice Book

- Planning and Classroom Management
- Reading and skill instruction
- Materials for reaching all learners

Teacher's Resource Blackline Masters

- Newsletters
- Selection Summaries
- Assignment Cards
- Observation Checklists
- Selection Tests

- Independent practice for skills

I ♥ READING BOOKS

- Decodable Text, Books 45–46

Instruction Transparencies/Masters and Strategy Posters

- Charts/ Transparencies
- Strategy Posters
- Blackline Masters

Reaching All Learners

Intervention Strategies for **Extra Support**

Instructional Activities for **Challenge**

Instructional Strategies for **English Language Learners**

Independent Activities for **Classroom Management**

Coordinated lessons, activities, and projects for additional reading instruction

For
- Classroom Teacher
- Extended Day
- Pull Out
- Resource Teacher
- Reading Specialist

Technology

Audio Selection
The Great Ball Game

Get Set for Reading CD-ROM
- Background building
- Vocabulary support
- Selection Summary in English and Spanish

Accelerated Reader®
- Practice quiz for the selection

www.eduplace.com
Log on to Education Place® for more activities related to the selection, including vocabulary support—
  e • **Glossary**
  e • **WordGame**

Leveled Books for Reaching All Learners

Leveled Readers and Leveled Practice

- Independent reading for building fluency
- Topic, comprehension strategy, and vocabulary linked to main selection
- Lessons in Teacher's Edition, pages T240–T243
- Leveled practice for every book

Technology

Leveled Readers
Audio available

Book Adventure®
- Practice quizzes for the Leveled Theme Paperbacks
  www.bookadventure.org

● BELOW LEVEL

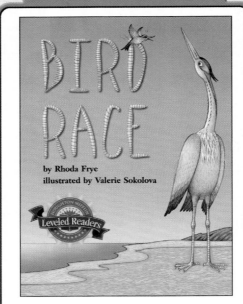

BIRD RACE
by Rhoda Frye
illustrated by Valerie Sokolova
Leveled Readers

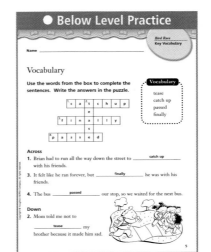

● Below Level Practice

Bird Race
Key Vocabulary

Name _____

Vocabulary

Use the words from the box to complete the sentences. Write the answers in the puzzle.

Vocabulary
tease
catch up
passed
finally

¹c a ²t c h u p
e
¹f i n a l l y
s
⁴p a s s e d

Across
1. Brian had to run all the way down the street to ____catch up____ with his friends.
3. It felt like he ran forever, but ____finally____ he was with his friends.
4. The bus ____passed____ our stop, so we waited for the next bus.

Down
2. Mom told me not to ____tease____ my brother because it made him sad.

● Below Level Practice

Bird Race
Comprehension Skill
Cause and Effect

Name _____

Comprehension

A cause tells why something happened. An effect tells what happened. Read the sentences below and tell whether the underlined phrase is a cause or an effect.

	Cause or Effect?
Humming-Bird likes to tease Heron because Heron is a slow flyer.	cause
Because Humming-Bird teases him, Heron asks Humming-Bird to race to the meadow.	effect
Humming-Bird has to rest at night because he is tired from flying so quickly and so far.	effect
Since he has flown slowly all day, Heron can keep flying at night.	cause
Humming-Bird has to work hard in the mornings because Heron is far ahead of him.	effect
Since he gets to the meadow first, Heron wins the race.	cause
The birds fly home together because they are still friends.	cause

---

▲ ON LEVEL

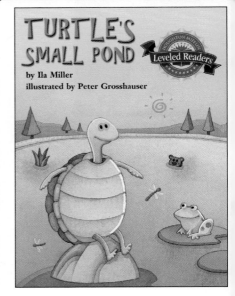

TURTLE'S SMALL POND
by Ila Miller
illustrated by Peter Grosshauser
Leveled Readers

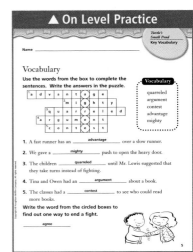

▲ On Level Practice

Turtle's
Small Pond
Key Vocabulary

Name _____

Vocabulary

Use the words from the box to complete the sentences. Write the answers in the puzzle.

Vocabulary
quarreled
argument
contest
advantage
mighty

⁴a d v a n t a g e
²m i g h t y
³q u a r r e l e d
⁴a r g u m e n t
c o n t e s t

1. A fast runner has an ____advantage____ over a slow runner.
2. We gave a ____mighty____ push to open the heavy door.
3. The children ____quarreled____ until Mr. Lewis suggested that they take turns instead of fighting.
4. Tina and Owen had an ____argument____ about a book.
5. The classes had a ____contest____ to see who could read more books.

Write the word from the circled boxes to find out one way to end a fight.

____agree____

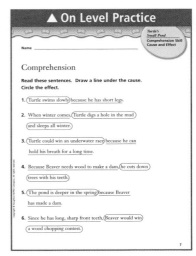

▲ On Level Practice

Turtle's
Small Pond
Comprehension Skill
Cause and Effect

Name _____

Comprehension

Read these sentences. Draw a line under the cause. Circle the effect.

1. Turtle swims slowly because he has short legs.
2. When winter comes, Turtle digs a hole in the mud and sleeps all winter.
3. Turtle could win an underwater race because he can hold his breath for a long time.
4. Because Beaver needs wood to make a dam, he cuts down trees with his teeth.
5. The pond is deeper in the spring because Beaver has made a dam.
6. Since he has long, sharp front teeth, Beaver would win a wood chopping contest.

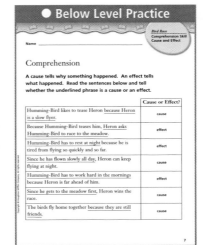

■ ABOVE LEVEL

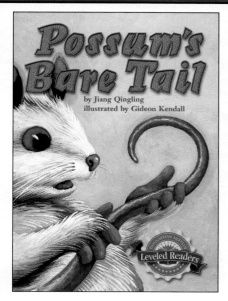

Possum's Bare Tail
by Jiang Qingling
illustrated by Gideon Kendall

Leveled Readers

■ Above Level Practice

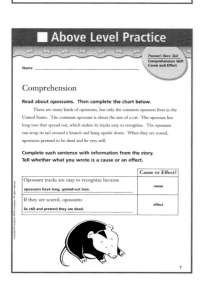

Name _____

Vocabulary

Find and circle five Vocabulary words. Write the words on the lines below.

A	H	U	M	I	L	I	A	T	I	O	N
B	A	C	S	H	C	E	C	P	T	R	E
G	R	E	G	A	I	D	C	N	L	R	T
R	E	A	S	H	A	M	E	D	F	E	V
O	R	C	D	R	K	U	P	Y	T	B	I
O	M	G	V	A	R	W	T	V	A	I	N
M	E	H	E	B	Y	S	H	A	E	N	T

Vocabulary
groom
vain
accept
ashamed
humiliation

1. _____groom_____   4. _____ashamed_____
2. _____vain_____   5. _____humiliation_____
3. _____accept_____

Pick two words from the box and write a sentence about each word.

Responses will vary.

_____

5

■ Above Level Practice

Name _____

Possum's Bare Tail
Comprehension Skill
Cause and Effect

Comprehension

Read about opossums. Then complete the chart below.

There are many kinds of opossums, but only the common opossum lives in the United States. The common opossum is about the size of a cat. The opossum has long toes that spread out, which makes its tracks easy to recognize. The opossum can wrap its tail around a branch and hang upside down. When they are scared, opossums pretend to be dead and lie very still.

Complete each sentence with information from the story. Tell whether what you wrote is a cause or an effect.

	Cause or Effect?
Opossum tracks are easy to recognize because opossums have long, spread-out toes.	cause
If they are scared, opossums lie still and pretend they are dead.	effect

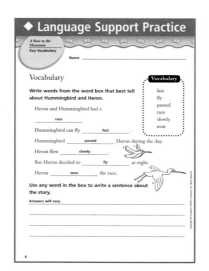

7

◆ LANGUAGE SUPPORT

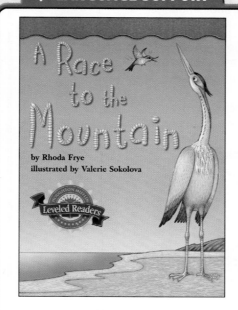

A Race to the Mountain
by Rhoda Frye
illustrated by Valerie Sokolova

Leveled Readers

◆ Language Support Practice

Name _____

A Race to the Mountain
Build Background

Build Background

Color and label the pictures of Heron and Hummingbird. Cut them out carefully and glue them to wooden sticks to make puppets.

Heron _____

Hummingbird _____

5

◆ Language Support Practice

A Race to the Mountain
Key Vocabulary

Name _____

Vocabulary

Write words from the word box that best tell about Hummingbird and Heron.

Vocabulary
fast
fly
passed
race
slowly
won

Heron and Hummingbird had a
_____race_____

Hummingbird can fly _____fast_____.

Hummingbird _____passed_____ Heron during the day.

Heron flew _____slowly_____.

But Heron decided to _____fly_____ at night.

Heron _____won_____ the race.

Use any word in the box to write a sentence about the story.

Answers will vary.

_____

6

Leveled Theme Paperbacks

- Extended independent reading in theme-related paperbacks
- Lessons in Teacher's Edition, pages R4–R9

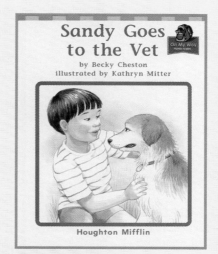

Sandy Goes to the Vet
by Becky Cheston
illustrated by Kathryn Mitter

Houghton Mifflin

Below Level

RAPTORS!
Written by Lisa McCourt
Illustrated by Monika Popowitz

On Level

RUSSELL E. ERICKSON
A Toad for Tuesday
"A small-scale *Wind in the Willows* with adventure and charm."—A.L.A. *Booklist*

Above Level

Daily Lesson Plans

Technology

Lesson Planner CD-ROM allows you to customize the chart below to develop your own lesson plans.

T Skill tested on Theme Skills Test and/or Integrated Theme Test

 WEEK 3 / **DAILY LESSON PLANS**

 80–90 minutes

Reading
Phonics
Comprehension

Leveled Readers
- Fluency Practice
- Independent Reading

DAY 1

Daily Routines, T186–T187
Phonics and Language Activities

Listening Comprehension, T188–T189
The Little Fly and the Great Moose

 **Phonics,** T190–T191
Vowel Pairs *oa, ow* **T**

Reading Decodable Text, T193–T195
Crow's Plan

Leveled Readers
Bird Race
Turtle's Small Pond
Possum's Bare Tail
A Race to the Mountain

Lessons and Leveled Practice, T240–T243

DAY 2

Daily Routines, T198–T199
Phonics and Language Activities

Building Background, T200

Key Vocabulary, T201
accept   argument   quarrel
advantage   penalty

Reading the Selection, T202–T213

Comprehension Strategy, T202
Summarize

Comprehension Skill, T202, T210
Cause and Effect **T**

Leveled Readers
Bird Race
Turtle's Small Pond
Possum's Bare Tail
A Race to the Mountain

Lessons and Leveled Practice, T240–T243

 20–30 minutes

Word Work
Vocabulary
High-Frequency Words
Spelling

DAY 1

Vocabulary, T187
Idioms

High-Frequency Words, T192
ago, field, half, war **T**

Spelling, T196
More Long *o* Words **T**

DAY 2

Vocabulary, T199
Find the Exact Word

High-Frequency Words, T198
Word Wall

Spelling, T214
Review, Practice: More Long *o* Words **T**

20–30 minutes

Writing and Oral Language
Writing
Grammar
Listening/Speaking/Viewing

DAY 1

Writing, T187
Daily Writing Prompt

Grammar, T197
Plural Possessive Nouns **T**

Daily Language Practice
1. Jake and i found a goald ring.
(Jake and I found a gold ring.)

Listening/Speaking/Viewing, T188–T189
Teacher Read Aloud

DAY 2

Writing, T215
A News Article

Grammar, T214
Practice: Plural Possessive Nouns **T**

Daily Language Practice
2. The childrens feet were colde.
(The children's feet were cold.)

Listening/Speaking/Viewing, T207, T213
Stop and Think, Wrapping Up

Target Skills of the Week

Phonics	Vowel Pairs *oa, ow*
Comprehension	Cause and Effect; Summarize
Vocabulary	High-Frequency Words; Parts of a Dictionary Entry
Fluency	Decodable Text; Leveled Readers

DAY 3

Daily Routines, T216–T217
Phonics and Language Activities

Rereading the Selection, T202–T213

Comprehension Check, T218
Responding, T218

Comprehension Skill, T220–T221
Cause and Effect **T**

Rereading for Understanding, T222
Visual Literacy: Perspective
Genre Lesson: Explanations in Fables

Leveled Readers

Bird Race
Turtle's Small Pond
Possum's Bare Tail
A Race to the Mountain

Lessons and Leveled Practice, T240–T243

Vocabulary, T217
Rhyme Time

High-Frequency Words, T216
Word Wall

Spelling, T223
Vocabulary Connection: More Long *o* Words **T**

Writing, T218
Writing a Folktale

Grammar, T223
Activity: Plural Possessive Nouns **T**

Daily Language Practice
3. Please holed this book for me
(Please hold this book for me.)

Listening/Speaking/Viewing, T218
Responding

DAY 4

Daily Routines, T224–T225
Phonics and Language Activities

Reading the Science Link, T226–T227

Comprehension: How to Read a Caption, T226

Phonics Review, T229
Words with *nd, nt, mp, ng, nk*

Reading Decodable Text, T230–T231
Brent Skunk Sings

Leveled Readers

Bird Race
Turtle's Small Pond
Possum's Bare Tail
A Race to the Mountain

Lessons and Leveled Practice, T240–T243

Vocabulary, T228
Parts of a Dictionary Entry **T**

High-Frequency Words, T224
Word Wall

Spelling, T232
Game, Proofreading: More Long *o* Words **T**

Writing, T233
Adding Details

Grammar, T232
Practice: Plural Possessive Nouns **T**

Daily Language Practice
4. Is this the rowd to the dance camp!
(Is this the road to the dance camp?)

Listening/Speaking/Viewing, T226
Discuss the Link

DAY 5

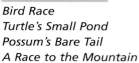

Daily Routines, T234–T235
Phonics and Language Activities

Comprehension: Rereading for Understanding, T236
Problem Solving
Compare and Contrast

Rereading for Fluency, T202–T213

Cross-Curricular Responding Activities, T219

Information and Study Skill, T237
Using Directions

Leveled Readers

Bird Race
Turtle's Small Pond
Possum's Bare Tail
A Race to the Mountain

Lessons and Leveled Practice, T240–T243

Vocabulary, T235
Vocabulary Expansion

High-Frequency Words, T234
Word Wall

Spelling, T238
Test: More Long *o* Words **T**

Writing, T235
Daily Writing Prompt

Grammar, T238
Improving Writing

Daily Language Practice
5. I drew a picture of the twins bote.
(I drew a picture of the twins' boat.)

Listening/Speaking/Viewing, T239
Giving Clear Directions

Managing Flexible Groups

Leveled Instruction and Leveled Practice

	DAY 1	DAY 2
WHOLE CLASS	• Daily Routines (TE pp. T186–T187) • Teacher Read Aloud (TE pp. T188–T189) • Phonics lesson (TE pp. T190–T191) • High-Frequency Words lesson (TE p. T192)	• Daily Routines (TE pp. T198–T199) • Get Set to Read, Strategy and Skill, Purpose Setting (TE pp. T200–T203) *After Reading at Small Group Time* • Wrapping Up (TE p. T213)
SMALL GROUPS		
Extra Support	**TEACHER-LED** • Read Phonics Library: *Crow's Plan.* (TE pp. T193–T195) • Selected I Love Reading Books: 45–46	**TEACHER-LED** • Read Main Selection. (TE pp. T202–T213) **Partner or Individual Reading** • Read with audio CD of Main Selection. • **Fluency Practice** Reread Phonics Library: *Crow's Plan.* (TE pp. T193–T195) OR selected I Love Reading Books: 45–46.
On Level	**TEACHER-LED** • Reread Transparency 4–21 aloud. (TE p. T192) • Read Phonics Library: *Crow's Plan.* (TE pp. T193–T195)	**TEACHER-LED** • Read Main Selection. (TE pp. T202–T213) • Begin Leveled Reader: On Level (TE p. T241) OR book from Bibliography. (TE pp. T6–T7) • **Fluency Practice** Reread Phonics Library: *Crow's Plan.* (TE pp. T193–T195) ✔
Challenge	**Partner or Individual Reading** • Read Phonics Library: *Crow's Plan.* (TE pp. T193–T195) • **Fluency Practice** Reread Little Big Book for this theme.	**Partner or Individual Reading** • Read Main Selection. (TE pp. T202–T213) • **Fluency Practice** Reread Phonics Library: *Crow's Plan.* (TE pp. T193–T195)
English Language Learners	**TEACHER-LED** • Read Phonics Library: *Crow's Plan.* (TE pp. T193–T195) • Selected I Love Reading Books: 45–46	**TEACHER-LED** • Selected I Love Reading Books: 45–46 • **Fluency Practice** Reread Phonics Library: *Crow's Plan.* (TE pp. T193–T195) ✔ **Partner or Individual Reading** • Read with audio CD of Main Selection.

Independent Activities

• Get Set for Reading CD-ROM OR audio CD of Anthology selection.
• Journals: selection notes, questions.
• Complete, review **Practice Book** (pp. 44–47, 51–53) and **Leveled Reader Practice Blackline Masters.** (TE pp. T240–T243)
• Assignment Cards. (**Teacher's Resource Blackline Masters** pp. 67–68)

✔ Opportunity to informally assess oral reading rate.

DAY 3

- Daily Routines (TE pp. T216–T217)

After Reading at Small Group Time
- Responding (TE p. T218)
- Comprehension lesson (TE pp. T220–T221)
- Rereading for Understanding (TE p. T222)

TEACHER-LED
- Read aloud from Main Selection to answer Guiding Comprehension. (TE pp. T202–T213)
- Begin Leveled Reader: Below Level (TE p. T240) OR book from Bibliography. (TE pp. T6–T7)

Partner or Individual Reading
- **Fluency Practice** Selected I Love Reading Books: 45–46

Partner or Individual Reading
- Reread Main Selection. (TE pp. T202–T213)
- Complete Leveled Reader: On Level (TE p. T241) OR book from Bibliography. (TE pp. T6–T7)
- **Fluency Practice** Selected I Love Reading Books: 45–46

TEACHER-LED
- Read aloud from Main Selection to answer Guiding Comprehension. (TE pp. T202–T213) ✔
- Begin Leveled Reader: Above Level (TE p. T242) OR book from Bibliography. (TE pp. T6–T7)

Partner or Individual Reading
- Complete Leveled Reader: Above Level (TE p. T242) OR book from Bibliography. (TE pp. T6–T7)

TEACHER-LED
- Reread Main Selection. (TE pp. T202–T213)

Partner or Individual Reading
- Selected I Love Reading Books: 45–46

DAY 4

- Daily Routines (TE pp. T224–T225)
- Link (TE pp. T226–T227)
- Phonics Review (TE p. T229)

TEACHER-LED
- Read Phonics Library: *Brent Skunk Sings.* (TE pp. T230–T231)
- Complete Leveled Reader: Below Level (TE p. T240) OR book from Bibliography. (TE pp. T6–T7)
- **Fluency Practice** Reread Phonics Library: *Brent Skunk Sings* (TE pp. T230–T231) OR Leveled Reader: Below Level. (TE p. T240) ✔

TEACHER-LED
- Read aloud from Main Selection to answer Guiding Comprehension. (TE pp. T202–T213)
- Read Phonics Library: *Brent Skunk Sings.* (TE pp. T230–T231)
- **Fluency Practice** Reread Link (TE pp. T226–T227) OR Leveled Reader: On Level. (TE p. T241) ✔

Partner or Individual Reading
- Read Phonics Library: *Brent Skunk Sings.* (TE pp. T230–T231)
- **Fluency Practice** Reread Main Selection and Link (TE pp. T202–T213, T226–T227) AND Phonics Library: *Brent Skunk Sings.* (TE pp. T230–T231)

TEACHER-LED
- Continue Main Selection. (TE pp. T202–T213)
- Begin Leveled Reader: Language Support (TE p. T243) OR On My Way Practice Reader. (TE pp. R4–R5)

Partner or Individual Reading
- **Fluency Practice** Read Phonics Library: *Brent Skunk Sings.* (TE pp. T230–T231)

DAY 5

- Daily Routines (TE pp. T234–T235)
- Comprehension Review lesson (TE p. T236)
- Information and Study Skill (TE p. T237)
- Responding: select from activities (TE p. T219)

TEACHER-LED
- Reread Phonics Library: *Brent Skunk Sings.* (TE pp. T230–T231)
- Read the On My Way Practice Reader. (TE pp. R4–R5)
- **Fluency Practice** Reread Phonics Library (TE pp. T193–T195, T230–T231) OR On My Way Practice Reader. (TE pp. R4–R5) ✔

Partner or Individual Reading
- Reread Link. (TE pp. T226–T227)
- Complete Theme Paperback: On Level (TE pp. R6–R7) OR book from Bibliography. (TE pp. T6–T7)
- **Fluency Practice** Reread Main Selection (TE pp. T202–T213) OR Leveled Reader: On Level. (TE p. T241)

TEACHER-LED
- **Fluency Practice** Reread Link (TE pp. T226–T227) OR Leveled Reader: Above Level. (TE p. T242) ✔

Partner or Individual Reading
- Complete Theme Paperback: Above Level (TE pp. R8–R9) OR book from Bibliography. (TE pp. T6–T7)

TEACHER-LED
- Reread Link. (TE pp. T226–T227)
- Complete Leveled Reader: Language Support (TE p. T243) OR On My Way Practice Reader. (TE pp. R4–R5)
- **Fluency Practice** Reread Phonics Library (TE pp. T193–T195, T230–T231). ✔

- Reread familiar selections.
- Read trade book from Leveled Bibliography. (TE pp. T6–T7)
- Responding activities. (TE pp. T218–T219)
- Activities related to *The Great Ball Game* at Education Place: www.eduplace.com

Turn the page for more independent activities.

Managing Flexible Groups **T183**

Classroom Management

Independent Activities

Assign these activities while you work with small groups.

Differentiated Instruction for Small Groups

- **Handbook for English Language Learners,** pp. 144–153

- **Extra Support Handbook,** pp. 140–149

Independent Activities

- Daily Routines, pp. T186, T198, T216, T224, T234

- Challenge/Extension Activities, pp. R19, R25, R31

- **Classroom Management Handbook,** Activity Masters CM4-9–CM4-12

- **Challenge Handbook,** Activity Masters CH4-5–CH4-6

Look for more activities in the Classroom Management Kit.

Social Studies Center

Name That Team!

👤 Singles	🕐 30 minutes
Objective	Draw a badge to represent a team.
Materials	Drawing paper, pencil, scissors, crayons or markers

Most sports teams have a name and a badge for their uniform. Think of a good name for each team in *The Great Ball Game*.

- Make a badge for each team. Include the team's name!

- Color and cut out the badges.

- Show your badges to the class. Explain how you picked the team's names and badge.

Drama Center

Animal Charades

👤👤👤 Groups	🕐 40 minutes
Objective	Play animal charades.
Materials	Index cards, pencils

Play animal charades.

- Make a card for each animal in *The Great Ball Game*. Shuffle the cards and place them face-down.

- Choose a card and read it to yourself.

- Act like the animal. Remember not to use words!

- Ask your classmates to guess what animal you are. For each guess, say *yes* or *no*. Do not give hints.

- Take turns playing and guessing.

Consider copying and laminating these activities for use in centers.

Science Center

Sort Them Again

Pairs	⏱ 30 minutes
Objective	Sort animals in different ways.
Materials	Writing paper and pencils

The animals in *The Great Ball Game* are sorted into two groups: Wings and Teeth. How else can they be sorted?

Reread *The Great Ball Game*. Look carefully at the pictures of the animals.

Think about their colors, features, sounds they make, what they eat, and how they move.

Sort the animals in different ways and show how you sorted them.

Art Center

Sports Picture

Singles	⏱ 40 minutes
Objective	Make a sports picture.
Materials	Drawing paper, construction paper, pencil, scissors, glue, markers

Look at the cut-paper pictures in *The Great Ball Game*. Make a cut-paper sports scene of your own.

- Think of a sport and answer these questions: *How many players are needed? What equipment is used? Where is the sport played?*

- Draw and cut out people playing the sport and the equipment.

- Glue down the cut-outs, and then draw a background.

- Display your picture.

Writing Center

A New Ending

Pairs	⏱ 30 minutes
Objective	Write a new ending to the story.
Materials	Writing paper, pencils

In *The Great Ball Game,* the Animals win because of Bat. What if the Birds had chosen Bat instead?

- Think of ways the story might end if Bat joined the Birds. Write your ideas.

- Choose one idea from your list.

- Use your notes to write a new story ending.

- Share your ending.

Day at a Glance
pp. T186–T197

Reading Instruction

Teacher Read Aloud

Phonics Instruction
Vowel Pairs *oa, ow*

Reading Decodable Text
Crow's Plan

• •

Leveled Readers, *T240–T243*

- ● *Bird Race*
- ▲ *Turtle's Small Pond*
- ■ *Possum's Bare Tail*
- ◆ *A Race to the Mountain*

Word Work

Vocabulary Review

High-Frequency Words

Spelling: More Long *o* Words

Writing & Oral Language

Writing Activity

Grammar: Plural Possessive Nouns

Listening/Speaking/Viewing

Daily Routines

Daily Message

Phonics Review Point to each word as you read aloud the Daily Message.

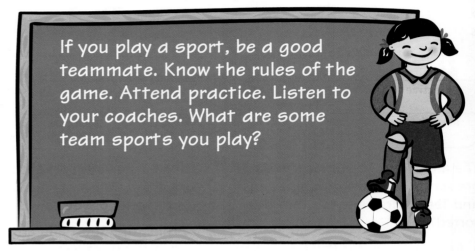

If you play a sport, be a good teammate. Know the rules of the game. Attend practice. Listen to your coaches. What are some team sports you play?

Have children

- read the Daily Message aloud, and discuss the question;
- find plural nouns; *(rules, coaches, sports)*
- read the words aloud and then circle them.

Word Wall

High-Frequency Word Review Briefly review these previously taught high-frequency words. Post the words on the Word Wall. Have children practice reading, chanting, spelling, and writing them.

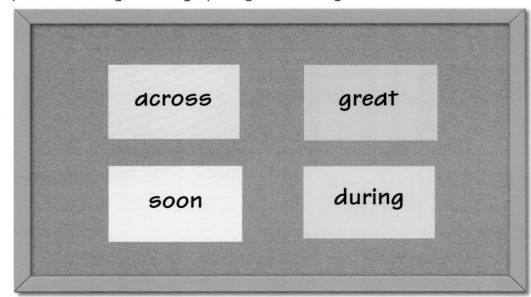

across   great

soon   during

Blackline Masters for these word cards appear on pp. R37, R38.

Vocabulary

Idioms Brainstorm with children idioms, or other expressions, that allude to animal behavior, such as *at a snail's pace*. List children's suggestions.

Idioms with Animal Names
busy bee
shed crocodile tears
playing possum
cunning as a fox
eagle eyes

busy bee

Daily Writing Prompt

Have children choose a topic to write about, or have them use the prompt below.

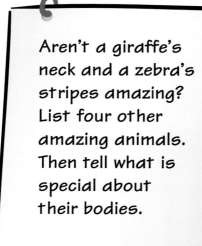

Aren't a giraffe's neck and a zebra's stripes amazing? List four other amazing animals. Then tell what is special about their bodies.

Daily Language Practice

Grammar Skill: Plural Possessive Nouns
Spelling Skill: More Long *o* Words

Display **Transparency 4–20**. Ask children to rewrite Sentence 1 correctly. Then model how to write it, and have children check their work.

Transparency 4–20
Daily Language Practice

Day 1

1. Jake and i found a goald ring.

Jake and **I** found a **gold** ring.

Day 3

3. Please holed this book for me

Please **hold** this book for me.

Day 4

4. Is this the rowd to the dance camp!

Is this the **road** to the dance camp?

Day 5

5. I drew a picture of the twins bote.

I drew a picture of the **twins' boat**.

TRANSPARENCY 4–20
TEACHER'S EDITION PAGES T187, T199, T217, T225, AND T235

Listening Comprehension

Building Background

Tell children that you are going to read aloud a story about how a small animal outsmarts a big animal.

- Ask children to discuss what might happen to animals that live near or in a river if the river dried up.

Fluency Modeling

Explain that as you read aloud, you will be modeling fluent oral reading. Ask children to listen carefully to your phrasing and expression, or tone of voice and emphasis.

COMPREHENSION SKILL

Cause and Effect

Explain that sometimes one event in a story makes another event happen.

- Why something happens is called the *cause*, or reason.
- What happens is called the *effect*.

Purpose Setting Read the story aloud, asking children to identify what happens and why it happens as they listen. Then use the Guiding Comprehension questions to assess children's understanding. Reread the story for clarification as needed.

Teacher Read Aloud

The Little Fly and the Great Moose

retold by Janeen R. Adil

A very long time ago, the Merrimac River flowed peacefully *slowly* through the wooded hills. Many beavers made their homes in the river, and great schools of fish lived in its pure, clean waters. So delicious was the water that thirsty animals would come to drink at the river from far and wide.

Now, in this long-ago time, the largest of all the animals was Moose. Even bigger than the mighty bear, Moose stood as tall as the highest tree. When he walked the ground shook beneath his heavy feet. And when he bellowed *roared*, birds flew before him in a panic.

One day, the giant creature learned of the Merrimac's sweet waters. I, too, will go there, Moose thought, and taste the water for myself.

When he reached the river, Moose immediately began to drink. The water pleased him, so he drank more and more. Soon the level of the water started to drop.

❶ This made the beavers very nervous. What would happen to their homes, the dams they had worked so hard to build from mud and sticks? "Help us," the beavers begged the rabbits. "We must stop Moose," they pleaded with the foxes. "Drive him away!" the beavers cried to the deer. But Moose was so big that no one—not even the bear—was brave enough to face him.

Meanwhile, Moose continued to drink from the river. The water dropped lower and lower, and now the fish were afraid. At least the beavers could move to a

new home, but what would the fish do if the river dried up? And they, too, began to beg for help.

At last, one creature volunteered to chase Moose away. It was Fly. "You are the smallest of us all!" exclaimed the animals. "How can you possibly make that huge creature leave?" And they laughed at Fly, thinking it was a fine joke.

Little Fly, though, had a plan. First she landed on one of Moose's legs and bit him. Moose simply brushed her off. Fly tried another leg, only this time she bit harder. Moose stamped his foot in annoyance. Then Fly buzzed quickly from spot to spot on Moose's brown hide, biting sharply as she went.

Moose was furious! He shook his immense head, snorted, stamped, and kicked. Up and down the river-bank he ran, trying to discover who was biting him. But since he couldn't see tiny Fly, Moose had no way to fight back. Finally he fled from the river as fast as he could run.

How proud little Fly was! She couldn't help boasting to the animals that she had driven Moose away. "You see," Fly told them, "my size didn't matter after all. I wasn't big enough or strong enough to fight Moose. But I was smart enough!"

Moose was gone, but beside the river were prints from his massive feet. Wherever he had stamped, the earth sank, and now the Merrimac came rushing in to fill the deep holes. No longer did the river flow quietly. Instead, it tumbled over falls and rushed noisily through rapids where Moose's feet had torn up the ground.

CRITICAL THINKING
Guiding Comprehension

❶ CAUSE AND EFFECT What do the animals fear will happen if the moose keeps drinking the water? (that the river will dry up, leaving them with no home)

❷ CAUSE AND EFFECT Why do the other animals laugh at Fly? (Fly seems too small to be able to make Moose leave.) *The Lion + The Mouse Story*

❸ CAUSE AND EFFECT According to the story, why does the Merrimac River have falls and rapids? (Moose's feet tore up the ground, and the water rushed into the deep holes.)

Discussion Options

Personal Response Ask children to tell why Moose's size did not help him fight back at Fly.

⭐ **Connecting/Comparing** Ask children to compare Fly and the ants in the selection *Ants*. How are these animals amazing?

English Language Learners

Language Development

Display a picture of a moose. Write the following words on index cards and explain the meanings: *bellows* (makes a loud noise); *annoyance* (something that causes trouble); *furious* (very mad or angry); *massive* (very large and solid); *immense* (of great size, huge). Invite volunteers to take turns picking cards and using the words to describe the moose in the story, pantomiming when possible.

OBJECTIVES

- Substitute phonemes.
- Read and write words with the vowel pairs *oa* and *ow* pronounced /ō/.

Target Skill Trace

Teach	p. T190
Reteach	p. R18
Review	p. 287; Theme 5, p. T73
See	*Handbook for English Language Learners*, p. 145; *Extra Support Handbook*, pp. 140–141, 146–147

Materials

- **Sound/Spelling Card,** *ocean*
- **Blending Routines Card 1**
- punchout letters and tray, one set per child

PHONICS: Vowel Pairs *oa, ow*

❶ Phonemic Awareness Warm-Up

Model how to substitute phonemes. Say *beat*. Have children repeat it. Ask what the vowel sound is. Tell children you will replace /ē/ with /ō/ and say a new word. Say *boat*. Repeat with *sip*, but have a volunteer replace /ĭ/ with /ō/ to say a new word. (soap)

❷ Teach Phonics

Connect sounds to letters. Write *boat* and *grow*, underlining the *oa* and *ow*. Blend each word.

- Display the **Sound/Spelling Card.** Point to *oa* and *ow* on the card. Explain that these letters go together and stand for one sound, long *o*.

- Draw a rowboat. Write the words below on the boat. Choose children to underline the *oa* or *ow* vowel pair in each word, say its sound, and point to its spelling on the **Sound/Spelling Card.**

- Use **Blending Routine 1** to help children read the words.

Review the letters that stand for the long o sound. Write *toe, crow, no, home,* and *load*. Point to a letter pattern on the **Sound/Spelling Card.** Choose a child to underline the same pattern in one of the words, read the word, and use it in a sentence.

Model how to decode longer words with *oa* and *ow*. Write *rowboat* and sound it out.

- Ask how many syllables there are in *rowboat*, and what vowel sound is in each syllable. (two, /ō/)
- Have a child underline the two letters that make the long *o* sound in each syllable. (*ow, oa*) Remind children that each vowel pair stands for a single sound and stays together in a syllable.
- Divide *rowboat* into syllables. Point out that it is a compound word. Help children sound out each syllable and blend the syllables to read the word.
- Repeat with the following words:

oat/meal   float/ing
grown/up   rain/bow
pil/low   shad/ow

❸ Guided Practice

Check understanding. Write *toad, hollow, slower,* and *The picture shows an oak tree in the snow.* Choose children to underline each vowel pair that stands for the long *o* sound. Ask a volunteer to point to each two-syllable word and tell how to divide it into syllables. Have children read the words and sentence.

Connect sounds to letters. Say *crow.* Have children spell *crow* with their punchout letters. Guide them by pointing to the appropriate vowel spelling on the **Sound/Spelling Card.** Display the word. Have children correct any mistakes. Repeat with *floats, bowl, yellow,* and *roadside.*

❹ Apply
Assign Practice Book page 44.

Practice Book page 44

The Great Ball Game
Phonics Skill Vowel Pairs
oa, ow

Name _____

A Walk Outside

Write the word from the box that completes each sentence.

Word Bank

low   toad   coat   crow   croak   willow

1. Ben put on his coat (1 point) .
2. He walked by a tall willow (1) tree.
3. He watched a crow (1) fly out of a tree.
4. It swooped low (1) to the ground.
5. Then Ben saw a toad (1) hopping by the pond.
6. A frog gave a loud croak (1) as the toad hopped by.

Now write each word under the animal that has the same vowel spelling.

oa   ow

coat (1)   willow (1)
toad (1)   crow (1)
croak (1)   low (1)

Monitoring Student Progress

If . . .	Then . . .
children score 8 or below on **Practice Book** page 44,	use the Reteaching lesson on page R18.
children meet the lesson objectives,	use the Challenge/ Extension activities on page R19.

OBJECTIVE

- Recognize new high-frequency words:

  ago   half
  field   war

Target Skill Trace

Teach	p. T192
Reteach	p. R24
Review	p. T198
See	*Handbook for English Language Learners*, pp. 147, 149; *Extra Support Handbook*, p. 144

Materials

- punchout high-frequency words for *The Great Ball Game*
- index cards, one high-frequency word per card or Word Wall Cards from p. R38.

Transparency 4–21

High-Frequency Words

Long <u>ago</u>, Animals and Birds played a ball game.

They played the game on a large <u>field</u>.

The Animals and Birds fought as if they were in a <u>war</u>.

More than <u>half</u> of the Animals were tired by the end of the game.

AMAZING ANIMALS *The Great Ball Game*
High-Frequency Words

ANNOTATED VERSION

TRANSPARENCY 4–21
TEACHER'S EDITION PAGE T192

Monitoring Student Progress

If...	Then...
children score below 3 on **Practice Book** page 45,	use the Reteaching lesson on page R24.
children are ready for more challenging material,	use the Challenge/Extension activities on page R25.

HIGH-FREQUENCY WORDS

❶ Teach

Introduce the high-frequency words. Display **Transparency 4–21.** Ask children to read the first sentence to themselves.

- Point to the word *ago*. Say it, and have children repeat it.
- Have children read the sentence along with you.
- Repeat, using the other sentences and underlined words.
- As needed, discuss the meaning of each word.

❷ Guided Practice

Have children give clues for the words. Pair children and have them use their punchout high-frequency words to play "I Spy."

- Have children take turns giving one or more clues about a new high-frequency word, such as its sounds, spelling, or meaning.
- Have partners hold up and read the word that fits the clues.
- After the initial round, have children add other previously learned high-frequency words and continue the activity.

❸ Apply

Assign Practice Book page 45.

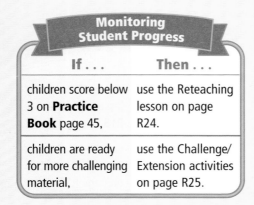

Practice Book page 45

The Great Ball Game
High-Frequency Words

Name _____

Write a Letter

Read this letter that Crane wrote to Bear.

Dear Bear,
*   Not long <u>ago</u>, you and I were friends. We would play in the <u>field</u> together. Now we are angry with each other. You play alone in <u>half</u> of the meadow, while I play in the other half. It feels like we are at <u>war</u>. I think we should talk about the problem. What do you think?*
*   Sincerely,*
*   Crane*

Pretend you are Bear. Write an answer to Crane. Use each of the underlined words in your answer.

Dear Crane,
(4 points)
_____
_____
_____
_____
_____
*   Sincerely,*
*   Bear*

Phonics Library

HOUGHTON MIFFLIN
Reading

Amazing Animals

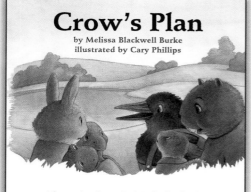

Crow's Plan

by Melissa Blackwell Burke
illustrated by Cary Phillips

The animals at <u>Oak</u> Lake had a big problem. They met in the <u>field</u> to speak about it.

"Long <u>ago</u>, Oak Lake <u>flowed</u> clean," said <u>Crow</u>. "Now trash <u>floats</u> in it. We must make this lake <u>flow</u> clean once more."

33

33

"How can we help?" <u>Toad</u> <u>croaked</u>. "We will make <u>war</u> on trash. <u>Follow</u> me!" said Crow.

<u>Half</u> the animals went around one side of Oak Lake. The rest went around the other side. They picked up trash and put it in trash cans.

34

"This lake looks good and clean," Toad croaked. "Let's keep it this way."

"We can wait in this <u>hollow</u> tree," Crow said. "Then we will <u>show</u> everyone how to take care of the lake. It must be our <u>goal</u>."

35

35

Word Key

Decodable words with *oa, ow* _____

High-Frequency Words _____

TARGET SKILL

PHONICS LIBRARY

Reading Decodable Text

OBJECTIVES

- Apply the Phonics/Decoding Strategy to decode words in context.
- Recognize high-frequency words in context.
- Reread to build fluency.

Have children preview *Crow's Plan*. Have them look at the pictures and predict what might happen in this story.

Model the Phonics/Decoding Strategy. Review the strategy. Then point to the word *Crow's* in the story title.

Think Aloud *I see that the first word has the vowel pair* ow, *which can stand for the long* o *sound. I also see an apostrophe* s *ending. If I try blending the word first without the ending, I say /krō/,* crow. *I know that a crow is a kind of bird. If I add the sound of* s, *the word is* crow's. *The story might be about a plan that a crow has.*

Apply the Phonics/Decoding Strategy. Have children read *Crow's Plan* with partners. Remind them to use the Phonics/Decoding Strategy.

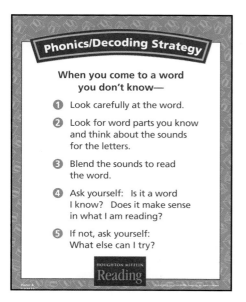

Phonics/Decoding Strategy

When you come to a word you don't know—

1 Look carefully at the word.

2 Look for word parts you know and think about the sounds for the letters.

3 Blend the sounds to read the word.

4 Ask yourself: Is it a word I know? Does it make sense in what I am reading?

5 If not, ask yourself: What else can I try?

HOUGHTON MIFFLIN
Reading

Prompts for Decoding

Support children as they read. Use prompts such as these:

- Look at the word *h-o-l-l-o-w* on page 35.
- What can you do if you don't know this word?
- Show me how you sound out the word.
- Now read the sentence. Does the word make sense? If not, ask yourself what else you can try.

Oral Language

Discuss the story. Ask children to answer the questions in complete sentences.

- What big problem do the animals at Oak Lake have? (There is trash floating in Oak Lake.)
- What will the animals do to solve the problem? (They will make a war on trash. They will pick up all the trash.)
- What happens when little raccoon throws his trash into the lake? (Crow catches it and puts it in the trash can.)
- What will the animals do if they see someone throw trash? (They will croak, moan, and bellow, and probably pick up the trash.)

Soon a raccoon family came to Oak Lake. The family ate a picnic in their <u>rowboat</u>. When they finished, the little raccoon tossed something. In a flash, Crow dove and got that trash in his beak before it hit Oak Lake.

36

Crow dropped that trash in a trash can. He flew back and <u>bellowed</u> at that family.

"I think I <u>know</u> why Crow is mad," the dad explained. "We won't <u>throw</u> trash again, <u>fellow</u>," he yelled up at Crow.

37

36

3

Crow went back to the hollow tree and spoke with the animals. "This is how we will show everyone. It must be our goal."

"Yes," they said. "You have our <u>oath</u>. If we see someone throw trash, we will <u>croak</u> or <u>moan</u> or <u>bellow</u>."

38

So when you hear animals croak or moan or bellow, think about this tale. And don't throw trash!

39

38

39

 Build Fluency

Model fluent reading.

- Read aloud pages 33 and 34. Make your voice different for the words that Crow and Toad speak.

- Have children read aloud the same pages in unison.

Have children practice fluent reading. Have groups of three reread the story aloud as a Readers' Theater, taking a different part each time. (narrator, Crow, and Toad and other animals) Encourage children to read with expression.

Home Connection
Hand out the take-home version of *Crow's Plan*. Ask children to reread the story with their families. (See the **Phonics Library Blackline Masters**.)

OBJECTIVE

- Write spelling words with long *o* patterns.

SPELLING WORDS

Basic

boat	load
cold	snow
road	hold *
blow	most
gold	toe†
old	do†

Review	Challenge
so *	goal*
show	rainbow

* *Forms of these words appear in the literature.*

† *These words are exceptions to the principle.*

Extra Support/ Intervention

Basic Word List Use only Basic Words 1–5, words with daggers, and the Review Words with children who have difficulty with this spelling principle.

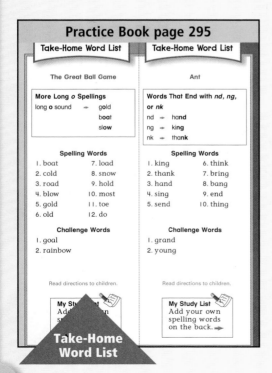

Practice Book page 295

Take-Home Word List	Take-Home Word List

The Great Ball Game

Ant

More Long *o* Spellings

long *o* sound → gold
boat
slow

Words That End with nd, ng, or nk

nd → hand
ng → king
nk → thank

Spelling Words

1. boat	7. load
2. cold	8. snow
3. road	9. hold
4. blow	10. most
5. gold	11. toe
6. old	12. do

Spelling Words

1. king	6. think
2. thank	7. bring
3. hand	8. bang
4. sing	9. end
5. send	10. thing

Challenge Words

1. goal
2. rainbow

Challenge Words

1. grand
2. young

Read directions to children.

Read directions to children.

My Study List
Add...

My Study List
Add your own spelling words on the back. →

Take-Home Word List

SPELLING: More Long *o* Words

❶ Teach the Principle

Pretest Say each sentence. Have children write only the underlined word.

Basic Words

1. I want to sail the **boat**.
2. The lake is **cold**.
3. Do not walk in the **road**.
4. Wind can **blow** down a tree.
5. The crown is made of **gold**.
6. I like to fix **old** bikes.
7. She has a big **load** of books.
8. I wear boots in the **snow**.
9. Can you **hold** this for me?
10. I ate **most** of my beans.
11. She bumped her **toe**!
12. He must **do** the dishes.

Challenge Words

13. My **goal** is to read three books.
14. We saw a **rainbow** after the storm.

Teach Write *cold, boat,* and *blow* at the top of three columns.

- Say each word. Ask children to repeat it and name the vowel sound they hear. (/ō/)
- Explain that these words show three different spellings for the long *o* sound: *o, oa,* and *ow.*
- Have children underline those spelling patterns.

Write *toe* and *do* in a separate column.

- Say each word and have children repeat it.
- Explain that these words are exceptions. The long *o* in *toe* is spelled *oe. Do* is spelled with a final *o,* but its sound is /o͞o/.

❷ Practice

Write *road, gold, old, load, snow, hold,* and *most.*

- Choose children to underline the long *o* spelling pattern, say each word, and name the vowel sound. Add each word to the appropriate column.
- Together, spell the words in each column.

❸ Apply

Practice/Homework Assign **Practice Book** page 295, the Take-Home Word List.

GRAMMAR: Plural Possessive Nouns

OBJECTIVES
- Identify plural possessive nouns.
- Explain possessive phrases.
- Learn academic language: *plural noun, plural possessive noun.*

❶ Teach

Read aloud two sample sentences.

- Write and read aloud *The <u>boys</u> played soccer. The <u>boys'</u> uniforms got dirty.*
- Point out the difference between *boys* and *boys',* explaining that the apostrophe is used to show belonging or ownership.
- Ask children whether each sentence tells about one boy or more than one boy.
- Ask which sentence tells about something that belongs to the boys.

Go over these points.

- A plural noun means more than one and usually ends in *s*. Write, for example, *the Animals.*
- A plural possessive noun shows that something belongs to more than one person, animal, or thing. These nouns usually end in *s'*. Write, for example, *the Animals' goal.*
- Some plural nouns, such as *children* and *mice,* do not end in *s*. To form the possessive of these nouns, add *'s*. Write, for example, *the children's pet.*

❷ Practice

Display Transparency 4–22. Ask children to read aloud each sentence, identify the plural possessive noun, and explain what belongs to whom or to what.

❸ Apply

Have each child write a sentence with a plural possessive noun. Pairs can then exchange papers, identify the plural possessive noun, and explain what belongs to whom or to what.

Transparency 4–22
Plural Possessive Nouns

1. There were twelve children at the <u>twins'</u> birthday party.
2. The twins passed out the <u>children's</u> party favors.
3. The <u>boys'</u> favors were in red bags and the <u>girls'</u> favors were in yellow ones.
4. The <u>candles'</u> wax dripped onto the cake.
5. The twins enjoyed their <u>friends'</u> singing.
6. Tim and Kim opened their <u>guests'</u> gifts.
7. After the games, Kim gave out the <u>winners'</u> prizes.
8. The children tied all the <u>balloons'</u> strings together.
9. Everyone helped clean up the <u>presents'</u> wrappings.
10. The children watched for their <u>parents'</u> cars to arrive.

Monitoring Student Progress

If . . .	Then . . .
children need help recognizing and forming plural possessive nouns,	use the Reteaching lesson on page R34.

Day at a Glance
pp. T198–T215

Reading Instruction

Background and Vocabulary
Reading the Anthology
The Great Ball Game

• • • • • • • • • • • • • • • • • •

Leveled Readers, *T240–T243*

- ● *Bird Race*
- ▲ *Turtle's Small Pond*
- ■ *Possum's Bare Tail*
- ◆ *A Race to the Mountain*

Word Work

Vocabulary Review
Word Wall
Spelling Practice

Writing & Oral Language

Writing: A News Article
Grammar Practice
Listening/Speaking/Viewing

Daily Routines

Daily Message

Phonics Review Point to each word as you read aloud the Daily Message.

Show you are a good sport. Cheer your team on. Don't groan when the other team scores. Other ways to be a good sport are

_____.

Have children

- read the Daily Message, discuss it, and ask volunteers to complete the last sentence;
- find and read aloud words with *oa, ow*. (*Show, groan*)

Word Wall

High-Frequency Word Review Briefly review these high-frequency words that were introduced on Day 1. Display the words and have children practice recognizing, chanting, spelling, and writing them.

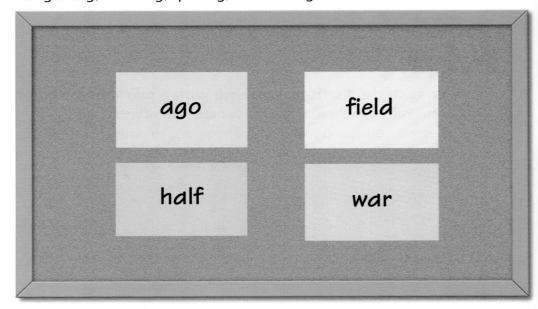

ago

field

half

war

Blackline Masters for these word cards appear on p. R38.

Vocabulary

Find the Exact Word Have children decide on exact words to describe animal calls. Distribute Activity Master 4–3 on page R42. Ask a volunteer to read aloud the different words that describe animal sounds. Then discuss the example.

Have children

- choose a word from the box that describes the sound an animal makes;
- write the word and complete the sentence to tell what happens;
- draw a picture to illustrate one sentence.

The lion roared, and the ground shook.

Daily Writing Prompt

Have children revise work they are currently writing, or have them use this prompt to begin a new writing activity.

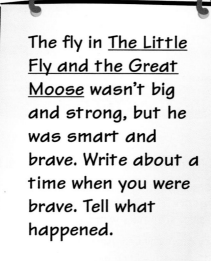

The fly in <u>The Little Fly and the Great Moose</u> wasn't big and strong, but he was smart and brave. Write about a time when you were brave. Tell what happened.

Daily Language Practice

Grammar Skill: Plural Possessive Nouns
Spelling Skill: More Long *o* Words

Display **Transparency 4–20.** Ask children to rewrite Sentence 2 correctly. Then model how to write it, and have children check their work.

Transparency 4–20
Daily Language Practice

Proofread each sentence. Correct any errors.

Day 1
1. Jake and i found a goald ring.

Day 2
2. The childrens feet were colde.

The **children's** feet were **cold**.

Please **hold** this book for me.

Day 4
4. Is this the rowd to the dance camp!

Is this the **road** to the dance camp?

Day 5
5. I drew a picture of the twins bote.

I drew a picture of the **twins' boat**.

TRANSPARENCY 4–20
TEACHER'S EDITION PAGES T187, T199, T217, T225, AND T

Building Background

Key Concept: Settling Arguments

Ask children to share good ways to settle an argument or disagreement. Then use "Ball Games" on Anthology pages 88–89 to build additional background and introduce Key Vocabulary.

- Have individuals read aloud the paragraph on page 88 and the captions on page 89.

- Have children identify the similarities and differences in each of the three photographs.

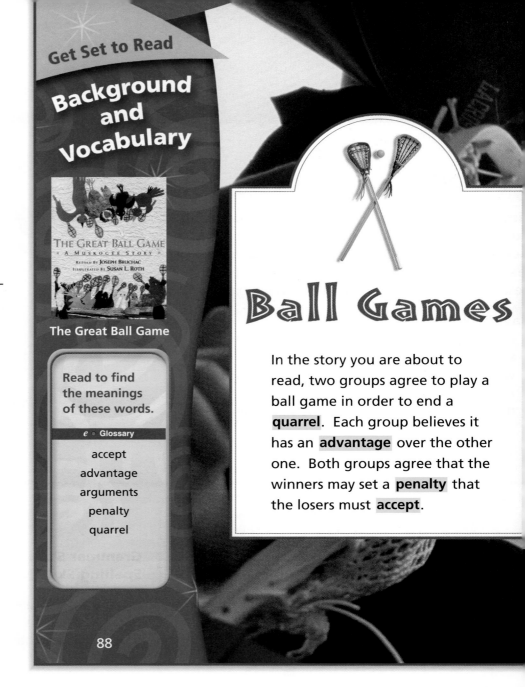

Get Set to Read

Background and Vocabulary

The Great Ball Game

Read to find the meanings of these words.

e ○ Glossary

accept

advantage

arguments

penalty

quarrel

Ball Games

In the story you are about to read, two groups agree to play a ball game in order to end a **quarrel**. Each group believes it has an **advantage** over the other one. Both groups agree that the winners may set a **penalty** that the losers must **accept**.

88

English Language Learners

Language Development

Beginning/Preproduction Have children draw a diagram of a bird or animal from the story. Have them label *fur, feet,* and *teeth,* or *wings, feathers,* and *beak.*

Early Production and Speech Emergence Have partners write rules for a game they enjoy playing in groups. Have them share their rules with the class.

Intermediate and Advanced Fluency Have children use reference materials to learn more about the animals mentioned in the story. Then have them create a class mural showing selected animals in their habitats. Have them include a paragraph detailing information about each animal depicted.

Ball games have been played in the Americas for hundreds of years.

Native Americans sometimes played these games as a way of settling **arguments**.

One game, which we now call lacrosse, was played with a deerskin ball and long poles that were used to toss the ball.

89

Introducing Vocabulary

Key Vocabulary

These words support the Key Concept and appear in the selection.

accept to agree to

advantage something that gives a benefit; something helpful

argument a disagreement

penalty a punishment for breaking rules

quarrel a type of disagreement

e • Glossary
e • WordGame

See Vocabulary notes on pages T204, T205, and T209.

Use Transparency 4–23.

- Read aloud the first sentence on the transparency.

- Model how to figure out the meaning of *arguments*, based on context clues.

- Ask children to use context clues to figure out the meaning of each Key Vocabulary word in the remaining sentences. Have children explain how they figured out each meaning.

- Ask children to look for these words as they read and to use them as they discuss the selection.

Practice/Homework Assign **Practice Book** page 46.

Transparency 4–23

Ball Game– Related Words

1. When teams play ball games, sometimes disagreements, or <u>arguments</u>, come up.

2. One team may feel that the other is winning because of some unfair <u>advantage</u>.

3. If a <u>quarrel</u> goes on for long, it may stop the game.

4. A referee, umpire, or judge can give a team a <u>penalty</u> for arguing.

5. To stay in the game, the team must <u>accept</u> this and move on.

Practice Book page 46

The Great Ball Game
Key Vocabulary

Name _____

Replacing Words

Read each sentence. Replace each word in dark print with a word from the box. Write the letters of that word in the spaces.

Vocabulary
accept   advantage   argument   penalty   quarrel

1. Two bear cubs had a big **disagreement**.
   a r g u m e n t (1 point)

2. One cub had an **edge** because he was bigger.
   a d v a n t a g e (1)

3. That cub thought that bigger was better. The other cub did not **agree** that this was true.
   a c c e p t (1)

4. Mother Bear heard the **disagreement**.
   q u a r r e l (1)

5. She said, "There will be a **punishment** if you two cubs do not settle this fight."
   p e n a l t y (1)

On another sheet of paper, write an ending to the story. Tell how you think the cubs will solve the argument.
Answers will vary. (3)

COMPREHENSION STRATEGY
Summarize

Teacher Modeling Read aloud the title and the author's and illustrator's names on Anthology page 91. Ask someone to read aloud the Strategy Focus. Then have individuals read aloud pages 92–93. Model how to summarize story events so far.

Think Aloud *If I want to tell a friend about the most important parts of this story, I need to tell who the story is about and what they are doing. My summary will be:* This story is about birds and animals who are arguing about which group is better. As I read, I can stop and sum up what I know so far to help me keep track of what is going on.

Test Prep Remind children that, when answering multiple-choice questions about cause and effect, they should look for a key word or phrase that tells them whether the question is asking about a cause or an effect.

COMPREHENSION SKILL
Cause and Effect

Introduce the Graphic Organizer.
Tell children that a Cause/Effect Chart can help them better understand story events.

- Display **Transparency 4–24.**
- Review Anthology pages 92–93. Have children help you complete the first sentence in the What Happens column. Have them do the same on **Practice Book** page 47.
- Children can fill in the rest of the sentences under What Happens as they read. They will complete the Why It Happens column in the Comprehension lesson.

THEME 4: Amazing Animals
(Anthology p. 90)

T202

Meet the Author
Joseph Bruchac

Joseph Bruchac's grandfather, a member of the Abenaki tribe, told him many traditional folk stories. Mr. Bruchac enjoys telling the stories that his grandfather passed on to him, as well as folktales from other Native American tribes.

Meet the Illustrator
Susan L. Roth

Susan L. Roth used cut paper collected from all over the world to make the illustrations for this book: red umbrella paper from Thailand, an envelope from Tibet, blue paper from Japan, and green paper from Italy.

Internet

To learn more about Joseph Bruchac and Susan L. Roth, visit Education Place.

www.eduplace.com/kids

90

Transparency 4–24
Cause-and-Effect Chart

AMAZING ANIMALS The Great Ball Game
Graphic Organizer Cause-and-Effect Chart

ANNOTATED VERSION

What Happens ➡	Why It Happens
(page 92) The Birds and Animals have a big argument	They think they are better than each other.
(page 94) The Birds and Animals decide to have a ball game	They want to settle the argument.
(page 96) Bat is left out of the game.	Bat has both teeth and wings.
(Page 104) Bat wins the game for the Animals	Bat can fly in the dark.
(page 108) Birds fly south each winter.	Bat gives the Birds a penalty.
(page 109) Bat comes flying every day at dusk	Bat wants to see if the Animals need him to play ball.

TRANSPARENCY 4–24
TEACHER'S EDITION PAGES T202 AND T220

Practice Book page 47

The Great Ball Game
Graphic Organizer Cause and Effect Chart

Name _____

Cause-Effect Chart

As you read the story, complete the chart below.

What Happens ➡	Why It Happens
(page 92) The Birds and Animals have a big argument **(1 point)**	They think they are better than each other. **(1)**
(page 94) The Birds and Animals decide to have a ball game **(1)**	They want to settle the argument. **(1)**
(page 96) Bat **(1)** is left out of the game.	Bat has both teeth and wings. **(1)**
(Page 104) Bat wins the game for the Animals **(1)**	Bat can fly in the dark. **(1)**
(page 108) Birds fly south **(1)** each winter.	Bat gives the Birds a penalty. **(1)**
(page 109) Bat comes flying every day at dusk **(1)**	Bat wants to see if the Animals need him to play ball. **(1)**

THE GREAT BALL GAME
◄ A MUSKOGEE STORY ►

RETOLD BY JOSEPH BRUCHAC
ILLUSTRATED BY SUSAN L. ROTH

Strategy Focus

Who will win the great ball game? As you read, stop and **summarize** the important parts of the story.

Purpose Setting

- Have children read the title, look at the cover illustration, and make predictions about what will happen in the ball game.

- Ask children to turn to Responding on Anthology page 110. Read the questions aloud. Encourage children to find answers to these questions as they read *The Great Ball Game*.

Journal ▶ Children can use their journals to record and revise their predictions, as well as write down their thoughts about the Birds' and Animals' argument and their decision for settling the quarrel.

Extra Support/Intervention

Preview pages 92–99.

pages 92–93 The Birds and the Animals are arguing about which group is better. Which group has wings? Which group has fur and teeth?

page 94 Bear and Crane are the leaders of each group. Why do you think they became leaders?

pages 96–99 What do you notice about Bat? Which group do you think Bat belongs with? Why?

Preview pages 100–109.

pages 100–102 The Birds and Animals play a game to decide who is better. Who do you think will win? Why?

page 103 Look at Bear and Crane. Who do you think is winning so far?

pages 104–105 Bat can see in the dark. How is this an advantage?

pages 106–109 Who do you think Bat will help, the Birds or the Animals?

Reading the Selection
(Anthology p. 91) **T203**

Long ago the Birds and Animals had a great argument.

"We who have wings are better than you," said the Birds.

92

"That is not so," the Animals replied. "We who have teeth are better."

The two sides argued back and forth. Their quarrel went on and on, until it seemed they would go to war because of it.

93

TARGET SKILL

READING STRATEGY

Phonics/Decoding

Vowel Sounds for *ar, or, ir*

Teacher/Student Modeling Write and say aloud the Key Vocabulary word *argument*. Underline *ar*. Point out that when a vowel is followed by *r*, its sound is sometimes affected. The letters *ar* are often pronounced /är/. Repeat this procedure for /ôr/ in *forth* and /ûr/ in *birds*. Then have children use what they know to blend the following words sound by sound: *first* (p. 94), *formed* (p. 96), *hard* (p. 100).

Vocabulary

argument a disagreement

quarrel a type of disagreement

Word Key

Decodable words with *oa* ______

High-Frequency Words ______

Vocabulary Words

REACHING ALL LEARNERS

English Language Learners

Ball Games

Have children look at Anthology page 91, the selection title page. Read the title aloud and ask the children what ball games they know of or play. List their responses on chart paper. Have an individual explain the basic rules of each game.

Then Crane, the leader of the Birds, and Bear, the leader of the Animals, had an idea.

"Let us have a ball game," Crane said. "The first side to score a <u>goal</u> will win the argument." **1**

94

"This idea is good," said Bear. "The side that loses will have to <u>accept</u> the <u>penalty</u> given by the other side." **2**

So they walked and flew to a <u>field</u>, and there they divided up into two teams.

On one side went all those who had wings. They were the Birds.

On the other side went those with teeth. They were the Animals.

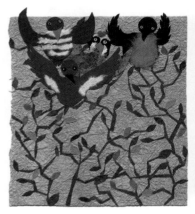

95

CRITICAL THINKING
Guiding Comprehension

1 CAUSE AND EFFECT How will the argument be won? (The first side to score a goal wins.)

2 NOTING DETAILS What will the winning side do? (Set a penalty for the losing side.)

 READING STRATEGY
Phonics/Decoding

Consonant Digraph: *th*

Teacher/Student Modeling Write *that*. Underline *th*. Remind children that *th* makes a single sound. Have children blend *that*. Write *other* and *teeth*. Have children look carefully for parts they know, think about the sounds for the letters, and blend sound by sound. Have children read the words in the sentences on page 95.

Vocabulary

penalty a punishment for breaking rules

accept to agree to

 Extra Support/Intervention

Strategy Modeling: Summarize

Use this example to model the strategy.

The Birds and Animals argue about whether it is better to have teeth or wings. They have a ball game to decide. The Birds are one team. The Animals are the other team.

Reading the Selection
(Anthology pp. 94–95) **T205**

But when the teams were formed, one creature was left out: Bat. He had wings *and* teeth! He flew back and forth between the two sides.

96

First he went to the Animals. "I have teeth," he said. "I must be on your side."

But Bear shook his head. "It would not be fair," he said. "You have wings. You must be a Bird."

97

CRITICAL THINKING
Guiding Comprehension

③ COMPARE AND CONTRAST How is Bat like both the Animals and the Birds? (Bat has wings like a bird and teeth like an animal.)

COMPREHENSION STRATEGY
Summarize

Teacher/Student Modeling Ask children which story events they would include in a summary of the story so far. If necessary, ask:

Who are the main characters in the story? How does the story begin? What happens in the middle of the story?

REACHING ALL LEARNERS **Extra Support/Intervention**

Review pages 90–99.

Before children join in Stop and Think, have them

- check the accuracy of their **predictions,**
- model the reading **strategies** they used,
- add to **Practice Book** page 47,
- **summarize** the story so far.

ASSIGNMENT CARD 10

I'm a Good Team Player

Persuasive Speaking

Imagine that you are Bat. Choose the team that you would like to be on—the Birds or the Animals.

Write a speech that would make the players want you on their team.

Read your speech to your classmates.

Theme 4: Amazing Animals

Teacher's Resource BLM page 67

THEME 4: Amazing Animals
(Anthology pp. 96–97)

So Bat flew to the other side. "Take me," he said to the Birds, "for you see I have wings."

But the Birds laughed at him. "You are too little to help us. We don't want you," they jeered.

98

Then Bat went back to the Animals. "Please let me join your team," he begged them. "The Birds laughed at me and would not accept me."

So Bear took pity on the little bat. "You are not very big," said Bear, "but sometimes even the small ones can help. We will accept you as an Animal, but you must hold back and let the bigger Animals play first."

99

Stop and Think

Critical Thinking Questions

1. **MAKING JUDGMENTS** If you could be on one of the teams in the story, which would you choose and why? (Answers should be supported with details from the selection.)

2. **MAKING INFERENCES** What do Bat's actions tell us about him? (He doesn't give up easily. He wants to be part of a team.)

Strategies in Action

Have children **Summarize** the story so far and model other strategies they used.

Discussion Options

Bring the entire class together to do either of these activities.

Review Predictions/Purpose Discuss whether predictions were accurate, revise predictions, and make new ones.

Share Group Discussions Have children share their questions for Assignment Card 11 and the results of their literature discussions.

ASSIGNMENT CARD 11

Literature Discussion

- What would you tell the characters in the story if you could talk to them?

- Do you think a ball game will really show which group is better? Why or why not?

- If you could choose to be on one of the teams, which would you choose? Why?

- How would you help the groups settle their argument?

Theme 4: Amazing Animals

Teacher's Resource BLM page 68

Monitoring Student Progress

If . . .	Then . . .
children have successfully completed the Extra Support activities on pages T203 and T206,	have them read the rest of the story cooperatively or independently.

Reading the Selection
(Anthology pp. 98–99) **T207**

Two poles were set up as the goalposts at each end of the field. Then the game began.

Each team played hard. On the Animals' side Fox and Deer were swift runners, and Bear cleared the way for them as they played. Crane and Hawk, though, were even swifter, and they stole the ball each time before the Animals could reach their goal.

4

5

6

100

101

CRITICAL THINKING
Guiding Comprehension

4 DRAWING CONCLUSIONS What can you tell about how the game is played? (The teams use poles with nets on the ends to try to toss the ball through the other team's goal; the first side to score a goal wins.)

5 MAKING INFERENCES Why do you think it's Bear's job to clear the way for his teammates? (He is the biggest and strongest.)

6 CAUSE AND EFFECT Why can't the Animals score a goal? (The swift Birds steal the ball each time.)

English Language Learners

Animal Characteristics
Have children go through the pages of the selection to identify different animals. Present characteristics of birds and mammals, such as *wings, four legs, tail, and horns.* Have children sort and chart the animals in the story according to these characteristics.

THEME 4: Amazing Animals
(Anthology pp. 100–101)

Soon it became clear that the Birds had the advantage. Whenever they got the ball, they would fly up into the air and the Animals could not reach them. The Animals guarded their goal well, but they grew tired as the sun began to set.

Just as the sun sank below the horizon, Crane took the ball and flew toward the poles. Bear tried to stop him, but stumbled in the dim light and fell. It seemed as if the Birds would surely win.

CRITICAL THINKING
Guiding Comprehension

7 PROBLEM SOLVING What do the Animals do to try to keep the Birds from scoring? (They guard their goal well.)

READING STRATEGY
Phonics/Decoding

Consonant Clusters

Teacher/Student Modeling Write *clear*. Underline *cl*. Remind children that each consonant in the cluster keeps its sound when blended. Have children blend *clear* sound by sound. Repeat this process with the following words with consonant clusters: *Crane, flew, stop.*

Vocabulary

advantage something that gives a benefit; something helpful

guarded protected; took care of

ASSIGNMENT CARD 12

Wow! What a Game!
Play-by-Play Description

Choose a partner. Discuss how the author uses words such as *flew*, *stole*, and *darted* to help you picture the action in the story.

Think of some other interesting action words.

Now, you and your partner can take turns pretending to be sports announcers telling about the ball game between the Birds and the Animals. See how exciting you can make your description using action words.

Theme 4: Amazing Animals

Teacher's Resource BLM page 68

Reading the Selection
(Anthology pp. 102–103) **T209**

Suddenly a small dark shape flew onto the field and stole the ball from Crane just as he was about to reach the poles. It was Bat. He darted from side to side across the field, for he did not need light to find his way. None of the Birds could catch him or block him.

104

105

Comprehension Preview

Cause and Effect

Teach

Remind children that a good way to understand what is happening in a story is to ask why something happens. Explain that they should be able to provide an answer, or reason, for every question. Write Why questions. Have children provide a reason (Cause) for each written question. Have them look for parts of the text that support their answers on Anthology pages 102–103. (Sample question and answer: Why do the birds have an advantage? They can fly up into the air with the ball.)

Practice/Apply

Have pairs continue to look for reasons why. Have them look on Anthology pages 106–107 for answers to these questions: *Why is Bat allowed to set the penalty for the Birds? Why must the Birds leave the land for half the year?*

Target Skill Trace	
Preview, Teach	pp. T188, T202, T210, T220
Reteach	p. R30
Review	p. T296; Theme 1, pp. T76, T224; Theme 3, p. T236; Theme 4, pp. T86, T168

This is how Bat came to be accepted as an Animal. He was allowed to set the penalty for the Birds. **8**

"You Birds," Bat said, "must leave this land for half of each year." **9**

Holding the ball, Bat flew right between the poles at the other end! The Animals had won!

106

107

CRITICAL THINKING

Guiding Comprehension

8 **PROBLEM SOLVING** Bat could help the Animals or the Birds. Why does he choose the Animals? (They accepted him on their team.)

9 **CAUSE AND EFFECT** What is Bat allowed to do at the end of the story? Why? (He's allowed to set the penalty for the Birds because he helped the Animals win.)

COMPREHENSION STRATEGY

Summarize

Student Modeling Have students summarize the story up to this point. If necessary, ask: *Which creature is this story mostly about? What problem does he solve?*

Strategy Modeling: Summarize

Use this example to model the strategy.

The Birds and the Animals have a ball game to decide which group is better. Bear lets Bat play with the Animals, even though he has both wings and teeth. Bat wins the game for the Animals. He decides the penalty: the Birds must leave the land for half of each year.

English Language Learners

Amazing Animals

Have children work in small groups to think of other fantastic things animals might do, for example *ride a bike, help children with their homework,* etc. Use this opportunity to review or introduce vocabulary related to everyday activities.

Reading the Selection
(Anthology pp. 106–107) **T211**

So it is that the Birds fly south each winter… **10**

108

And every day at dusk Bat still comes flying to see if the Animals need him to play ball. **11** **12**

109

CRITICAL THINKING
Guiding Comprehension

10 **FANTASY AND REALISM** What real bird behavior does this folktale attempt to explain? (seasonal migration)

11 **FANTASY AND REALISM** What real bat behavior does this story attempt to explain? (the reason bats appear at dusk)

12 **FANTASY AND REALISM** How can you tell that this is not a realistic story? (Birds and animals don't talk or play ball games.)

Extra Support/Intervention

Selection Review

Before Wrapping Up, have children

- check the accuracy of their **predictions,**
- model the reading **strategies** they used,
- review and complete **Practice Book** page 47,
- **summarize** the entire story.

On Level	Challenge

Have small groups discuss the story, using their own questions and questions from Think About the Selection on Anthology page 110.

THEME 4: Amazing Animals
(Anthology pp. 108–109)

Wrapping Up

Critical Thinking Questions

1. **MAKING INFERENCES** What do you think the Animals and Birds learned from the ball game? (Sample response: Small animals can help in important ways.)

2. **PREDICTING OUTCOMES** How might the outcome have been different if Bat had played for the Birds? (The Birds would probably have won, and Bat would have set a penalty for the Animals.)

3. **MAKING JUDGMENTS** If you were to be a team captain for a second ball game, which creatures would you pick for your team? Explain your thinking. (Answers will vary but should be supported with factual details.)

Strategies in Action

Have individuals **Summarize** the entire story and model other strategies they used.

Discussion Options

Bring the entire class together to do either of these activities.

Review Predictions/Purpose Revisit children's predictions and discuss their accuracy.

Share Group Discussions Have children share their reactions to the ball game and questions from their discussion groups.

Monitoring Student Progress

If . . .	Then . . .
children have difficulty completing Wrapping Up activities,	pair each child who has difficulty with a child who can summarize the story easily to review story events.

Challenge

Word Practice

Have children use the Challenge Words to write some quotes that a bird might say while flying south for the winter.

Practice Book page 48

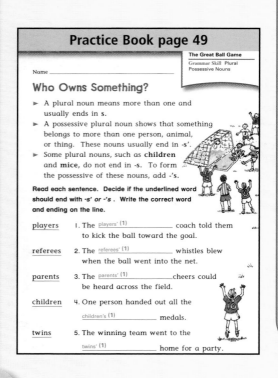

Name _____

The Great Ball Game
Spelling More Long o
Spellings

The Long o Sound?

Most of the Spelling Words have the long o sound spelled o, oa, or ow.
  Example: go, boat, slow

► The word **toe** is special. The vowels **oe** spell the long o sound in **toe**.
► The word **do** is special. The vowel **o** does not spell the long o sound in **do**.

Write each Spelling Word under the correct column.

long o sound spelled o	long o sound spelled oa
cold **(1)**	boat **(1)**
gold **(1)**	road **(1)**
old **(1)**	load **(1)**
hold **(1)**	
most **(1)**	long o sound spelled ow
	blow **(1)**
	snow **(1)**

Write the special words that have a star next to them. Circle the word that has the long o sound.

(toe) **(1)**   do **(1)**

Spelling Words
1. boat
2. cold
3. road
4. blow
5. gold
6. old
7. load
8. snow
9. hold
10. most
11. toe*
12. do*

Practice Book page 49

Name _____

The Great Ball Game
Grammar Skill Plural
Possessive Nouns

Who Owns Something?

► A plural noun means more than one and usually ends in **s**.
► A possessive plural noun shows that something belongs to more than one person, animal, or thing. These nouns usually end in **-s'**.
► Some plural nouns, such as **children** and **mice**, do not end in **-s**. To form the possessive of these nouns, add **-'s**.

Read each sentence. Decide if the underlined word should end with **-s'** or **-'s** . Write the correct word and ending on the line.

players   1. The players' **(1)** _____ coach told them to kick the ball toward the goal.

referees   2. The referees' **(1)** _____ whistles blew when the ball went into the net.

parents   3. The parents' **(1)** _____ cheers could be heard across the field.

children   4. One person handed out all the children's **(1)** _____ medals.

twins   5. The winning team went to the twins' **(1)** _____ home for a party.

PRACTICE

SPELLING: More Long *o* Words

Review the Principle Write and say *load*, *gold*, and *snow*. Review that these words show three different spellings for the long *o* sound: *oa*, *o*, and *ow*.

Write the Basic Words with a line where the vowels should be. Say each Basic Word, and have a child write the spelling pattern for the missing long *o* vowel sound. Together spell each word.

Practice/Homework Assign **Practice Book** page 48.

PRACTICE

GRAMMAR: Plural Possessive Nouns

Review the Skill Have volunteers read aloud the information about plural possessive nouns at the top of **Practice Book** page 49.

Practice/Homework Assign **Practice Book** page 49.

A plural possessive noun shows that something belongs to more than one person, animal, or thing.

WRITING: A News Article

❶ Teach

Discuss the characteristics of a good news article.

- Tell children that a news article must get the reader's attention and give a lot of information quickly and clearly.

- Begin a chart by writing *Who? What? When? Where? Why?* and *How?* as headings. Have someone read the questions aloud. Tell children that a news article should answer these questions.

Display the news article on Transparency 4–25; read it aloud.

- Choose a child to read the article's title or headline. Tell children that a good headline often gives the main idea of the article and makes the reader want to find out more.

- Have children help you fill in the chart with details from the article that answer each question.

Display and discuss the guidelines on Transparency 4–26.

❷ Practice/Apply

Assign Practice Book page 50. Have children write news articles about class events. Have pairs read each other's articles and write *who, what, when, where, why,* and *how* above sentences that answer these questions. Publish the articles in a class newspaper.

DAY 2

WRITING

The Great Ball Game

OBJECTIVES

- Identify the characteristics of a good news article.
- Write a news article.
- Learn academic language: *news article, headline.*

Transparency 4–25

A News Article

Young Joggers Help Sick Children

In a jog-a-thon to raise money for Children's Hospital, second graders from Bowles School jogged one hundred miles and raised more than five hundred dollars. The event was held Saturday morning at Jones Park, and 68 second graders from Bowles School jogged along the lake while a large crowd watched and cheered them on. The students had asked friends and family to pledge money for each half-mile they jogged. Many of the runners ran one and a half miles, and some ran two. Tina Golden was one of the runners who ran two miles. "I stayed in Children's Hospital when I had an operation. I really wanted to help the sick children who go there. All my pledges added up to eleven dollars for every half-mile, so I raised forty-four dollars!" said Tina proudly. The runners plan to take the money to the hospital next Friday. While they are there, the Bowles students will visit sick children and read them books.

ANNOTATED VERSION | AMAZING ANIMALS *The Great Ball Game* Writing Skill A News Article

TRANSPARENCY 4–25 TEACHER'S EDITION PAGE T215

Practice Book page 50

Name _____

The Great Ball Game
Writing Skill Writing a News Article

In the News

Use the picture to gather information for writing an article about the baseball game. Answer the questions.

Welcome to Oklahoma City for the Little League Baseball Finals June 13–16

SCORE
BEARS 3 TIGERS 2

Question	Information
Who?	The Bears **(1 point)**
What?	won Little League Baseball Finals **(1)**
When?	June 13–16 **(1)**
Where?	Oklahoma City **(1)**
Why?	Possible answer: They beat the Tigers. **(1)**
How?	The Bears got three runs; Tigers got only two runs. **(1)**

Use the information you wrote to write a news article about the game on another sheet of paper. Remember to add details that will catch a reader's interest. Answers will vary. **(4)**

Transparency 4–26

Guidelines for Writing a News Article

- Write a headline that makes a reader want to know more about the topic.

- Start with a sentence that tells what the article is about and that grabs the reader's attention.

- Tell important facts first. Answer the questions <u>who</u>, <u>what</u>, <u>when</u>, <u>where</u>, <u>why</u>, and <u>how</u>.

- After telling important facts, add details that will interest the reader.

ANNOTATED VERSION | AMAZING ANIMALS *The Great Ball Game* Writing Guidelines News Article

TRANSPARENCY 4–26 TEACHER'S EDITION PAGE T215

Day at a Glance
pp. T216–T223

Reading Instruction

Responding

Comprehension Instruction
Cause and Effect

Rereading for Understanding

• • • • • • • • • • • • • • • • • •

Leveled Readers, *T240–T243*

● *Bird Race*

▲ *Turtle's Small Pond*

■ *Possum's Bare Tail*

◆ *A Race to the Mountain*

Word Work

Vocabulary Review

Word Wall

Spelling Practice

Writing & Oral Language

Writing Activity

Grammar Practice

Listening/Speaking/Viewing

Daily Routines

Daily Message

Phonics Review Point to each word as you read aloud the Daily Message.

Think about games on the playground. Which game is the slowest and dullest? Which game is the best? Do you like to throw or kick a ball? Can you score a goal?

Have children

• read the Daily Message aloud, and discuss the questions;
• find words with *oa, ow;* (*slowest, throw, goal*)
• read the words aloud and then circle them.

Word Wall

Speed Drill Have children review and practice these and other previously taught high-frequency words. Also have them practice reading a few decodable words that feature the new phonics skills.

• Have children take turns holding up a card for partners to read.
• Have individuals read the words to you quickly.

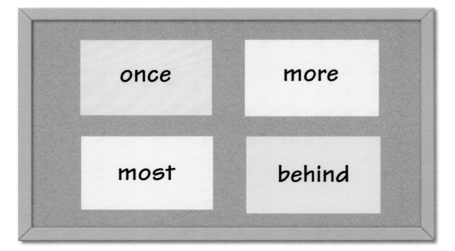

once   more

most   behind

Blackline Masters for these word cards appear on p. R39.

Vocabulary

Rhyme Time First, write *goat,* and brainstorm words that rhyme. Write children's responses. Then write the riddle *What is a jacket for a goat?* and the answer *a goat coat.* Next, list the animal names shown.

Have children
- write riddles about one animal that has a rhyming pair for an answer such as *dry fly;*
- illustrate their riddles;
- share their riddles with someone at home.

fly	mouse
hen	hare
whale	moose
hound	mole

What is a fly with an umbrella?

Daily Writing Prompt

Have children revise work they are currently writing, or have them use this prompt to begin a new writing activity.

Write an answer to this letter to give the child some advice. The child says:

I never get to do what my sister does because I am too little. What can I do?

Daily Language Practice

Grammar Skill: Plural Possessive Nouns
Spelling Skill: More Long *o* Words

Display **Transparency 4–20.** Ask children to rewrite Sentence 3 correctly. Then model how to write it, and have children check their work.

Transparency 4–20

AMAZING ANIMALS *The Great Ball Game*
Grammar Skill Plural Possessive Nouns
Spelling Skill More Long o Words *Spellings (o, oa, ow)*

Daily Language Practice

Proofread each sentence. Correct any errors.

Day 1
1. Jake and i found a goald ring.

   Jake and I found a **gold** ring.

Day 2

Day 3
3. Please holed this book for me

   Please **hold** this book for me.

4. Is this the rowd to the dance camp.

   Is this the **road** to the dance camp?

Day 5
5. I drew a picture of the twins bote.

   I drew a picture of the **twins' boat.**

TRANSPARENCY 4–20
TEACHER'S EDITION PAGES T187, T199, T209, T217, T227

Responding

Comprehension Check

Have children reread or finish reading the selection. Then assign **Practice Book** page 51 to assess children's comprehension of the selection.

Think About the Selection

Have children discuss or write answers. Sample answers are provided; accept reasonable responses.

1. **NOTING DETAILS** It explains why birds fly south for the winter and why bats fly at dusk.

2. **MAKING INFERENCES** The Animals probably would have lost the game and had to accept a penalty.

3. **PREDICTING OUTCOMES** Accept responses that indicate Bat's point of view.

4. **PROBLEM SOLVING** Accept responses that state the reader's opinion and support it with an explanation.

5. ⭐ **Connecting/Comparing** Accept reasonable responses that identify similarities and differences between teams.

Responding

Think About the Selection

1. What event in nature does this tale explain?

2. How might the story have been different if Bat had not played the game?

3. If Bat had helped the Birds win, what sort of penalty might he have set for the Animals?

4. Do you think the story shows a good way to settle an argument? Why or why not?

5. ⭐ **Connecting/Comparing** All of the animals in this theme work in teams. Describe each type of team, and then compare two or more teams.

Expressing

Writing a Folktale

Bears go to sleep for the winter. Spiders make webs. Moths fly toward lights. Think of an animal. Write a folktale that explains why the animal acts the way it does.

Tips
• Observe a pet or other animal to get ideas.
• Use a story map to organize your ideas.

110

Practice Book page 51

Name _____

The Great Ball Game
Comprehension Check

Ball Game Clues

Use the clues to complete the puzzle.

1. The Animals and the Birds had a big _____. (1)
2. The _____ thought they were better because they had teeth. (1)
3. The Birds thought they were better because they had _____. (1)
4. They decided to play a ball _____ to decide who was better. (1)
5. Little _____ had both wings and teeth. (1)
6. Bat made the winning _____. (1)
7. The Birds had to fly _____ each winter because they had lost. (1)

```
        ¹a r g u m e n t
      ²a n i m a l s
      ³w i n g s
        ⁴g a m e
        ⁵b a t
    ⁶g o a l
        s o u t h
```

Write the letters from the boxes in dark print to answer this question.

8. Which team won the ball game? (1)

   a n i m a l s

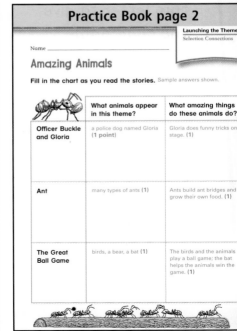

Practice Book page 2

Name _____

Launching the Theme
Selection Connections

Amazing Animals

Fill in the chart as you read the stories. Sample answers shown.

	What animals appear in this theme?	What amazing things do these animals do?
Officer Buckle and Gloria	a police dog named Gloria (1 point)	Gloria does funny tricks on stage. (1)
Ant	many types of ants (1)	Ants build ant bridges and grow their own food. (1)
The Great Ball Game	birds, a bear, a bat (1)	The birds and the animals play a ball game; the bat helps the animals win the game. (1)

Science

Make a Fact File

List what you've learned about bats from reading this selection. Then look for information about bats in an encyclopedia or science book. Make a bat fact file using the information you've collected.

Social Studies

Create Game Rules

The Birds and Animals played a game without any written rules. Write a set of rules for them to follow when playing their game. Explain how rules can help them play together fairly.

 Internet

Take a Web Field Trip

Learn more about amazing animals. Visit Education Place to discover interesting facts about all kinds of animals.

www.eduplace.com/kids

111

Additional Responses

Personal Response Invite volunteers to share their personal responses to *The Great Ball Game* orally in small groups.

Journal ► Ask children to write in their journals about the message they think the author wanted this story to send.

Selection Connections Remind children to add to **Practice Book** page 2.

 **REACHING ALL LEARNERS**

Extra Support/ Intervention	English Language Learners

Writing Support

Tell children that facts about the animals they chose can help them write folktales explaining why the animals act the way they do. Help children read age-appropriate reference materials and take notes. Instruct them to refer to their notes and include facts as they write.

Supporting Comprehension

Beginning/Preproduction Ask children to draw and label a diagram of another animal or bird to play in the game.

Early Production and Speech Emergence Ask yes-no questions to give children a chance to demonstrate understanding without relying on expressive language ability.

Intermediate and Advanced Fluency Have children develop questions about the story they can ask other English language learners. Remind children that they should be able to answer their own questions.

Monitoring Student Progress

End-of-Selection Assessment

Selection Test Use the test on pages 123–124 in the **Teacher's Resource Blackline Masters** to assess selection comprehension and vocabulary.

Student Self-Assessment Have children assess their reading with questions such as

- Which part of the story did I find the most enjoyable? Why did I like that part the best?

- Which strategy helped me the most as I read text that presented a problem?

Responding
(Anthology p. 111) **T219**

OBJECTIVE

- Identify cause-and-effect relationships in a story.

Target Skill Trace

Preview, Teach	pp. T188, T202, T210, T220
Reteach	p. R28
Review	p. T296; Theme 1, p. T76, p. T224; Theme 3, p. T236
See	*Extra Support Handbook,* pp. 142–143, 148–149

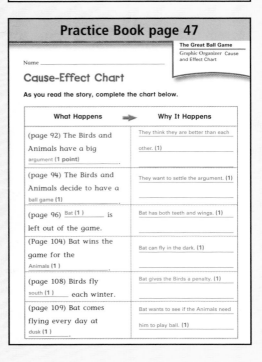

Transparency 4–24

Cause-and-Effect Chart

What Happens ➡	Why It Happens
(page 92) The Birds and Animals have a big argument .	They think they are better than each other.
(page 94) The Birds and Animals decide to have a ball game .	They want to settle the argument.
(page 96) Bat is left out of the game.	Bat has both teeth and wings.
(Page 104) Bat wins the game for the Animals .	Bat can fly in the dark.
(page 108) Birds fly south each winter.	Bat gives the Birds a penalty.
(page 109) Bat comes flying every day at dusk .	Bat wants to see if the Animals need him to play ball.

TRANSPARENCY 4–24
TEACHER'S EDITION PAGES T202 AND T220

AMAZING ANIMALS The Great Ball Game
Graphic Organizer: Cause-and-Effect Chart

ANNOTATED VERSION

Practice Book page 47

The Great Ball Game
Graphic Organizer: Cause and Effect Chart

Name _____

Cause-Effect Chart

As you read the story, complete the chart below.

What Happens ➡	Why It Happens
(page 92) The Birds and Animals have a big argument (1 point)	They think they are better than each other. (1)
(page 94) The Birds and Animals decide to have a ball game (1)	They want to settle the argument. (1)
(page 96) Bat (1) is left out of the game.	Bat has both teeth and wings. (1)
(Page 104) Bat wins the game for the Animals (1)	Bat can fly in the dark. (1)
(page 108) Birds fly south (1) each winter.	Bat gives the Birds a penalty. (1)
(page 109) Bat comes flying every day at dusk (1)	Bat wants to see if the Animals need him to play ball. (1)

COMPREHENSION: Cause and Effect

❶ Teach

Display the Graphic Organizer on Transparency 4–24. Use this Cause/Effect Chart to review what children recorded about cause-and-effect relationships in the story.

- Have children read the events in the first column on **Practice Book** page 47.
- Talk about the words children used to fill in the blanks in the first column. Write the words on the transparency.
- Have children find and read parts of the text to support their answers.

Modeling Point out that sometimes one thing in a story makes another thing happen.

- Read aloud the first sentence in the What Happens column. Then point to the column labeled Why It Happens. Ask children to explain why the Birds and Animals have an argument. (Each group thinks it is better than the other.) Then read aloud the second sentence in the What Happens column, and model filling out Why It Happens, or the cause.

Think Aloud *I know what happens in this story:* the Birds and the Animals decide to play a game. *If I ask myself why they want to do that, I know the answer.* They want to play the game in order to settle an argument. *Whenever I ask myself* what happened, *I am looking for an* effect. *When I ask* why it happened, *I am looking for a* cause.

Tell children that thinking about what happens (the effect) and why things happen (the cause) can show them how events in a story are connected.

❷ Guided Practice

Have children review the sentences in the first column and record the cause of those events. Have them work independently or in pairs.

- Have children discuss what questions they asked themselves to figure out what to write in the second column.
- Have children refer to the text to support their answers.

❸ Apply

Assign Practice Book pages 52–53. Have children apply this skill as they read their Leveled Readers for this week. You may also select books from the Leveled Bibliography for this theme (pages T6–T7).

✔️ **Test Prep** When answering multiple-choice questions about cause and effect, children should circle the key word or phrase that tells them whether the question is asking about a cause (why something happened) or an effect (what happened).

Leveled Readers and Leveled Practice

Children at all levels apply the comprehension skill as they read their Leveled Readers. See lessons on pages T240–T243.

● **BELOW LEVEL**   ▲ **ON LEVEL**   ■ **ABOVE LEVEL**   ◆ **LANGUAGE SUPPORT**

Reading Traits

Teaching children to recognize and describe cause-and-effect relationships is one way of encouraging them to "read beyond the lines" of a story. This comprehension skill supports the reading trait **Integrating for Synthesis**.

Practice Book page 52

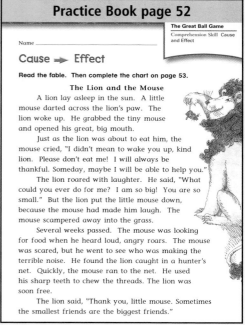

The Great Ball Game
Comprehension Skill Cause and Effect

Name _____

Cause ➡ Effect

Read the fable. Then complete the chart on page 53.

The Lion and the Mouse

A lion lay asleep in the sun. A little mouse darted across the lion's paw. The lion woke up. He grabbed the tiny mouse and opened his great, big mouth.

Just as the lion was about to eat him, the mouse cried, "I didn't mean to wake you up, kind lion. Please don't eat me! I will always be thankful. Someday, maybe I will be able to help you."

The lion roared with laughter. He said, "What could you ever do for me? I am so big! You are so small." But the lion put the little mouse down, because the mouse had made him laugh. The mouse scampered away into the grass.

Several weeks passed. The mouse was looking for food when he heard loud, angry roars. The mouse was scared, but he went to see who was making the terrible noise. He found the lion caught in a hunter's net. Quickly, the mouse ran to the net. He used his sharp teeth to chew the threads. The lion was soon free.

The lion said, "Thank you, little mouse. Sometimes the smallest friends are the biggest friends."

Practice Book page 53

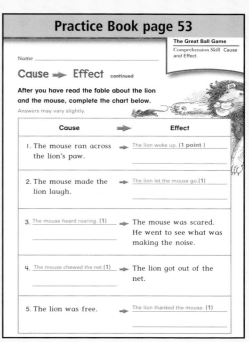

The Great Ball Game
Comprehension Skill Cause and Effect

Name _____

Cause ➡ Effect *continued*

After you have read the fable about the lion and the mouse, complete the chart below.

Answers may vary slightly.

Cause	➡	Effect
1. The mouse ran across the lion's paw.	➡	The lion woke up. (1 point)
2. The mouse made the lion laugh.	➡	The lion let the mouse go.(1)
3. The mouse heard roaring. (1)	➡	The mouse was scared. He went to see what was making the noise.
4. The mouse chewed the net.(1)	➡	The lion got out of the net.
5. The lion was free.	➡	The lion thanked the mouse. (1)

Monitoring Student Progress

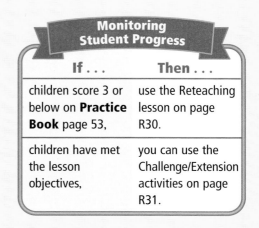

If . . .	Then . . .
children score 3 or below on **Practice Book** page 53,	use the Reteaching lesson on page R30.
children have met the lesson objectives,	you can use the Challenge/Extension activities on page R31.

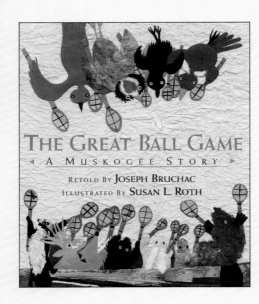

REREADING FOR UNDERSTANDING

Visual Literacy: Perspective

Teach Remind children that perspective

- is the viewpoint from which an illustrator depicts a scene,
- can show different views of the same setting.

Have children look at Anthology pages 100–101. Explain that both of these scenes show the playing field, but that one is an aerial view. Tell children that this is called a "bird's-eye view," seen as if a bird were flying overhead and looking down.

Practice/Apply Have children select their favorite illustration from the selection. Ask them to explain to a partner how they determined what vantage point the illustrator used.

Genre Lesson: Explanations in Fables

Teach Tell children that *The Great Ball Game* is a retelling of a Muskogee fable. Fables such as this often

- teach a lesson about behavior,
- explain why something in nature happens.

Tell children that this fable teaches the lesson that ability sometimes matters more than size or strength. It also explains why birds fly south for the winter.

Practice/Apply Have children think of other fables they have read. Encourage them to discuss what lessons the fables teach or what events they explain. Remind children of the tales they read in Theme 2, *Focus on Fables*.

SPELLING: More Long *o* Words

Vocabulary Connection Write the Basic Words.

boat	blow	load	most
cold	gold	snow	toe
road	old	hold	do

Word Groups Have children say and spell the Basic Word that belongs with each set of words listed.

- car, plane, _____ (boat)
- street, highway, _____ (road)
- rain, wind, _____ (snow)
- finger, leg, _____ (toe)
- hot, cool, _____ (cold)
- red, brown, _____ (gold)

Have children use each Basic Word in an oral sentence.

Practice/Homework Assign **Practice Book** page 54.

GRAMMAR: Plural Possessive Nouns

Apostrophe Challenge Have each child write three plural nouns that name people or animals and the possessives of the same nouns on six index cards. Put the cards for each group in a bag or box. Have small groups sit in circles to play a game of plurals and possessives.

- Have a player take a card, show the word to the group, and use the word in a sentence.
- If the group agrees that the word was used correctly, the player gets one point.
- The game continues around the circle until all cards are used. The player with the most points wins.

Practice Book page 54

The Great Ball Game

Spelling Skill More long *o* Spellings

Name _____

Spelling Spree

Word Games Think how the words in each group are alike. Write the missing Spelling Words.

Spelling Words

1. street, path, road (1 point) _____
2. silver, copper, gold (1) _____
3. rain, sleet, snow (1) _____
4. grab, grip, hold (1) _____
5. finger, nose, toe (1) _____
6. all, some, most (1) _____
7. chilly, cool, cold (1) _____
8. ship, raft, boat (1) _____
9. fill, pack, load (1) _____
10. make, act, do (1) _____

Spelling Words
1. boat
2. cold
3. road
4. blow
5. gold
6. old
7. load
8. snow
9. hold
10. most
11. toe*
12. do*

Materials
- six index cards for each child
- bag or box for each group

Day at a Glance
pp. T224–T233

Reading Instruction

Science Link
Phonics Review
Reading Decodable Text
Brent Skunk Sings

• • • • • • • • • • • • • • • • • • •

Leveled Readers, *T240–T243*
- ● *Bird Race*
- ▲ *Turtle's Small Pond*
- ■ *Possum's Bare Tail*
- ◆ *A Race to the Mountain*

Word Work

Vocabulary Instruction
Parts of a Dictionary Entry
Word Wall
Spelling Practice

Writing & Oral Language

Improving Writing
Grammar Practice
Listening/Speaking/Viewing

Daily Routines

Daily Message

Strategy Review Remind children of the Phonics/Decoding Strategy. Guide them in applying it to selected words in today's message.

Some birds are common, and we see them often. Other birds are unusual, such as the crane and the hawk. Can you name some of each? We seldom see bats. How are they like birds? How are they different?

Read aloud the entire Daily Message with children, pointing to each word as you read. Ask children to read the message aloud. Then have volunteers answer the questions, and discuss their responses.

Word Wall

Tic-Tac-Toe Briefly review the high-frequency words from this week's Word Wall. Then have children use the words to play tic-tac-toe.

Have pairs of children
- create a tic-tac-toe board using nine words;
- read a word aloud before putting an *X* or an *O* on it.

a go	most	great
once	war	half
more	soon	during

Vocabulary

Key Vocabulary Review Briefly review the words and their meanings. Then distribute twelve index cards to pairs of children.

Have partners
- write each vocabulary word on a card and each definition on its own index card;
- shuffle all the cards together and place them face down;
- take turns turning two cards over and trying to match each word to its definition.

accept   guarded
advantage   penalty
argument   quarrel

Daily Writing Prompt

Have children revise work they are currently writing, or have them use this prompt to begin a new writing activity.

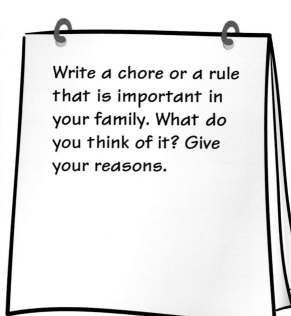

Write a chore or a rule that is important in your family. What do you think of it? Give your reasons.

Daily Language Practice

Grammar Skill: Plural Possessive Nouns
Spelling Skill: More Long *o* Words

Display **Transparency 4–20.** Ask children to rewrite Sentence 4 correctly. Then model how to write it, and have children check their work.

Transparency 4–20

Daily Language Practice

Proofread each sentence. Correct any errors.

Day 1
1. Jake and i found a goald ring.

    Jake and I found a **gold** ring.

Day 2
2. The childrens feet were colde.

    The **children's** feet were **cold**.

Day 4

4. Is this the rowd to the dance camp!

    Is this the **road** to the dance camp?

5. I drew a picture of the twins bote.

    I drew a picture of the **twins' boat**.

Science Link

Bat Attitude

from 3–2–1 Contact
by Lynn O'Donnell

Veronica Thomas has been crazy about bats ever since she could walk. Her room is littered with bat puppets, bat key chains, bat books, and glow-in-the-dark bat T-shirts.

Veronica's obsession with bats might have something to do with her dad's job. He's the curator of mammals at the Wildlife Conservation Society (Bronx Zoo) in New York City. Veronica saw her first bat there when she was just a year old.

Batgirl Forever

You might think Veronica wants to be a bat expert when she grows up. But her dream is to become a paleontologist. Paleontologists are scientists who study animal fossils. "Who knows?" says Veronica. "Maybe someday I'll find a fossil of a bat."

112

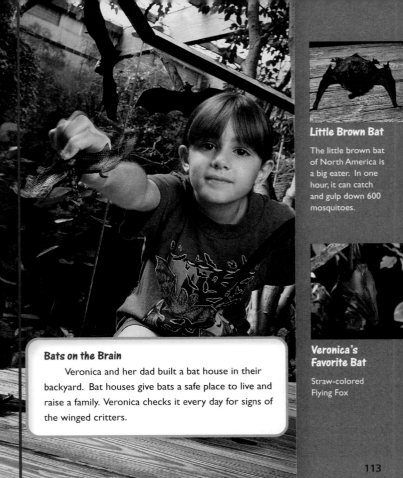

Bats on the Brain

Veronica and her dad built a bat house in their backyard. Bat houses give bats a safe place to live and raise a family. Veronica checks it every day for signs of the winged critters.

Little Brown Bat

The little brown bat of North America is a big eater. In one hour, it can catch and gulp down 600 mosquitoes.

Veronica's Favorite Bat

Straw-colored Flying Fox

113

Science Link

Skill: How to Read a Caption

• **Introduce** the article by reading aloud the title and author's name. Explain that "Bat Attitude" is a nonfiction article from *3-2-1 Contact* magazine.

• **Discuss** the Skill Lesson on Anthology page 112. Explain that captions are titles or short explanations that give readers information about illustrations or photographs.

• **Model** reading captions for information. Then work with children to complete the first column of the K-W-L chart. Ask them what they would like to learn about bats. Fill in their responses in the second column.

• **Assign** children to summarize important information. Together, read pages 112–115. Ask children to tell what they learned about bats and Veronica's love for them. Then write their responses in the third column of the K-W-L chart.

K	W	L
What I Know Some bats fly at night. Bats have furry bodies.	**What I Want to Learn** How do bats find their food in the dark? Are bats types of birds?	**What I Learned**

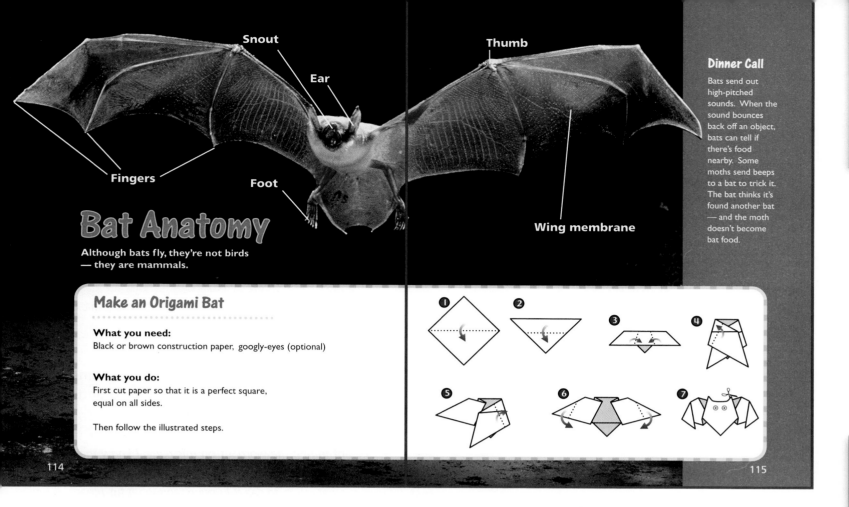

Bat Anatomy

Snout

Ear

Fingers

Foot

Thumb

Wing membrane

Although bats fly, they're not birds — they are mammals.

Dinner Call

Bats send out high-pitched sounds. When the sound bounces back off an object, bats can tell if there's food nearby. Some moths send beeps to a bat to trick it. The bat thinks it's found another bat — and the moth doesn't become bat food.

Make an Origami Bat

What you need:
Black or brown construction paper, googly-eyes (optional)

What you do:
First cut paper so that it is a perfect square, equal on all sides.

Then follow the illustrated steps.

114

115

Wrapping Up

Critical Thinking Questions

Ask children to read aloud parts of the text that support each answer. Then review the K-W-L chart with children.

1. **SUMMARIZING** In your own words, explain how Veronica shows she has a "bat attitude." (Sample response: Her room is decorated with bat things. She has a bat house at home. She is not afraid of bats.)

2. **DRAWING CONCLUSIONS** Why does Veronica know so much about bats? (Her dad is in charge of mammals at the Bronx Zoo, so he showed her the bats at his zoo.)

3. **MAKING INFERENCES** How do you know Veronica's dad likes bats? (He works at a zoo and built a bat house at home.)

4. **COMPARE AND CONTRAST** How are "Bat Attitude" and *The Great Ball Game* alike and different? (Sample response: Both mention bats; the article is a true story, but *The Great Ball Game* is a made-up story.)

Quotations

Teach

Explain that authors sometimes use people's exact words. Identify the quotation on page 112, and point out that readers understand more about Veronica when her exact words are used. Note how her words are enclosed with quotation marks.

Practice/Apply

- Ask how the author might have told readers the same information on page 112 without using Veronica's exact words.

- Have children interview each other, asking their opinion about bats. Have children write the opinions as paragraphs, including exact words and quotation marks. Discuss the impact of using exact words.

Science Link
(Anthology pp. 114–115)

INSTRUCTION

OBJECTIVES

- Identify the entry word and definition in a dictionary entry.
- Use sample sentences and pictures to understand word meanings.
- Learn academic language: *entry word, definition, sample sentence.*

Target Skill Trace

Teach	p. T228
Review	p. T288
See	*Handbook for English Language Learners,* p. 151

TARGET SKILL

VOCABULARY:
Parts of a Dictionary Entry

❶ Teach

Review the parts of a dictionary entry. Display **Transparency 4–27.**

- Review that all entry words on a page are in alphabetical order. Explain that *fang* is a dictionary entry word.
- Read the definition for *fang*. Tell children that this part of the entry explains what the word means.
- Read the sample sentence.
- Point out the picture. Tell children that pictures are sometimes included in an entry to make the meaning easier to understand.

Model how to find entry words and meanings.

Think Aloud *I want to find the word* fur *on this page. I know the words are in alphabetical order, so I find* fur *near the end of the* F *section. First, I'll read the definition to see if I understand what* fur *means. If I need more information, I'll read the sample sentence.*

❷ Guided Practice

Use Transparency 4–27.

- Have children identify each entry word and read its definition.
- Ask which entries have pictures and which have sample sentences.
- Have partners write answers to the questions.

❸ Apply

Assign Practice Book page 55.

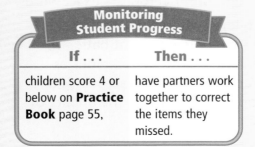

Transparency 4–27

Parts of a Dictionary Entry

fang A long, pointed tooth that an animal uses to grip or tear its prey. *The tiger sank its fangs into its prey.*

fox A wild animal that is part of the dog family. A fox has a pointed nose, large ears, a bushy tail, and a coat of thick fur.

fur The soft, thick hair that covers many animals' bodies. *The snowshoe rabbit's fur turns white in winter.*

goalie A player who stays by the goal to keep the ball from going into the goal area.

Questions

1. Which entry has a picture—*fur* or *fox*?
2. What entry word is listed after *fur*?
3. What is the meaning of *goalie*?

AMAZING ANIMALS: The Great Ball Game
Vocabulary Skill: Parts of a Dictionary Entry
ANNOTATED VERSION
TRANSPARENCY 4–27
TEACHER'S EDITION PAGE T228

Monitoring Student Progress

If . . .	Then . . .
children score 4 or below on **Practice Book** page 55,	have partners work together to correct the items they missed.

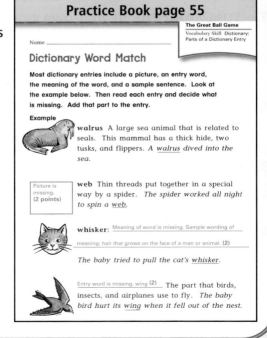

Practice Book page 55

The Great Ball Game
Vocabulary Skill: Dictionary: Parts of a Dictionary Entry

Name _____

Dictionary Word Match

Most dictionary entries include a picture, an entry word, the meaning of the word, and a sample sentence. Look at the example below. Then read each entry and decide what is missing. Add that part to the entry.

Example

walrus A large sea animal that is related to seals. This mammal has a thick hide, two tusks, and flippers. *A* walrus *dived into the sea.*

Picture is missing. (2 points)
web Thin threads put together in a special way by a spider. *The spider worked all night to spin a* web.

whisker: Meaning of word is missing. Sample wording of meaning: hair that grows on the face of a man or animal. (2) *The baby tried to pull the cat's* whisker.

Entry word is missing. wing (2) The part that birds, insects, and airplanes use to fly. *The baby bird hurt its* wing *when it fell out of the nest.*

PHONICS: Words with *nd, nt, mp, ng, nk*

❶ Review

Review the pattern. Use *hand, went, lamp, wing, think, longest,* and *ending* to model and explain these concepts:

- The consonants *nd, nt,* and *mp* often appear together in words. The sound of each letter is heard when they are blended.

- The consonants *ng* and *nk* form one sound that is different from their separate letter sounds.

- The letters *nd, nt, mp, ng,* and *nk* stay together in a syllable.

❷ Guided Practice

Assign Practice Book page 56. Also have children play Word-0.

Word-0

Get ready to play.

- Divide children into groups of three. Have each child fold a paper into eight boxes, and label each box with *nd, nt, mp, ng,* or *nk,* repeating three letter pairs.

- Have each group make word cards for *skunk, bank, drinking; sound, landing, command; jumped, stamp, shrimp; sting, kingdom, sang; went, plant,* and *footprint.*

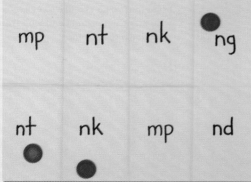

Play the game.

- The caller reads the words. Players listen to each word and put a marker on the letter pair whose sound they hear.

- The caller names the correct letter pair and its sound. If correct, the child's marker remains. The first player to cover all the letters wins.

OBJECTIVE

- Read and write words with *nd, nt, mp, ng,* and *nk.*

Review Skill Trace

Teach	p. T120
Reteach	p. R14
Review	pp. T229, T279
See	*Handbook for English Language Learners,* p. 149

Materials

- drawing paper, paper squares for word cards
- buttons or other markers

Practice Book page 56

The Great Ball Game
Phonics Review Words with *nd, nt, mp, ng, nk*

Name _____

Tongue Twister Sentences

Write the three rhyming words in each sentence.

1. The pig spilled pink ink in the sink.
   pink (1 point)   ink (1)   sink (1)

2. The tiger sent a tent that was bent.
   sent (1)   tent (1)   bent (1)

3. The band got a hand from animals sitting in the stand.
   band (1)   hand (1)   stand (1)

4. The cat likes to tramp on the lamp at camp.
   tramp (1)   lamp (1)   camp (1)

5. The skunk fell off the trunk and went kerplunk!
   skunk (1)   trunk (1)   kerplunk (1)

6. The goat with the long beard played the wrong song.
   long (1)   wrong (1)   song (1)

PHONICS LIBRARY

Reading Decodable Text

OBJECTIVES

- Apply the Phonics/Decoding Strategy to decode words in context.
- Reread to build fluency.

Have children preview *Brent Skunk Sings*.

Have children model the Phonics/ Decoding Strategy. Have a volunteer read the story title and tell how to figure out each word. Ask children to tell how they can figure out other new words.

Apply the Phonics/Decoding Strategy. Have children read the story independently. If necessary, use prompts such as these for *yanked* (page 43):

- Find the word *y-a-n-k-e-d*. What sound does *nk* stand for? What sound does the ending *-ed* have?
- Blend the word. Does the word make sense in the sentence?

Word Key

Decodable words with *nd, nt, mp, ng, nk* ———

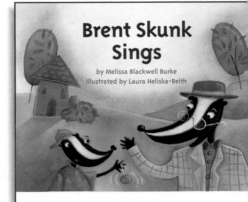

Brent Skunk Sings

by Melissa Blackwell Burke
illustrated by Laura Heliska-Beith

It was time for <u>Brent Skunk</u> to make his first trip to the <u>dentist</u>.

"This bird is the best dentist in this <u>land</u>," <u>Granddad Frank</u> said. "He is quite nice. When we go, he will clean your teeth <u>and</u> check them out. It will not hurt a bit."

41

4

Brent Skunk was afraid.

"This dentist visit won't take long," Granddad Frank said. "And you can <u>bring</u> that yo-yo you like so much."

So Brent Skunk and Granddad Frank <u>went</u> down to the dentist.

42

Brent Skunk and Granddad Frank sat in the waiting room.

When it was time to see the dentist, Granddad Frank <u>found</u> Brent Skunk <u>behind</u> a <u>plant</u>.

Granddad Frank <u>yanked</u> Brent Skunk out.

43

42

4

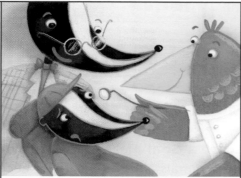

Granddad Frank set Brent Skunk down. Brent Skunk slumped.

Just then, the dentist came in.

"Brent Skunk, you'll be fine. We'll just count and clean and check those teeth. Let me get my lamp on so we can see. Open wide, please."

44

But Brent Skunk kept his mouth closed tight. He just sat there blinking.

"We'll get you a new toy with a string when we are through," the dentist said. "Now please open up."

Brent Skunk still kept his mouth closed tight.

45

"This skunk has me stumped!" the dentist said. "What do you think we can try, Frank?"

"He opens wide when he laughs. We need to make him laugh. Can you do a stunt with that yo-yo?" Granddad Frank asked.

The dentist did three stunts. And Brent Skunk laughed, but with his hand over his mouth.

46

"I've got it!" Granddad Frank said. "Brent can't pass up a chance to sing. How about it, Brent?"

So Brent Skunk sang, and opened wide.

The dentist counted and cleaned and checked Brent's teeth.

It did not hurt a bit.

47

Oral Language

Discuss the story. Ask children to answer in complete sentences.

- Why is Brent Skunk afraid? (This is his first trip to the dentist.)
- Why does the dentist do stunts with the yo-yo? (He wants to make Brett laugh so he will open his mouth.)
- How does Granddad get Brent to open his mouth? (Granddad gets Brent to sing.)

Build Fluency

Model fluent reading.

- Read aloud page 46 and 47 with expression.
- Have children find sentences that are exclamations, questions, and telling sentences on these pages. Call on children to read them aloud.
- Divide children into groups of three to present a Readers' Theater. Assign each group two or three pages.
- Have group members decide who will read the words of the narrator, the dentist, and Granddad Frank. When groups can read fluently, have them present their part of the story.

Home Connection

Hand out the take-home version of *Brent Skunk Sings*. Ask children to reread the story with their families. (See the **Phonics Library Blackline Masters**.)

Reading Decodable Text   **T231**

SPELLING: More Long *o* Words

Score a Goal Have children play this game in two teams of two, the Animals and the Birds. For each group of four, duplicate a rectangular "playing field" with a goal at each end, labeled with the team's name. Have group members make a ball-shaped card for each Basic and Review word. Explain the game.

- Cards are placed face-down in a stack.
- An Animal player chooses a card and reads the word aloud for a Birds player to spell.
- If the word is spelled correctly, the player places the word card in his or her goal. If the word is misspelled, the word card is returned to the stack.
- Teams alternate reading and spelling the words. The team with the most "goals" wins.

Practice/Homework Assign **Practice Book** page 57 for proofreading and writing practice.

Practice Book page 57

The Great Ball Game
Spelling Skill More Long *o* Spellings

Name _____

Proofreading and Writing

Proofreading Circle the four Spelling Words in this story that are not spelled correctly. Write each of the words correctly on the lines.
Allow 1 point for each word that is circled correctly.

The wind began to (blo) harder. The air was getting very cold. The birds flew faster. They wanted to get to the ocean before the (snoe) came. It wouldn't be long now. In fact, there was the water ahead. Soon the birds saw a boat below. All they had to (dow) was follow the (oald) bird. He had traveled the path for many years.

Spelling Words
1. boat
2. cold
3. road
4. blow
5. gold
6. old
7. load
8. snow
9. hold
10. most
11. toe*
12. do*

blow (**1 point**) _____   do (**1**) _____

snow (**1**) _____   old (**1**) _____

✎ **Writing Sentences** Some birds fly thousands of miles to get to a warmer place. What would it be like to be one of those birds? Write about it on a separate sheet of paper. Use Spelling Words from the list.
Responses will vary. (**2**)

GRAMMAR: Plural Possessive Nouns

Practice/Homework Assign **Practice Book** page 58.

The rabbits' ears are floppy.

Practice Book page 58

The Great Ball Game
Grammar Skill Plural Possessive Nouns

Name _____

Nouns That Belong

► A plural noun usually ends in -s.
► A possessive plural noun shows that something belongs to more than one person, animal, or thing. These nouns usually end in -s'.
► Some plural nouns, such as **children** and **mice**, do not end in -s. To form the possessive, add -'s.

Rewrite each sentence. Use the correct possessive noun.

1. The [rabbits] ears are floppy.

The rabbits' ears are floppy. (**1 point**)

2. The [birds] babies are hungry.

The birds' babies are hungry. (**1**)

3. The [mice] cage is dirty.

The mice's cage is dirty. (**1**)

4. The [sheep] wool is soft.

The sheep's wool is soft. (**1**)

IMPROVING WRITING: Adding Details

❶ Teach

Writing Traits: Ideas Explain to children that it is important for news writers to include interesting details because readers want to understand exactly what happened. The more exact the details they give, the clearer the reader will be able to picture the events described.

Model how to add details.

- Write *There was a big game.*
- Explain that by adding details that tell who, where, when, why, and how, the writer can help readers picture this event.
- Write *Last Friday there was a big ball game in the field by the river.*
- Have children identify the details that have been added and what questions they answer.

❷ Practice

Write *The birds went away.*

- Have children copy the sentence and rewrite it by adding details that tell when, where, why, and how.
- Tell children they can rewrite the sentence so that it relates to *The Great Ball Game,* or create an original sentence.
- Have children share and discuss their new sentences.

❸ Apply

Assign Practice Book page 59. Then have children look at the newspaper articles they wrote to see if they can add details to help readers picture more clearly what happened.

Portfolio Opportunity

Save children's completed newspaper articles as examples of their writing development.

Practice Book page 59

The Great Ball Game
Writing Skill Writing a News Article

Name _____

Add Details to the Story

Read the news article. Rewrite sentences on the lines below. Add details that will make your sentences more interesting.

Zoo Opens New Snake House
The zoo opened a new snake house. People came to see it on Friday. Visitors found all kinds of snakes. A zookeeper fed the snakes. Mr. Diaz, the zoo manager, said, "People have always wanted to see bigger snakes. We were lucky to have a person donate the money for this exhibit." The zoo is open every day.

1. The zoo opened a new snake house.
   Answers will vary. **(1 point)**

2. People came to see it on Friday.
   (1)

3. Visitors found all kinds of snakes.
   (1)

4. A zookeeper fed the snakes.
   (1)

5. The zoo is open every day.
   _____

Day at a Glance
pp. T234–T239

Reading Instruction

Rereading for Understanding
and Fluency
Study Skill: Using Directions

• • • • • • • • • • • • • • • • • • •

Leveled Readers, *T240–T243*
- ● *Bird Race*
- ▲ *Turtle's Small Pond*
- ■ *Possum's Bare Tail*
- ◆ *A Race to the Mountain*

Word Work

Vocabulary Expansion
Word Wall
Spelling Test: More Long *o* Words

Writing & Oral Language

Writing Activity
Grammar: Improving Writing
Listening/Speaking/Viewing:
Giving Clear Directions

Daily Routines

Daily Message

Strategy Review Remind children of the Phonics/Decoding Strategy. Guide
them in applying it to selected words in today's message.

Good Morning, Class!
You can have fun with tongue
twisters. Here's one to
practice: The blind black
bat balanced on the
bamboo branch.

Ask children to read aloud the entire Daily Message. Point to each word as
they read.

Word Wall

Cumulative Review Review previously taught high-frequency words. Have
children choose two or more words and use them in a sentence. Then discuss
how some of the words are related. Illustrate how *idea* relates to *head*.
(Sample response: You get an idea in your head.) Continue the discussion
with the remaining word pairs. Have children draw pictures that illustrate
the relationships.

idea   head

listen   story

pull   climb

Vocabulary

Vocabulary Expansion Remind children that the birds in the story all have wings, and that the creatures called animals all have teeth. Point out that the animal team members also have fur, so they are all part of an animal group called *mammals*.

Have children tell what else they know about birds and mammals.

Record their ideas on word webs, such as the ones shown.

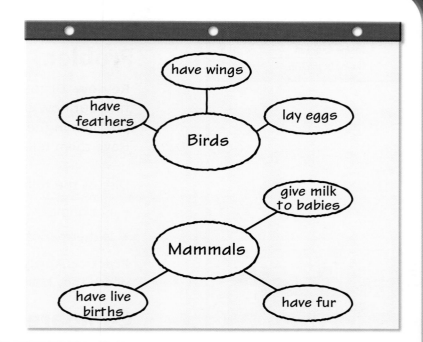

Daily Writing Prompt

Have children revise work they are currently writing, or have them use this prompt to begin a new writing activity.

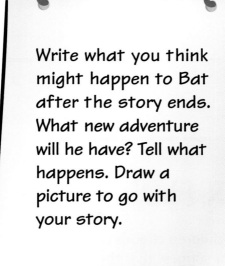

Write what you think might happen to Bat after the story ends. What new adventure will he have? Tell what happens. Draw a picture to go with your story.

Daily Language Practice

Grammar Skill: Plural Possessive Nouns
Spelling Skill: More Long o Words

Display **Transparency 4–20.** Ask children to rewrite Sentence 5 correctly. Then model how to write it, and have children check their work.

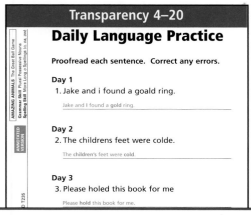

Transparency 4–20

Daily Language Practice

Proofread each sentence. Correct any errors.

Day 1
1. Jake and i found a goald ring.

   Jake and I found a **gold** ring.

Day 2
2. The childrens feet were colde.

   The **children's** feet were **cold.**

Day 3
3. Please holed this book for me.

   Please **hold** this book for me.

Day 5

5. I drew a picture of the twins bote.

   I drew a picture of the **twins' boat**.

Review Skill Trace	
Teach	Theme 3, pp. T220–T221
	Theme 2, pp. T66–T67
Reteach	Theme 3, p. R38
	Theme 2, p. R28
▶ Review	Theme 4, p. T236
	Theme 6, p. T84
	Theme 5, p. T146

COMPREHENSION: Rereading for Understanding

Problem Solving

Review Discuss the fact that readers often read stories in order to find out how characters solve a problem. Have children identify a problem in the story. (The Birds and Animals have a disagreement.) Have them tell how the characters try to solve the problem. (They have a ball game to decide which group is better.)
Discuss the following:

- Is a game a good way to settle a disagreement?
- Is there another way to solve the problem?

Practice/Apply Have children think about and discuss ways in which they have solved or attempted to solve problems.

Compare and Contrast

Review Point out that in this story children encounter two groups that are different in some ways and alike in others.

- Draw a Venn diagram with the labels Birds, Both, and Animals.
- Have children think of ways in which the Birds and the Animals are alike and different. Record their responses in the appropriate areas of the diagram. (Birds: have wings; Both: play ball; Animals: have teeth)

Practice/Apply Have children use the diagram to tell in their own words how the Birds and the Animals are alike and different.

REREADING FOR FLUENCY

Rereading the Selection Have children choose part of the story to reread orally in small groups, or suggest that they reread Anthology pages 94–96. If children are not reading with feeling and expression, model for them.

STUDY SKILL:
Using Directions

OBJECTIVES
- Read and restate directions.
- Follow written directions.

❶ Teach

Discuss directions. Tell children that directions tell how to do something. Then discuss these tips for using directions correctly.

⭐ Read all the directions.

⭐ Gather any materials you might need.

⭐ Follow the steps. Look for words, such as *first* and *last*.

⭐ Ask questions about anything you do not understand.

Display Transparency 4–28 and read the directions. Work with children to draw a cat's face.

❷ Practice/Apply

Have children answer questions about Transparency 4–28.

- How many steps are there? (5)

- What would happen if you left out a step? Could you follow the steps in a different order? If so, how? (Parts of the face would be missing; yes, draw the ears before the eyes and nose.)

Have children complete the assignable activity below.

Transparency 4–28

Using Directions

How to Draw a Cat Face

1. First, draw a large circle.

2. Second, draw two little circles for the eyes.

3. Next, draw a triangle for the nose.

4. Then draw two triangles on top of the circle for ears.

5. Last, draw lines on each side of the nose for whiskers.

TRANSPARENCY 4–28
TEACHER'S EDITION PAGE T237

AMAZING ANIMALS The Great Ball Game
Information and Study Skills Using Directions

ANNOTATED VERSION

Follow Directions

- Draw a house. First, draw a yellow square.

- Then draw a blue triangle for a roof.

- Next, draw a small red rectangle in the middle of the square for a door.

- Then, use a black crayon to draw two small squares on each side of the rectangle for windows.

OBJECTIVES

- Write spelling words with long *o* patterns.
- Proofread sentences for use of apostrophes to improve writing.

Transparency 4–29

AMAZING ANIMALS The Great Ball Game
Grammar Skill Improving Your Writing

ANNOTATED VERSION

Proofreading for Apostrophes

1. The Parents' Club made the children's costumes for The Great Ball Game.

2. Everyone was invited to the students' play.

3. They glued fur onto men's shirts to make the animal costumes.

4. The bird costumes were made of feathers and women's scarves.

5. The visitors' chairs were arranged in rows.

6. Before the play, the actors waited in the teachers' workroom.

7. The visitors were quiet so they could hear the actors' lines.

8. The birds' team stood on a table and pretended to fly.

9. Everyone on the animals' team crawled or walked on their knees.

10. At the end of the play, the actors were happy to hear their fans' applause.

TRANSPARENCY 4–29
TEACHER'S EDITION PAGE T238

Practice Book page 60

The Great Ball Game
Grammar Skill Plural Possessive Nouns

Name _____

More Than One

Mrs. Howard wrote a list of chores for her pet shop. She made some mistakes. Read the list. Decide whether an ' or an 's should be added to the animal name in each sentence. Rewrite the sentence.

Things to Do

1. Mix the dogs food in their bowls.

    Mix the dogs' food in their bowls. (1 point)

2. Clean out the cats boxes.

    Clean out the cats' boxes. (1)

3. Fill the mice water bottles.

    Fill the mice's water bottles. (1)

4. Get a helper to put the puppies toys in the pen.

    Get a helper to put the puppies' toys in the pen. (1)

5. Wash the walls of the fish tanks.

    Wash the walls of the fish's tanks. (1)

SPELLING: More Long *o* Words

Test

Say each underlined word, read the sentence, and then repeat the word. Have children write only the underlined word.

Basic Words

1. I want to sail the **boat**.
2. The lake is **cold**.
3. Do not walk in the **road**.
4. Wind can **blow** down a tree.
5. The crown is made of **gold**.
6. I like to fix **old** bikes.
7. She has a big **load** of books.
8. I wear boots in the **snow**.
9. Can you **hold** this for me?
10. I ate **most** of my beans.
11. She bumped her **toe**!
12. He must **do** the dishes.

Challenge Words

13. My **goal** is to read three books.
14. We saw a **rainbow** after the storm.

GRAMMAR: Improving Writing

Proofreading for Apostrophes

Teach Demonstrate how to proofread for apostrophes. Remind children that a noun that shows possession needs an apostrophe. Review the rules for placing apostrophes correctly. Display the first sentence on **Transparency 4–29.**

- Read the sentence, and guide children to place apostrophes in the words *Parents'* and *children's*.

- Repeat with the remaining sentences.

Have children proofread for apostrophes in a sample of their own writing.

Practice/Apply Assign **Practice Book** page 60.

LISTENING & SPEAKING:
Giving Clear Directions

❶ Teach

Explain the importance of giving clear directions.
Demonstrate by giving each direction below to volunteers. Ask the class to compare the two directions and the results.

- Move your feet and hands.

- Face the class and clap while you march in place. March for eight steps and stop.

Share these tips for giving clear directions.

⭐ Tell the purpose of the directions.

⭐ Tell exactly what the listener must do.

⭐ Tell each step in order. Use time-order words.

⭐ Use short, easy-to-understand sentences.

⭐ Include details and exact verbs to make each step clear.

❷ Practice

Have partners make up a simple routine. Ask children to write what to do to complete their routine. Suggest that children follow the directions to see if they make sense.

❸ Apply

Have partners complete the activity below.

Give Directions

- Together, teach the group the simple routine you practiced.

- Make sure everyone understands each step.

- Have the class follow your directions.

- Ask the class how to make your directions better.

OBJECTIVES

- Give clear directions.
- Listen to and repeat directions.

 English Language Learners
REACHING ALL LEARNERS

Using Direction Words

First, review direction words, such as *up*, *down*, *left*, and *forward*. Then describe simple actions, such as *step forward*. Have children mimic the actions. Next, give the same directions, but have children complete them without you as a model. Lastly, ask children to give directions for simple tasks, using direction words. Encourage the rest of the group to follow the directions.

LISTENING & SPEAKING

The Great Ball Game

Bird Race

Summary *In a race to a far-away meadow, Humming-Bird takes the lead over his friend Heron. Humming-Bird rests each night, while Heron continues to fly. Humming-Bird has to work hard to catch up the next day. After several days Heron reaches the meadow first. The birds realize that Humming-Bird is a faster flyer, but Heron has won the race. The friends fly home together.*

Vocabulary

Introduce the Key Vocabulary and ask children to complete the BLM.

tease to make fun of in a playful way, *p. 2*

catch up to come up from behind, *p. 6*

passed went by, *p. 7*

finally after a long while; at last, *p. 9*

Building Background and Vocabulary

Explain to children that this story is about what happens when Humming-Bird and Heron have a race. Ask children to talk about races they have seen or taken part in. Use some of the language of the book and key vocabulary as you guide children through the text.

Comprehension Skill: Cause and Effect

Have children read the Strategy Focus on the book flap. Remind children to use the strategy and to think about causes and effects as they read the book. (See the Leveled Readers Teacher's Guide for **Vocabulary and Comprehension Practice Masters.**)

Responding

Have partners discuss how to answer the questions on the inside back cover.

Think About What You Have Read Sample answers:

1. Heron and Humming-Bird
2. Heron keeps on flying.
3. Possible response: Yes. They could try a shorter race to see if Humming-Bird will win.

Making Connections Responses will vary.

Building Fluency

Model Read aloud pages 2–3. Ask a volunteer to read the part of Humming-Bird as you read the narration and Heron.

Practice Ask partners to read pages 11 and 12, practicing two-character dialogue.

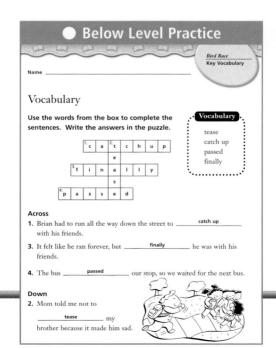

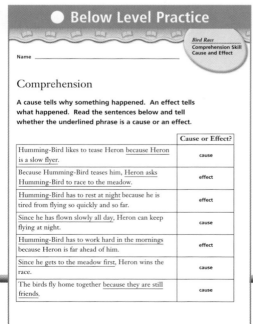

Turtle's Small Pond

Summary *Turtle thinks that he has the best pond in the world. One spring he finds that his pond has been changed by the dam built by Beaver. The two decide to have a race across the pond to decide who will stay. Although Turtle wins with a clever trick, the two decide to share the pond. Together they have the best pond in the world.*

Vocabulary

Introduce the Key Vocabulary and ask children to complete the BLM.

quarreled* had a disagreement, *p. 6*

argument* a disagreement, *p. 6*

contest competition, usually for a prize, *p. 7*

advantage* something that gives a benefit; something helpful, *p. 8*

mighty having or showing great power, strength, or force, *p. 14*

*Forms of these words are Anthology Key Vocabulary words.

Building Background and Vocabulary

Explain to children that this story is about what happens when Turtle and Beaver have a race to decide who gets to live in the pond. Ask children to talk strategies they know to win races. Use some of the language of the book and key vocabulary as you guide children through the text.

Comprehension Skill: Cause and Effect

Have children read the Strategy Focus on the book flap. Remind children to use the strategy and to think about causes and effects as they read the book. (See the Leveled Readers Teacher's Guide for **Vocabulary and Comprehension Practice Masters.**)

Responding

Have partners discuss how to answer the questions on the inside back cover.

Think About What You Have Read Sample answers:

1. He discovers that Beaver built a dam that has changed the pond.
2. They want to decide who can live at the pond.
3. They talk about an underwater contest, a wood-chopping contest, and a swimming contest.
4. Possible response: No. The contest was to swim across the pond, and Turtle cheated by holding on to Beaver's tail.

Making Connections Responses will vary.

Building Fluency

Model Read aloud page 5. Emphasize the sentence with the exclamation point.

Practice Have children read aloud pages 10, 14, and 15 to practice emphasizing sentences with exclamation points.

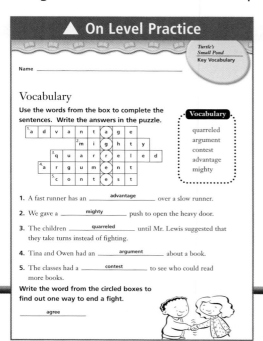

▲ On Level Practice

Turtle's Small Pond Key Vocabulary

Name _____

Vocabulary

Use the words from the box to complete the sentences. Write the answers in the puzzle.

Vocabulary
quarreled
argument
contest
advantage
mighty

1. A fast runner has an ___advantage___ over a slow runner.
2. We gave a ___mighty___ push to open the heavy door.
3. The children ___quarreled___ until Mr. Lewis suggested that they take turns instead of fighting.
4. Tina and Owen had an ___argument___ about a book.
5. The classes had a ___contest___ to see who could read more books.

Write the word from the circled boxes to find out one way to end a fight.
___agree___

▲ On Level Practice

Turtle's Small Pond Comprehension Skill Cause and Effect

Name _____

Comprehension

Read these sentences. Draw a line under the cause. Circle the effect.

1. Turtle swims slowly because he has short legs.
2. When winter comes, Turtle digs a hole in the mud and sleeps all winter.
3. Turtle could win an underwater race because he can hold his breath for a long time.
4. Because Beaver needs wood to make a dam, he cuts down trees with his teeth.
5. The pond is deeper in the spring because Beaver has made a dam.
6. Since he has long, sharp front teeth, Beaver would win a wood chopping contest.

Possum's Bare Tail

Summary
This Cherokee folktale tells how Possum got his bare tail. Possum is quite vain about his thick, shiny, beautiful tail and he loves to brag about it to everyone. Rabbit gets tired of hearing Possum brag and decides to teach Possum a lesson. Rabbit gets Cricket to give Possum's tail a special shampooing —which leaves Possum's tail bare. Possum does indeed learn a lesson.

Vocabulary

Introduce the Key Vocabulary and ask children to complete the BLM.

groom to clean and brush, *p. 3*

vain showing too much pride, *p. 5*

accept* to agree to, *p. 6*

ashamed felt guilty or embarrassed, *p. 15*

humiliation the state of being disgraced or embarrassed in a very public way, *p. 16*

*Forms of these words are Anthology Key Vocabulary words.

■ ABOVE LEVEL

Building Background and Vocabulary

Explain to children that this story is about how Possum got his bare tail and learned a lesson about bragging. Use some of the language of the book and key vocabulary as you guide children through the text.

Comprehension Skill: Cause and Effect

Have children read the Strategy Focus on the book flap. Remind children to use the strategy and to think about causes and effects as they read the book. (See the Leveled Readers Teacher's Guide for **Vocabulary and Comprehension Practice Masters.**)

Responding

Have partners discuss how to answer the questions on the inside back cover.

Think About What You Have Read . Sample answers:

1. He is very proud of his beautiful tail.
2. Rabbit has Cricket use a special shampoo on Possum's tail. The shampoo causes Possum to lose all the fur on his tail.
3. Possible response: Rabbit's plan is clever.
4. Possum played dead for the rest of the party, so that the guests would not pay any more attention to him.

Making Connections Responses will vary.

Building Fluency

Model Read aloud pages 2–3. Define page 2 as an introduction and show how to transition to the body of the tale.

Practice Ask partners to read aloud pages 15 and 16, having them practice the transition from the story to its conclusion.

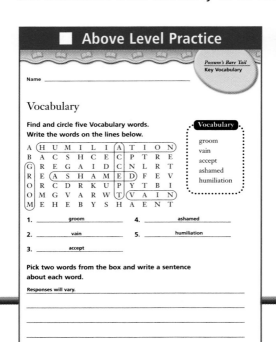

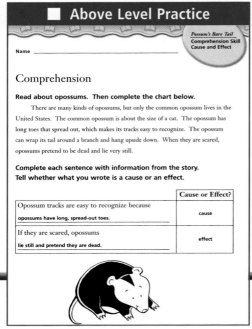

Leveled Readers

A Race to the Mountain

Summary *Hummingbird and Heron have a race to see who can arrive first at a far-off field near a mountain. Hummingbird is a fast flyer, and Heron flies slowly. But Hummingbird has to rest each night, and Heron makes up for lost time. In the end, slow and steady Heron wins the race.*

Vocabulary

Introduce the Key Vocabulary and ask children to complete the BLM.

fly to travel through the air, *p. 2*

fast quick, *p. 2*

slowly with little speed, *p. 2*

race a contest to find out who is the fastest, *p. 2*

passed moved on; left someone or something behind, *p. 5*

won came in first; was the best in a contest or race, *p. 11*

◆ LANGUAGE SUPPORT

Building Background and Vocabulary

Read and discuss the phrase *Slow and steady wins the race*. Encourage children to share what they know about the phrase. You may want to choose volunteers to act out the phrase under your direction. Distribute **Build Background Practice Master** and have children use it to make character puppets.

Comprehension Skill: Cause and Effect

Have children read the Strategy Focus on the book flap. Remind children to use the strategy and to notice why things happen as they read the book. (See the Leveled Readers Teacher's Guide for **Build Background, Vocabulary,** and **Graphic Organizer Masters.**)

Responding

Have partners discuss how to answer the questions on the inside back cover.

Think About What You Have Read Sample answers:

1. Hummingbird slept at night.
2. Hummingbird had to fly very fast in the day because Heron kept flying while Hummingbird slept at night
3. Answers will vary.

Making Connections Responses will vary.

Building Fluency

Model Have children follow along in their books as they listen to pages 2–3 of the recording on the audio CD.

Practice Have students read aloud with the recording until they are able to read the text on their own accurately and with expression. If children made the puppets on the **Build Background Practice Master,** have small groups read and act out a scene with their puppets.

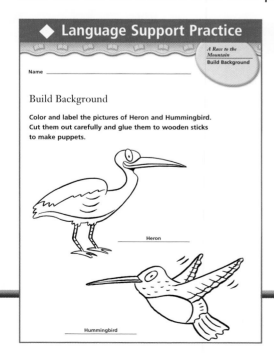

Connecting and Comparing Literature

Check Your Progress

Use these Paired Selections to help students make connections with other theme literature and to wrap up the theme.

Little Grunt and the Big Egg
Genre: Fantasy

Little Grunt and his family adopt George, a baby dinosaur who grows so big that he no longer fits in the family cave. The Grunts send George away, but he returns in time to rescue them from an erupting volcano.

Mighty Dinosaurs
Genre: Nonfiction

Dinosaurs were giant lizards that lived millions of years ago. They came in many different shapes and sizes, and scientists study their fossils to learn more about them.

OVERVIEW

Preparing for Tests

Skill Review

Use these lessons and supporting activities to review tested skills in this theme.

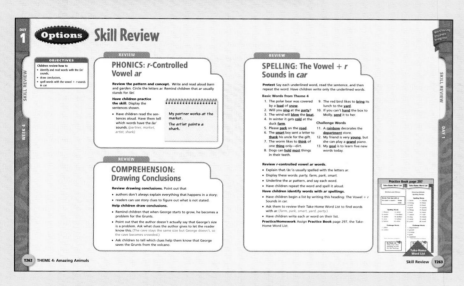

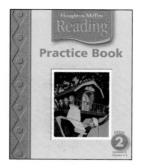

• Independent
  practice for skills

• Charts/
  Transparencies
• Strategy Posters
• Blackline Masters

Taking Tests: Strategies

Use this material to prepare for tests, to teach strategies, and to practice test formats.

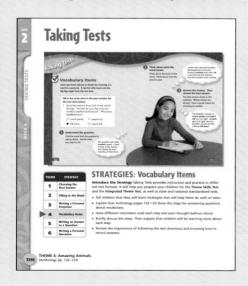

Technology

Audio Selections
Little Grunt and the Big Egg

Mighty Dinosaurs

www.eduplace.com
Log on to Education
Place® for vocabulary
support—
  e•Glossary
  e•WordGame

Theme Wrap-Up Overview   T245

Theme Connections

Anthology Literature

Activities to help students think critically

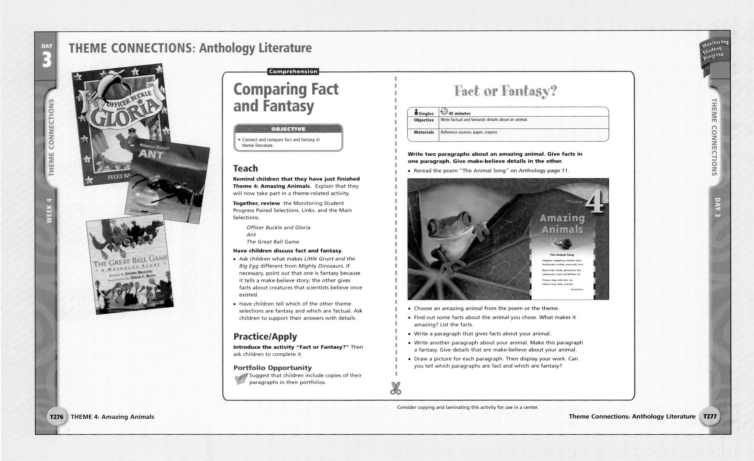

THEME CONNECTIONS: Anthology Literature

DAY 3

Comprehension

Comparing Fact and Fantasy

OBJECTIVE
• Connect and compare fact and fantasy in theme literature.

Teach

Remind children that they have just finished **Theme 4: Amazing Animals.** Explain that they will now take part in a theme-related activity.

Together, review the Monitoring Student Progress Paired Selections, Links, and the Main Selections.

Officer Buckle and Gloria
Ant
The Great Ball Game

Have children discuss fact and fantasy.
• Ask children what makes *Little Grunt and the Big Egg* different from *Mighty Dinosaurs.* If necessary, point out that one is fantasy because it tells a make-believe story; the other gives facts about creatures that scientists believe once existed.
• Have children tell which of the other theme selections are fantasy and which are factual. Ask children to support their answers with details.

Practice/Apply

Introduce the activity "Fact or Fantasy?" Then ask children to complete it.

Portfolio Opportunity
Suggest that children include copies of their paragraphs in their portfolios.

Fact or Fantasy?

Singles	45 minutes	
Objective	Write factual and fantastic details about an animal.	
Materials	Reference sources, paper, crayons	

Write two paragraphs about an amazing animal. Give facts in one paragraph. Give make-believe details in the other.

• Reread the poem "The Animal Song" on Anthology page 11.

theme **4**
Amazing Animals

The Animal Song

• Choose an amazing animal from the poem or the theme.
• Find out some facts about the animal you chose. What makes it amazing? List the facts.
• Write a paragraph that gives facts about your animal.
• Write another paragraph about your animal. Make this paragraph a fantasy. Give details that are make-believe about your animal.
• Draw a picture for each paragraph. Then display your work. Can you tell which paragraphs are fact and which are fantasy?

Consider copying and laminating this activity for use in a center.

T276 THEME 4: Amazing Animals

Theme Connections: Anthology Literature T277

THEME CONNECTIONS

DAY 3

Three Main Selections

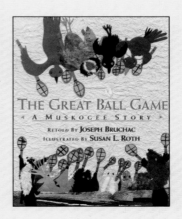

Leveled Books

...ctivities to help students connect and compare

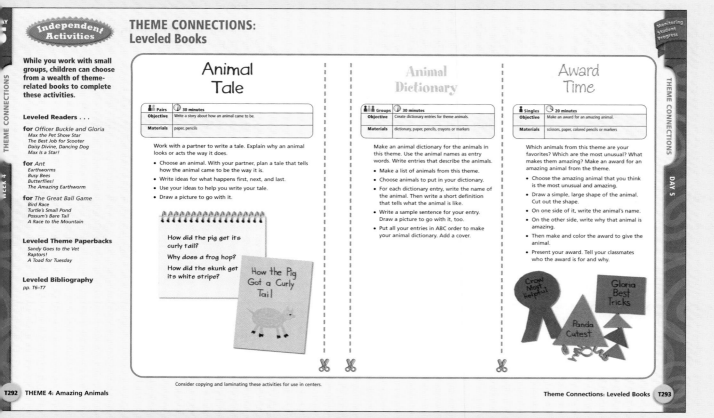

Independent Activities

While you work with small groups, children can choose from a wealth of theme-related books to complete these activities.

Leveled Readers . . .

for *Officer Buckle and Gloria*
Max the Pet Show Star
The Best Job for Scooter
Daisy Divine, Dancing Dog
Max Is a Star!

for *Ant*
Earthworms
Busy Bees
Butterflies!
The Amazing Earthworm

for *The Great Ball Game*
Bird Race
Turtle's Small Pond
Possum's Bare Tail
A Race to the Mountain

Leveled Theme Paperbacks
Sandy Goes to the Vet
Raptors!
A Toad for Tuesday

Leveled Bibliography
pp. T6–T7

THEME CONNECTIONS:
Leveled Books

Animal Tale

👥 Pairs	🕑 30 minutes
Objective	Write a story about how an animal came to be.
Materials	paper, pencils

Work with a partner to write a tale. Explain why an animal looks or acts the way it does.

- Choose an animal. With your partner, plan a tale that tells how the animal came to be the way it is.
- Write ideas for what happens first, next, and last.
- Use your ideas to help you write your tale.
- Draw a picture to go with it.

How did the pig get its curly tail?

Why does a frog hop?

How did the skunk get its white stripe?

How the Pig Got a Curly Tail

Animal Dictionary

👥 Groups	🕑 30 minutes
Objective	Create dictionary entries for theme animals.
Materials	dictionary, paper, pencils, crayons or markers

Make an animal dictionary for the animals in this theme. Use the animal names as entry words. Write entries that describe the animals.

- Make a list of animals from this theme.
- Choose animals to put in your dictionary.
- For each dictionary entry, write the name of the animal. Then write a short definition that tells what the animal is like.
- Write a sample sentence for your entry. Draw a picture to go with it, too.
- Put all your entries in ABC order to make your animal dictionary. Add a cover.

Award Time

👤 Singles	🕑 20 minutes
Objective	Make an award for an amazing animal.
Materials	scissors, paper, colored pencils or markers

Which animals from this theme are your favorites? Which are the most unusual? What makes them amazing? Make an award for an amazing animal from the theme.

- Choose the amazing animal that you think is the most unusual and amazing.
- Draw a simple, large shape of the animal. Cut out the shape.
- On one side of it, write the animal's name.
- On the other side, write why that animal is amazing.
- Then make and color the award to give the animal.
- Present your award. Tell your classmates who the award is for and why.

Crow Most Helpful

Panda Cutest

Gloria Best Tricks

Consider copying and laminating these activities for use in centers.

THEME CONNECTIONS   WEEK 4   THEME CONNECTIONS   DAY 5

...welve Leveled Readers

The Best Job for Scooter

Max the Pet Show Star

Max Is a Star!

Butterflies!

Busy

THE AMAZING EARTHWORM

Possum's Bare Tail

TURTLES SMALL POND

BIRD

A Race to the Mountain

Three Leveled Theme Paperbacks

Sandy Goes to the Vet
by Becky Cheston
illustrated by Kathryn Mitter

Houghton Mifflin

RAPTORS!
Written by Lisa McCourt
Illustrated by Marsha Popović

RUSSELL E. ERICKSON
A Toad for Tuesday
"A small-scale *Wind in the Willows* adventure and charm." —ALA Booklist

Daily Lesson Plans

Technology

Lesson Planner CD-ROM allows you to customize the chart below to develop your own lesson plans.

T Skill tested on Theme Skills Test and/or Integrated Theme Test

---

 60–80 minutes

Connecting and Comparing Literature

CHECK YOUR PROGRESS

Leveled Readers
- Fluency Practice
- Independent Reading

 60–80 minutes

Preparing for Tests

TAKING TESTS: Strategies

SKILL REVIEW OPTIONS

High-Frequency Words

Phonics

Comprehension

Vocabulary

Grammar

Spelling

Prompts for Writing

DAY 1

Daily Routines, T252–T253

Introducing Paired Selections

Key Vocabulary, T255

disaster	lava
earthquake	pitch
erupting	volcano

Reading the Selection, T256–T261
Little Grunt and the Big Egg

Comprehension Strategy, T256
Question T

Stop and Think, T261

Connecting and Comparing
Drawing Conclusions, T257
Cause and Effect, T259
Problem Solving, T261

Leveled Readers
Max the Pet Show Star
The Best Job for Scooter
Daisy Divine, Dancing Dog
Max Is a Star!

High-Frequency Words, T252 T

Phonics, T262
r-Controlled Vowel *ar* T

Comprehension, T262
Drawing Conclusions T

Spelling, T263
The Vowel + *r* Sounds in *car* T

Prompts for Writing, T253
An Invitation
Writing Times T

DAY 2

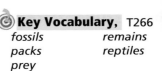

Daily Routines, T264–T265

Key Vocabulary, T266

fossils	remains
packs	reptiles
prey	

Reading the Selection, T267–T269
Mighty Dinosaurs

Think and Compare, T269

Connecting and Comparing
Text Organization, T267

Leveled Readers
Earthworms
Busy Bees
Butterflies!
The Amazing Earthworm

Vocabulary Items, T270
Introduce the Strategy.

High-Frequency Words, T264 T

Phonics, T271
r-Controlled Vowels *or, ore* T
Words with *nd, nt, mp, ng, nk* T

Vocabulary, T272
Dictionary Entry Words T

Grammar, T272
Words for Nouns T

Spelling, T273
Words That End with *nd, ng,* or *nk* T

Prompts for Writing, T265
A Poem
Using *I* and *me* T

Target Skills of the Week

Phonics
Comprehension
Vocabulary
Fluency

Monitoring
Student
Progress

DAILY LESSON PLANS

DAY 3

Daily Routines, T274–T275

Theme Connections: Anthology Literature, T276–T277
Comparing Fact and Fantasy

Rereading for Fluency, T280
Little Grunt and the Big Egg

Classroom Management Activities, T250–T251

Leveled Readers
Bird Race
Turtle's Small Pond
Possum's Bare Tail
A Race to the Mountain

Vocabulary Items, T278
Understand the Question.
Think About What the Word Means.

High-Frequency Words, T274 **T**

Phonics, T279
Base Words and Endings *-s, -es, -ies* **T**

Comprehension, T280
Text Organization **T**

Vocabulary, T281
Using a Thesaurus **T**

Spelling, T281
Spelling Game

Prompts for Writing, T275
News Article

DAY 4

Daily Routines, T282–T283

Theme Connections: Anthology Literature, T284–T285
Comparing Authors' Viewpoints

Rereading for Fluency, T288
Mighty Dinosaurs

Classroom Management Activities, T250–T251

Leveled Readers
Choose from among the Leveled Readers for the theme.

Vocabulary Items, T286
Narrow the Choices.
Then Choose the Best Answer.

High-Frequency Words, T282 **T**

Phonics, T287
Vowel Pairs *oa, ow* **T**

Vocabulary, T288
Parts of a Dictionary Entry **T**

Grammar, T289
Singular Possessive Nouns **T**

Spelling, T289
More Long *o* Words **T**

Prompts for Writing, T283
Taking Notes for a Research Report

DAY 5

Daily Routines, T290–T291

Theme Connections: Leveled Books, T292–T293

Rereading for Fluency, T296
Selected Stories from Theme 4
Phonics Library

Classroom Management Activities, T250–T251

Leveled Readers
Choose from among the Leveled Readers for the theme.

Vocabulary Items, T294
Test Practice

High-Frequency Words, T290 **T**

Phonics, T295
Cumulative Review **T**

Comprehension, T296
Cause and Effect **T**

Grammar, T297
Plural Possessive Nouns **T**

Spelling, T297
Test

Prompts for Writing, T291
Research Report **T**

Classroom Management

Independent Activities

Assign these activities anytime during the week while you work with small groups.

Suggest that children include copies of their work in their portfolios.

Look for more activities in the **Classroom Management Kit.**

Science Center

Dinosaur Facts

👥 **Pairs**	🕐 **30 minutes**
Objective	Use dinosaur facts to identify a dinosaur.
Materials	writing paper

Use facts from *Mighty Dinosaurs* to figure out what kind of dinosaur George was.

- How are meat eaters different from plant eaters? Make a list of dinosaur facts about meat eaters. Then make a list about plant eaters.

- Think about George. What did he eat? What did he look like? Write sentences that describe George.

- What kind of dinosaur do you think George is? Write a paragraph to tell why.

Folktale Center

Another Game

👤 **Singles**	🕐 **20 minutes**
Objective	Write a new folktale ending.
Materials	writing and drawing paper, crayons or markers

Imagine that George plays on a team in *The Great Ball Game*. Think how the ending might change.

- Decide whether George plays with the Birds or the Animals. Think about how he helps his team win. How does he use his neck and tail? Does his size help the team?

- Write a new story ending. Explain what happens when George plays.

- Draw a picture that shows George playing the game.

George stretches his long neck and gets the ball.

Consider copying and laminating these activities for use in centers.

Technology Center

Animal Research

Groups	🕐 45 minutes
Objective	Use the Internet or an encyclopedia to do animal research.
Materials	computer, encyclopedia, writing paper, scissors, crayons, glue

Choose an amazing animal that was not in this theme. Use the Internet or an encyclopedia to find out about that animal.

- Log on to the Internet. Type the animal name. Click on a site.
- Read about the animal. What makes it amazing? Take notes about what you find out.
- Print a picture of the animal, or draw your own. Then write about the animal. Tell what you learned.

Worker bees get nectar and make it into honey. They build and take care of the nests.

Language Arts Center

Word Search

🧍 Singles	🕐 30 minutes
Objective	Create a word search puzzle.
Materials	graph paper

Make a word search. Use amazing animal words.

- Look for ten important words about amazing animals in the theme selections. Write the words to make a Word Bank for your puzzle.
- Then write the words on the graph paper. Write some up and down. Write some across. Put one letter in each box.
- Fill in the puzzle with other letters. Put one letter in each box until your puzzle is full.
- Trade puzzles with a partner. Find and circle all the words in the Word Box. Can you figure out what stories the words are from?

Art Center

Create an Amazing Animal

🧍🧍 Pairs	🕐 20 minutes
Objective	Create a unique animal.
Materials	coffee can, colored paper, yarn, material scraps, crayons, markers, glue

Create your own *really* amazing animal!

- Think about the animals in this theme. What are their best features? What helps the animals survive?
- Create your own animal that has the best of everything. Give your animal the best features of each animal in the theme.
- Make your animal out of a tin can. Use scraps of paper, yarn, crayons, and other materials to create it. Then give your animal a name.
- Share your amazing animal. Tell what makes it special.

DAY 1
week 4

Day at a Glance
pp. T252–T263

Reading Instruction

Introduction

Key Vocabulary

Reading
Little Grunt and the Big Egg

Stop and Think

Connecting and Comparing
Drawing Conclusions
Cause and Effect
Problem Solving

Skill Review Options

High-Frequency Words

Phonics
r-Controlled Vowel *ar*

Comprehension
Drawing Conclusions

Spelling
The Vowel + *r* Sounds in *car*

Prompts for Writing
An Invitation
Writing Times

Daily Routines

Daily Message

Phonics Review Point to each word as you read aloud the Daily Message.

Near and far, on farms and in cities, animals can be everywhere. Do rabbits live in your backyard? Have you seen toads in your garden? What other animals do you see near your home?

Have children
- read aloud the Daily Message and discuss the questions,
- find, read, and circle words with the /är/ sounds. (*far, farms, backyard, garden*)

Word Wall

High-Frequency Word Review Review these high-frequency words and their meanings. For each word, have children make up a question that the word answers.

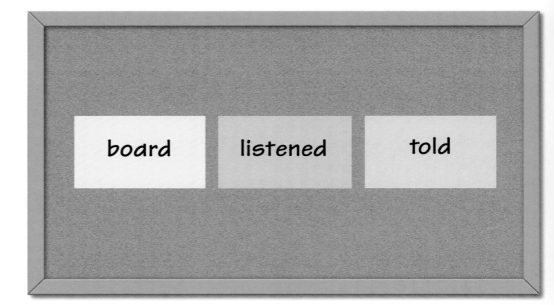

board   listened   told

Vocabulary

Vocabulary Expansion Create a word web for *Pet*.

- Ask children to name kinds of pets, and record their responses.
Have children discuss pets they have had or known.
Ask children to complete and illustrate this sentence:

If I could have any pet at all, it would be ___.

If I could have any pet at all, it would be <u>an elephant.</u>

Daily Writing Prompt

An Invitation Use this prompt to review how to write an invitation. Remind children to write the time of the event correctly as *A.M.*, *P.M.*, or *o'clock*.

This weekend a dog show is coming to Boxer Park. Big dogs perform in the morning, and little dogs star in the afternoon. Write an invitation to a friend. Ask the friend to go to the dog show with you.

Connecting and Comparing Literature

Theme Wrap-Up

Check Your Progress

What made the animals in this theme amazing to you? Get ready to read and compare two more selections about amazing animals. Then practice some test–taking skills.

On pages 12–14, Joseph Bruchac describes how much fun it is to watch animals. What would you tell him about the animals in this theme?

Think about what makes the animals amazing in the next two selections. How do they compare with the other amazing animals in this theme?

116

Read and Compare

Little Grunt and the Big Egg A Prehistoric Fairy Tale · Tomie dePaola

Find out what happens when a boy finds the biggest egg he has ever seen.

Try these strategies:
Predict and Infer
Summarize

Mighty Dinosaurs

Discover facts about dinosaurs that lived on earth millions of years ago.

Try these strategies:
Monitor and Clarify
Question

Strategies in Action *Be sure to use all your reading strategies as you read these selections.*

117

Use Paired Selections: Check Your Progress

Have children read page 116. Ask:

• Which animal in this theme do you think was the most amazing? Why? (Responses will vary.)

Have children read page 117. Ask:

• How do you think the story about Little Grunt will be like other theme selections? (Sample response: The egg will hatch into another amazing animal.)

• How might *Mighty Dinosaurs* be like the other selections in this theme? (Sample response: It will give facts about an amazing animal, like *Ant*.)

Strategies in Action Remind children to use all their reading strategies as they read these Paired Selections.

THEME 4: Amazing Animals
(Anthology pp. 116–117)

Transparency 4–30

AMAZING ANIMALS *Little Grunt and the Big Egg*
Monitoring Student Progress Key Vocabulary
ANNOTATED VERSION

Volcano Words

The floor began to <u>pitch</u> and shake under Lana's feet. It moved up and down.

"The ground is shaking!" she yelled. "Are we having an <u>earthquake</u>?"

"No," Lana's father said. "Mount San is <u>erupting</u>. You can see the clouds of gas and ashes bursting out of the mountain and flying up into the night sky." The two stared at the amazing sight.

"Well, scientists have been warning us that the <u>volcano</u> was ready to start erupting," noted Lana. "Look at the bright orange glow. Is that hot <u>lava</u> flowing out of the volcano and down its sides?"

"Yes it is," Dad replied. "The ashes and lava will completely destroy everything near the volcano. That would be a real <u>disaster</u> if anyone lived nearby. Luckily, no one does!"

TRANSPARENCY 4–30
TEACHER'S EDITION PAGE T255

Selection 1

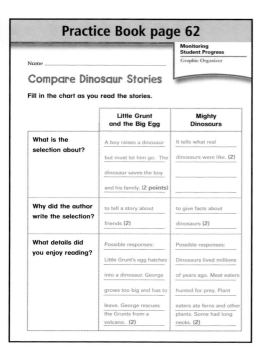

Little Grunt and the Big Egg

A Prehistoric Fairy Tale

Tomie dePaola

Introducing Vocabulary

Key Vocabulary
These words appear in the selection.

disaster something that causes damage or destruction

earthquake a shaking of the ground

erupting bursting out

lava melted rock that flows from a volcano

pitch to rise and fall

volcano an opening in the earth that spews out lava, ash, and hot gases

e • **Glossary**
e • **WordGame**

See Vocabulary notes on pages T256–T260 for additional words to preview.

Use Transparency 4–30.

- Read aloud the first paragraph on the transparency.

- Model how to use context clues to figure out what *pitch* means.

- Help children use context clues to figure out the meanings of the other Key Vocabulary words. Ask how children figured out each meaning.

Practice/Homework Assign **Practice Book** page 61.

Introduce the Graphic Organizer. Tell children to fill in **Practice Book** page 62 as they read the Paired Selections.

Word Key

Vocabulary Words

Practice Book page 61

Name _____

Monitoring Student Progress
Key Vocabulary

Volcano Words

Use a word from the box to complete each sentence. Write the word in the puzzle.

Vocabulary

disaster pitch earthquake volcano erupting lava

Across
3. The ground shakes during an ____. (2 points)
4. Something that's ____ shoots out rocks or gas. (2)
6. A ____ is a mountain that shoots out melted rock and ash. (2)

Down
1. If there is a ____, there is usually a lot of damage. (2)
2. Hot, melted rock is called ____. (2)
5. When something begins to ____, it begins to move up and down. (2)

Crossword: 3-across EARTHQUAKE, 4-across ERUPTING, 6-across VOLCANO; with DISASTER down at d-i-s-a-s-t-e-r, LAVA, PITCH

Practice Book page 62

Name _____

Monitoring Student Progress
Graphic Organizer

Compare Dinosaur Stories

Fill in the chart as you read the stories.

	Little Grunt and the Big Egg	Mighty Dinosaurs
What is the selection about?	A boy raises a dinosaur but must let him go. The dinosaur saves the boy and his family. **(2 points)**	It tells what real dinosaurs were like. **(2)**
Why did the author write the selection?	to tell a story about friends **(2)**	to give facts about dinosaurs **(2)**
What details did you enjoy reading?	Possible responses: Little Grunt's egg hatches into a dinosaur. George grows too big and has to leave. George rescues the Grunts from a volcano. **(2)**	Possible responses: Dinosaurs lived millions of years ago. Meat eaters hunted for prey. Plant eaters ate ferns and other plants. Some had long necks. **(2)**

Reading the Paired Selections **T255**

Little Grunt and the Big Egg

written and illustrated by Tomie dePaola

Little Grunt and his family live in a mountain cave. One day Little Grunt brings home the biggest egg he has ever seen. The whole family is surprised when the egg hatches into a baby dinosaur. The Grunts agree to let Little Grunt keep the dinosaur as a pet.

"I'm going to call him George," said Little Grunt. Little Grunt and George became great pals.

But there was a problem. The cave stayed the same size, but George didn't. He began to grow.

1

118

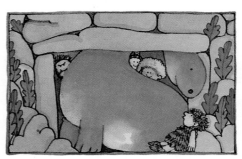

And GROW.
And GROW.
The cave got very crowded.

And there were other problems.

George wasn't housebroken.

George ate ALL the leaves off ALL the trees and ALL the bushes ALL around the cave. But still he was hungry.

George liked to play — rough. George stepped on things. And when he sneezed — well, it was a disaster.

2

119

TARGET SKILL

COMPREHENSION STRATEGY

Question

Teacher Modeling: Remind children that thinking of questions about important story details can help them check their understanding of the story. Have someone read aloud page 118. Then model the strategy.

Think Aloud *I know that most stories have a problem, so I ask, "What is the story problem?" When I answer that George grows to be too big for the cave, it helps me understand the story.*

CRITICAL THINKING

Guiding Comprehension

1 **STORY STRUCTURE** What is the problem at the beginning of the story? (Sample response: George grows too big to live in the cave and be a pet.)

2 **DRAWING CONCLUSIONS** How do the grownup Grunts feel about George? (Sample response: angry, upset; he's too big, isn't housebroken, and breaks things.)

THEME 4: Amazing Animals
(Anthology pp. 118–119)

Vocabulary

disaster something that causes damage or destruction

REACHING ALL LEARNERS

Extra Support/Intervention

Preview the selection.

pages 118–120 How can you tell that George, the dinosaur, and the boy, Little Grunt, are friends? Do you think Little Grunt's family likes George? Why or why not?

pages 121–123 Chief Rockhead Grunt decides that George is causing too many problems. How do you think Little Grunt feels about having to send him away?

pages 124–125 Why do you think Granny is pointing to the volcano nearby? What might be happening?

page 126 Why is everyone climbing on George?

"Ooga, ooga! Enough is enough!" said the Grunts.

"Either that dinosaur goes, or I go," said Unca Grunt.

"I spend all day getting food for him," said Ant Grunt.

"Achoo!" said Papa Grunt. "I told you I was allergic to him."

"He stepped on all my cooking pots and broke them," said Mama Grunt.

"I guess it wasn't a good idea to keep him," said Granny Grunt. "How about a nice *little* cockroach. They make nice pets."

"I'm in charge here," said Chief Rockhead Grunt. "And I say, *That giant lizard goes!*"

"Ooga, ooga! Yes! Yes!" said all the Grunts.

"But you promised," said Little Grunt.

120

121

Connecting and Comparing

Drawing Conclusions

- How do Little Grunt and Officer Buckle from *Officer Buckle and Gloria* feel about their animal pals? Explain. (Sample responses: They both love their pals. Little Grunt feeds George leaves and cuddles with him. Officer Buckle takes Gloria for ice cream and hugs her.)

- In what ways are George and Bat from *The Great Ball Game* alike? (Sample responses: Both want to fit in with other characters; both help their friends.)

Vocabulary

allergic having a bad reaction to something, such as food or animal hair

Challenge

Additional Reading

Other Books by Tomie dePaola Children may be interested in reading other stories written by Tomie dePaola, including *Strega Nona: Her Story* and *Tony's Bread*. To learn more about the author, visit *Education Place*®. **www.eduplace.com/kids**

Reading the Paired Selections
(Anthology pp. 120–121)

T257

The next morning, Little Grunt took George away from the cave, out to where he had found him in the first place.

"Good-bye, George," said Little Grunt. "I'll sure miss you."

"Waaargh," said George.

3 Big tears rolled down both their cheeks. Sadly, Little Grunt watched as George walked slowly into the swamp.

"I'll never see him again," sobbed Little Grunt.

122

The days and months went by, and Little Grunt still missed George. He dreamed about him at night and drew pictures of him by day.

"Little Grunt certainly misses that dinosaur," said Mama Grunt.

"He'll get over it," said Papa Grunt.

"It's nice and peaceful here again," said Ant and Unca Grunt.

"I still say a cockroach makes a nice pet," said Granny Grunt.

"Ooga, ooga. Torches out. Everyone in bed," said Chief Rockhead.

123

CRITICAL THINKING
Guiding Comprehension

3 DRAWING CONCLUSIONS Why do tears roll down Little Grunt's and George's cheeks? (Possible response: They're sad because they'll never see each other again.)

4 CAUSE AND EFFECT What effect does the erupting volcano have on the Grunt family? (Sample response: They're very upset; they realize they can't escape the lava.)

5 PREDICTING OUTCOMES What do you think will happen? (George will probably help the Grunts.)

 READING STRATEGY
Phonics/Decoding

Teacher/Student Modeling Write *Grunt*. Underline the *nt*. Remind children to say the sound of both *n* and *t*. Have children read *Grunt*. Repeat with *found, swamp,* and *wonk*.

THEME 4: Amazing Animals
(Anthology pp. 122–123)

T258

Vocabulary

swamp muddy land that is often filled with water

 English Language Learners

Language Support

Read aloud the first sentence on page 123. Explain that the phrase *the days and months went by* shows the passing of time from one month to the next. Then discuss the meaning of *He'll get over it*. Point out that the Grunts meant that Little Grunt would stop missing George.

That night, the cave started to shake. The floor began to pitch, and loud rumblings filled the air.

"Earthquake!" cried the Grunts, and they rushed to the opening of the cave.

"No, it's not," said Granny Grunt. "Look! Volcano!"

And sure enough, the big volcano was erupting all over the place. Steam and rocks and black smoke shot out of the top. Around the cave, big rocks and boulders tumbled and bounced.

124

"We're trapped! We're trapped!" shouted the Grunts. "What are we going to do?"

"Don't ask me!" said Chief Rockhead. "I resign."

"Now we have no leader," cried Ant Grunt.

"Now we're really in trouble!" shouted Papa Grunt.

The lava was pouring out of the volcano in a wide, flaming river and was heading straight for the cave.

There wasn't enough time for the Grunts to escape. ❹
All of a sudden, the Grunts heard a different noise. ❺
"Waaargh! Wonk!"

125

Connecting and Comparing

Cause and Effect

- Why do George in *Little Grunt and the Big Egg* and Gloria in *Officer Buckle and Gloria* both feel sad? (Sample response: They miss their buddies or pals.)

- What problem do the Grunts have? How is this like problems faced by other theme characters? (Possible response: The Grunts are in danger because of the volcano. The children in *Officer Buckle and Gloria* are in trouble because they don't follow Officer Buckle's safety tips.)

COMPREHENSION STRATEGY

Question

Teacher/Student Modeling: Remind children that asking questions helps them check their understanding of the story. Have them model asking questions about the erupting volcano. (Possible questions: *What new problem do the Grunts have? Why can't the Grunts escape?*)

Vocabulary

pitch to rise and fall

rumblings deep, long rolling sounds

earthquake a shaking of the ground

volcano an opening in the earth that spews out lava, ash, and hot gases

erupting bursting out

resign give up or quit a job

lava melted rock that flows from a volcano

 Challenge

Volcanoes

Challenge children to find out what happens when a volcano erupts. Then have them draw and label the parts of a volcano.

Reading the Paired Selections
(Anthology pp. 124–125)

"It's George," cried Little Grunt. "He's come to save us."

❻ "Ooga, ooga! Quick!" said the Grunts as they all jumped on George's long neck and long back and long tail.

And before you could say Tyrannosaurus rex, George
❼ carried them far away to safety.

126

CRITICAL THINKING
Guiding Comprehension

❻ **NOTING DETAILS** How does George rescue the Grunts? (They climb onto him, and he carries them to safety.)

❼ **MAKING INFERENCES** How do you think the Grunts feel about George now? Why? (Possible response: They are grateful because he has saved them.)

Continue the Graphic Organizer Have children share the details they noted on their **Graphic Organizers** on **Practice Book** page 62.

THEME 4: Amazing Animals
(Anthology p. 126)

T260

Vocabulary

Tyrannosaurus rex a large, meat-eating dinosaur

REACHING ALL LEARNERS

Extra Support/Intervention

Selection Review

Before children join in Stop and Think, have them

- take turns modeling **Question** and other strategies they used,
- check and revise **Practice Book** page 62,
- summarize the story.

Stop and Think

Critical Thinking Questions

1. **FANTASY AND REALISM** Could the events in this story really have happened? Why or why not? (Sample responses: No. Dinosaurs and people never lived together or at the same time in history; dinosaurs aren't pets.)

2. **AUTHOR'S VIEWPOINT** How do you think the author feels about friendship? How do you know? (Sample responses: He feels that friends should take care of one another. He shows Little Grunt taking care of George, and vice versa.)

3. **COMPARE AND CONTRAST** Think about times when you said good-bye to a friend or helped a friend. How were your feelings like the feelings of characters from this theme? (Responses will vary but should include details from the stories and from children's personal experiences.)

Strategies in Action Have children model how they used Question and other strategies to help them understand *Little Grunt and the Big Egg*. (Sample response: I asked myself these questions: *Why are the Grunts in danger? How does George help Little Grunt?*)

Connecting and Comparing

Problem Solving

- Ask children to explain how George is able to help the Grunts solve their problem of needing to escape from the flowing lava. (He carries them away from danger.)

- Have children describe a problem that the ants from *Ant* must solve. Then have them compare problems and solutions from *Ant* with ones from *Little Grunt and the Big Egg*. (Sample responses: The ants in *Ant* work together to gather food and build their tunnels. In both *Ant* and *Little Grunt and the Big Egg*, animals help others, and everyone benefits from working together.)

- Ask children to complete **Practice Book** page 63 independently.

Practice Book page 63

Monitoring Student Progress

Connecting and Comparing

Name _____

Problem Solving

For each story, answer the questions on the chart.
Responses will vary. Sample responses are given.

	What problems do the story characters face?	How do the characters solve it?
Little Grunt and the Big Egg	Little Grunt and his family must escape from the volcano. **(2 points)**	George rescues the family. **(2)**
The Great Ball Game	The animals are losing the ball game. **(2)**	Bat scores the winning goal. **(2)**

How are the solutions in the stories alike?

One animal helps the other characters. **(2)**

Monitoring Student Progress

If . . .	Then . . .
children had difficulty answering Guiding Comprehension questions,	guide them in reading aloud relevant portions of the text and discussing their answers.

Reading the Paired Selections T261

 **Skill Review**

OBJECTIVES

Children review how to
- identify and read words with the /är/ sounds,
- draw conclusions,
- spell words with the vowel + *r* sounds in *car*.

REVIEW

PHONICS: *r*-Controlled Vowel *ar*

Review the pattern and concept. Write and read aloud *barn* and *garden*. Circle the letters *ar*. Remind children that *ar* usually stands for /är/.

Have children practice the skill. Display the sentences shown.

- Have children read the sentences aloud. Have them tell which words have the /är/ sounds. (*partner, market, artist, shark*)

My partner works at the market.

The artist paints a shark.

REVIEW

COMPREHENSION: Drawing Conclusions

Review drawing conclusions. Point out that

- authors don't always explain everything that happens in a story;
- readers can use story clues to figure out what is not stated.

Help children draw conclusions.

- Remind children that when George starts to grow, he becomes a problem for the Grunts.

- Point out that the author doesn't actually say that George's size is a problem. Ask what clues the author gives to let the reader know this. (The cave stays the same size but George doesn't, so the cave becomes crowded.)

- Ask children to tell which clues help them know that George saves the Grunts from the volcano.

SPELLING: The Vowel + *r* Sounds in *car*

Pretest Say each underlined word, read the sentence, and then repeat the word. Have children write only the underlined words.

Basic Words from Theme 4

1. The polar bear was covered by a **load** of **snow**.
2. Will you **sing** at the **party**?
3. The wind will **blow** the **boat**.
4. In winter it gets **cold** at the duck **farm**.
5. Please **park** on the **road**.
6. The **smart** boy sent a letter to **thank** his uncle for the gift.
7. The worm likes to **think** of one **thing** only—dirt.
8. Dogs can **hold** **most** things in their teeth.
9. The red bird likes to **bring** its lunch to the **yard**.
10. If you can't **hand** the box to Molly, **send** it to her.

Challenge Words

11. A **rainbow** decorates the **department** store.
12. My friend is very **young**, but she can play a **grand** piano.
13. My **goal** is to learn five new words today.

Review *r*-controlled vowel *ar* words.

- Explain that /är/ is usually spelled with the letters *ar*.
- Display these words: *party, farm, park, smart.*
- Underline the *ar* pattern, and say each word.
- Have children repeat the word and spell it aloud.

Have children identify words with *ar* spellings.

- Have children begin a list by writing this heading: The Vowel + *r* Sounds in *car.*
- Ask them to review their Take-Home Word List to find words with *ar.* (*farm, park, smart, yard, party.*)
- Have children write each *ar* word on their list.

Practice/Homework Assign **Practice Book** page 297, the Take-Home Word List.

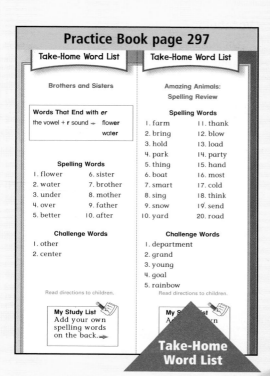

Practice Book page 297

Take-Home Word List	Take-Home Word List
Brothers and Sisters	Amazing Animals: Spelling Review

Words That End with *er*
the vowel + r sound → flower
water

Spelling Words
1. flower	6. sister
2. water	7. brother
3. under	8. mother
4. over	9. father
5. better	10. after

Challenge Words
1. other
2. center

Read directions to children.

My Study List
Add your own spelling words on the back.➡

Spelling Words
1. farm	11. thank
2. bring	12. blow
3. hold	13. load
4. park	14. party
5. thing	15. hand
6. boat	16. most
7. smart	17. cold
8. sing	18. think
9. snow	19. send
10. yard	20. road

Challenge Words
1. department
2. grand
3. young
4. goal
5. rainbow

Read directions to children.

My Study List
Add your own

Take-Home Word List

Skill Review

Day at a Glance
pp. T264–T273

Reading Instruction

Key Vocabulary

Reading
  Mighty Dinosaurs

Think and Compare

Connecting and Comparing
  Text Organization

Taking Tests

Vocabulary Items
  Introduce the Strategy.

Skill Review Options

High-Frequency Words

Phonics
  r-Controlled Vowel *or, ore*
  Words with *nd, nt, mp, ng, nk*

Vocabulary
  Dictionary: Entry Words

Grammar
  Words for Nouns

Spelling
  Words That End with *nd, ng,*
  or *nk*

Prompts for Writing
  A Poem
  Using *I* and *me*

Daily Routines

Daily Message

Phonics Review Point to each word as you read aloud the Daily Message.

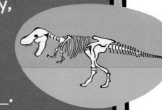

> If you go on a dinosaur hunt and
> find any bones, here's what to do:
> • Don't dump them in a pile!
> • Sort them very carefully,
>   thinking all the while.
> • Store them in a
>   special place. Then
>   _____ stand back and ___.

Have children
- read the Daily Message aloud, and suggest the rhyming word that best completes the message; (*smile*)
- identify words with the *r*-controlled vowel sounds spelled *or* or *ore* and words with *nd, nt, mp,* or *nk*. (*sort, store; hunt, find, dump, thinking, stand*)

Word Wall

High-Frequency Word Review Display these high-frequency words, and review their meanings. Have children write clues for these and other Word Wall words and then use their work to make crossword puzzles.

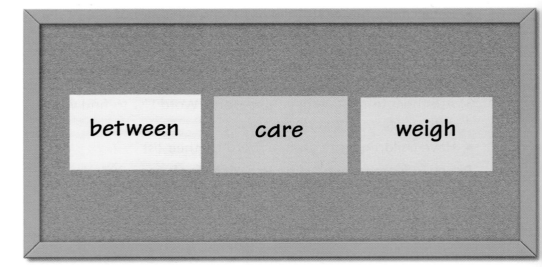

between   care   weigh

Vocabulary

Vocabulary Expansion Explain that the next selection gives information about real dinosaurs.

- Create a word web for *dinosaurs*. Have children help you complete it by naming related words.
- Ask children to draw pictures that illustrate concepts from the word web.

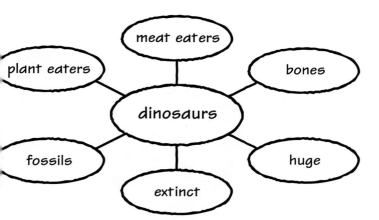

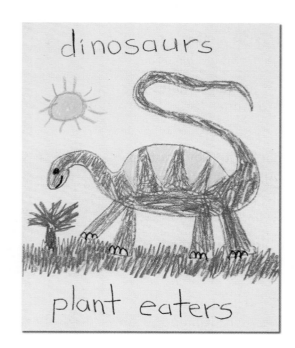

Daily Writing Prompt

Poem Use this prompt to review with children how to write a poem about themselves. Remind children to use *I* and *me* correctly.

In <u>Little Grunt and the Big Egg</u>, a boy finds a giant dinosaur egg. Suppose you found a giant egg. What might be inside? Write a poem about a giant egg and what you would do if you found one.

Introducing Vocabulary

Key Vocabulary

These words appear in the selection.

fossils plant or animal remains that have changed to stone

packs groups of animals

prey an animal hunted by another animal for food

remains things left behind after something has died

reptiles cold-blooded animals, such as snakes, turtles, and lizards

 e • Glossary
e • WordGame

See Vocabulary notes on pages T267 and T268 for additional words to preview.

Use Transparency 4–31.

- Have someone read aloud the first two parts of the dialogue.

- Model how to use context clues to figure out the meaning of *fossils*.

- Have children use context clues to figure out the meaning of the remaining Key Vocabulary words. Ask how children figured out each meaning.

- Ask children to look for these words as they read and to use them as they discuss the selection.

Practice/Homework Assign **Practice Book** page 64.

Selection 2

Mighty Dinosaurs

THE NATURE COMPANY • YOUNG DISCOVERIES LIBRARY

Transparency 4–31
Dinosaur Words

Host: Dr. Topp, tell us what you have found near the river.
Dr. Topp: We have just found more dinosaur fossils. When these creatures died many, many years ago, their bodies were covered with soil and sand. Over time, the dinosaur bones, teeth, and other remains turned to stone and became part of the rock around them. We study these fossils to learn more about what dinosaurs were like.
Host: Were dinosaurs reptiles?
Dr. Topp: Yes, we think that many dinosaurs were cold-blooded animals, just like snakes and lizards.
Host: Did all dinosaurs hunt for prey?
Dr. Topp: No, only meat-eating dinosaurs hunted other animals for their meals. They usually ate fish, insects, and often other dinosaurs. Some hunted alone, while others hunted in packs with other dinosaurs.

TRANSPARENCY 4–31
TEACHER'S EDITION PAGE T266

AMAZING ANIMALS Mighty Dinosaurs
Monitoring Student Progress Key Vocabulary

ANNOTATED VERSION

Practice Book page 64

Monitoring
Student Progress
Key Vocabulary

Name _____

Dinosaur Words

Read the sentences. Complete them with the correct words from the box.

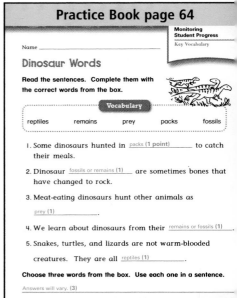

Vocabulary				
reptiles	remains	prey	packs	fossils

1. Some dinosaurs hunted in ___packs (1 point)___ to catch their meals.

2. Dinosaur ___fossils or remains (1)___ are sometimes bones that have changed to rock.

3. Meat-eating dinosaurs hunt other animals as ___prey (1)___.

4. We learn about dinosaurs from their ___remains or fossils (1)___

5. Snakes, turtles, and lizards are not warm-blooded creatures. They are all ___reptiles (1)___.

Choose three words from the box. Use each one in a sentence.

Answers will vary. (3)

_____

_____

Mighty Dinosaurs

by Judith Simpson

The Age of Dinosaurs

Dinosaurs roamed the Earth millions of years ago. Dinosaur means "terrible lizard" and, like lizards, dinosaurs were reptiles. We know a lot about dinosaurs from their remains, which we have found buried in rocks and beneath sand. Dinosaurs had knobby or pebbly skin and laid eggs. Some walked on two legs, others moved on all four. Dinosaurs fed on different things — some ate only plants, others ate meat and hunted for their food.

Dinosaurs came in different shapes and sizes. Some had very large bodies and tiny heads. Some dinosaurs had spikes or bumps on their backs. Others had horns or crests on their heads. Their skin was thick and rough. People did not live on Earth until long after dinosaurs died out.

127

Connecting and Comparing

Text Organization

- How is *Mighty Dinosaurs* like *Ant*? How is it different? (Possible responses: Both give facts about a kind of animal and have captions for pictures. *Mighty Dinosaurs* is broken into sections with the topics named in the headings; *Ant* has photographs, and *Mighty Dinosaurs* has drawings.)

- How does the way the text is organized help you find information in *Mighty Dinosaurs* and in *Ant*? (Accept reasonable responses that include various text features such as headings, captions, or photographs.)

Extra Support/Intervention

Preview the selection.

- Look at the dinosaurs in the pictures. How are they alike? How are they different? What do you know about them?

- Look at the dinosaur bones on page 130. What can you tell about the dinosaur from looking at its teeth? What can you learn from reading the caption?

- What do you think you might learn about dinosaurs from this selection?

Vocabulary

roamed wandered; moved around

reptiles cold-blooded animals, such as snakes, turtles, and lizards

remains things left behind after something has died

crests natural growths on animals' heads

Reading the Paired Selections
(Anthology p. 127)   **T267**

Meat Eaters

Meat-eating dinosaurs had good eyesight and a strong sense of smell. They had much larger brains than plant-eating dinosaurs, so they could plan attacks to catch their prey. Some meat eaters lived on eggs, insects, lizards, small furry animals, and fish. Others gathered in packs to kill dinosaurs that were much bigger than themselves. *Tyrannosaurus* could be three times as tall as a man and was one of the largest meat-eating dinosaurs.

◀*Tyrannosaurus* was one of the last dinosaurs on Earth.

128

Plant Eaters

Not all dinosaurs were fierce hunters. Some ate only plants. For most of the age of dinosaurs, the weather was warm and wet. Plants grew easily and there were lots to choose from. Plant-eating dinosaurs needed large amounts of food to give them energy. Some roamed the land grazing on low-growing ferns. Others had long necks and, like giraffes, could stretch up to reach leaves from the tops of the tallest trees.

①

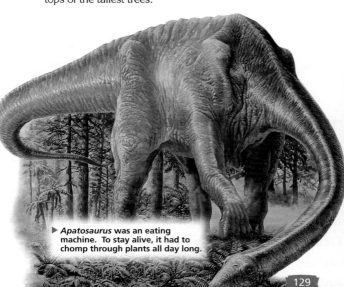

▶ *Apatosaurus* was an eating machine. To stay alive, it had to chomp through plants all day long.

129

CRITICAL THINKING

Guiding Comprehension

① **COMPARE AND CONTRAST** How were meat eaters different from plant eaters? (Possible response: Meat eaters used their larger brains to hunt other dinosaurs. Plant eaters ate ferns and other plants.)

② **MAKING JUDGMENTS** Do you think it is important to study dinosaur fossils? Why or why not? (Responses will vary but should include details from the selection and from children's personal knowledge.)

TARGET SKILL

COMPREHENSION STRATEGY

Question

Student Modeling Have children ask and answer questions about what they have read. Ask how asking questions helps them check their understanding of *Mighty Dinosaurs*.

Vocabulary

prey an animal hunted by another animal for food

packs groups of animals

grazing feeding on grass or other plants

fossils (page 130) plant or animal remains that have changed to stone

REACHING ALL LEARNERS

Extra Support/Intervention

Selection Review

Before children join in Think and Compare, have them

- model the strategies they used,
- review and complete **Practice Book** page 62,
- summarize main ideas in the selection.

THEME 4: Amazing Animals
(Anthology pp. 128–129)

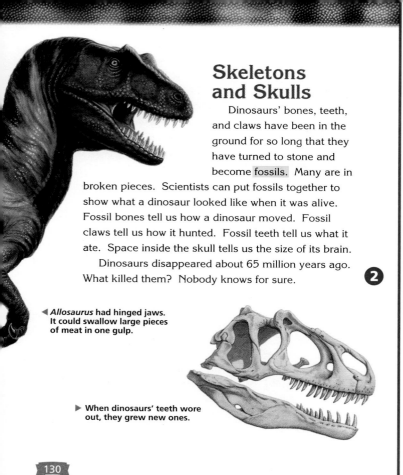

Skeletons and Skulls

Dinosaurs' bones, teeth, and claws have been in the ground for so long that they have turned to stone and become fossils. Many are in broken pieces. Scientists can put fossils together to show what a dinosaur looked like when it was alive. Fossil bones tell us how a dinosaur moved. Fossil claws tell us how it hunted. Fossil teeth tell us what it ate. Space inside the skull tells us the size of its brain.

Dinosaurs disappeared about 65 million years ago. What killed them? Nobody knows for sure. **2**

◀ *Allosaurus* had hinged jaws. It could swallow large pieces of meat in one gulp.

▶ When dinosaurs' teeth wore out, they grew new ones.

130

Think and Compare

1. Compare *Little Grunt and the Big Egg* with *Mighty Dinosaurs*. Tell some things that George does that real dinosaurs could not do.

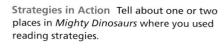
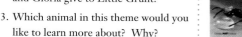

2. What safety tips could Officer Buckle and Gloria give to Little Grunt?

3. Which animal in this theme would you like to learn more about? Why?

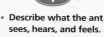

4. In this theme, which characters show how important it is to work together? Give reasons for your answers.

Strategies in Action Tell about one or two places in *Mighty Dinosaurs* where you used reading strategies.

Write a Journal Entry

Write a journal entry from the point of view of an ant that lived during the dinosaur age. Tell what happened one day when the ant looked up and saw a dinosaur!

Tips
- Describe what the ant sees, hears, and feels.
- Use details about ants and dinosaurs from the stories in this theme.

131

Think and Compare

Discuss or Write Have children answer the questions. Sample answers are provided; accept reasonable responses.

1. George lives with people and carries them to safety.

2. Do not let dinosaurs live in a cave with you. Do not live next to a volcano.

3. Responses will vary.

4. Officer Buckle and Gloria work better as a team. Ants gather food and build colonies together. Bat helps his team win the game. George helps the Grunts escape the volcano.

Strategies in Action Have children take turns modeling Question and other reading strategies.

Finish the Graphic Organizer. Have children share and discuss their completed **Graphic Organizers** on **Practice Book** page 62.

English Language Learners

Supporting Comprehension

Beginning/Preproduction Point to and name the parts of dinosaurs, such as their bodies, heads, necks, bones, teeth, and claws. Then have children point to and name the dinosaur parts.

Early Production and Speech Emergence Ask children to name and describe their favorite animal character in this theme. Encourage them to use color, shape, and size words.

Intermediate and Advanced Fluency Ask children to choose one selection and use the pictures to retell the story to a partner.

Monitoring Student Progress

If . . .	Then . . .
children had difficulty answering two or more Think and Compare questions,	guide them in reading aloud relevant portions of the text and discussing their answers.

Reading the Paired Selections
(Anthology pp. 130–131)

Taking Tests

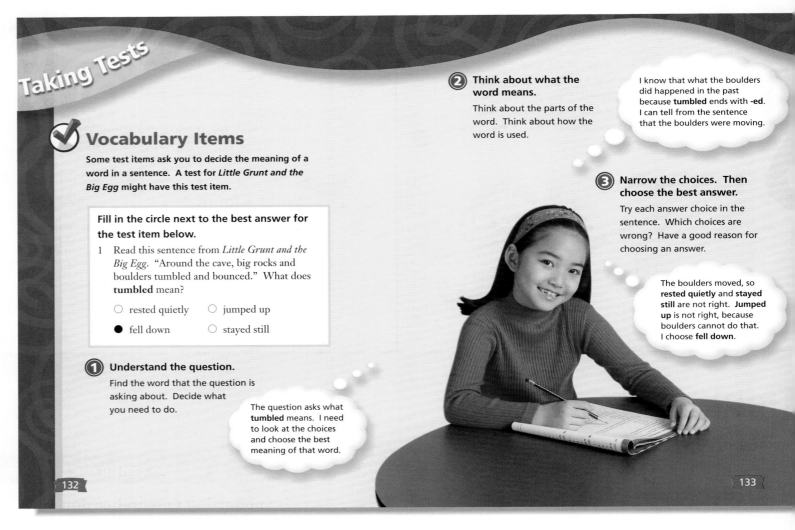

STRATEGIES: Vocabulary Items

Introduce the Strategy Taking Tests provides instruction and practice in different test formats. It will help you prepare your children for the **Theme Skills Test** and the **Integrated Theme Test**, as well as state and national standardized tests.

THEME	STRATEGY
1	**Choosing the Best Answer**
2	**Filling in the Blank**
3	**Writing a Personal Response**
▶ **4**	**Vocabulary Items**
5	**Writing an Answer to a Question**
6	**Writing a Personal Narrative**

- Tell children that they will learn strategies that will help them do well on tests.
- Explain that Anthology pages 132–133 show the steps for answering questions about vocabulary.
- Have different volunteers read each step and each thought balloon aloud.
- Briefly discuss the steps. Then explain that children will be learning more about each step.
- Review the importance of following the test directions and knowing how to record answers.

THEME 4: Amazing Animals
(Anthology pp. 132–133)

Skill Review

REVIEW

PHONICS: *r*-Controlled Vowels *or, ore;* Words with *nd, nt, mp, ng, nk*

Review the concepts.

- Display *more* and *fort,* and underline the letters *or* and *ore.* Have children read each word. Point out that the letters *or* and *ore* often stand for /ôr/.

- Display *land, dent,* and *damp,* and underline the last two consonants in each word. Have children read each word. Remind them that these consonants keep their own sounds.

- Display *ring* and *thank,* and underline the last two consonants in each word. Have children read each word. Review that *ng* stands for the sound at the end of *ring* and that *nk* stands for the sound at the end of *thank.*

Have children read words.

- Display these words, and have children read them: *trunk, jumper, landing, strong, spent, horn, before.*

- Challenge children to write a rhyming word for each of the words. Have them read their words. (Possible responses: *skunk, bumper, standing, wrong, bent, torn,* and *store*)

Have children practice the phonics skills. Assign **Practice Book** page 65.

SKILL REVIEW

DAY 2

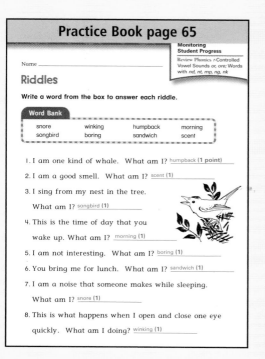

Practice Book page 65

Monitoring Student Progress

Review Phonics *r*-Controlled Vowel Sounds *or, ore;* Words with *nd, nt, mp, ng, nk*

Name _____

Riddles

Write a word from the box to answer each riddle.

Word Bank

| snore | winking | humpback | morning |
| songbird | boring | sandwich | scent |

1. I am one kind of whale. What am I? humpback **(1 point)**

2. I am a good smell. What am I? scent **(1)**

3. I sing from my nest in the tree.
   What am I? songbird **(1)**

4. This is the time of day that you
   wake up. What am I? morning **(1)**

5. I am not interesting. What am I? boring **(1)**

6. You bring me for lunch. What am I? sandwich **(1)**

7. I am a noise that someone makes while sleeping.
   What am I? snore **(1)**

8. This is what happens when I open and close one eye
   quickly. What am I doing? winking **(1)**

Options Skill Review

OBJECTIVES

Children review how to
- find entry words in a dictionary;
- identify and use pronouns;
- spell words that end with *nd, ng,* or *nk.*

Materials
- dictionary for each pair of children

VOCABULARY: Dictionary Entry Words

Review how to find and use entry words.

- Dictionary entry words are listed in alphabetical order.
- Guide words can help to find the pages where entry words appear.
- Definitions, or word meanings, are given after the entry words.

Model how to find the entry word *dinosaur*.

- Use guide words to find the page in the dictionary. Point out the entry word *dinosaur*.
- Have a child read the meaning of *dinosaur*.

Have children find entry words. Have pairs of children find the entry words *boulder, fierce,* and *skull*. Have partners read aloud each definition and use the word correctly in a sentence.

Practice Book page 66

Name _____

Monitoring
Student Progress
Review Grammar Words
for Nouns

Writing Pronouns

Read each sentence. Replace the word or words in dark print with the pronouns *she, he, it,* or *they*. Rewrite each sentence.

1. **Little Grunt and George** were pals.
   They were pals. **(2 points)**

2. **Aunt Grunt** got food for George.
   She got food for George. **(2)**

3. **The cave** became very crowded.
   It became very crowded. **(2)**

4. **Chief Rockhead Grunt** said that George had to go.
   He said that George had to go. **(2)**

5. Later **the Grunts** needed George's help.
   Later they needed George's help. **(2)**

GRAMMAR: Words for Nouns

Review pronouns. Remind children that

- a noun names a person, a place, or a thing;
- a pronoun is a word that takes the place of a noun.

Ask children to identify pronouns. Write sentences such as those shown. Have someone read aloud the sentences. Have children identify each pronoun in the second sentence and tell which noun it replaces. (*he/boy; it/egg*)

Practice/Homework. Assign **Practice Book** page 66.

> The boy found an egg.
> He found it.

SPELLING: Words That End with *nd, ng,* or *nk*

Review words that end with *nd, ng,* or *nk*.

- Write *hand, sing,* and *think*. Circle the *nd, ng,* and *nk*.
- Remind children that the /nd/ sounds are usually spelled *nd*, as in *hand*; that /ng/ is usually spelled *ng*, as in *sing*; and that /nk/ is usually spelled *nk*, as in *think*.

Have children write words that end with *nd, ng,* or *nk*.

- Say each of these words, and have children use their punchout letter cards to spell it: *thank, bring, thing,* and *send*.
- Ask children to spell a rhyming word for each of the spelling words they made.

Practice/Homework Assign **Practice Book** page 67.

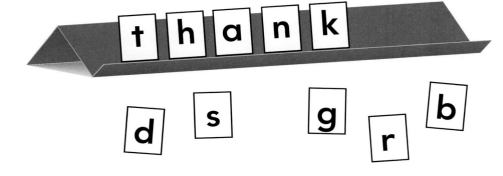

Materials
- punchout letter cards and tray for each child

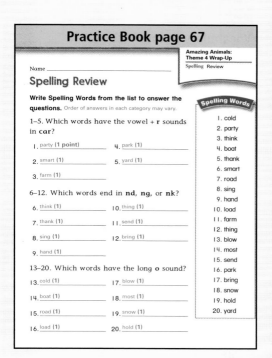

Practice Book page 67

Amazing Animals:
Theme 4 Wrap-Up

Name _____

Spelling Review

Spelling Review

Write Spelling Words from the list to answer the
questions. Order of answers in each category may vary.

Spelling Words

1–5. Which words have the vowel + r sounds
in c**ar**?

1. party (1 point)   4. park (1)

2. smart (1)   5. yard (1)

3. farm (1)

6–12. Which words end in **nd, ng,** or **nk**?

6. think (1)   10. thing (1)

7. thank (1)   11. send (1)

8. sing (1)   12. bring (1)

9. hand (1)

13–20. Which words have the long o sound?

13. cold (1)   17. blow (1)

14. boat (1)   18. most (1)

15. road (1)   19. snow (1)

16. load (1)   20. hold (1)

1. cold
2. party
3. think
4. boat
5. thank
6. smart
7. road
8. sing
9. hand
10. load
11. farm
12. thing
13. blow
14. most
15. send
16. park
17. bring
18. snow
19. hold
20. yard

DAY 3
week 4

Day at a Glance
pp. T274–T281

Reading Instruction

Theme Connections
Anthology Literature

Rereading for Fluency
Little Grunt and the Big Egg

Taking Tests

Vocabulary Items
Understand the Question.
Think About What the Word Means.

Skill Review Options

High-Frequency Words

Phonics
Base Words and Endings *-s, -es, -ies*

Comprehension
Text Organization

Vocabulary
Using a Thesaurus

Spelling
Spelling Game

Prompts for Writing
News Article

Daily Routines

Daily Message

Phonics Review Point to each word as you read aloud the Daily Message.

Good morning, Class,
Can you guess this riddle?
* We are pets.
* We are small enough to fit in boxes.
* We are the babies of dogs.
* Our name rhymes with <u>guppies.</u>

Have children
* read aloud the Daily Message and guess the answer to the riddle; (puppies)
* find, read, and circle nouns with endings *-s, -es, -ies*. (*pets, boxes; babies, guppies*)

Word Wall

High-Frequency Word Review Display these high-frequency words, and discuss their meanings. Then have partners take turns using their punchout letter cards to spell each word. Also have them use it in an oral sentence.

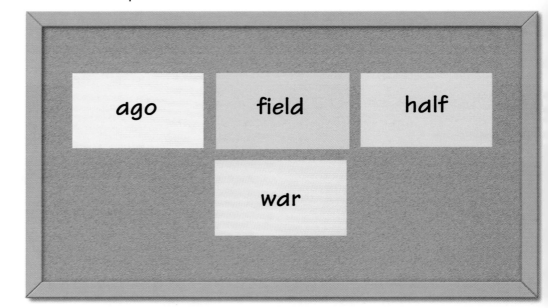

ago   field   half

war

Vocabulary

Entry Words Have partners take turns playing a dictionary game. Tell children that they will guess entry words. Have children take turns finding an entry word in the dictionary and saying the entry words that come before and after it. Tell the partner to use those words as clues to find the entry word, read the definition, and then to use it in a sentence.

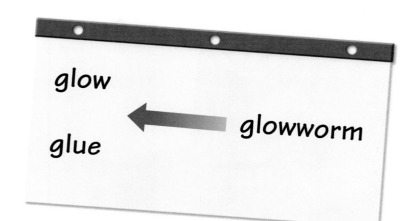

glow

glue

glowworm

Daily Writing Prompt

News Article Use this prompt to review writing a news article. Remind children to include interesting details to tell readers what happened.

Write a news article about an event from this theme, such as the volcano that erupted or a dinosaur fossil that was found. Answer these questions: Who? What? When? Where? Why? How?

THEME CONNECTIONS: Anthology Literature

Comprehension

Comparing Fact and Fantasy

OBJECTIVE

- Connect and compare fact and fantasy in theme literature.

Teach

Remind children that they have just finished Theme 4: Amazing Animals. Explain that they will now take part in a theme-related activity.

Together, review the Monitoring Student Progress Paired Selections, Links, and the Main Selections.

> *Officer Buckle and Gloria*
> *Ant*
> *The Great Ball Game*

Have children discuss fact and fantasy.

- Ask children what makes *Little Grunt and the Big Egg* different from *Mighty Dinosaurs*. If necessary, point out that one is fantasy because it tells a make-believe story; the other gives facts about creatures that scientists believe once existed.

- Have children tell which of the other theme selections are fantasy and which are factual. Ask children to support their answers with details.

Practice/Apply

Introduce the activity "Fact or Fantasy?" Then ask children to complete it.

Portfolio Opportunity

 Suggest that children include copies of their paragraphs in their portfolios.

Fact or Fantasy?

Singles	🕐 **45 minutes**	
Objective	Write factual and fantastic details about an animal.	
Materials	Reference sources, paper, crayons	

Write two paragraphs about an amazing animal. Give facts in one paragraph. Give make-believe details in the other.

- Reread the poem "The Animal Song" on Anthology page 11.

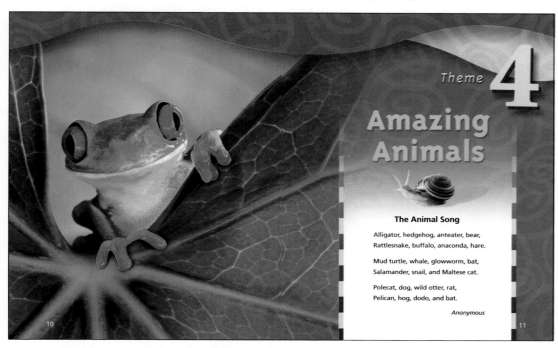

- Choose an amazing animal from the poem or the theme.
- Find out some facts about the animal you chose. What makes it amazing? List the facts.
- Write a paragraph that gives facts about your animal.
- Write another paragraph about your animal. Make this paragraph a fantasy. Give details that are make-believe about your animal.
- Draw a picture for each paragraph. Then display your work. Can you tell which paragraphs are fact and which are fantasy?

Consider copying and laminating this activity for use in a center.

TAKING TESTS: Vocabulary Items

Understand the Question.

Review the steps for completing vocabulary items. Have children refer to Anthology pages 132–133.

Display Transparency 4–32 and discuss Step 1. Have a volunteer read aloud Step 1. Discuss the parts of the step briefly.

- Compare Question 1 and Question 2 to the test question on Anthology page 132.
- Explain that both questions are based on *Little Grunt and the Big Egg* on Anthology pages 118–126.
- Explain that the answer choices for these questions will be given later.

Model Step 1. Model how to apply the step to Question 1.

Think Aloud *First, I will circle the word that the question is asking about: resign. Next, I will decide what I need to do. Will I choose an answer that is almost the same as resign or one that is the opposite? I see the words means about the same as. I will choose a word or phrase that is almost the same as resign.*

Complete Transparency 4–32. For Question 2, help children use Step 1 to find the word that the question is asking about and to decide what they need to do.

Think About What the Word Means.

Display Transparency 4–33 and model Step 2. Have a volunteer read aloud Step 2. Briefly discuss it.

Model Step 2. Model using the step to think about the parts of the word in Question 1 and how the word is used.

Think Aloud *First, I will think about the parts of the word resign. It must mean something that happens in the present time, because it doesn't end in -ed. Next, I will think about how the word is used. This is what the Chief says after the volcano starts erupting and the Grunts are trapped. Right after the Chief uses the word resign, Ant Grunt says "Now we have no leader."*

Complete Transparency 4–33. For Question 2, help children use Step 2 to think about the parts of the word and how the word is used.

Transparency 4–32

Vocabulary Items

AMAZING ANIMALS
Monitoring Student Progress
Taking Tests: Vocabulary Items

ANNOTATED VERSION

Step 1: Understand the Question.
- Find the word that the question is asking about.
- Decide what you need to do.

Use Step 1 to understand each of these questions about *Little Grunt and the Big Egg.*

1. On page 125, what does the word *resign* mean?

   Use the Think Aloud on Teacher's Edition page T278 to model using Step 1 to understand this question.

2. Read this sentence from the story. "'It's nice and peaceful here again,' said Ant and Unca Grunt." Which word means the opposite of *peaceful*?

   - **Word the question asks about:** *peaceful*
   - **Context:** The question includes the sentence from the story where the word is used.
   - **What you need to do:** I need to find a word that means the opposite of *peaceful*.

TRANSPARENCY 4–32
TEACHER'S EDITION PAGE T278

Transparency 4–33

Vocabulary Items

AMAZING ANIMALS
Monitoring Student Progress
Taking Tests: Vocabulary Items

ANNOTATED VERSION

Step 2: Think About What the Word Means.
- Think about the parts of the word.
- Think about how the word is used.

Use Step 2 to think about what the word means in both of these questions.

1. On page 125, what does the word *resign* mean?

   Use the Think Aloud on Teacher's Edition page T278 to model using Step 2 to think about what the word means in this question.

2. Read this sentence from the story. "'It's nice and peaceful here again,' said Ant and Unca Grunt." Which word means the opposite of *peaceful*?

   - **Parts of the word:** *peace* and *-ful*
   - **Context:** Ant and Unca Grunt wanted George to leave because he caused so many problems. This sentence comes after George leaves. The word *nice* gives a clue that they like it better after George is gone. *Peaceful* must mean something good.

TRANSPARENCY 4–33
TEACHER'S EDITION PAGE T278

Options Skill Review

REVIEW

PHONICS: Base Words and Endings -s, -es, -ies

OBJECTIVE
- Children review how to read base words with endings -s, -es, and -ies.

Review the skill. Remind children of the following conventions:

- The ending -s, -es, or -ies makes a noun mean "more than one."

- In most words that end in y, the y is changed to i before -es is added.

Model reading base words with plural endings.

- Write these words: *dinosaurs, bodies.*

- Read each word. Help children identify the base word and the ending. (*dinosaur, -s; body, -ies*)

- Write each base word. Ask children how the base word changed before the ending was added. (no change; y to i)

> dinosaurs
> dinosaur

> bodies
> body

Have children read base words with -s, -es, and -ies.

- Display the sentences shown.

- Have children read the sentences, find the base words with endings, and identify the endings.

- Ask volunteers to write each base word and to tell how it changed before the ending was added.

> What wishes do you make on your birthday? (wish<u>es</u>)
>
> Several bunnies hopped into the garden. (bunn<u>ies</u>)
>
> What is in those big boxes? (box<u>es</u>)
>
> Three ponies stood in the field. (pon<u>ies</u>)
>
> In the fishbowl swam three guppies. (gupp<u>ies</u>)

Skill Review

OBJECTIVES

Children review how to
- use captions, pictures, and headings to understand text;
- read fluently;
- use a thesaurus to find exact words;
- review spelling patterns.

Practice Book page 68

Name _____

Monitoring
Student Progress

*Review Comprehension
Text Organization*

Text Organization

Fill in this chart with main ideas
and details from *Mighty Dinosaurs.*

Main Ideas	Details
Page 128 Some dinosaurs were meat eaters. **(1 point)**	Page 128 Possible responses: Meat eaters had good eyesight and smell. They had large brains. They caught prey. Some hunted in packs. **(5)**
Page 129 Some dinosaurs were plant eaters. **(1)**	Page 129 Possible responses: Plant eaters needed a lot of food. Some ate ferns. Others ate leaves from tall trees. **(3)**

What does the picture on page 128 help you understand?
Possible response: Tyrannosaurus rex was a fierce, meat-eating dinosaur. **(1)**

What does the caption on page 129 tell you? _____

Apatosaurus had to eat plants all day long. **(1)**

REVIEW

COMPREHENSION: Text Organization

Review text organization. Remind children of these concepts:

- Nonfiction selections often have pictures, captions, and headings that go along with the text.
- Readers can use pictures, captions, headings, and text to find main ideas and details about something.

Help children use text features. Ask children to identify the topic of the selection on Anthology pages 127–130. (dinosaurs)

- Have children read aloud the heading, "Skeletons and Skulls," on Anthology page 130. Ask what children learn from the heading. (the main idea of the page; that the section will tell more about dinosaur skeletons and skulls)
- Ask children what details they learn from the captions. (Allosaurus had hinged jaws; dinosaurs grew new teeth.)
- Have volunteers read aloud the page. Discuss details that support the main idea. Record children's responses.

Have children fill in a text organization chart. Assign **Practice Book** page 68.

REVIEW

REREADING FOR FLUENCY

Rereading the Selection Have children choose a favorite part of *Little Grunt and the Big Egg* to practice reading independently, or suggest that they practice reading page 125 to a partner. If children need practice reading accurately and with expression, model the reading.

Monitoring
Student
Progress

VOCABULARY: Using a Thesaurus

Review what children have learned about using a thesaurus.

- A thesaurus is a book that gives synonyms for words.
- The entries in a thesaurus are in alphabetical order.

Model using a thesaurus to find a more exact word.

- Display this sentence: *Some dinosaurs were* <u>big</u>.
- Look up *big* in a children's thesaurus and read aloud the entries. Ask children to help you select a word to use in place of *big*. *(gigantic, huge, enormous)*

Have children use a thesaurus. Have groups of children use a thesaurus to find more exact words to replace the underlined words in sentences such as the ones shown.

Practice/Homework Assign **Practice Book** page 69.

A bee is <u>small</u>.

Little Grunt was <u>sad</u>.

The volcano made a big <u>sound</u>.

Materials

- children's thesaurus, one per group
- 12 duplicated dinosaur bone shapes

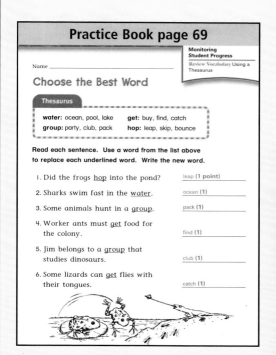

Practice Book page 69

Monitoring
Student Progress
Review Vocabulary Using a
Thesaurus

Name _____

Choose the Best Word

Thesaurus

water: ocean, pool, lake   **get:** buy, find, catch
group: party, club, pack   **hop:** leap, skip, bounce

Read each sentence. Use a word from the list above to replace each underlined word. Write the new word.

1. Did the frogs <u>hop</u> into the pond?   leap (1 point)
2. Sharks swim fast in the <u>water</u>.   ocean (1)
3. Some animals hunt in a <u>group</u>.   pack (1)
4. Worker ants must <u>get</u> food for the colony.   find (1)
5. Jim belongs to a <u>group</u> that studies dinosaurs.   club (1)
6. Some lizards can <u>get</u> flies with their tongues.   catch (1)

SPELLING: Dinosaur Game

- Display these words: *smart, park, bring, send, think, thank, hand, sing, farm, thing, yard, party.*
- Ask small groups to write a clue for each word on a bone shaped card. Then have children place the bones face-down.
- Explain the rules: The first player says, "I'm looking for a dinosaur bone" and draws a "bone." The player must read the clue aloud, guess the word, and spell it correctly to keep the bone. Play continues until all the "bones" are collected.

Practice/Homework Assign **Practice Book** page 70.

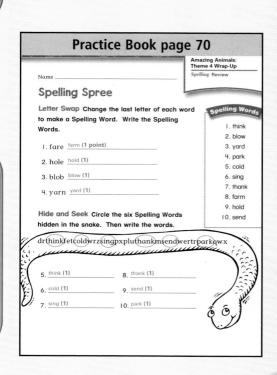

Practice Book page 70

Amazing Animals:
Theme 4 Wrap-Up
Spelling Review

Name _____

Spelling Spree

Letter Swap Change the last letter of each word to make a Spelling Word. Write the Spelling Words.

1. fare   farm (1 point)
2. hole   hold (1)
3. blob   blow (1)
4. yarn   yard (1)

Hide and Seek Circle the six Spelling Words hidden in the snake. Then write the words.

drthinkfetcoldwrzsingpxpluthankmsendwertrparkqwx

5. think (1)   8. thank (1)
6. cold (1)   9. send (1)
7. sing (1)   10. park (1)

Spelling Words
1. think
2. blow
3. yard
4. park
5. cold
6. sing
7. thank
8. farm
9. hold
10. send

Day at a Glance
pp. T282–T289

Reading Instruction

Theme Connections
Anthology Literature

Rereading for Fluency
Mighty Dinosaurs

Taking Tests

Vocabulary Items
Narrow the Choices.
Choose the Best Answer.

Skill Review Options

High-Frequency Words

Phonics
Vowel Pairs *oa, ow*

Comprehension
Categorize and Classify

Vocabulary
Parts of a Dictionary Entry

Grammar
Singular Possessive Nouns

Spelling
More Long *o* Words

Prompts for Writing
Taking Notes for a Research Report

Daily Routines

Daily Message

Phonics Review Point to each word as you read aloud the Daily Message.

Granny Grunt said that a cockroach would make a good pet. Do you know what might be a better pet for Little Grunt? Will it live in the cave or roam outside? Be sure it will not grow too big!

Have children
- read aloud the Daily Message and discuss the questions;
- find, read, and circle words with the vowel pairs *oa* or *ow*. (*cockroach, know, roam, grow*)

Word Wall

High-Frequency Word Review Briefly review these high-frequency words and discuss their meanings. Then have children write a short advertisement using all the words and others from the Word Wall.

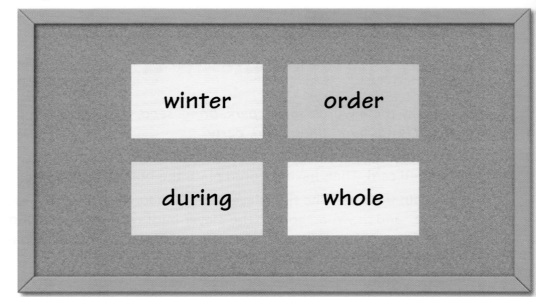

winter   order

during   whole

Vocabulary

Thesaurus Review Remind children that a thesaurus is a book that contains synonyms for words.

Display the sentences shown.
Ask children to use a thesaurus to find a more exact word for each underlined word. Have children reread the sentences aloud, replacing the underlined words with synonyms. Ask children to tell why they chose the synonyms that they did.
Have children write and illustrate new sentences that use several of the synonyms they chose.

I had a <u>good</u> dream last night.
Dinosaurs <u>walked</u> out of an anthill.
The ants ate <u>big</u> amounts of plant leaves.
In my dream, a tiger <u>jumped</u>.

Daily Writing Prompt

Taking Notes Use this prompt to review how to find and take notes on facts for a research report. Tell children that they will be using the notes they take today to write a paragraph on Day 5.

Take notes for a research report about how animals work together. Reread Anthology pages 68 and 74. Take notes about how some ants work together. Reread Anthology page 128. Take notes about how meat-eating dinosaurs worked together.

THEME CONNECTIONS: Anthology Literature

Comparing Authors' Viewpoints

OBJECTIVE

- Connect and compare authors' viewpoints.

Teach

Explain that children will now take part in an activity about Theme 4: *Amazing Animals*. As needed, review the Monitoring Student Progress Paired Selections, Links, and Main Selections they have read.

> *Officer Buckle and Gloria*
> *Ant*
> *The Great Ball Game*

Discuss the authors' viewpoints.

- Ask children to tell whether the author of each selection wrote it to entertain, give information, persuade, or describe. Suggest that children use **Practice Book** page 2 to recall the selections. Encourage children to support their answers with selection details.

- Have children discuss how they think the various authors feel about the selection topics. What is important to each author? Ask children to describe possible ways that an author's purpose for writing might be affected by his or her opinion on the topic. Also have children tell what was the same and different about their reading experiences.

Practice/Apply

Introduce the activity "Read This!" Then ask children to complete it independently.

Read This!

👤 Singles	🕐 40 minutes
Objective	Make an advertisement for a selection.
Materials	poster board, crayons or markers

Advertise a theme selection. Make a poster to persuade someone to read it.

- Choose the selection that you like best in Theme 4. Pretend you are its author. Think about why you wrote it. Make a list of things that make the selection a good one for others to read.

- Create an advertisement for your selection. Write its title. Then write sentences to convince others to read it. Tell why the selection is so good. Remember your purpose—you want someone to read it!

- Draw a picture to include on your poster. Show the animal from the selection doing something amazing.

onsider copying and laminating this activity for use in a center.

TAKING TESTS: Vocabulary Items

Narrow the Choices. Then Choose the Best Answer.

Review the steps for vocabulary test items. Have children refer to Anthology pages 132–133.

Display Transparency 4–34 and discuss Step 3. Have a volunteer read aloud Step 3.

- Briefly discuss the parts of this step.
- Emphasize that many words have more than one meaning and that the best answer will fit the meaning of the word in the selection.

Model Step 3. Model how to narrow the answer choices and then choose the best answer for Question 1.

Think Aloud *I will start by narrowing the choices. The first choice is wrong because the Chief just stopped being their leader. He is not about to start anything. I can tell that the third choice is wrong because it does not make sense if I put it in the sentence: "Don't ask me!" said Chief Rockhead. "I* <u>think</u>.*"*

Two choices are left. I can guess, but I would rather be sure I am choosing the best answer. The last choice is wrong because forgetting would not keep the Chief from being the leader. The second choice must be right. Let me make sure. If the Chief quits, then the people would have no leader. Yes, the second choice is the best answer.

Complete Transparency 4–34. Help children use Step 3 to choose the best answer to Question 2.

Transparency 4–34

Vocabulary Items

AMAZING ANIMALS
Monitoring Student Progress
Taking Tests: Vocabulary Items

ANNOTATED VERSION

Step 3: Narrow the Choices. Then Choose the Best Answer.
- Try each answer choice. Which choices are wrong?
- Have a good reason for choosing an answer.

Use Step 3 to choose the best answer for each of these questions.

1. On page 125, what does the word *resign* mean?
   ○ start
   ○ quit
   ○ think
   ○ forget

   Use the Think Aloud on Teacher's Edition page T286 to model using Step 3 to narrow the choices and choose the best answer.

2. Read this sentence from the story. "'It's nice and peaceful here again,' said Ant and Unca Grunt." Which word means the opposite of *peaceful*?
   ○ soft   ○ warm
   ○ calm   ○ noisy

   - **Wrong answers:** First choice (*soft*), because the opposite of *soft* is *hard* and that doesn't have anything to do with the fact George left; Second choice (*calm*), because calm means about the same as *peaceful*; Third choice (*warm*), because the opposite of *warm* is *cool* and this also wouldn't show how things change after George left
   - **Right answer:** Fourth choice (*noisy*), because *noisy* is the opposite of *peaceful*; Ant and Unca Grunt are happy that the cave is peaceful, or quiet, again

TRANSPARENCY 4–34
TEACHER'S EDITION PAGE T286

English Language Learners

If English language learners don't know the answer to a vocabulary question right away, tell them to skip it and come back to it later. After they have answered all the other questions in that section of the test, they should try answering the vocabulary questions that they skipped. Offer these steps.

- Sound out the word. Is it familiar? Do you remember hearing it before?
- Think about the context again. Look carefully at the words that come before and after the word. What is the author trying to say?
- If you can eliminate at least two answer choices, it is usually worth guessing.

REVIEW

PHONICS: Vowel Pairs
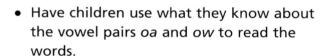

Review the sound/spelling patterns.

- Display and read *coat* and *grow*.
- Point out that the letters *oa* and *ow* usually stand for one vowel sound—the long *o* sound. Refer children to those spellings on the **Sound/Spelling Card** *ocean*.

Model reading words with *oa* and *ow*.

Display *lower, coasting, showboat, shallow*.

- Have children use what they know about the vowel pairs *oa* and *ow* to read the words.
- Have children group the words by the spelling for long *o*. Ask which word could go in both groups. (*showboat*)

Have children read words with the vowel pairs. Display the paragraph shown.

- Have pairs of children read the paragraph aloud.
- Ask children to write the words with the long *o* sound on index cards. Also have them underline the letters that stand for long *o*.
- Tell children to sort the words into groups by the spelling for long *o*. (*flowed, window, below, crow, mower, tomorrow; toad, croaked, oak, moaned*)

OBJECTIVE
- Children review how to identify and read words with vowel pair *oa* or *ow*.

Materials
- **Sound/Spelling Card** *ocean*
- 10 index cards for each pair of children

Warm air flowed into my room through the bedroom window. A toad croaked in the grass below. Then a crow landed in the oak tree, and I heard a lawn mower. I moaned and tried to sleep. Tomorrow would come too soon.

 **Skill Review**

OBJECTIVES

Children review how to

- read fluently;
- use parts of a dictionary entry to find word meanings;
- identify and use singular possessive nouns;
- spell more words with long *o*.

REVIEW

 ## REREADING FOR FLUENCY

Rereading *Mighty Dinosaurs* Have children work in pairs to reread part of *Mighty Dinosaurs* orally, or suggest that children reread page 130. If children need practice reading accurately and with expression, model the reading.

Materials

- dictionary for each pair of children

REVIEW

VOCABULARY: Parts of a Dictionary Entry

Review the parts of a dictionary entry.

- Each alphabetized word in a dictionary is an entry word.
- The definition explains the meaning of the entry word.
- A sample sentence shows how to use the entry word in a sentence.
- A picture may be included to help make the meaning clearer.

Model finding an entry word and meaning.

- Use guide words to find *colony* in a dictionary.
- Read the definition and the sample sentence.
- Ask children to use *colony* in their own sentences.

Have children use dictionary entries to learn word meanings.

- Have partners look up words such as *hinge, rumble, skull*.
- Have pairs read the definitions. Then have children use the words in sentences that suggest their meanings.

GRAMMAR: Singular Possessive Nouns

Review singular possessive nouns.

- A possessive noun is a noun that shows ownership.
- An apostrophe and *s* are added to form the possessive of a singular noun.

Ask children to identify and use singular possessive nouns.

- Display these phrases. Have children identify the singular possessive noun in the second phrase and tell what words it replaced. (*boy's; of the boy*)

> the pet of the boy
> the boy's pet

- Have children use possessive nouns in sentences that describe things their classmates have. Ask other children to identify the possessive nouns and tell what is owned.

Practice/Homework Assign **Practice Book** page 71.

Practice Book page 71

Name _____

Monitoring Student Progress
Review Grammar Singular Possessive Nouns

Writing Possessive Nouns

Rewrite each sentence below by changing the underlined words to show who or what owns something. Remember to add the apostrophe.

1. The <u>pet of the boy</u> was a dinosaur.
   The boy's pet was a dinosaur. **(2 points)**

2. The <u>cave of the family</u> was too small.
   The family's cave was too small. **(2)**

3. The <u>pots of the mother</u> were broken.
   The mother's pots were broken. **(2)**

4. The <u>new home of George</u> was the swamp.
   George's new home was the swamp. **(2)**

5. The Grunts rode on the <u>neck of the dinosaur</u>.
   The Grunts rode on the dinosaur's neck. **(2)**

6. The dinosaur took the Grunts away from the <u>eruption of the volcano</u>.
   The dinosaur took the Grunts away from the volcano's eruption. **(2)**

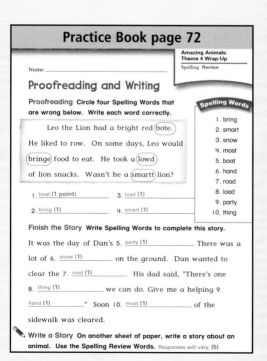

SPELLING: More Long *o* Words

Review long *o* spellings.

- Display *snow, boat, cold*. Have children read each word. Then ask them to name the vowel sound in the words. (long *o*)
- Point out the spellings for long *o*: *o, ow,* and *oa*.

Have children spell long *o* words. Display each incomplete sentence pair.

- Ask volunteers to read each pair of sentences, using words that rhyme with the underlined words to complete them. Have children spell each rhyming word.

> This can <u>float</u>. It's called a ____. (*boat*)
>
> The grass did <u>grow</u>! It's time to ____. (*mow, go*)
>
> Will it <u>snow</u>? I don't ____. (*know*)

Practice Homework Assign **Practice Book** page 72.

Practice Book page 72

Name _____

Amazing Animals: Theme 4 Wrap-Up
Spelling Review

Proofreading and Writing

Proofreading Circle four Spelling Words that are wrong below. Write each word correctly.

Leo the Lion had a bright red (bote.) He liked to row. On some days, Leo would (bringe) food to eat. He took a (lowd) of lion snacks. Wasn't he a (smartt) lion?

1. boat **(1 point)**   3. load **(1)**
2. bring **(1)**   4. smart **(1)**

Spelling Words
1. bring
2. smart
3. snow
4. most
5. boat
6. hand
7. road
8. load
9. party
10. thing

Finish the Story Write Spelling Words to complete this story.

It was the day of Dan's 5. party **(1)** _____. There was a lot of 6. snow **(1)** _____ on the ground. Dan wanted to clear the 7. road **(1)** _____. His dad said, "There's one 8. thing **(1)** _____ we can do. Give me a helping 9. hand **(1)** _____." Soon 10. most **(1)** _____ of the sidewalk was cleared.

✏ **Write a Story** On another sheet of paper, write a story about an animal. Use the Spelling Review Words. Responses will vary. **(5)**

Day at a Glance
pp. T290–T297

Reading Instruction

Theme Connections
Leveled Books

Rereading for Fluency
Selected Theme 4 Phonics
Library stories

Taking Tests

Vocabulary Items
Test Practice

Skill Review Options

High-Frequency Words

Phonics
Cumulative Review

Comprehension
Cause and Effect

Grammar
Plural Possessive Nouns

Spelling
Test

Prompts for Writing
Research Report

Daily Routines

Daily Message

Phonics Review Point to each word as you read aloud the Daily Message.

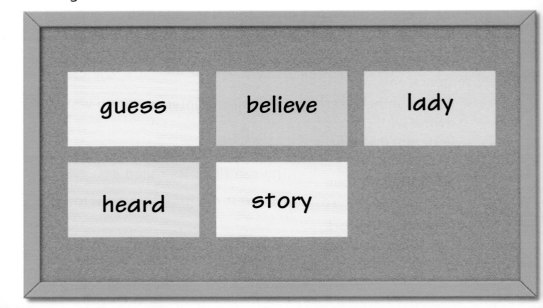

Do you know the answers to these tricky animal questions?
• How many babies do cockroaches have at one time? Do they have more or fewer than ten?
• Why do wolves howl after dark?

Have children
• read aloud the Daily Message and guess the answers; (about 32; to communicate with other wolves)
• circle and read words with *r*-controlled vowel sounds; words with the long *o* sound; and plural nouns. (*more, or, dark; know, cockroaches; questions, answers, babies, cockroaches, wolves*)

Word Wall

High-Frequency Word Review Briefly review these high-frequency words and their meanings. Have children use the words to write a story about an amazing animal.

guess   believe   lady

heard   story

Vocabulary

Dictionary Entries Display this sentence: *Do ats have gills?* Have children use dictionaries to ook up the word *gills,* find its meaning, and then nswer the question.

Provide partners with unfamiliar words, such as those shown. Have them use a dictionary to find the words.

Have partners make up questions with the words. Ask other children to look up the words and answer the questions.

graze   fierce
extinct   migrate

Daily Writing Prompt

Research Report Use this prompt to review writing a draft of a research report. Have children use the notes they took on Day 4. Remind children to include a title.

Write a paragraph for a report about how animals work together. Use the facts from the notes you took about ants and dinosaurs. Remember to use your own words.

While you work with small groups, children can choose from a wealth of theme-related books to complete these activities.

Leveled Readers . . .

for *Officer Buckle and Gloria*
Max the Pet Show Star
The Best Job for Scooter
Daisy Divine, Dancing Dog
Max Is a Star!

for *Ant*
Earthworms
Busy Bees
Butterflies!
The Amazing Earthworm

for *The Great Ball Game*
Bird Race
Turtle's Small Pond
Possum's Bare Tail
A Race to the Mountain

Leveled Theme Paperbacks

Sandy Goes to the Vet
Raptors!
A Toad for Tuesday

Leveled Bibliography

pp. T6–T7

THEME CONNECTIONS: Leveled Books

Animal Tale

👥 **Pairs**	🕐 30 minutes
Objective	Write a story about how an animal came to be.
Materials	paper, pencils

Work with a partner to write a tale. Explain why an animal looks or acts the way it does.

- Choose an animal. With your partner, plan a tale that tells how the animal came to be the way it is.
- Write ideas for what happens first, next, and last.
- Use your ideas to help you write your tale.
- Draw a picture to go with it.

How did the pig get its curly tail?

Why does a frog hop?

How did the skunk get its white stripe?

How the Pig Got a Curly Tail

Consider copying and laminating these activities for use in centers.

Animal Dictionary

👤👤👤 Groups	🕐 30 minutes
Objective	Create dictionary entries for theme animals.
Materials	dictionary, paper, pencils, crayons or markers

Make an animal dictionary for the animals in this theme. Use the animal names as entry words. Write entries that describe the animals.

- Make a list of animals from this theme.

- Choose animals to put in your dictionary.

- For each dictionary entry, write the name of the animal. Then write a short definition that tells what the animal is like.

- Write a sample sentence for your entry. Draw a picture to go with it, too.

- Put all your entries in ABC order to make your animal dictionary. Add a cover.

Award Time

👤 Singles	🕐 20 minutes
Objective	Make an award for an amazing animal.
Materials	scissors, paper, colored pencils or markers

Which animals from this theme are your favorites? Which are the most unusual? What makes them amazing? Make an award for an amazing animal from the theme.

- Choose the amazing animal that you think is the most unusual and amazing.

- Draw a simple, large shape of the animal. Cut out the shape.

- On one side of it, write the animal's name.

- On the other side, write why that animal is amazing.

- Then make and color the award to give the animal.

- Present your award. Tell your classmates who the award is for and why.

TAKING TESTS: Vocabulary Items

Test Practice

Remind children to mark answers carefully.

- Be sure to mark your answer in the correct place.
- Be careful to fill in the answer bubble completely.
- When you change an answer, be sure to erase it completely.

Discuss how to check answers.

- Take a break before checking answers. Stretch, stare out the window, or close your eyes. Relax for a minute.
- Focus on the test questions that gave you trouble.

Assign Practice Book pages 73–74.

- Provide children with practice answering vocabulary questions about *Mighty Dinosaurs* on Anthology pages 127–130.
- Read the directions aloud.
- Emphasize that children should use all three steps to choose the best answer for each question.

Practice Book page 73

Name _____

Monitoring
Student Progress

Taking Tests Vocabulary
Items

Test Practice

Read each vocabulary question about *Mighty Dinosaurs*. Use the three steps you've learned to choose the best answer. Then fill in the circle beside the best answer.

1. Read this sentence from the story. "We know a lot about dinosaurs from their remains, which we have found buried in rocks and beneath sand." What does **remains** mean? (3 points)

   ○ staying late   ○ going away
   ● parts that are left   ○ pieces of rock

2. The author writes, "Dinosaurs had knobby or pebbly skin and laid eggs." Which word means the opposite of **knobby**? (3)

   ○ rough   ● smooth
   ○ pretty   ○ hard

3. On page 127, what does the word **crests** mean? (3)

   ○ teeth for biting or chewing
   ● body parts that stick up
   ○ leafy plants
   ○ hats to shade their eyes

Continue on page 74.

Practice Book page 74

Name _____

Monitoring
Student Progress

Taking Tests Vocabulary
Items

Test Practice continued

4. Which word means about the same as **packs** on page 128? (3 points)

   ○ meals
   ○ bundles
   ● groups
   ○ claws

5. Read this sentence from the story. "Not all dinosaurs were fierce hunters." Which word means the opposite of **fierce**? (3)

   ● gentle
   ○ angry
   ○ dangerous
   ○ hungry

6. Read this sentence from the story. "Plant-eating dinosaurs needed large amounts of food to give them energy." What does **energy** mean? (3)

   ○ a tool to move things around
   ○ a happy feeling
   ○ a light to see with
   ● the strength to do things

Additional Resources

Teacher's Assessment Handbook

Suggests more strategies for preparing children for standardized tests

REVIEW

PHONICS: Cumulative Review

Review the patterns. Use these words to review the skills:

m<u>ar</u>ket	thi<u>nk</u>	rainb<u>ow</u>	foxes
c<u>or</u>n	gra<u>nd</u>	c<u>oa</u>ch	snakes
m<u>ore</u>	spli<u>nt</u>		ladies
	cla<u>mp</u>		
	ri<u>ng</u>		

- For each word in column 1, point to the underlined letters and remind children of the sound they stand for. Then ask volunteers to read the words.

- Follow a similar procedure for columns 2 and 3. Review the sounds the underlined letters stand for. Then have children read the words.

- For column 4, have children read the plural nouns. Then remind them that the endings *-s, -es,* or *-ies* can be added to some base words to make them mean "more than one" and that *y* often changes to *i* before the ending *-es* is added. Ask children to identify the base words and the endings.

Have children read words with the patterns. Display these words: *glowing, pretend, patches, forgotten, chores, toaster.* Have children use what they know about letters and sounds to help them read the words. Then ask them to use the words in sentences.

Have children apply their phonics skills. Assign **Practice Book** page 75.

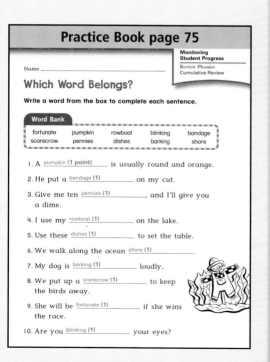

Practice Book page 75

Name _____

Monitoring Student Progress
Review Phonics
Cumulative Review

Which Word Belongs?

Write a word from the box to complete each sentence.

Word Bank

fortunate	pumpkin	rowboat	blinking	bandage
scarecrow	pennies	dishes	barking	shore

1. A <u>pumpkin **(1 point)**</u> is usually round and orange.
2. He put a <u>bandage **(1)**</u> on my cut.
3. Give me ten <u>pennies **(1)**</u>, and I'll give you a dime.
4. I use my <u>rowboat **(1)**</u> on the lake.
5. Use these <u>dishes **(1)**</u> to set the table.
6. We walk along the ocean <u>shore **(1)**</u>.
7. My dog is <u>barking **(1)**</u> loudly.
8. We put up a <u>scarecrow **(1)**</u> to keep the birds away.
9. She will be <u>fortunate **(1)**</u> if she wins the race.
10. Are you <u>blinking **(1)**</u> your eyes?

Skill Review

OBJECTIVES

Children review how to
- identify cause-and-effect relationships;
- read fluently;
- identify plural possessive nouns;
- apply spelling principles.

Practice Book page 76

Monitoring
Student Progress

Review Comprehension
Cause and Effect

Name _____

Cause-Effect Chart

Complete the chart for *Little Grunt and the Big Egg*.

Cause	➡	Effect
1. An egg hatches into a baby dinosaur.		The Grunts are surprised. (1)
2. George gets too big for the cave. (1 point)		George is sent away.
3. Little Grunt takes George back to the swamp.		George and Little Grunt cry. (1)
4. A volcano starts erupting. (1)		The cave begins to shake.
5. George carries the Grunts away from the volcano.		The Grunts are safe. (1)

Monitoring Student Progress

Fluency Check

Consider conducting fluency checks with individuals to monitor their reading development. See the guidelines on page T299.

REVIEW

COMPREHENSION: Cause and Effect

Review cause and effect. Remind children that

- sometimes one thing in a story causes another thing to happen;
- the cause tells why something happens, and the effect is what happens.

Have children identify causes and effects. Remind children that George must leave the cave in *Little Grunt and the Big Egg*.

- Ask what causes that event to happen. (George gets too big.)
- Have children tell which event is the cause and which is the effect. (Cause: George gets too big. Effect: George has to leave.)
- Have children name other events that have cause-and-effect relationships in other stories from the theme. Also ask children to identify the cause and effect. (Sample responses: Ants dig tunnels under the ground, so they must carry the dirt above ground to form anthills. The volcano erupted, so the Grunts' lives were in danger.)

Have children practice recognizing causes and effects. Assign **Practice Book** page 76.

REVIEW

 ## REREADING FOR FLUENCY

Rereading Selected Phonics Library Stories Have children work in pairs to reread orally a Phonics Library story. If children need practice reading accurately and with expression, model the reading.

GRAMMAR: Plural Possessive Nouns

Review plural possessive nouns. Display the words *dinosaurs, dinosaurs', children,* and *children's.* Remind children that

- a plural possessive noun, such as *dinosaurs',* shows that something belongs to more than one person, animal, or thing;
- most plural possessive nouns end in *s'.*

Have students identify plural possessive nouns.

- Display phrases such as these: *the girls' toys, the boy's rocks, the cook's pots, the trees' leaves.*
- Have children read each phrase and identify the possessive noun in it. Ask whether the possessive noun is a singular or a plural possessive noun and how children know. (*girls',* plural; *boy's,* singular; *cook's,* singular; *trees',* plural)

SPELLING: Test

Test Have children write only the underlined words.

Basic Words

1. The polar bear was covered by a **load** of **snow**.
2. Will you **sing** at the **party**?
3. The wind will **blow** the **boat**.
4. In winter it gets **cold** at the duck **farm**.
5. Please **park** on the **road**.
6. The **smart** boy sent a letter to **thank** his uncle for the gifts.
7. The worm likes to **think** of one **thing** only—dirt.
8. Dogs can **hold** **most** things in their teeth.
9. The red bird likes to **bring** its lunch to the **yard**.
10. If you can't **hand** the box to Molly, **send** it to her.

Challenge Words

11. A **rainbow** decorates the **department** store.
12. My friend is very **young**, but she can play a **grand** piano.
13. My **goal** is to learn five new words today.

Assessing Student Progress

Monitoring Student Progress

Preparing for Testing

Throughout the theme, your children have had opportunities to read and think critically, to connect and compare, and to practice and apply new and reviewed skills and reading strategies.

Monitoring Student Progress

For Theme 4, *Amazing Animals,* children have read the paired selections—*Little Grunt and the Big Egg* and *Mighty Dinosaurs*—and made connections between these and other selections in the theme. They have practiced strategies for Vocabulary Items, and they have reviewed all the tested skills taught in this theme, as well as some tested skills taught in earlier themes. Your children are now ready to have their progress formally assessed in both theme assessments and standardized tests.

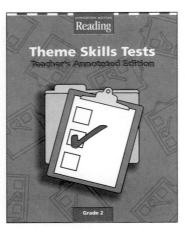

Testing Options

The **Integrated Theme Test** and the **Theme Skills Test** are formal group assessments used to evaluate children's performance on theme objectives. In addition to administering one or both of these tests, you may wish to assess children's oral reading fluency.

Integrated Theme Test
- Assesses children's progress as readers and writers in a format that reflects instruction
- Integrates reading and writing skills: comprehension strategies and skills, high-frequency words and vocabulary, spelling, grammar, and writing
- Includes authentic literary passages to test children's reading skills in context

Theme Skills Test
- May be used as a pretest or administered following the theme
- Assesses children's mastery of discrete reading and language arts skills taught in the theme: comprehension skills, high-frequency words and vocabulary, spelling, grammar, writing, and information and study skills
- Consists of individual skill subtests, which can be administered separately

Fluency Assessment

Oral reading fluency is a useful measure of a child's development of rapid automatic word recognition. Children who are on level in Grade 2 should be able to read, accurately and with expression, an appropriate level text at the approximate rates shown in the table below.

Early Grade 2	Mid-Grade 2	Late Grade 2
53–82 words correct per minute	78–106 words correct per minute	94–124 words correct per minute

- You can use the **Leveled Reading Passages Assessment Kit** to assess fluency or a **Leveled Reader** from this theme at the appropriate level for each child.

For some children you may check their oral fluency rate three times during the year. If children are working below level, you might want to check their fluency rate more often. Children can also check their own fluency by timing themselves reading easier text.

Consider decoding and comprehension, as well as reading rate, when evaluating children's reading development.

- For information on how to select appropriate text, administer fluency checks, and interpret results, see the **Teacher's Assessment Handbook,** pp. 25–28.

Using Multiple Measures

In addition to the tests mentioned on page T298, multiple measures might include the following:

- Observation Checklist from this theme
- Research Report from the Reading-Writing Workshop
- Other writing, projects, or artwork
- One or more items selected by the student

Children's progress is best evaluated through multiple measures. Multiple measures of assessment can be collected in a portfolio. The portfolio provides a record of children's progress over time and can be useful when conferencing with the child, parents, or other educators.

Turn the page to continue.

Technology

Managing Assessment

**The Learner Profile®
CD-ROM** lets you record, manage, and report your assessment of children's progress electronically.

You can

- record children's progress on objectives in Theme 4.

- add or import additional objectives, including your state standards, and track your children's progress against these.

- record and manage results from the **Integrated Theme Test** and the **Theme Skills Test** for Theme 4, as well as results from other reading assessments.

- organize information about children's progress and generate a variety of student assessment reports.

- use *Learner Profile® To Go* to record children's progress throughout the day on a handheld computer device and then upload the information to a desktop computer.

Using Assessment to Plan Instruction

You can use the results of theme assessments to determine an individual child's needs for additional skill instruction and to modify instruction during the next theme. For more detail, see the test manuals or the **Teacher's Assessment Handbook**.

This chart shows Theme 4 resources for differentiating additional instruction. As you look ahead to Theme 5, you can plan to use the corresponding Theme 5 resources.

Differentiating Instruction

Assessment Shows	Use These Resources	
Difficulty with Comprehension **Emphasize** Oral comprehension, strategy development, story comprehension, vocabulary development	• **Get Set for Reading CD-ROM** • Reteaching: Comprehension, *Teacher's Edition,* pp. R26; R28; R30 • Selection Summaries in *Teacher's Resource Blackline Masters,* pp. 31–33	• *Extra Support Handbook,* pp. 122–123, 128–129; 132–133, 138–139; 142–143, 148–149
Difficulty with Word Skills Phonics High-Frequency Words Vocabulary **Emphasize** Word skills; phonics; reading for fluency; phonemic awareness	• **Get Set for Reading CD-ROM** • *Phonics Library,* Theme 4 • *I Love Reading Books* • Reteaching: Phonics, *Teacher's Edition,* pp. R10; R12; R14; R16; R18 • Reteaching: High-Frequency Words, *Teacher's Edition,* pp. R20; R22; R24	• *Extra Support Handbook,* pp. 120–121, 124, 126–127; 130–131, 134, 136–137; 140–141, 144, 146–147 • *Handbook for English Language Learners,* pp. 124–125, 126–127, 128–129, 130, 132; 134–135, 136–137, 138–139, 140, 142; 144–145, 146–147, 148–149, 150, 152 • *Lexia Phonics CD-ROM: Primary Intervention*
Difficulty with Fluency **Emphasize** Reading and rereading of independent level text, vocabulary development	• *Phonics Library,* Theme 4 • Leveled Bibliography, *Teacher's Edition,* pp. T6–T7 • Below Level **Theme Paperback**	• Below Level **Leveled Readers**. *See* Below Level lesson, *Teacher's Edition,* pp. T90; T172; T240
Difficulty with Writing **Emphasize** Complete sentences, combining sentences, choosing exact words	• *Handbook for English Language Learners,* pp. 133; 143; 153 • Reteaching: Grammar Skills, *Teacher's Edition,* pp. R32; R33; R34	• Improving Writing, *Teacher's Edition,* pp. T83, T88; T102; T165, T170; T233, T238
Overall High Performance **Emphasize** Independent reading and writing, vocabulary development, critical thinking	• Challenge/Extension Activities: Phonics and High-Frequency Words, *Teacher's Edition,* pp. R11; R13; R15; R17; R19; R21; R23; R25 • Challenge/Extension Activities: Comprehension, *Teacher's Edition,* pp. R27; R29; R31	• Reading Assignment Cards, *Teachers' Resource Blackline Masters,* pp. 63–68 • Above Level **Theme Paperback** • Above Level **Leveled Readers**. *See* Above Level lesson, *Teacher's Edition,* pp. T92; T174; T242 • Challenge Activity Masters, *Challenge Handbook,* CH4–1 to CH4–6

BIOGRAPHY

Literature

BIOGRAPHY

1 Decodable Text

Phonics Library

* *Where Do I Start?*

2 Background and Vocabulary

3 Main Selections

4 Write a Biography

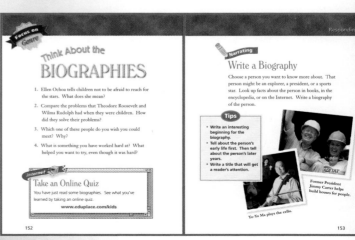

Instructional Support

Planning and Practice

- Planning and classroom management
- Reading and skill instruction
- Materials for reaching all learners

- Independent practice for skills, Level 2.2

- Charts/ Transparencies
- Strategy Posters
- Blackline Masters

Technology

Audio Selections

Reach for the Stars: The Ellen Ochoa Story

President Theodore Roosevelt

Wilma Rudolph: Olympic Track Champion

www.eduplace.com

Log on to Education Place for vocabulary support—
- **e•Glossary**
- **e•WordGame**

Leveled Books for Reaching All Learners

Leveled Readers and Leveled Practice

- Independent reading for building fluency

- Topic, comprehension strategy, and comprehension skill linked to selections

- Lessons in Teacher's Edition, pages T362–T365

- Leveled practice for every book

Technology

Leveled Readers
Audio available

● BELOW LEVEL

Florence Griffith Joyner
Olympic Champion

by Joelle Campbell

▲ ON LEVEL

Mae Jemison
Making Dreams Come True

by C. M. Thorsen

● Below Level Practice

Vocabulary

Use the clues to complete the crossword puzzle. Choose your answers from the words in the box.

Vocabulary
college
coach
Olympics
champion
medal

Across
1. a person who wins races or games
4. a person who helps athletes improve their skills

Down
1. a school to go to after high school
2. a metal disk awarded as a prize
3. games and races that people from all over the world compete in

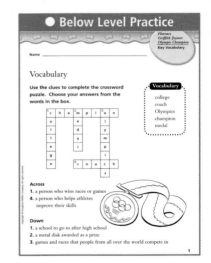

▲ On Level Practice

Vocabulary

Use the words from the box to complete the sentences.

Vocabulary
launched
astronauts
voyage
curiosity
universe
weightlessness

1. The ___astronauts___ flew into space.
2. NASA ___launched___ the space shuttle.
3. The men and women on board would ___voyage___ to the moon.
4. The moon, planets, and stars are all part of the ___universe___.
5. In space, people float because of ___weightlessness___.
6. Each astronaut felt great ___curiosity___ about what they might find on the moon.

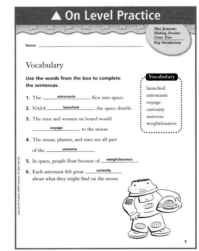

● Below Level Practice

Writing

Check your biography. Make sure you have shown why your person is so special. Read each sentence in the checklist. Does your biography contain that part? If so, put a checkmark in the box. If not, add that part to your biography. By revising it, you will make your biography even better! **Answers will vary.**

☐ I wrote a good title. It tells the most interesting fact about the person.

☐ I wrote a strong beginning. I think it will grab readers' attention.

☐ I told about the person's early life first.

☐ I told about each important event.

☐ I put the events in the order in which they happened.

☐ I wrote a strong ending. It tells why the person is so special.

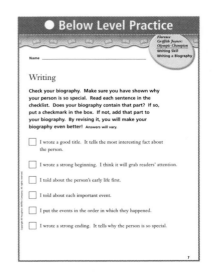

▲ On Level Practice

Writing

Check your biography. Make sure you have shown why your person is so special. Read each sentence in the checklist. Does your biography contain that part? If so, put a checkmark in the box. If not, add that part to your biography. By revising it, you will make your biography even better! **Answers will vary.**

☐ I wrote a title that tells an interesting fact about the person.

☐ I wrote an interesting beginning. I think it will grab the readers' attention.

☐ I presented the facts in the right order.

☐ I told about the person's early life.

☐ I told about each important event.

☐ I put the events in the order in which they happened.

☐ I wrote a strong ending. It tells why I think that this person is special.

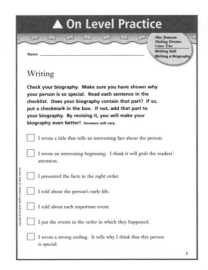

■ ABOVE LEVEL

Theodore Roosevelt:
Friend of Nature
by Gary Miller

Leveled Readers

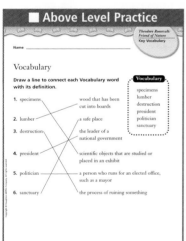

■ Above Level Practice

Name _____

Vocabulary

Draw a line to connect each Vocabulary word with its definition.

Vocabulary
specimens
lumber
destruction
president
politician
sanctuary

1. specimens — wood that has been cut into boards
2. lumber — a safe place
3. destruction — the leader of a national government
4. president — scientific objects that are studied or placed in an exhibit
5. politician — a person who runs for an elected office, such as a mayor
6. sanctuary — the process of ruining something

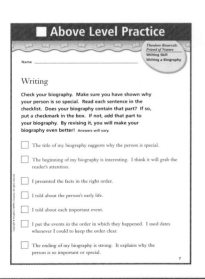

■ Above Level Practice

Name _____

Writing

Check your biography. Make sure you have shown why your person is so special. Read each sentence in the checklist. Does your biography contain that part? If so, put a checkmark in the box. If not, add that part to your biography. By revising it, you will make your biography even better! Answers will vary.

☐ The title of my biography suggests why the person is special.

☐ The beginning of my biography is interesting. I think it will grab the reader's attention.

☐ I presented the facts in the right order.

☐ I told about the person's early life.

☐ I told about each important event.

☐ I put the events in the order in which they happened. I used dates whenever I could to keep the order clear.

☐ The ending of my biography is strong. It explains why the person is so important or special.

◆ LANGUAGE SUPPORT

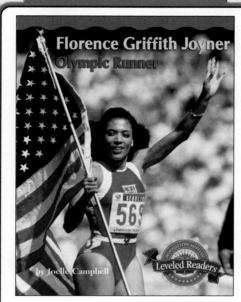

Florence Griffith Joyner
Olympic Runner

by Joelle Campbell

Leveled Readers

◆ Language Support Practice

Name _____

Build Background

Label and color the medals. Then match them to the teams.

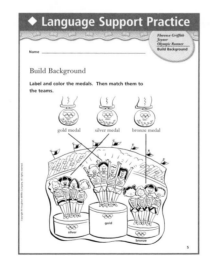

gold medal   silver medal   bronze medal

◆ Language Support Practice

Name _____

Vocabulary

Use the words in the box to label what is in the picture.

Vocabulary
champion
coach
medal
Olympics
prizes
team

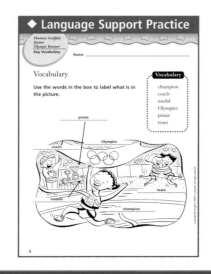

Suggestions for Independent Reading

- Recommended trade books for independent reading in the genre

Helen Keller: Courage in the Dark

(Random)
by Johanna Hurwitz

Happy Birthday, Martin Luther King

(Scholastic)
by Jean Marzollo

A Picture Book of George Washington

(Holiday)
by David A. Adler

Roberto Clemente: Athlete and Hero

(Modern Curriculum)
by Diana Pérez, Ph.D.

Daily Lesson Plans

Technology

Lesson Planner CD-ROM allows you to customize the chart below to develop your own lesson plans.

T Skill tested on Theme Skills Test and/or Integrated Theme Test

 80–90 minutes

Reading
Phonics
Comprehension

Leveled Readers
• Fluency Practice
• Independent Reading

 20–30 minutes

Word Work
Vocabulary
High-Frequency Words
Spelling

 20–30 minutes

Writing and Oral Language
Writing
Grammar
Listening/Speaking/Viewing

DAY 1

Daily Routines, T312–T313
Phonics and Language Activities

Listening Comprehension, T314–T315
Meet Dr. Seuss

Phonics, T316–T317
Words with *r*-Controlled Vowels
Word Endings, Final Syllables *-tion, -ture*

Reading Decodable Text, T319–T321
Where Do I Start?

Leveled Readers
Florence Griffith-Joyner
Mae Jemison
Theodore Roosevelt
Florence Griffith-Joyner

Lessons and Leveled Practice, T362–T365

Vocabulary, T313
Exact Verbs

High-Frequency Word Review, T318
about, afraid, beautiful, believe, friend, near, surprised, watch, write, years

Spelling, T322
The Vowel + *r* Sounds in *for* and *before*

Writing, T313
Daily Writing Prompt

Grammar, T323
Nouns and Pronouns Together

Daily Language Practice
1. Where were you borne.
(Where were you born?)

Listening/Speaking/Viewing, T314–T315
Teacher Read Aloud

DAY 2

Daily Routines, T324–T325
Phonics and Language Activities

Building Background, T326

Genre Vocabulary, T327
biography   event   information
champion   fact   president

Reading the Selection, T328–T337

Comprehension Strategy, T328
Evaluate

Comprehension Skill, T328
Understanding a Biography

Responding, T338
Comprehension Check, T338

Leveled Readers
Florence Griffith-Joyner
Mae Jemison
Theodore Roosevelt
Florence Griffith-Joyner

Lessons and Leveled Practice, T362–T365

Vocabulary, T325
Categories

High-Frequency Words, T324
Word Wall

Spelling, T341
Review, Practice: The Vowel + *r* Sounds in *for* and *before*

Writing, T339, T340
Write a Biography

Grammar, T341
Practice: Nouns and Pronouns Together

Daily Language Practice
2. This merning Jan ate two apple.
(This morning Jan ate two apples.)

Listening/Speaking/Viewing, T331, T337, T33:
Stop and Think, Wrapping Up, Responding

Target Skills of the Week

Phonics	*r*-Controlled Vowels; Word Endings, *-tion, -ture*
Comprehension	Understanding Biography; Evaluate
Vocabulary	High-Frequency Words; Abbreviations
Fluency	Decodable Text; Leveled Readers

Focus On Genre

DAY 3

Daily Routines, T342–T343
Phonics and Language Activities

Rereading the Selection, T328–T337

Comprehension Skill, T344–T345
Understanding a Biography

Rereading for Understanding, T346
Writer's Craft: Using Quotations; Use of Paragraphs and Topic Sentences

Leveled Readers
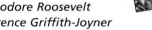
Florence Griffith-Joyner
Mae Jemison
Theodore Roosevelt
Florence Griffith-Joyner

Lessons and Leveled Practice, T362–T365

Vocabulary, T343
Multiple-Meaning Words

High-Frequency Words, T342
Word Wall

Spelling, T347
Vocabulary Connection: The Vowel + *r* Sounds in *for* and *before*

Writing, T340
Continue Writing a Biography

Grammar, T347
Activity: Nouns and Pronouns Together

Daily Language Practice
3. My friend carl has for pets.
(My friend Carl has four pets.)

Listening/Speaking/Viewing, T346
Rereading for Understanding

DAY 4

Daily Routines, T348–T349
Phonics and Language Activities

Preparing for Discussion, T350
Small Group Discussion

Phonics Review, T353
Game: Let's Go Fishing (Vowel Pairs)

Information and Study Skill, T355
Using Text Features

Leveled Readers
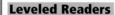
Florence Griffith-Joyner
Mae Jemison
Theodore Roosevelt
Florence Griffith-Joyner

Lessons and Leveled Practice, T362–T365

Vocabulary, T352
Abbreviations

High-Frequency Words, T348
Word Wall

Spelling, T354
Game, Proofreading: The Vowel + *r* Sounds in *for* and *before*

Writing, T351
Dates and Time-Order Words

Grammar, T354
Practice: Nouns and Pronouns Together

Daily Language Practice
4. Mom beeped the car horen at the Dog.
(Mom beeped the car horn at the dog.)

Listening/Speaking/Viewing, T350
Preparing for Discussion

DAY 5

Daily Routines, T356–T357
Phonics and Language Activities

Comprehension: Rereading for Understanding Visualizing, T358
Literature Discussion, T359

Rereading for Fluency, T328–T337

Leveled Readers

Florence Griffith-Joyner
Mae Jemison
Theodore Roosevelt
Florence Griffith-Joyner

Lessons and Leveled Practice, T362–T365

Vocabulary, T357
Vocabulary Expansion

High-Frequency Words, T356
Word Wall

Spelling, T360
Test: The Vowel + *r* Sounds in *for* and *before*

Writing, T360
Publishing a Biography

Grammar, T359
Proofreading for Capital Letters

Daily Language Practice
5. The sporte Ed likes best is running?
(The sport Ed likes best is running.)

Listening/Speaking/Viewing, T361
Making Introductions

DAILY LESSON PLANS

Focus on Biography

Managing Flexible Groups

		DAY 1	**DAY 2**
WHOLE CLASS		• Daily Routines (TE pp. T312–T313) • Teacher Read Aloud (TE pp. T314–T315) • Phonics lesson (TE pp. T316–T317) • High-Frequency Word Review lesson (TE p. T318)	• Daily Routines (TE pp. T324–T325) • Background, Vocabulary, Strategy and Skill, Purpose Setting (TE pp. T326–T329) ***After Reading at Small Group Time*** • Wrapping Up, Responding (TE pp. T337–T338)
SMALL GROUPS	**Extra Support**	**TEACHER-LED** • Read Phonics Library: *Where Do I Start?* (TE pp. T319–T321) • Selected I Love Reading Books: 33–39	**TEACHER-LED** • Read Biographies. (TE pp. T328–T336) —————————————— **Partner or Individual Reading** • Read with audio CD of Biographies. • **Fluency Practice** Reread Phonics Library: *Where Do I Start?* (TE pp. T319–T321) OR selected I Love Reading Books: 33–39.
	On Level	**TEACHER-LED** • Reread Transparency 4–2 aloud. (TE p. T318) • Read Phonics Library: *Where Do I Start?* (TE pp. T319–T321)	**TEACHER-LED** • Read Biographies. (TE pp. T328–T336) • Begin Leveled Reader: On Level (TE p. T363) OR book from Bibliography. (TE pp. T6–T7) • **Fluency Practice** Reread Phonics Library: *Where Do I Start?* (TE pp. T319–T321) ✔
	Challenge	**Partner or Individual Reading** • Read Phonics Library: *Where Do I Start?* (TE pp. T319–T321) • Select from Suggestions for Independent Reading (TE p. T305) • **Fluency Practice** Reread *Little Grunt and the Big Egg.* (TE pp. T256–T260)	**Partner or Individual Reading** • Read Biographies. (TE pp. T328–T336) • **Fluency Practice** Reread Phonics Library: *Where Do I Start?* (TE pp. T319–T321)
	English Language Learners	**TEACHER-LED** • Read Phonics Library: *Where Do I Start?* (TE pp. T319–T321) • Selected I Love Reading Books: 33–39	**TEACHER-LED** • Selected I Love Reading Books: 33–39 • **Fluency Practice** Reread Phonics Library: *Where Do I Start?* (TE pp. T319–T321) ✔ —————————————— **Partner or Individual Reading** • Read with audio CD of Biographies

Independent Activities

- Audio CD of Anthology biographies.
- Journals: selection notes, questions.
- Complete, review **Practice Book** (pp. 77–82, 86, 88) and **Leveled Reader Practice Blackline Masters.** (TE pp. T362–T365)

✔ Opportunity to informally assess oral reading rate.

DAY 3

Daily Routines (TE pp. T342–T343)

After Reading at Small Group Time
- Comprehension lesson (TE pp. T344–T345)
- Rereading for Understanding (TE p. T346)

TEACHER-LED

Read aloud from Biographies to answer Guiding Comprehension. (TE pp. T328–T331)
Begin Leveled Reader: Below Level (TE p. T362) OR book from Bibliography. (TE pp. T6–T7)

Partner or Individual Reading

Fluency Practice Phonics Library, Week 1 (TE pp. T37–T39 or T80–T81)

Partner or Individual Reading
- Reread Biographies. (TE pp. T328–T336)
- Complete Leveled Reader: On Level (TE p. T363) OR book from Bibliography. (TE pp. T6–T7)
- **Fluency Practice** Phonics Library, Week 1 (TE pp. T37–T39 or T80–T81)

TEACHER-LED

Read aloud from Biographies to answer Guiding Comprehension. (TE pp. T328–T336) ✔
Begin Leveled Reader: Above Level (TE p. T364) OR book from Bibliography. (TE pp. T6–T7)

Partner or Individual Reading
- Complete Leveled Reader: Above Level (TE p. T364) OR book from Bibliography. (TE pp. T6–T7)

TEACHER-LED

Read aloud from Biographies to answer Guiding Comprehension. (TE pp. T328–T331)
Preview Leveled Reader: Language Support. (TE p. 365)

Partner or Individual Reading

Fluency Practice Phonics Library, Week 1 (TE pp. T37–T39 or T80–T81)

DAY 4

- Daily Routines (TE pp. T348–T349)
- Preparing for Discussion (TE p. T350)
- Phonics Review (TE p. T353)
- Information and Study Skill (TE p. T355)

TEACHER-LED

- Read aloud from Biographies to answer Guiding Comprehension. (TE pp. 332–336)
- Complete Leveled Reader: Below Level (TE p. T362) OR book from Bibliography. (TE pp. T6–T7)
- **Fluency Practice** Phonics Library, Week 2 (TE pp. T123–T125 or T162–T163) OR Leveled Reader: Below Level (TE p. T362) ✔

TEACHER-LED

- Read aloud from Biographies to answer Guiding Comprehension. (TE pp. T328–T336)
- **Fluency Practice** Phonics Library, Week 2 (TE pp. T123–T125 or T162–T163) OR Leveled Reader: On Level (TE p. T363) ✔

Partner or Individual Reading
- **Fluency Practice** Reread *Mighty Dinosaurs* (TE pp. T267–T269) OR Leveled Reader: Above Level. (TE p. T364)
- Select from Suggestions for Independent Reading. (TE p. T305)

TEACHER-LED

- Read aloud from Biographies to answer Guiding Comprehension. (TE pp. T332–T336)
- Read Leveled Reader: Language Support. (TE p. T365)

Partner or Individual Reading
- **Fluency Practice** Phonics Library, Week 2 (TE pp. T123–T125 or T162–T163)

DAY 5

- Daily Routines (TE pp. T356–T357)
- Comprehension: Visualizing (TE p. T358)
- Literature Discussion (TE p. T359)

TEACHER-LED

- Reread Biographies. (TE pp. T328–T336)
- **Fluency Practice** Phonics Library, Week 3 (TE pp. T193–T195 or T230–T231) OR Leveled Reader: Below Level (TE p. T362) ✔

Partner or Individual Reading
- Reread Biographies or *Little Grunt and the Big Egg* and *Mighty Dinosaurs* (TE pp. T328–T336, T256–T260, T267–T269)
- **Fluency Practice** Phonics Library, Week 3 (TE pp. T193–T195 or T230–T231) OR Leveled Reader: On Level (TE p. T363)

TEACHER-LED

- **Fluency Practice** Reread Biographies (TE pp. T328–T336) OR Leveled Reader: Above Level. (TE p. T364) ✔

Partner or Individual Reading
- Suggestions for Independent Reading (TE p. T305) OR Bibliography (TE pp. T6–T7).

TEACHER-LED

- Reread Biographies. (TE pp. T328–T336)
- Complete Leveled Reader: Language Support. (TE p. T365)
- **Fluency Practice** Phonics Library, Week 3 (TE pp. T193–T195 or T230–T231) OR selected I Love Reading Books: 33–39 ✔

- Reread familiar selections.
- Read trade book from Leveled Bibliography (TE pp. T6–T7) OR Suggestions for Independent Reading. (TE p. 305)
- Activities related to *Focus on Biography* at Education Place: www.eduplace.com

Turn the page for more independent activities.

Classroom Management

Independent Activities

Assign these activities while you work with small groups.

Differentiated Instruction for Small Groups

- **Leveled Readers** Below Level, On Level, Above Level, Language Support

- **Lessons and Leveled Practice** pp. T362–T365

Independent Activities

- Daily Routines, pp. T312, T324, T342, T348, T356

Drama Center

Biographies

👥 **Groups**	🕐 **40 minutes**
Objective	Role-play a scene from a biography.
Materials	Paper, pencil, props, costumes

Choose a scene from a biography to perform.

- Reread the biography. Think about what the person says and does.

- Decide on parts for each group member. Remember, you will need a narrator.

- Read the biography aloud. Add movements, props, and costumes.

- Perform your biography for the class.

Social Studies Center

Terrific Timelines

👤 **Singles**	🕐 **30 minutes**
Objective	Make a timeline.
Materials	Paper, ruler, pencil

Make a timeline of your school year.

- Draw a line across your paper.

- Write the month you started school at the left end of the line and today's month at the right.

- Write one important event for each month. It could be a special thing you did or learned.

- Share your timeline with classmates.

September	October	November	December
Started second grade	learned about whales and the ocean	field trip to a museum	sang in a concert

---

Look for more activities in the **Classroom Management Kit.**

Consider copying and laminating these activities for use in centers.

Art Center

Body Biographies

Pairs	⏱ 40 minutes
Objective	Write a biography.
Materials	Butcher paper, markers, scissors

Make a body biography!

Have a partner trace your body on a piece of paper. Cut out the shape.

Write information about yourself on your cut-out. When were you born? What is your favorite sport?

Draw pictures of your favorite books, toys, foods, colors, or games. Fill in your whole body!

Display your body biography.

Writing Center

Diary Entry

👤 Singles	⏱ 30 minutes
Objective	Write a diary entry.
Materials	Paper, pencil

Pretend you are someone in a biography you have read.

• Write one or two diary entries.

• Write the date. Tell what happened. Use lots of details. Make the entry seem like it was written by this person.

• Read your diary entry to a partner. Can he or she guess who this person is?

Music Center

Biography of a Musician

👥 Pairs	⏱ 40 minutes
Objective	Learn about a famous musician.
Materials	Encyclopedia or computer with Internet access, paper, pencil

Write a short biography of a musician, composer, or performer.

• Find facts about this person in an encyclopedia or on the Internet.

• Jot down important facts about him or her.

• Draw a picture of the musician on a poster. Write what you learned about this person on the poster, next to your picture.

• Share your work with classmates.

Day at a Glance
pp. T312–T323

Reading Instruction

Teacher Read Aloud

Phonics Instruction
Words with *r*-Controlled Vowels
Word Endings, Final Syllables
-tion, -ture

Reading Decodable Text
Where Do I Start?

• • • • • • • • • • • • • • • •

Leveled Readers, *T362–T365*

- ● *Florence Griffith-Joyner: Olympic Champion*
- ▲ *Mae Jemison: Making Dreams Come True*
- ■ *Theodore Roosevelt: Friend of Nature*
- ◆ *Florence Griffith-Joyner: Olympic Runner*

Word Work

Vocabulary Review

High-Frequency Word Review

Spelling: The Vowel + *r* Sounds in *for* and *before*

Writing & Oral Language

Writing Activity

Grammar: Nouns and Pronouns Together

Listening/Speaking/Viewing

Daily Routines

Daily Message

Phonics Review Point to each word as you read aloud the Daily Message.

Get set to meet some good role models. You might like to follow in their footsteps and set a goal for yourself. When you grow up, what would you like to do?

Have children

- read the Daily Message aloud, and discuss the question;
- find words with vowel pairs *oa, ow;* (*follow, goal, grow*)
- read the words aloud and then circle them.

Word Wall

High-Frequency Word Review Briefly review these high-frequency words that were taught in Grade 1. Post the words on the Word Wall. Have children practice reading, chanting, spelling, and writing them.

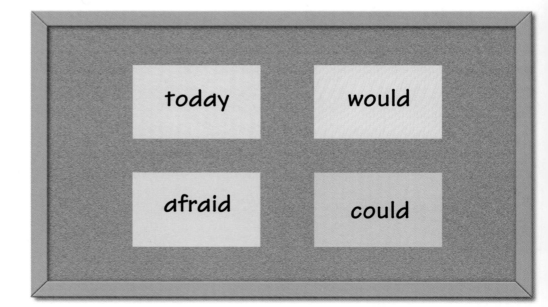

today   would

afraid   could

Vocabulary

Exact Verbs Write *run* and ask a volunteer to pan-mime the action in slow motion. Then have children brainstorm exact verbs that describe ways to run.

Begin a list of exact verbs, writing children's responses. (Examples: *dash, jog, gallop, sprint, race, rush, scurry*) You may want volunteers to pantomime or illustrate words that they suggest. Encourage children to use a thesaurus.

Verbs to Describe Running

gallop	rush
sprint	dash
race	jog

Daily Writing Prompt

Have children choose a topic to write about, or have them use the prompt below.

It's thirty years in the future, and you are famous. You are on the cover of a magazine. Write a paragraph that explains why you are famous. Draw yourself on the magazine cover.

Daily Language Practice

Grammar Skill: Proofreading
Spelling Skill: The Vowel + *r* Sounds in *for* and *before*

Display **Transparency F4–1.** Ask children to rewrite Sentence 1 correctly. Then model how to write it, and have children check their work.

Transparency F4–1
Daily Language Practice

Day 1
1. Where were you borne.

  Where were you **born**?

Day 3
3. My friend carl has for pets.

  My friend **Carl** has **four** pets.

Day 4
4. Mom beeped the car horen at the Dog.

  Mom beeped the car **horn** at the **dog**.

Day 5
5. The sporte Ed likes best is running?

  The **sport** Ed likes best is running.

TRANSPARENCY F4–1
TEACHER'S EDITION PAGES T313, T325, T343, T349, T357

Listening Comprehension

Building Background

Tell children that they will be reading three biographies. They will learn what makes a good biography and try writing a biography. Explain that you will begin by reading aloud a biography of Dr. Seuss.

- Display several books written by Dr. Seuss. Ask children if they know them or others.

Fluency Modeling

Explain that as you read aloud, you will be modeling fluent oral reading. Ask children to listen carefully to your phrasing and expression, or tone of voice or emphasis.

COMPREHENSION SKILL

Understanding Biographies

Discuss how biographies differ from other stories. (Sample answers: A biography is a true story about a person's life. It usually begins with the early years of a person's life and then goes to later years.)

Purpose Setting Read the selection aloud, asking children to note interesting facts about Dr. Seuss as they listen. Then use the Guiding Comprehension questions to assess children's understanding. Reread the selection for clarification as needed.

Teacher Read Aloud

Meet Dr. Seuss
by Sarah M. Healey

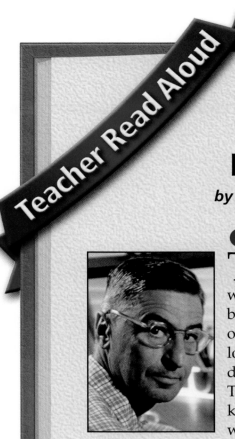

❶ Theodor Seuss Geisel, the man who wrote *The Cat in the Hat*, was born in Springfield, Massachusetts, on March 2, 1904. As a boy, Ted loved drawing. Although his animal drawings were a bit silly-looking, Ted's father encouraged him to keep drawing. As an adult, Ted wrote and illustrated over fifty children's books.

❷ Ted took his first art class in high school, where he was asked to draw a vase of flowers. Unhappy with his work, Ted turned his paper upside-down and began drawing the flowers that way. Ted's teacher was upset and told him he must always draw right-side up. So Ted quit the class and took no more art because there were too many rules to follow.

In college, Ted wrote stories and drew funny pictures for the college magazine. He also began signing his middle name, Seuss, on some work.

After college, Ted went to school in England, but he liked drawing more than studying and filled his notebooks with pictures. His friend, Helen Palmer, loved his work and encouraged him to do more. Ted agreed, and in 1927 he returned to America.

Ted began to take drawing more seriously by creating funny cartoons. Soon after selling his first "Seuss" cartoon, he moved to New York City, married Helen, and got a job writing advertisements. Then Ted began signing "Dr. Seuss" on his work.

3 In 1936 while on a boat trip, Ted noticed the rhythm of the ship's engines. Soon he began thinking up rhymes to go with the rhythmic, chugging sounds. Six months later, Ted succeeded in turning those rhymes into his first children's story.

Ted sent his story to dozens of publishers, but none of them wanted to publish such an unusual book. Then one day Ted's luck changed. As he walked down a New York City street with the story under his arm, Ted ran into a college friend. This friend just happened to be a children's book editor, so Ted showed him the story. In 1937 *And to Think That I Saw It on Mulberry Street* was published, and Dr. Seuss's writing career was underway.

By the time World War II began, Ted had written books such as *The 500 Hats of Bartholomew Cubbins* and *Horton Hatches the Egg*. He was now a full-time book author, but he joined the army in 1943 and made educational films for the military.

After the war, Ted and Helen moved to California, and Ted continued to write. It took him just a week to write *The Grinch Who Stole Christmas* but another two months to fix the ending. (Ted liked to joke that he was part Grinch himself.) Ted wrote *The Cat in the Hat* after being challenged to write a book from a list of only 225 words. He used the first rhyming words on the list, *cat* and *hat,* for the title. Ted wrote *Green Eggs and Ham* when he was challenged to use only fifty words. Children loved his books because they were fun and easy to read.

Ted's last book as Dr. Seuss was *Oh, the Places You'll Go!* A best seller with adult readers, Ted was thrilled that adults as well as children enjoyed his work. Theodor Geisel died on September 24, 1991, but his books continue to be popular. Readers still get caught up in the funny rhymes and silly-looking characters created by the man known as Dr. Seuss.

CRITICAL THINKING
Guiding Comprehension

Focus On Genre

❶ UNDERSTANDING BIOGRAPHY Who was Theodor Seuss Geisel? (He was the writer Dr. Seuss, who wrote *The Cat in the Hat* and other children's books.)

❷ UNDERSTANDING BIOGRAPHY What did you learn about Dr. Seuss's personality from the description of what happened in art class in high school? (Sample answer: He had his own ideas about art and didn't believe in so many rules.)

❸ UNDERSTANDING BIOGRAPHY Why did Dr. Seuss begin writing rhymes? (He noticed the rhythm of a ship's engines and began to think up rhymes to go with the sounds.)

Discussion Options

Personal Response Ask children to tell why they think Theodor Geisel is a good choice for a biography.

⭐ **Connecting/Comparing** Ask children why a biography about Dr. Seuss fits in the theme *Amazing Animals.*

 English Language Learners

Supporting Comprehension

Have students say the title *The Cat in the Hat* aloud. Point out that "Cat" and "Hat" rhyme, or have the same ending sound. Help students make a two-column list of rhyming words. (For example, "street"/ "eat," "hats"/"cats," "eggs"/"legs," "who"/ "you," "ham"/"am") Ask students to work in pairs to write a sentence that uses two rhyming words.

OBJECTIVES

- Isolate phonemes.
- Read and write words with *r*-controlled vowels.

Materials

- **Sound/Spelling Cards** *artist, orange, bird*

PHONICS: Words with *r*-Controlled Vowels

❶ Phonemic Awareness Warm-Up

Model how to isolate phonemes. Say *farm,* /f//är//m/. Identify /är/ as the vowel plus *r* that children hear. Repeat with *storm* and /ôr/. Then say *first, herd,* and *hurt.* Ask children what vowel plus *r* sounds they hear in these words. (/ûr/) Have them say the sounds in each word.

❷ Teach

Connect sounds to letters. Write *farm, storm, first, herd,* and *hurt.* Underline the vowel plus *r* in each word. Display the **Sound/Spelling Cards** and name the picture on each.

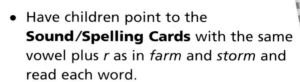

- Have children point to the **Sound/Spelling Cards** with the same vowel plus *r* as in *farm* and *storm* and read each word.

- Point to *ir, er,* and *ur* on the **Sound/Spelling Card** *bird.* Explain that these letters all stand for /ûr/. Have children read *first, herd,* and *hurt.*

Model how to decode longer words. Write *order.* Underline *or* and *er.*

- Divide this VCCV word into syllables between *r* and *d*. Point out that, instead of short vowel sounds, the word has *r*-controlled vowel sounds. Have a volunteer read the word.

- Repeat with *after, forests, return, hardly,* and *birthday.* Have volunteers underline each *r*-controlled vowel. Help children divide each word into syllables and read it.

❸ Guided Practice

Check children's understanding. Write *doctors, member, third, starting,* and *church.* Have children read each word. Have them write *morning, girl, stars,* and *later.* Display the words, and have children correct their work.

❹ Apply

Assign Practice Book page 77.

Practice Book page 77

Focus on Biography
Phonics Skill Words with
r-Controlled Vowels

Name _____

Word Search

Find and circle ten words with *ar, or, er, ir,* and *ur.* Write the words on the lines below. Read them to a partner.

Order of answers will vary.

Words with *ar*
1. card **(1 point)**
2. car *or* cars **(1)**
3. start *or* tart **(1)**

Words with *or*
4. important, port, *or* or **(1)**
5. short **(1)**
6. porch **(1)**

Words with *er, ir,* and *ur*
7. serve **(1)**
8. dirt **(1)**
9. bird **(1)**
10. burn *or* urn **(1)**

Monitoring Student Progress

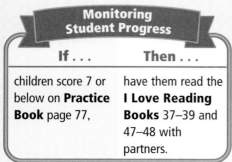

If...	Then...
children score 7 or below on **Practice Book** page 77,	have them read the **I Love Reading Books** 37–39 and 47–48 with partners.

TARGET SKILL
PHONICS: Word Endings, Final Syllables *-tion* and *-ture*

OBJECTIVES

- Read and write words with *-ed, -ing, -er, -est, -ful,* and *-ly* endings.
- Read and write words with the final syllable *-tion* or *-ture.*

❶ Teach

Review previously learned word endings. Write *speaking, asked, shorter, fastest, playful,* and *loudly.*

- Choose children to point to each word and say its ending. Review that *-ing* means an action is happening now, *-ed* means an action has already happened, *-er* and *-est* are used to compare items and mean "more and most," *-ful* means full of, and *-ly* means in a certain way.

- Have volunteers cover the ending of each word, read the base word, and then add the ending to read the word.

Review the syllables *-tion* and *-ture*. Write *picture* and *nation.* Have children pronounce the final syllable in these words.

- Have children sound out the first syllable in each word and add the ending to read the words.

❷ Guided Practice

Check children's understanding.

- Write the sentences below. Choose children to underline words with endings or final syllables *-tion* and *-ture.*

- Have others read each word and explain how they figured it out. Read the sentences together.

What will happen in <u>future</u> space travel?

<u>Conservation</u> means <u>taking</u> care of our land, water, and air.

Teddy Roosevelt <u>wanted</u> people to be <u>careful</u> about <u>nature</u>.

Wilma was the <u>youngest</u> member of the 1956 Olympic track team.

Wilma <u>nearly</u> <u>dropped</u> the baton in the relay race.

---

❸ Apply

Assign Practice Book page 78.

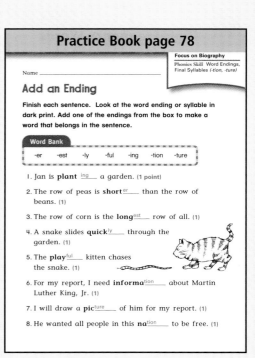

Practice Book page 78

Focus on Biography
Phonics Skill Word Endings,
Final Syllables *(-tion, -ture)*

Name _____

Add an Ending

Finish each sentence. Look at the word ending or syllable in dark print. Add one of the endings from the box to make a word that belongs in the sentence.

Word Bank

| -er | -est | -ly | -ful | -ing | -tion | -ture |

1. Jan is **plant** _ing___ a garden. (1 point)

2. The row of peas is **short** _er___ than the row of beans. (1)

3. The row of corn is the **long** _est_ row of all. (1)

4. A snake slides **quick** _ly___ through the garden. (1)

5. The **play** _ful_ kitten chases the snake. (1)

6. For my report, I need **informa** _tion___ about Martin Luther King, Jr. (1)

7. I will draw a **pic** _ture___ of him for my report. (1)

8. He wanted all people in this **na** _tion___ to be free. (1)

Monitoring Student Progress

If . . .	Then . . .
children score 6 or below on **Practice Book** page 78,	review the pronunciation of the endings and give children more practice sounding out base words and adding these endings.

REVIEW

OBJECTIVE

- To recognize previously taught high-frequency words.

about	*near*
afraid	*surprised*
beautiful	*watch*
believe	*write*
friend	*years*

Materials

- Index cards with the high-frequency words, one per card

HIGH-FREQUENCY WORDS

❶ Teach

Review the high-frequency words in the word box. Display Transparency F4–2. Tell children that the words in the box are found in the biographies.

- Point to each word. Have children chant it by saying its letters aloud.

- Ask a volunteer to read the word. Have the class repeat it.

❷ Guided Practice

Have children choose the word that best completes each sentence.

- Have volunteers read a sentence and tell which word from the box will complete it.

- Write each correct word on the transparency and reread the sentences together.

- Post the words on the Word Wall.

- Have volunteers use each word in an oral sentence.

❸ Apply

Assign Practice Book page 79.

Transparency F4–2

High-Frequency Words

TRANSPARENCY F4–2
TEACHER'S EDITION PAGE T318

THEME 4 Focus on Biography
High-Frequency Words
ANNOTATED VERSION

friend	about	beautiful	near	write
believe	watch	surprised	afraid	years

1. If you ___believe___ you can do it, you can!

2. Do not be ___afraid___ to try new things.

3. My ___friend___ is learning how to scuba dive.

4. I wish I could ___watch___ the stars from space.

5. After the rain stopped, I saw a ___beautiful___ rainbow.

6. Kim is nine ___years___ old today.

7. Kim was ___surprised___ when she got a kitten for her birthday.

8. The kitten sleeps in a basket ___near___ Kim's bed.

9. It will take Jack ___about___ a week to read this book.

10. Jack will ___write___ a book report when he finishes.

Monitoring Student Progress

If . . .	Then . . .
children score 7 or below on **Practice Book** page 79,	have them copy the words and practice reading them to partners; review alphabetical order.
children are ready for more challenging material,	have them write stories using the high-frequency words.

Practice Book page 79

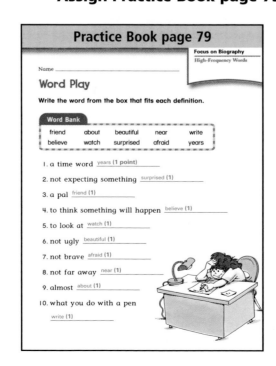

Focus on Biography
High-Frequency Words

Name _____

Word Play

Write the word from the box that fits each definition.

Word Bank

friend	about	beautiful	near	write
believe	watch	surprised	afraid	years

1. a time word ___years (1 point)___

2. not expecting something ___surprised (1)___

3. a pal ___friend (1)___

4. to think something will happen ___believe (1)___

5. to look at ___watch (1)___

6. not ugly ___beautiful (1)___

7. not brave ___afraid (1)___

8. not far away ___near (1)___

9. almost ___about (1)___

10. what you do with a pen ___write (1)___

Something was wrong. I had to write a biography. I couldn't think of anyone to <u>write about</u>. I had no idea what to say.

"I don't know where to <u>start</u>," I said. "I'm stumped!"

49

49

"Think of someone brave or with a <u>special</u> talent," said Dad. "Is there someone you know with a neat job?"

I thought and thought. "I could write about your <u>friend Mr. Parks</u>!" I said.

50

1. What did you like to do when you were little?

2. What did you want to be when you grew up?

3. How did you choose the job you do now?

4. What are you proud of doing?

Dad called Mr. Parks. I wrote down many of my <u>questions</u>.

51

51

Word Key

Decodable words with *r*-controlled vowels, with endings, and with *-tion*, *-ture* ———

Review High-Frequency Words ———

Reading Decodable Text

OBJECTIVES

- Apply the Phonics/Decoding Strategy to decode words in context.
- Recognize high-frequency words in context.
- Reread to build fluency.

Have children preview *Where Do I Start?* Ask them to predict who the girl might write a biography about.

Model the Phonics/Decoding Strategy. Review the strategy. Then point to the word *talent* on page 50.

Think Aloud *I see a vowel-consonant-vowel pattern. If I divide the word before* l, *the vowel* a *ends the first syllable, so I say the long* a *sound. The word is /tā//lĕnt/. I don't know that word. So I'll divide it after the* l *and say the short* a *sound, /tăl//ĕnt/. Oh, I know that word.* Talent *is something that you do well.*

Apply the Phonics/Decoding Strategy. Have children read *Where Do I Start?* with partners. Remind them to use the Phonics/Decoding Strategy as they read.

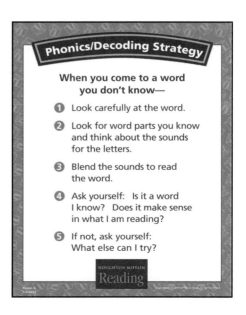

Phonics/Decoding Strategy

When you come to a word you don't know—

❶ Look carefully at the word.

❷ Look for word parts you know and think about the sounds for the letters.

❸ Blend the sounds to read the word.

❹ Ask yourself: Is it a word I know? Does it make sense in what I am reading?

❺ If not, ask yourself: What else can I try?

PHONICS LIBRARY

Focus on Biography

Prompts for Decoding

Support children as they read. Use prompts such as these:

- Look at the word *c-r-e-a-t-u-r-e-s* on page 53.

- Can you find an ending you know how to say?

- What vowel sound might the letters *ea* stand for in the first syllable?

- Sound out the first part of the word. Add the ending.

- Read the sentence. Does the word make sense in it?

Oral Language

Discuss the story. Ask children to answer the questions in complete sentences.

- Who is telling this story? (A girl is telling it.)

- Why is the girl stumped? (She doesn't know who to write a biography about or where to start.)

- Who does the girl write her biography about? (She writes about Mr. Parks.)

- What does this person do? (He takes pictures of sea animals.)

- What does the girl learn about Mr. Parks? (He goes to work on a boat and lives on the seacoast; he takes pictures of sea horses, whales, and sharks; his pictures are in nature books and magazines.)

Mr. Parks came that night. We sat in the kitchen and I asked my questions. I used a notebook to take notes.

I already knew that Mr. Parks takes pictures of sea animals. I found out that he lives on the seacoast and goes to work on a boat.

52

When he was a boy, Mr. Parks liked to watch ocean animals. Now he takes pictures of creatures like sea horses, whales, and sharks. His pictures can be seen in nature books and magazines.

53

52   5

Mr. Parks told me many stories. Once he saw a large, dark bump on the ocean floor. At first he thought it was a sandbar. Then he thought it could be a monster. As he got closer, he saw that it was a sunken ship!

54

We talked and talked. Before Mr. Parks left, I thanked him for his help.

When he was gone, I groaned loudly. "What's wrong now?" asked my dad.

"I took so many notes," I said. "I'll need to give my hand a rest before I start!"

55

54

55

 ## Build Fluency

Model fluent reading.

- Read aloud the last page of the story with expression.

- Have children identify who asks a question and who answers it. Have volunteers read the words each person says.

- Have all the children read the same page in unison.

Have children practice fluent reading.

- Have partners each choose another story page.

- Tell them to read their page silently first to decide on phrasing and to note any words they can't read. Partners can figure out these words together.

- Then have partners read their pages aloud. Encourage them to read smoothly, grouping words together and pausing briefly after punctuation marks.

Home Connection

Hand out the take-home version of *Where Do I Start?* Ask children to reread the story with their families. (See the **Phonics Library Blackline Masters.**)

Reading Decodable Text **T321**

OBJECTIVE

- Write spelling words with the vowel + *r* sounds in *for* and *before*.

SPELLING WORDS

Basic

born*	horn
core	sport*
short	torn
morning	sort
fork	snore
four†	fort

Review
more*
store

Challenge
forty*
forest*

*Forms of these words appear in the literature.

†These words are exceptions to the principle.

Extra Support/ Intervention

Basic Word List You may want to use only Basic Words 1–5 and the Review Words with children who need extra support.

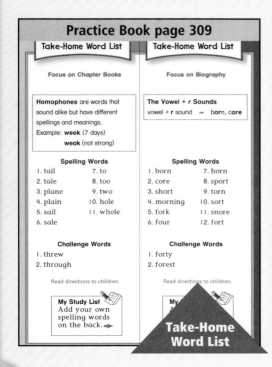

Practice Book page 309

Take-Home Word List	Take-Home Word List
Focus on Chapter Books	*Focus on Biography*
Homophones are words that sound alike but have different spellings and meanings. Example: **week** (7 days) **weak** (not strong)	The Vowel + *r* Sounds vowel + r sound → born, core
Spelling Words	**Spelling Words**
1. tail 7. to	1. born 7. horn
2. tale 8. too	2. core 8. sport
3. plane 9. two	3. short 9. torn
4. plain 10. hole	4. morning 10. sort
5. sail 11. whole	5. fork 11. snore
6. sale	6. four 12. fort
Challenge Words	**Challenge Words**
1. threw	1. forty
2. through	2. forest
Read directions to children.	*Read directions to children.*

My Study List Add your own spelling words on the back. ➡

Take-Home Word List

SPELLING: The Vowel + *r* Sounds in *for* and *before*

❶ Teach the Principle

Pretest Say each sentence. Have children write only the underlined words.

Basic Words

1. When were you **born**?
2. Don't eat the apple **core**.
3. We took a **short** trip.
4. I jog every **morning**.
5. His **fork** is beside his plate.
6. Anna has **four** boxes.
7. The car **horn** beeped.
8. Is baseball the **sport** she likes?
9. One page in the book is **torn**.
10. They will **sort** the beads.
11. Do you **snore** every night?
12. My friends made a snow **fort**.

Challenge Words

13. They found **forty** shells.
14. We saw many trees in the **forest**.

Teach Write *born* and *core*.

- Point to each word, say it, and have children repeat it.

- Explain that each word has a vowel sound that is neither short nor long because the vowel is followed by *r*. Have children say /ôr/.

- Underline the *or* in *born* and the *ore* in *core*. Explain that /ôr/ can be spelled *or* or *ore*.

- Next, write *four* and underline *our*. Explain that in this word, the letters *our* spell /ôr/.

❷ Practice

Add the remaining Basic Words to the correct columns. Ask children to read each word and underline the letters that spell /ôr/.

❸ Apply

Practice/Homework Assign **Practice Book** page 309, the Take-Home Word List.

GRAMMAR: Nouns and Pronouns Together

❶ Teach

Review the following:

- A noun names a person, place, or thing.
- A pronoun is a word that can take the place of a noun.

Write *Abraham Lincoln, Mary, cabin, Abe and Mary* in one column. Write *she, they, it,* and *he* in a second column.

- Have children draw a line from the noun to the pronoun that can take its place.

Display Transparency F4–3. Have a child read aloud the first paragraph. Underline each pronoun *he.*

- Explain that it is clear that *he* stands for *Abraham Lincoln,* but repeating *he* over and over again makes the paragraph boring.
- Use the transparency to model how to replace two of the pronouns *he* with *Lincoln* or *Abe.*

❷ Practice

Have a child read aloud the second paragraph on the transparency.

- Tell children that they will read biographies about Ellen Ochoa, who went into space, and Wilma Rudolph, who won three Olympic gold medals.
- Ask which pronoun is used to take the place of the nouns *Ellen* and *Wilma* in the second sentence. (*They*)
- Reread the two sentences beginning with *she.*
- Explain that it isn't clear to whom the word *she* refers in each sentence. Ask children which noun, *Wilma* or *Ellen,* they would use in place of each *she* to make the paragraph less confusing.

❸ Apply

Read the third paragraph together. Ask children which pronoun is repeated many times. (it) Have children rewrite the paragraph, replacing *it* twice with a noun. Write changes on the transparency.

GRAMMAR

Focus on Biography

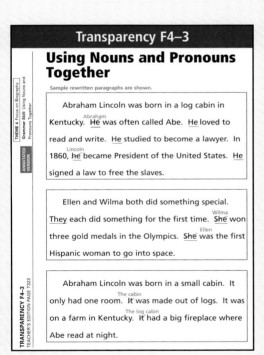

Transparency F4–3

Using Nouns and Pronouns Together

Sample rewritten paragraphs are shown.

THEME 4 Focus on Biography
Grammar Skill Using Nouns and Pronouns Together

ANNOTATED VERSION

> Abraham Lincoln was born in a log cabin in Kentucky. *Abraham* He was often called Abe. He loved to read and write. He studied to become a lawyer. In 1860, *Lincoln* he became President of the United States. He signed a law to free the slaves.

> Ellen and Wilma both did something special. They each did something for the first time. *Wilma* She won three gold medals in the Olympics. *Ellen* She was the first Hispanic woman to go into space.

> Abraham Lincoln was born in a small cabin. It *The cabin* only had one room. It was made out of logs. It was on a farm in Kentucky. *The log cabin* It had a big fireplace where Abe read at night.

TRANSPARENCY F4–3
TEACHER'S EDITION PAGE T323

Monitoring Student Progress

If . . .	Then . . .
children need help identifying pronouns,	provide additional sentences and have children replace the pronouns with nouns.

Day at a Glance
pp. T324–T341

Reading Instruction

Background and Genre
Vocabulary

Reading the Biographies

Responding

• • • • • • • • • • • • • • • • • •

Leveled Readers, T362–T365

- ● *Florence Griffith-Joyner: Olympic Champion*
- ▲ *Mae Jemison: Making Dreams Come True*
- ■ *Theodore Roosevelt: Friend of Nature*
- ◆ *Florence Griffith-Joyner: Olympic Runner*

Word Work

Vocabulary Review

Word Wall

Spelling Practice

Writing & Oral Language

Writing: A Biography

Grammar Practice

Listening/Speaking/Viewing

Daily Routines

Daily Message

Phonics Review Point to each word as you read aloud the Daily Message.

Some people have fun at their jobs. They get paid for drawing cartoons, playing ball, or riding horses. What do we call people whose job it is to explore outer space?

Have children

- read the Daily Message aloud, and discuss the question;
- find words with *r*-controlled vowels; (*cartoons, horses, explore, outer*)
- read the words aloud and then circle them.

Word Wall

High-Frequency Word Review Display these high-frequency words that were taught in Grade 1. Have children practice recognizing, chanting, spelling, and writing them.

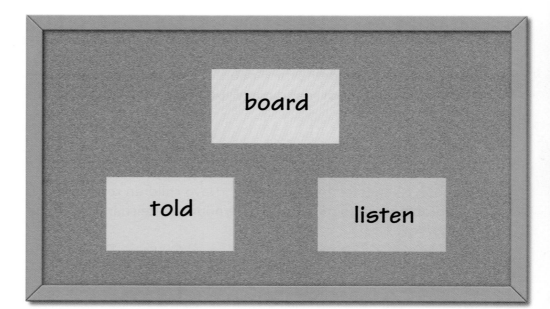

board

told

listen

Vocabulary

Five-Finger Categories Give children colored drawing paper in the shape of a large hand, or have children trace their hands. Ask them to write a category, such as *Machines That Fly,* on the palm. Then, on each finger, have them write a word that fits in that category.

Daily Writing Prompt

Have children revise work they are currently writing, or have them use this prompt to begin a new writing activity.

Do you have a favorite Dr. Seuss book? Dr. Seuss liked to draw funny pictures and write rhyming words. Write some silly rhyming sentences the way Dr. Seuss would. Then draw a picture to go with them.

Daily Language Practice

Grammar Skill: Proofreading
Spelling Skill: The Vowel + *r* Sounds in *for* and *before*

Display **Transparency F4–1.** Ask children to rewrite Sentence 2 correctly. Then model how to write it, and have children check their work.

Transparency F4–1

Daily Language Practice

Proofread each sentence. Correct any errors.

Day 1

Day 2

2. This merning Jan ate two apple.

This **morning** Jan ate two **apples.**

Day 4

4. Mom beeped the car horen at the Dog.

Mom beeped the car **horn** at the **dog.**

Day 5

5. The sporte Ed likes best is running?

The **sport** Ed likes best is running.

TRANSPARENCY F4–1
TEACHER'S EDITION PAGES T313, T325, T343, T349, T397

Building Background

Key Concept: Understanding Biography

Connecting to the Genre Tell children that they will read three biographies in this section. They will learn that a biography is a true story about someone's life, and they will try writing a biography of their own.

Read aloud the text on Anthology page 135, including the titles listed under Contents. Have children name people whose lives they think would make good biographies or who they would like to know more about. List these names on the board or chart paper. (Responses might include people whom children admire, such as sports heroes, authors, presidents, or musicians.)

 Journal ▶ Have children think of people they personally admire and would like to write about. Have them list those names in their journals. Children can use their lists as a basis for writing biographies of their own.

Focus on Genre

BIOGRAPHY

134

REACHING ALL LEARNERS

English Language Learners

Beginning/Preproduction Ask questions that focus on the meanings of Genre Vocabulary words. Have children use the vocabulary words in short oral answers.

Early Production and Speech Emergence Have children list names of individuals whose lives they think would make interesting biographies. Have them record each name and write a short phrase explaining who the person is, for example: *Abraham Lincoln: 16th President of the United States.*

Intermediate and Advanced Fluency Have children think of individuals who would make interesting subjects for biographies. Have them choose an individual and write a short paragraph about him or her.

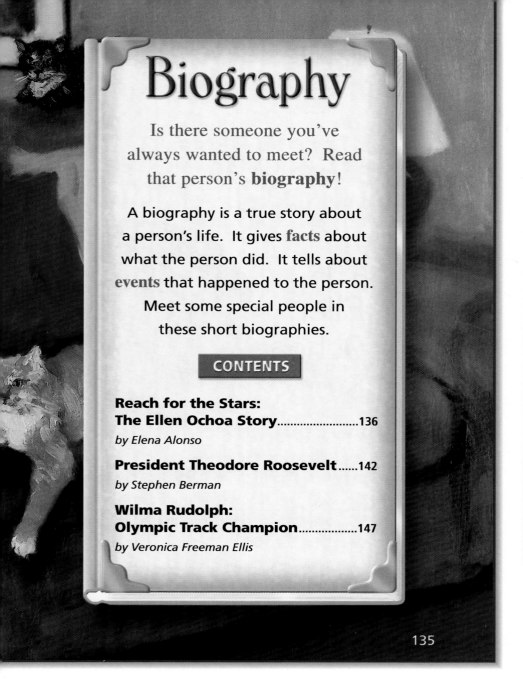

Biography

Is there someone you've always wanted to meet? Read that person's **biography**!

A biography is a true story about a person's life. It gives **facts** about what the person did. It tells about **events** that happened to the person. Meet some special people in these short biographies.

CONTENTS

135

Introducing Vocabulary

Genre Vocabulary

These words support the Key Concept.

biography a true story about some-one's life

champion the winner of a game or contest; the best of all

event something that happens, especially something important

fact something that has really happened or that really exists

information knowledge about an event or subject

president the leader of a country or a group

**e • Glossary
e • WordGame**

See Vocabulary notes on pages T328, T330, T331, and T332.

Display Transparency F4–4.

- Read aloud the paragraph with the underlined Genre Vocabulary.
- Read the first definition and then read the words in the right-hand column.
- Help children use context clues from the paragraph to choose a word that fits the first definition. Draw a line from that definition to the word it defines. (information)
- For each remaining item, ask children to match each definition to its corresponding word.

Ask children to use these words as they discuss the biographies.

Practice/Homework Assign **Practice Book** page 80.

Introducing Vocabulary
(Anthology p. 135) **T327**

Transparency F4–4

Biography Words

I will write a <u>biography</u> about the life of a famous person. I will find true <u>facts</u> about important <u>events</u> in this person's life. I might write about a sports <u>champion</u> who has won many awards or medals. But I think I will write about a <u>president</u> and tell why he was a good leader for our nation. I will look up <u>information</u> in a reference book.

1. knowledge about a subject or event — champion
2. something that can be proved to be true — president
3. the best of all — biography
4. the leader of a country — event
5. a true story about a person's life — fact
6. something that happens that is important — information

Practice Book page 80

Focus on Biography
Genre Vocabulary

Name _____

Biography Words

Write the word from the box that means the same as the underlined word or words in each sentence.

Vocabulary

| biography | events | information |
| fact | champion | president |

1. My sister Elena is the <u>best of all</u> on the school math team.
   champion **(1 point)**

2. Elena tells me about all the <u>important things that happen</u> at her school.
   events **(1)**

3. She knows <u>things we know for sure</u> about many subjects.
   facts **(1)**

4. She said the <u>leader</u> of the United States lives and works in the White House.
   president **(1)**

5. Someday I'm going to write a <u>true story of the life</u> of Elena.
   biography **(1)**

6. I have plenty of <u>knowledge</u> about Elena that I can include.
   information **(1)**

COMPREHENSION STRATEGY

Evaluate

Teacher Modeling Read aloud the title and author on Anthology page 136. Ask children to read pages 136–137 silently, look at the pictures, and think about whether they will enjoy reading this biography. Model how to Evaluate.

Think Aloud *I think I'm going to like this biography because I like stories about space exploration and astronauts. The photographs look interesting, and the topic is one I enjoy. I think the selection will be interesting and informative.*

COMPREHENSION SKILL

Understanding Biography

Introduce the Graphic Organizer.

Tell children that using the Biography Notes Chart can help them keep track of important details and information.

- Display **Transparency F4–5**.
- Model how to complete the first item.
- Have children complete the chart on **Practice Book** page 81 as they read the biography of Ellen Ochoa.

Vocabulary

space shuttle a vehicle that carries people into space and returns to Earth

astronauts people trained to fly in a space shuttle

THEME 4: Focus on Biography
(Anthology p. 136)

T328

REACH FOR THE STARS

The Ellen Ochoa Story

BY ELENA ALONSO

It was April 17, 1993. The space shuttle *Discovery* was about to return to Earth after more than nine days in space. One of the five astronauts on board, Dr. Ellen Ochoa, had just made history. Dr. Ochoa had become the first Hispanic woman to travel in space.

❶

136

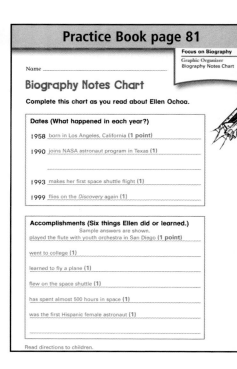

Transparency F4–5

Biography Notes Chart

Complete this chart as you read about Ellen Ochoa.

Sample answers are shown.

Dates (Write what happened in each year.)
1958 born in Los Angeles, California
1990 joins NASA astronaut program in Texas
1993 makes her first space shuttle flight
1999 flies on the *Discovery* again

Accomplishments (Write six things Ellen did or learned.)
played the flute with youth orchestra in San Diego
went to college
learned to fly a plane
flew on the space shuttle
spent almost 500 hours in space
was the first Hispanic female astronaut

TRANSPARENCY F4–5
TEACHER'S EDITION PAGES T328, T344

THEME 4 Focus on Biography
Graphic Organizer Biography Outline

ANNOTATED VERSION

Practice Book page 81

Focus on Biography
Graphic Organizer
Biography Notes Chart

Name _____

Biography Notes Chart

Complete this chart as you read about Ellen Ochoa.

Dates (What happened in each year?)
1958 born in Los Angeles, California (1 point)
1990 joins NASA astronaut program in Texas (1)
1993 makes her first space shuttle flight (1)
1999 flies on the *Discovery* again (1)

Accomplishments (Six things Ellen did or learned.)
Sample answers are shown.
played the flute with youth orchestra in San Diego (1 point)
went to college (1)
learned to fly a plane (1)
flew on the space shuttle (1)
has spent almost 500 hours in space (1)
was the first Hispanic female astronaut (1)

Read directions to children.

Discovery lifts off.

Ellen Ochoa was <u>born</u> in 1958 in Los Angeles, <u>California</u>. She was eleven <u>years</u> old when astronauts walked on the moon for the first time. She didn't dream then that some day she too would become an astronaut.

137

Building Background

Remind children that biographies are true stories of people's lives and tell about real events. Tell children that many biographies are about people who inspire us to work hard and have hope. Then refer to the phrase in the title of Ellen Ochoa's biography: *Reach for the Stars*. Ask how that phrase might be an important clue about what Ellen Ochoa does.

Purpose Setting

Tell children that people often read biographies to learn more about a job or career that might interest them. Ask children to think about possible future jobs and careers as they read.

CRITICAL THINKING

Guiding Comprehension

1 **AUTHOR'S VIEWPOINT** How does the author tell you that Dr. Ochoa is special? (She says that Dr. Ochoa made history by becoming the first Hispanic woman in space.)

Extra Support/Intervention

Preview the biographies.

pages 136–139 What sort of work do you think Dr. Ellen Ochoa does? Explain.

pages 140–141 Do you think Dr. Ochoa enjoys her work? Why?

pages 142–143 When do you think Theodore Roosevelt was president of the United States? Explain.

pages 144–145 Describe what you see in the photographs.

page 146 What are these bears usually called? Where do you think the name might have come from?

pages 147–151 Wilma Rudolph was an Olympic champion. Describe what you see Wilma doing on these pages.

Word Key

Decodable words with *r*-controlled vowels; word endings, and syllables *-tion, -ture* _____
Review High-Frequency Words _____
Vocabulary Words _____

Reading the Selection **T329**
(Anthology p. 137)

The crew of
Discovery, 1993

❷ "At that time, there weren't any women astronauts and also very few who were scientists," she says. "So it didn't occur to me when I was in school that this was something I could grow up and do."

❸ Today, Ellen enjoys speaking to children about her work as an astronaut. She encourages children, especially girls, to study math and science.

Ellen's favorite subjects in school were math and music. She also played the flute. In fact, she became so good at it that she was asked to play with a youth orchestra in San Diego.

138

The space shuttle's
cargo bay

139

CRITICAL THINKING
Guiding Comprehension

❷ **MAKING INFERENCES** Why do you think there were few women scientists when Ellen Ochoa was a girl? (Sample answer: Few girls and women studied math and science before then.)

❸ **MAKING INFERENCES** Why do you think Dr. Ochoa encourages girls to study math and science? (Sample answer: She probably wants more girls to become astronauts and scientists.)

Vocabulary

scientists people who use special tests to become experts on the world around us

encourages gives someone hope or confidence

REACHING ALL LEARNERS **Extra Support/Intervention**

Review pages 136–141.

Before children join in Stop and Think, have them

- take turns modeling **Evaluate** and other strategies they used;

- check and revise **Practice Book** page 81;

- **summarize** the important parts of the selection.

THEME 4: Focus on Biography
(Anthology pp. 138–139)

"Only you put limitations on yourself about what you can achieve, so don't be afraid to reach for the stars."

Several years after college, Ellen decided that she really wanted to learn how to be an astronaut. She moved to Houston, Texas, where the NASA space program is located. Meanwhile, she took up a new hobby: she learned how to fly an airplane!

In 1990, NASA picked Ellen for its astronaut program. Three years later, she made her first space shuttle flight. Her job was to work a robotic arm that can send small satellites into space and then catch them again.

Ellen Ochoa with her son

Ellen Ochoa flew with six other astronauts on the _Discovery_ in 1999.

Since her first flight, Ellen has spent almost 500 hours in space. On one trip, Ellen and her team traveled 4 million miles in 235 hours and 13 minutes!

Ellen is proud to be the first Hispanic female astronaut. She tells children to work hard to become whatever they want to be. She says, "Only you put limitations on yourself about what you can achieve, so don't be afraid to reach for the stars."

140 141

Stop and Think

Critical Thinking Questions

1. **AUTHOR'S VIEWPOINT** Why does the author tell about how hard Dr. Ochoa works? (She admires Dr. Ochoa and wants to point out that her success resulted from hard work.)

2. **DRAWING CONCLUSIONS** What are two possible meanings of "Reach for the Stars"? (It's what astronauts do when they go into space, and what people do to achieve goals.)

Strategies in Action

Have volunteers model evaluate and other strategies they used. Be sure children summarize the selection.

Discussion Options

Bring the entire class together to do either of these activities.

Review Purpose Have children discuss whether or not they found Ellen Ochoa's biography inspiring, and why.

Make Predictions Ask children to make predictions about the next two biographies.

Vocabulary

limitations things that make it difficult to do what you want to do

robotics mechanical; made to do some of the same things a human being can do

Monitoring Student Progress

If . . .	Then . . .
children have successfully completed the Extra Support activities on pages T329 and T330,	have them read the remaining biographies either cooperatively or independently.

Reading the Selection
(Anthology pp. 140–141) **T331**

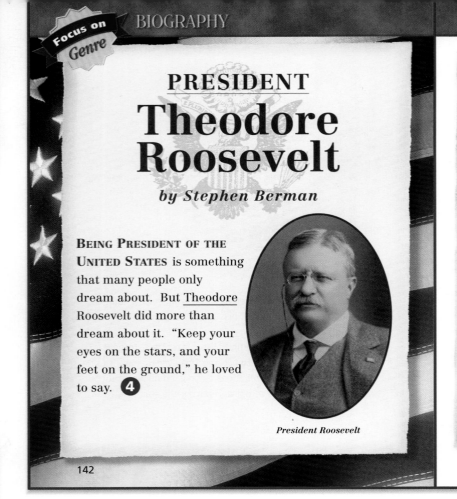

PRESIDENT
Theodore Roosevelt

by Stephen Berman

BEING PRESIDENT OF THE UNITED STATES is something that many people only dream about. But Theodore Roosevelt did more than dream about it. "Keep your eyes on the stars, and your feet on the ground," he loved to say. **4**

President Roosevelt

142

President Roosevelt and his family

TR, as his friends called him, was born in 1858 in New York City. When he was very young, he was sick with asthma. Later, he started exercising every day. He became strong and fit. He learned to love sports and the outdoors.

TR loved to read and write too. Most of all, he loved nature. When he was seven years old, he started the Roosevelt Museum of Natural History in his family's house. It was filled with bones and skins and skulls of animals he had found. His love of nature remained an important part of his life when he was president.

143

Purpose Setting

Ask children to look for elements of a biography as they read about two more famous people, a United States president and an Olympic champion.

READING STRATEGY

Phonics/Decoding

r-Controlled Vowels

Teacher/Student Modeling Write *important*. Remind children that *o* followed by *r* usually stands for the /ôr/. Have children read the word. Then write *forty-two* and *Rushmore*. Have children blend the sounds in each syllable to read each word.

Vocabulary

asthma an illness that makes it hard for people to breathe

fit in good health

THEME 4: Focus on Biography
(Anthology pp. 142–143)

An image of Theodore Roosevelt's face is carved in stone, sixty feet high, at Mount Rushmore in South Dakota.

Theodore Roosevelt was elected vice president in 1900. When President William McKinley was killed less than a year later, TR became president. He was only forty-two years old, the youngest president ever.

Theodore Roosevelt and a friend look out on Yosemite National Park.

144

While TR was president, he made laws to create national forests and national parks. That's how he became known as the "Conservation President."

Theodore Roosevelt was president from 1901 to 1909. He died ten years later on January 16, 1919. He was sixty years old.

Today we can still enjoy the beautiful parks he **5** **6** helped create.

Theodore Roosevelt National Park, North Dakota

145

CRITICAL THINKING
Guiding Comprehension

4 **MAKING INFERENCES** What does Theodore Roosevelt mean when he says *Keep your eyes on the stars, and your feet on the ground?* (It is important to dream, but also to be practical and realistic.)

5 **AUTHOR'S VIEWPOINT** How does the author connect Theodore Roosevelt's childhood to his work? (TR's love of nature as a child led him to create parks and national forests when he became president.)

6 **MAKING INFERENCES** Why do you think Theodore Roosevelt loved nature so much? (As a boy, Roosevelt had asthma and couldn't play outdoors. Once he was able to be outdoors, nature became very important to him.)

REACHING ALL LEARNERS **Extra Support/Intervention**

Strategy Modeling: Evaluate

Use this example to model the strategy.

The author says that TR always loved nature and even started his own museum when he was seven years old. Later he says that when TR was president, he made laws to create national parks and forests. I think the author does a good job of explaining how TR's love of nature led him to become known as the "Conservation President."

Reading the Selection
(Anthology pp. 144–145)   **T333**

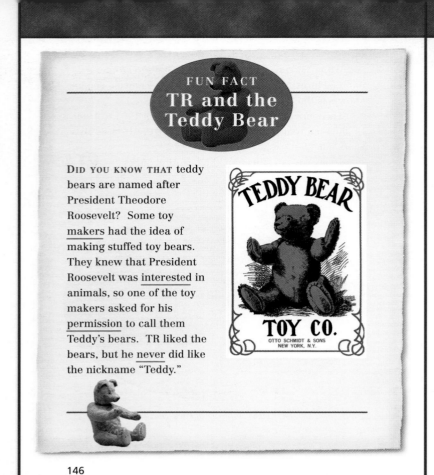

BIOGRAPHY

WILMA RUDOLPH

OLYMPIC TRACK CHAMPION

BY VERONICA FREEMAN ELLIS

ALL EYES WATCHED the little girl walking down the aisle. Wasn't she Wilma Rudolph, who always wore a brace on her left leg? Yes, she was. But that Sunday morning in church, Wilma was walking without her brace. Everyone was surprised, but Wilma had always known that she would walk again someday.

7 **8**

146

147

CRITICAL THINKING

Guiding Comprehension

7 **DRAWING CONCLUSIONS** How would you describe Wilma Rudolph from what you read about her on the first page of her biography? (She was tough, courageous, and determined.)

8 **COMPARE AND CONTRAST** How are Wilma Rudolph and Theodore Roosevelt alike? (Both TR and Wilma Rudolph were sickly as children. Both were determined to become strong and fit and were able to achieve those goals.)

REACHING ALL LEARNERS

English Language Learners

Using Words to Describe

Have children find photographs of people doing things children admire, such as helping someone, showing courage, or being a friend. Have them label the pictures. Children can use these words and images when they write their own biographies.

THEME 4: Focus on Biography
T334 (Anthology pp. 146–147)

Wilma wins the 100–meter dash.

Wilma runs a 400–meter relay.

Wilma receives one of her three gold medals.

"The doctors told me I would never walk," said Wilma many years later, "but my mother told me I would, so I believed my mother."

Wilma Rudolph was born in Bethlehem, Tennessee, in 1940. Just before her fifth birthday, Wilma became very ill. Her illness caused her to lose the use of her left leg.

9

148

Wilma was determined to walk. She did exercises every day to make her leg stronger. Even though doctors had put a steel brace on her leg, Wilma practiced walking every day without it. When she was twelve years old, she took off her brace for good.

At sixteen, Wilma Rudolph became the youngest member of the 1956 U.S. Olympic track team. That year she won a bronze medal in the relay race.

10

149

CRITICAL THINKING

Guiding Comprehension

9 DRAWING CONCLUSIONS Why do you think the authors of Theodore Roosevelt's and Wilma Rudolph's biographies tell about childhood health problems? (to show that these people were courageous even as children, and to show how they overcame difficulties and achieved their goals)

10 AUTHOR'S VIEWPOINT Why do you think the author of Wilma Rudolph's biography mentions the 1956 Olympics? (She probably wants to point out how much of an achievement it was for Wilma to win a bronze medal only four years after taking off her leg brace.)

REACHING ALL LEARNERS

English Language Learners

Using Words and Photographs

Invite children to retell the story of Wilma Rudolph's life in their own words. Encourage them to use selection photographs and captions to support their retellings of Wilma's Olympic victories.

Focus on Biography

In 1960, Wilma became <u>world</u> famous. At the Olympics in Rome, Italy, she won a gold medal for the 100-<u>meter</u> dash. She won a second gold medal for the 200-meter dash.

It was time for the 400-meter relay race. Wilma was the final <u>runner</u> on her team. It was up to her to cross the finish line. When her teammate handed her the baton, Wilma <u>nearly</u> dropped it! Her team fell to <u>third</u> place, but Wilma didn't give up. She ran as hard as she could — and she won.

Wilma Rudolph became the first American woman to win three gold medals in track at the same Olympics. The little girl who had been <u>told</u> she would never walk was now the <u>fastest</u> woman runner in the world!

Wilma retired from running in 1962. She became a second-grade <u>teacher</u> and a high school track coach. She started the Wilma Rudolph <u>Foundation</u>, which teaches young athletes that they, too, can be champions.

12

11 **IMPORTANT DATES AND EVENTS**

1940
Wilma Rudolph is born on June 23.

1956
She wins a bronze medal at the Olympics.

1960
She wins three gold medals at the Rome Olympics.

1962
Wilma retires from running.

1981
She starts the Wilma Rudolph Foundation.

1983
Wilma is elected to the U.S. Olympic Hall of Fame.

1994
She dies on November 12, in Brentwood, Tennessee.

150

151

CRITICAL THINKING
Guiding Comprehension

11 **TEXT ORGANIZATION** Why do you think the author uses a timeline to show the events of Wilma Rudolph's life? (to show when the events in her life took place)

12 **COMPARE AND CONTRAST** How does the Wilma Rudolph story show that she, like Ellen Ochoa and Theodore Roosevelt, had her "eyes on the stars"? (It demonstrates how Wilma Rudolph overcame tremendous obstacles to become a champion runner, a coach, and a teacher.)

COMPREHENSION STRATEGY
Evaluate

Student Modeling Have children model how to Evaluate. If necessary, ask: *Do you like to read true stories about people's lives? Does the author do a good job of describing Wilma Rudolph and telling about her goals?*

THEME 4: Focus on Biography
(Anthology pp. 150–151)

REACHING ALL LEARNERS
Extra Support/Intervention

Review pages 142–151.

Before children join in Wrapping Up, have them

● take turns modeling **Evaluate** and other strategies they used,

● check and complete **Practice Book** page 81,

● **summarize** the important events in both biographies.

Wrapping Up

Critical Thinking Questions

1. **COMPARE AND CONTRAST** How is Wilma Rudolph's biography like or unlike others you have read? (Sample answer: Both Wilma and Theodore Roosevelt overcame difficulties and achieved goals. Each person had a different career in a different time and place.)

2. **MAKING GENERALIZATIONS** What elements of a biography do you find in each story? (facts and true events that happened during people's lives)

Strategies in Action

Have children evaluate how well each biography presented its subject and the challenges each faced.

Discussion Options

Bring the entire class together to do either of these activities.

Review Predictions/Purpose Have children discuss which biographies they found inspiring, and why.

Share Ideas Ask children to discuss how biographies may influence the people who read them.

REACHING ALL LEARNERS Challenge

Creating a Timeline

Invite children to create a timeline showing important class events, such as trips, celebrations, or the arrival of a new student.

Monitoring Student Progress

If . . .	Then . . .
children have trouble answering the Critical Thinking questions,	have them form small groups and refer to the biographies as they discuss possible answers to the questions.

Responding

Comprehension Check

Have children reread or finish reading the biographies. Then assign **Practice Book** page 82 to assess children's comprehension of the biographies.

Think About Biographies

Discuss or Write Have children answer the questions on Anthology page 152. Answers will vary; sample answers are shown; accept reasonable responses.

1. **MAKING INFERENCES** Ellen means that you should not be afraid to try new and difficult things, even if they seem hard or impossible to do at first.

2. **COMPARE AND CONTRAST** Both were sick as children. Theodore Roosevelt had asthma; Wilma Rudolph lost the use of her left leg. Both solved their problems by doing exercises every day to become stronger.

3. **MAKING JUDGMENTS** Answers will vary but should include a reason why that person would be interesting to meet.

4. **PROBLEM SOLVING** (Answers will vary but should include a personal example and explanation of how they worked hard at something or solved a problem.)

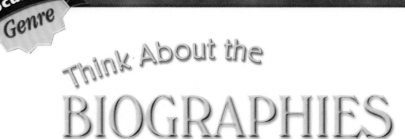

Think About the BIOGRAPHIES

1. Ellen Ochoa tells children not to be afraid to reach for the stars. What does she mean?

2. Compare the problems that Theodore Roosevelt and Wilma Rudolph had when they were children. How did they solve their problems?

3. Which one of these people do you wish you could meet? Why?

4. What is something you have worked hard at? What helped you want to try, even though it was hard?

Internet

Take an Online Quiz

You have just read some biographies. See what you've learned by taking an online quiz.

www.eduplace.com/kids

152

Practice Book page 82

Focus on Biography
Comprehension Check

Name _____

Key Events

Fill in the chart by answering the questions about each person.

	Ellen Ochoa	Theodore Roosevelt	Wilma Rudolph
What happened in their childhood?	Responses will vary. (2 points)	Responses will vary. (2)	Responses will vary. (2)
What school subjects did they work hard at?	Responses will vary. (2)	Responses will vary. (2)	Responses will vary. (2)
What did they do when they grew up?	Responses will vary. (2)	Responses will vary. (2)	Responses will vary. (2)

Narrating

Write a Biography

Choose a person you want to know more about. That person might be an explorer, a president, or a sports star. Look up facts about the person in books, in the encyclopedia, or on the Internet. Write a biography of the person.

Tips

Write an interesting beginning for the biography.

Tell about the person's early life first. Then tell about the person's later years.

Write a title that will get a reader's attention.

Former President Jimmy Carter helps build houses for people.

Yo-Yo Ma plays the cello.

153

Write a Biography

Have children read and briefly discuss the writing assignment on Anthology page 153. Before children begin writing their biographies, present the writing lesson on page T340.

 REACHING ALL LEARNERS

Extra Support/ Intervention	English Language Learners

Writing Support

Reread a section of the Read Aloud "Meet Dr. Seuss." Help children take notes by listing words and phrases in time order to tell about parts of Dr. Seuss's life. Ask children how to turn the notes into complete sentences. Write the completed sentences.

Supporting Comprehension

Beginning/Preproduction Have children pantomine the people featured in this section. The other children guess the person's name.

Early Production and Speech Emergence Have children create illustrations of the people featured in this section. Guide them to include speech balloons with dialogue.

Intermediate and Advanced Fluency Have children write a paragraph about their favorite biography. Have them share it with the rest of the class.

Monitoring Student Progress

End-of-Selection Assessment

Student Self-Assessment Have children assess their reading with questions such as

- How did the author help me understand each person?

- What did I like and dislike about each biography?

- Which biography did I enjoy most? Why?

Responding
(Anthology p. 153) **T339**

- Do research to find important facts about a person.
- Plan and write a biography.

Transparency F4–6

Guidelines for Writing a Biography

- Give your biography a title.

- Start with a sentence that tells whom you are writing about.

- Tell only the most important events and accomplishments.

- Write about the facts in the order that they happened in the person's life.

- Use exact verbs to tell what the person did.

- Give some details that show what the person is like.

- Use different kinds of sentences.

- Use your own words. Don't copy from a book.

THEME 4 • Focus on Biography
Writing Guidelines for a Biography

ANNOTATED VERSION

TRANSPARENCY F4–6
TEACHER'S EDITION PAGE T340

Practice Book page 83

Focus on Biography
Writing Skill A Biography

Name _____

Biography Facts Chart

Take notes about a person's life. Write a fact in each row. Use your own words. Number the facts in the order you will write about them. Write and number more facts on another paper. (6 points)

My biography is about _____

Notes will vary.

WRITING: A Biography

❶ Teach

Review the characteristics of a biography.

- It is a true story about a person's life.

- It gives facts about what the person did.

- It tells about events that happened in the person's life.

Brainstorm a list of people children would like to learn more about. Suggest categories, such as explorers, inventors, presidents, sports stars, and authors. Have children decide about whom they will write.

Discuss how to get started writing a biography.

- Tell children that good biographers take notes from reference sources before writing. Since children can't tell everything about a person's life, they should choose the most important facts.

- Brainstorm and list the type of facts that should be included, such as important dates and events and accomplishments.

- Tell children that notes should be brief and written in their own words, using single words and phrases. Later they will write the notes as complete sentences.

Display and discuss the guidelines on Transparency F4–6. Then help children find appropriate books or encyclopedias in the school library.

❷ Practice/Apply

Assign Practice Book page 83. Ask children to find information about the person for their biography in reference sources.

- Have children use this page to take notes for writing a two- to three-paragraph biography.

- Have children number their facts in the order they will write about them.

- Then have them begin their biographies, writing out their notes in complete sentences.

SPELLING: The vowel + *r* Sounds in *for* and *before*

Review the Principle Remind children that /ôr/ is usually spelled *or* or *ore*. Choose a Basic Word and make a short line for each letter. Write *or* or *ore* in the correct position in the word. Say the word. Have a child write the missing letters to spell the word. Continue with other Basic Words.

Practice/Homework Assign **Practice Book** page 84.

GRAMMAR: Nouns and Pronouns Together

Review the Skill Have volunteers read aloud the information at the top of **Practice Book** page 85. Have children first name some nouns and tell which pronoun can take the place of each noun.

Practice/Homework Assign **Practice Book** page 85.

What is a pronoun?

A pronoun is a word that takes the place of a noun. <u>She</u>, <u>he</u>, <u>they</u>, and <u>it</u> are pronouns.

Focus On Genre

Challenge

Word Practice

Children can make a dictionary page. Have them write five Spelling Words that begin with *f*, including the Challenge Words, in alphabetical order. Have them add a definition and either a sentence or a picture for each word.

Practice Book page 84

Focus on Biography
Spelling Skill The Vowel + *r*
Sounds in *for* or *before*

Name _____

Or? Ore?

► You hear the vowel + r sounds in **born** and **core**. These sounds are spelled **or** or **ore**.

Spelling Words
1. born
2. core
3. short
4. morning
5. fork
6. four
7. horn
8. sport
9. torn
10. sort
11. snore
12. fort

Write the Spelling Words that have the vowel +r sounds spelled as *or*.

1. born (1 point)   6. sport (1)
2. short (1)   7. torn (1)
3. morning (1)   8. sort (1)
4. fork (1)   9. fort (1)
5. horn (1)

Write the Spelling Words that have the vowel + *r* sounds spelled as *ore*.

10. core (1)   11. snore (1)

Write the Spelling Word that does not follow the spelling pattern.

12. four (1)

Practice Book page 85

Focus on Biography
Grammar Skill Nouns and
Pronouns Together

Name _____

Replace the Pronouns

Read this book report. Find two places where the pronoun *he* can be replaced by a noun. Draw a circle around each pronoun you want to replace. (2 points)

George Washington was our first President. He was born in Virginia in 1732. He was a general in the army. He led many battles against Great Britain. He helped to win freedom for the United States. He has a monument named after him.

Rewrite the book report. Replace each pronoun you circled with *George* or *Washington*. (2 points)

The replacement of the pronoun *he* will vary.

_____
_____
_____
_____
_____

Spelling and Grammar T341

Day at a Glance
pp. T342–T347

Reading Instruction

Comprehension Instruction
Understanding a Biography
Rereading for Understanding

Leveled Readers, T362–T365

- ● *Florence Griffith-Joyner: Olympic Champion*
- ▲ *Mae Jemison: Making Dreams Come True*
- ■ *Theodore Roosevelt: Friend of Nature*
- ◆ *Florence Griffith-Joyner: Olympic Runner*

Word Work

Vocabulary Review
Word Wall
Spelling Practice

Writing & Oral Language

Writing Activity
Grammar Practice
Listening/Speaking/Viewing

Daily Routines

Daily Message

Phonics Review Point to each word as you read aloud the Daily Message.

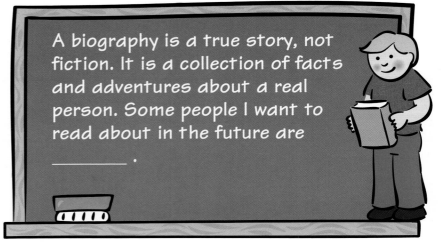

A biography is a true story, not fiction. It is a collection of facts and adventures about a real person. Some people I want to read about in the future are _____ .

Have children

- read the Daily Message, discuss it, and ask volunteers to complete the last sentence;
- find and read aloud words with final syllables *-tion, -ture*. (*fiction, collection, adventures, future*)

Word Wall

Speed Drill Have children review and practice these and other previously taught high-frequency words. Also have them practice reading a few decodable words that feature new phonics skills.

- Have children take turns holding up a card for partners to read.
- Have individuals read the words to you quickly.

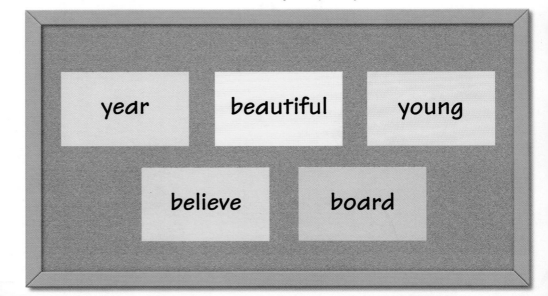

year   beautiful   young

believe   board

Vocabulary

Multiple-Meaning Words Distribute **Activity Master 4–4** on page R43 and provide dictionaries. Discuss alternative meanings for the words *shuttle*, *board*, *store*, and *space*. Have children use a dictionary to write alternative meanings for the underlined words. Then ask children to write a sentence, using one of the words, and draw a picture to go with it.

A space shuttle is an aircraft that makes trips between Earth and space.

Daily Writing Prompt

Have children revise work they are currently writing, or have them use this prompt to begin a new writing activity.

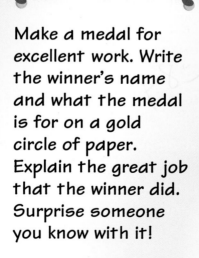

Make a medal for excellent work. Write the winner's name and what the medal is for on a gold circle of paper. Explain the great job that the winner did. Surprise someone you know with it!

Daily Language Practice

Grammar Skill: Proofreading
Spelling Skill: The Vowel + *r* Sounds in *for* and *before*

Display **Transparency F4–1.** Ask children to rewrite Sentence 3 correctly. Then model how to write it, and have children check their work.

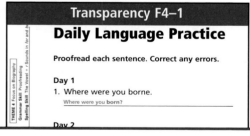

Transparency F4–1
Daily Language Practice

Proofread each sentence. Correct any errors.

Day 1
1. Where were you borne.
   Where were you **born**?

Day 2

Day 3
3. My friend carl has for pets.
   My friend **Carl** has **four** pets.

Day 5
5. The sporte Ed likes best is running?
   The **sport** Ed likes best is running.

OBJECTIVES

- Explain what a biography is.
- List important facts about a person, including dates and accomplishments.

Target Skill Trace

Preview, Teach	pp. T314, T328, T344

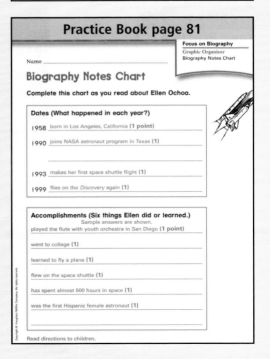

COMPREHENSION: Understanding a Biography

❶ Teach

Review characteristics of a biography.

- It is a true story about someone's life.
- It includes facts about the person's life, including important accomplishments.
- It often lists the years or dates of important happenings, and tells them in the same order they occured.

Have children share responses from their Biography Notes Charts. Have them refer to **Practice Book** page 81. Record the information on **Transparency F4–5**.

- Explain that Ellen Ochoa is still living today. Her biography begins when she was born (1958) and continues until the date the author recorded the last event (1999).
- The biographies of Theodore Roosevelt and Wilma Rudolph tell about the most important facts of their entire lives.

Modeling Model how to use picture captions to learn more information about a person in a biography.

Think Aloud *I look at the pictures and read the captions in Ellen Ochoa's biography. They help me understand more about Ellen's life. I see pictures of what Ellen looks like, how the space shuttle* Discovery *lifts off, and the astronauts she worked with. I learn from captions that she has a young son and that she flew on the* Discovery *in 1999.*

❷ Guided Practice

Have small groups discuss "President Theodore Roosevelt." List the dates 1858, 1900, 1901–1909, and 1919.

- Have children tell what happened on each date and make a group list of Roosevelt's accomplishments.
- Have children look at the pictures and captions and discuss what additional information they learn. (Sample answer: Theodore Roosevelt's face is carved in stone on Mount Rushmore; there is park named after him.)
- Have groups share their responses with the whole class.

❸ Apply

Assign Practice Book page 86. Have children complete the Biography Notes Chart for Wilma Rudolph. They can also apply this skill as they read other biographies in their Leveled Readers for this week or books from the Suggestions for Independent Reading for this theme on page T305.

✔ **Test Prep** Tell children that reading tests may ask them to identify the genre of a passage. Emphasize that children can identify a biography by checking to see if the passage tells about a real person and gives facts about what happened in that person's life and the dates they occurred.

Leveled Readers and Leveled Practice

Children at all levels apply the comprehension skill as they read their Leveled Readers on pages T362–T365.

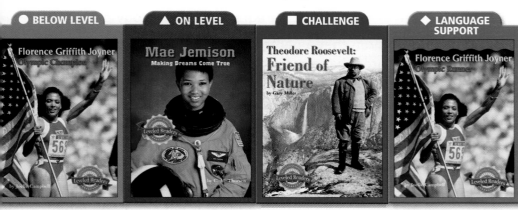

● **BELOW LEVEL** — Florence Griffith Joyner Olympic Champion

▲ **ON LEVEL** — Mae Jemison Making Dreams Come True

■ **CHALLENGE** — Theodore Roosevelt: Friend of Nature by Gary Miller

◆ **LANGUAGE SUPPORT** — Florence Griffith Joyner Olympic Runner

Reading Traits

Teaching children to think about genre is one way of encouraging them to "read the lines" of a selection. This comprehension skill supports the reading trait **Decoding Conventions**.

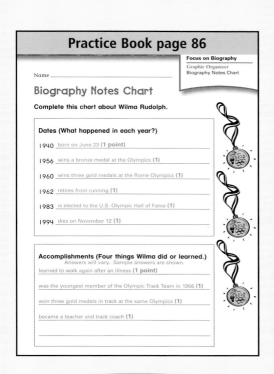

Practice Book page 86

Focus on Biography
Graphic Organizer
Biography Notes Chart

Name _____

Biography Notes Chart

Complete this chart about Wilma Rudolph.

Dates (What happened in each year?)
1940 — born on June 23 **(1 point)**
1956 — wins a bronze medal at the Olympics **(1)**
1960 — wins three gold medals at the Rome Olympics **(1)**
1962 — retires from running **(1)**
1983 — is elected to the U.S. Olympic Hall of Fame **(1)**
1994 — dies on November 12 **(1)**

Accomplishments (Four things Wilma did or learned.)
Answers will vary. Sample answers are shown.

learned to walk again after an illness **(1 point)**

was the youngest member of the Olympic Track Team in 1956 **(1)**

won three gold medals in track at the same Olympics **(1)**

became a teacher and track coach **(1)**

Monitoring Student Progress

If . . .	Then . . .
children score 7 or below on **Practice Book** page 86,	help them find main ideas and dates to retell the most important facts.

REREADING FOR UNDERSTANDING

Writer's Craft: Using Quotations

Teach Remind children that a quotation is one person's words repeated exactly by another person.

- Read the quotation on Anthology page 142.
- Point out the quotation marks. Ask who loved to say these words. (Theodore Roosevelt)

Have children find the quotation on Anthology page 141.

- Have a child read the words between the quotation marks. Ask who said these exact words that the author included in the biography. (Ellen Ochoa)

Practice/Apply Have children work in pairs to write quotations that they are familiar with. Have them identify the speaker. Allow time for children to share their work.

Writer's Craft: Use of Paragraphs and Topic Sentences

Teach Read aloud the first paragraph on Anthology page 149.

- Remind children that a paragraph usually begins with a word that is indented, has a main or topic sentence, and includes supporting details.
- Identify these features in the first paragraph. (indented word *Wilma*; topic sentence: *Wilma was determined to walk*; supporting details: did exercises every day; had a steel brace on her leg; practiced walking every day)

Practice/Apply Have pairs of children read the second paragraph on page 149 and identify the word that is indented, the topic sentence, and one detail.

SPELLING: The Vowel + *r* Sounds in *for* and *before*

Vocabulary Connection Write the Basic Words, and read the clues. Have children say and spell the spelling word that answers each clue.

- all cars have one (horn)
- the opposite of long (short)
- soccer is an example (sport)
- the first part of each day (morning)

- often built in a tree (fort)
- a sound sometimes made when you sleep (snore)

Ask children to use each Basic Word in an oral sentence.

Practice/Homework Assign **Practice Book** page 87.

GRAMMAR: Nouns and Pronouns Together

Stick the Noun on the Pronoun

Copy the paragraph shown, leaving space between lines.

- Choose a child to circle the pronoun *they*.
- Have children suggest nouns that can replace two or three pronouns in the paragraph.
- Write each noun suggested on a self-stick note. Have a child place it over the pronoun. Read the revised story together.
- Then try a different way of replacing two pronouns, and read the story again.

    Wilbur and Orville Wright were
brothers and did many interesting
things. They invented the first
airplane. Orville built his own press.
They started a weekly paper. They
made bicycles to sell. Then they
became interested in flying. They
built a glider that stayed in the air
for 59 seconds on its first flight.

Day at a Glance
pp. T348–T355

Reading Instruction

Phonics Review

Study Skills: Using Text Features

Preparing for Discussion

• •

Leveled Readers, *T362–T365*

- ● *Florence Griffith-Joyner: Olympic Champion*
- ▲ *Mae Jemison: Making Dreams Come True*
- ■ *Theodore Roosevelt: Friend of Nature*
- ◆ *Florence Griffith-Joyner: Olympic Runner*

Word Work

Vocabulary Instruction
  Abbreviations and Acronyms

Word Wall

Spelling Practice

Writing & Oral Language

Improving Writing

Grammar Practice

Listening/Speaking/Viewing

Daily Routines

Daily Message

Phonics Review Point to each word as you read aloud the Daily Message.

> Hello, Boys and Girls,
> Wilma Rudolph believed that she could walk and run. She was hopeful and didn't give up. She became a winner and proudly _____ .

Have children
- read the Daily Message, discuss it, and ask volunteers to complete the last sentence;
- find and read aloud words with endings *-ful, -ly*. (hopeful, proudly)

Word Wall

Using the Senses Review the high-frequency words from this week's Word Wall by having children see, trace, and hear them.

Have partners take turns
- pointing to a word and saying it;
- tracing the word on their arms or desks, saying the letters;
- using the word in an oral sentence.

Vocabulary

Genre Vocabulary Review Briefly review these words and their meanings: *biography, champion, event, fact, information,* and *president.* Then assign one word to each of several small groups.

- Have children write words or ideas they associate with the selected word.
- Allow time for sharing ideas.

biography
champion
event
fact
information
president

biography

true story
famous person
Dr. Seuss
dates

Daily Writing Prompt

Have children revise work they are currently writing, or have them use this prompt to begin a new writing activity.

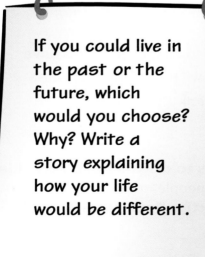

If you could live in the past or the future, which would you choose? Why? Write a story explaining how your life would be different.

Daily Language Practice

Grammar Skill: Proofreading
Spelling Skill: The Vowel + *r* Sounds in *for* and *before*

Display **Transparency F4–1.** Ask children to rewrite Sentence 4 correctly. Then model how to write it, and have children check their work.

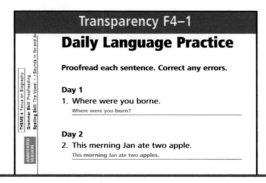

Transparency F4–1

Daily Language Practice

Proofread each sentence. Correct any errors.

Day 1
1. Where were you borne.
   Where were you born?

Day 2
2. This merning Jan ate two apple.
   This morning Jan ate two apples.

Day 4
4. Mom beeped the car horen at the Dog.
   Mom beeped the car **horn** at the **dog.**

The **sport** Ed likes best is running.

COMPREHENSION: Preparing for Discussion

Biographies

Have children review the Anthology biographies. Assign **Practice Book** page 88 to use for small group and class literature discussions.

Prepare children to discuss biographies in small groups.

- Point out that biographies can be written about people who lived in the past or people who are still living.

- Explain that many biographies begin when the person is born and tell true facts about his or her life in the same order that they occurred in the person's life.

- Share these tips. You may want to display them in the classroom.

Tips for Discussing the Biographies

⭐ Take turns asking questions about Ellen, TR, or Wilma. The answers must be found in their biographies.

⭐ First, name the person. Then ask a question. Speak clearly.

⭐ Call on a classmate to answer the question.

⭐ Listen carefully to the questions and answers.

⭐ Wait for your classmate to respond. If you have more to add or disagree with the answer, raise your hand and ask to speak.

Divide children into small groups to discuss the biographies. Have them ask questions about the people in the biographies and then share their responses from **Practice Book** pages 82 and 88.

Practice Book page 88

Focus on Biography
Preparing for Discussion

Name _____

We Are All the Same

Answer the question.

Ellen Ochoa, Theodore Roosevelt, and Wilma Rudolph are alike in many ways. Which way do you think is the most important?

(4 points)

_____
_____
_____

Fill in the chart.

This is How I Am Like Ellen Ochoa	This is How I Am Like Theodore Roosevelt	This is How I Am Like Wilma Rudolph
Responses will vary. (2 points)	Responses will vary. (2)	Responses will vary. (2)

IMPROVING WRITING: Dates and Time-Order Words

OBJECTIVES

- Identify time-order words and dates in a biography.
- Revise writing to include more dates and time-order words.

❶ Teach

Writing Traits: Organization Children may have difficulty arranging events in time order. Explain that a biography usually tells the events in a person's life in the order in which they happened. A biography makes more sense if it clearly tells when each event happened.

- Tell children that time-order words tell when something happened.

- List and read these time-order words and phrases: *first, after that, soon, then, later, next, when, during, now, finally,* and *last.*

- Explain that dates also help to make time order clear. Write *1940* and *November 12, 1994* as examples.

- Point out and briefly discuss the timeline of Wilma Rudolph's life on Anthology pages 150–151. Explain that this timeline uses dates instead of time-order words to show the sequence of important events in Wilma's life between 1940 and 1994.

❷ Practice

Display Transparency F4–7. Read the brief biography of Wilma Rudolph in the first box.

- Have children identify the time-order words or phrases. Circle these on the transparency.

- Repeat with the biography of Walt Disney in the second box.

❸ Apply

Assign Practice Book page 89. Ask children to check their biographies to see if they have used dates and other time-order words and to decide if they would like to add more.

Portfolio Opportunity

✔ Save children's biographies as examples of their writing development.

Transparency F4–7

Time-Order Words

Wilma Rudolph

In 1940, Wilma Rudolph was born. When she was five, she got very sick. After that, she worked hard to walk again. Soon, she was running too! She won a bronze medal at the Olympics in 1956. Later, she won three gold medals at the Olympics.

The Amazing Walt Disney

Walt Disney was born in 1901 in Chicago. After he went to art school there, he began to draw cartoons. Walt made up the character Mickey Mouse in 1928. People loved this mouse, and Walt used his own voice for Mickey. Soon Walt began to make long cartoon movies. *Snow White and the Seven Dwarfs* is just one of them. Later, he set up big theme parks. Before he died, Walt won many prizes for his work.

ANNOTATED VERSION
THEME 4 Focus on Biography
Writing Skill Improving Your Writing

TRANSPARENCY F4–7
TEACHER'S EDITION PAGE T351

Practice Book page 89

Focus on Biography
Writing Skill Time-Order Words

Name _____

When Did It Happen?

Read the paragraphs about Dr. Seuss. Circle the time-order words and dates. (9 points)

Dr. Seuss was born on March 2, 1904. He liked to draw. During college, he wrote stories and drew funny pictures. Next, he began creating funny cartoons.

Then Dr. Seuss sold his first cartoon and moved to New York City. Next, he got a job writing ads. Dr. Seuss wrote his first story in 1937. After World War II, he wrote The Cat in the Hat and many other books for children.

Dr. Seuss died on September 24, 1991. Today, children around the world read and love his books.

On another sheet of paper, write five sentences about events in your life. Put them in the order that they happened. Use time-order words. (5)

WRITING

Focus on Biography

OBJECTIVE

● Identify abbreviations and the words they stand for.

VOCABULARY: Abbreviations

❶ Teach

Introduce abbreviations. Explain that an abbreviation is a short way of saying or writing the name of a person, street, state, month, day, or title.

● Read aloud the first sentence on Anthology page 143: *TR, as his friends called him, was born in 1858 in New York City.*

● Explain that the letters *TR* are Theodore Roosevelt's initials, the first letter in both his first and last names.

Give other examples of abbreviations.

● Write *St., Mr., CA,* and *Sept.* Explain what each abbreviation stands for. (*Street, Mister, California, September*) Call attention to the capital letters and period at the end of all the abbreviations except CA.

Model how to figure out the meaning of an abbreviation in the context of a sentence. Write *My friend lives at 20 Clark Rd.*

Think Aloud   Rd. *is probably an abbreviation for a longer word. It must have something to do with where the friend lives. Oh, maybe it is short for* Road. *I know that* r *and* d *are the first and last letters in* road *and an abbreviation often ends with a period.*

❷ Guided Practice

Write *Dr., TV, TX, Mr., Ave.,* and *Oct.* in one column and *Texas, television, Doctor, October, Avenue,* and *Mister* in the second column.

● Have volunteers draw a line to match each abbreviation with the word it stands for.

● Note which abbreviations use punctuation and which do not.

❸ Apply

Assign Practice Book page 90.

Practice Book page 90

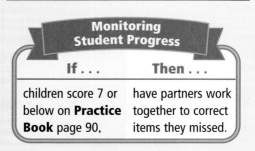

Focus on Biography
Vocabulary Skill
Abbreviations

Name _____

Add Abbreviations

1–6. Read the story. When you find a word missing, choose an abbreviation from the box. Write it on the line. Then read the story again. (6 points)

Word Bank

| St. | Thurs. | T.C. | Aug. | Mrs. | Mr. |

I saw Mr.___ Clark walking his dog on Elm St.___. He had the letters T.C.___ for Tim Clark on his shirt pocket. I asked when he was going to have a yard sale. He said it would be on Aug.___ 24. Then I stopped to talk with Mrs.___ Miller. She invited me to a birthday party for Sam on Thurs.___, July 16.

Now choose two abbreviations. Write a sentence using each one. Sentences will vary. (2 points)

7. _____

8. _____

Monitoring Student Progress

If . . .	Then . . .
children score 7 or below on **Practice Book** page 90,	have partners work together to correct items they missed.

PHONICS: Vowel Pairs

❶ Review

Review the pattern. Write the example words below, underlining the vowel pair. Review these concepts.

- The vowel pairs *ai* and *ay* in *braid* and *gray* stand for the long *a* sound.

- The vowel pairs *ee* and *ea* in *green* and *squeak* stand for the long *e* sound.

- The vowel pairs *ow* and *ou* in *cloud* and *town* stand for the /ou/ sound.

- The vowel pair *ow* can also have the long *o* sound as in the word *grow*. Try both sounds for *ow* before reading the word.

❷ Guided Practice/Apply

Assign Practice Book page 91. Also have children play Let's Go Fishing.

Let's Go Fishing

Get ready to play.

- Cut out twenty or more fish shapes.
- Write a word on each fish. Use *spray, haystack, playful, beach, paintbrush, freely, round, frown, slow, downtown, scream, mouth, meeting, painful, crayon, shower, surround, speeding, neatly,* and *rainbow.*

Play the game.

- Set up a "fish pond" and place the fish in it.
- Show children how to catch a fish.
- Assign children to small groups. Have them take turns catching fish and reading the words.

Focus On Genre

OBJECTIVE

- Read and write words with vowel pairs.

Materials

- Fish cut from construction paper or oak tag; markers
- paper clips to attach to each fish
- fishing pole made from a pencil or stick, string, and a magnet
- blue paper or a tub for a fish pond

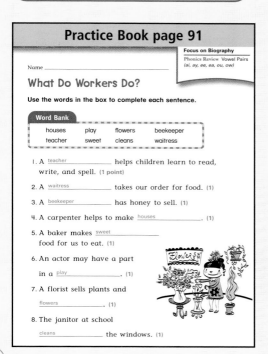

Practice Book page 91

Focus on Biography
Phonics Review Vowel Pairs
(ai, ay, ee, ea, ou, ow)

Name _____

What Do Workers Do?

Use the words in the box to complete each sentence.

Word Bank

| houses | play | flowers | beekeeper |
| teacher | sweet | cleans | waitress |

1. A _teacher_ helps children learn to read, write, and spell. (1 point)
2. A _waitress_ takes our order for food. (1)
3. A _beekeeper_ has honey to sell. (1)
4. A carpenter helps to make _houses_ . (1)
5. A baker makes _sweet_ food for us to eat. (1)
6. An actor may have a part in a _play_ . (1)
7. A florist sells plants and _flowers_ . (1)
8. The janitor at school _cleans_ the windows. (1)

PHONICS REVIEW

Focus on Biography

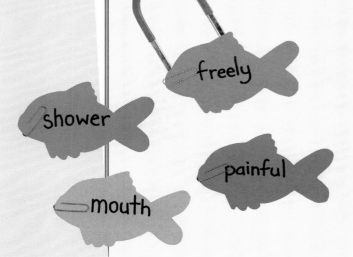

Practice Book page 92

Focus on Biography
Spelling Skill The Vowel + r
Sounds in *for* or *before*

Name _____

Proofreading and Writing

Proofreading Circle four Spelling Words that are incorrect. Then write each word correctly.

Max was short for his age but that never stopped him! He was the surt of boy who wanted to try everything.
His favorite sport was soccer. So every murning he would practice kicking the ball. Then he would run up and down the field four times. Max said that he was bourn to play soccer!

Spelling Words
1. born
2. core
3. short
4. morning
5. fork
6. four
7. horn
8. sport
9. torn
10. sort
11. snore
12. fort

1. short (1 point) 3. morning (1)

2. sort (1) 4. born (1)

Write Questions Write the name of someone you want to learn more about. List questions you would like to be able to answer by reading that person's biography. Use Spelling Words from the list. (2 points)

SPELLING: The Vowel + *r* Sounds in *for* and *before*

Blast Off! Provide pairs of children with this week's spelling list and a large rocket ship pattern. Have them each trace and cut out a rocket ship from construction paper.

- To play the game, Player 1 chooses a spelling word and gives a clue for that word.
- Player 2 names and spells the word. If correct, the player writes the word on his or her rocket ship.
- Partners take turns giving clues and spelling the words.
- A player's rocket ship "blasts off" when he or she has correctly written six spelling words.

Practice/Homework Assign **Practice Book** page 92 for proofreading and writing practice.

GRAMMAR: Nouns and Pronouns Together

Practice/Homework Assign **Practice Book** page 93.

Five children are in the race.

They run very fast.

Anna wins the race.

She gets a gold medal.

Todd claps for his sister.

He is very proud of her.

Practice Book page 93

Focus on Biography
Grammar Skill Nouns and
Pronouns Together

Name _____

Make It Clear!

Read the story below. Circle the pronouns *he*, *she*, and *they*.

Tom and Kate are twins. Rob and Pam are their brother and sister. Yesterday, he rode his bike to the lake. They went to play soccer at North Field. On Monday, she will finish her clay vase at school. He will take a trumpet lesson.

Rewrite the story on the lines below. Replace *he*, *she*, and *they* with nouns from the story.

(Score **2 points** each for replacing the pronouns *he* (Tom or Rob),

They (any two people: Tom, Kate, Rob, Pam), *she* (Kate or Pam), and

He (Tom or Rob).

_____

_____

_____

Share your story with a partner. They may be different stories, but are both stories clear?

STUDY SKILL: Using Text Features

① Teach

Discuss photographs and captions. Ask questions about text features in "Wilma Rudolph: Olympic Track Champion."

- Ask why the photograph of Wilma Rudolph is included on Anthology page 147. (It shows what she looks like, and tells readers more about the person being described.)

- Ask children to read the captions on pages 148 and 149 and tell what information they give. (They tell what Wilma is doing in the pictures.)

Explain timelines. Point out that timelines show events in the order they happened. Discuss the timeline on pages 150–151 and ask questions about it.

- Read aloud its title and Important Dates and Events.

- Ask what happened first. (Wilma Rudolph was born in 1940.)

- Point out the year and event labels. Ask what happened in 1960. (Wilma won three gold medals at the Olympics.)

② Practice/Apply

Have children complete the assignable activity below.

All About You

- Make a timeline of what you did last week. Write days of the week as labels. Tell something you did each day.

- Choose one day from your timeline. Draw a picture of what you did. Write a caption to go with it.

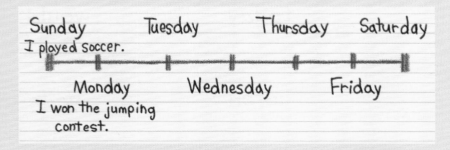

OBJECTIVES

- Interpret information in biography text features.
- Learn academic language: *photographs, captions, timeline.*

Materials

- Anthology pages 147–151
- drawing paper
- markers or crayons

Focus On Genre

INFORMATION & STUDY SKILLS

Focus on Biography

DAY 5 week 5

Day at a Glance
pp. T356–T361

Reading Instruction

Rereading for Understanding
Visualizing

Rereading for Fluency

Literature Discussion

• • • • • • • • • • • • • • • • •

Leveled Readers, T362–T365

● *Florence Griffith-Joyner: Olympic Champion*

▲ *Mae Jemison: Making Dreams Come True*

■ *Theodore Roosevelt: Friend of Nature*

◆ *Florence Griffith-Joyner: Olympic Runner*

Word Work

Vocabulary Expansion

Word Wall

Spelling Test: The Vowel + *r* Sounds in *for* and *before*

Writing & Oral Language

Writing Activity

Grammar: Improving Writing

Listening/Speaking/Viewing: Making Introductions

Daily Routines

Daily Message

Strategy Review Point to each word as you read aloud the Daily Message.

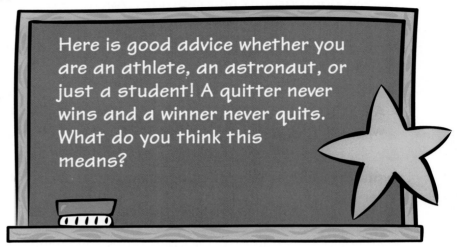

Here is good advice whether you are an athlete, an astronaut, or just a student! A quitter never wins and a winner never quits. What do you think this means?

Read aloud the entire Daily Message with children, pointing to each word as you read. Ask children to read the message aloud. Then have volunteers answer the question, and discuss their responses.

Word Wall

Cumulative Review Use word cards to review all high-frequency words posted on the Word Wall.

Have partners
• write numerals 1–6 on six index cards;
• place selected word cards and number cards face-down on a desk;
• draw a number card, pick up that number of word cards, and read aloud the words.

4

today	would
listen	year

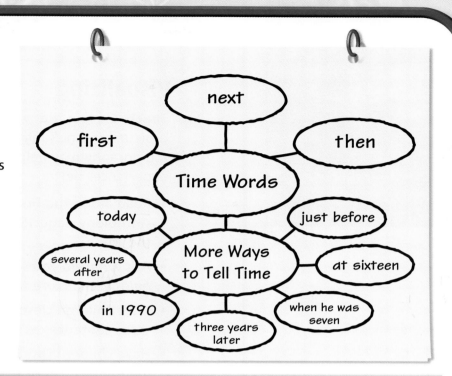

Vocabulary

Vocabulary Expansion Explain that most biographies tell about events in people's lives in the order that they happened. Then work with children to brainstorm words and phrases that help organize the order of events.

- Begin a word web as shown with the time words *first, next,* and *then.*
- Have children use a thesaurus or page through the selection to name other words and phrases that tell more about when key events happened.
- Add children's suggestions to a web similar to the one shown.

Daily Writing Prompt

Have children revise work they are currently writing, or have them use this prompt to begin a new writing activity.

> Write a diary entry. Tell about a time you wanted to quit but didn't. Use words that tell about time.

Daily Language Practice

Grammar Skill: Proofreading
Spelling Skill: The Vowel + *r* Sounds in *for* and *before*

Display **Transparency F4–1.** Ask children to rewrite Sentence 5 correctly. Then model how to write it, and have children check their work.

Transparency F4–1

Daily Language Practice

Proofread each sentence. Correct any errors.

Day 1
1. Where were you borne.
   Where were you **born?**

Day 2
2. This merning Jan ate two apple.
   This **morning** Jan ate two **apples.**

Day 3
3. My friend carl has for pets.
   My friend **Carl** has **four** pets.

Day 5
5. The sporte Ed likes best is running?
   The **sport** Ed likes best is running.

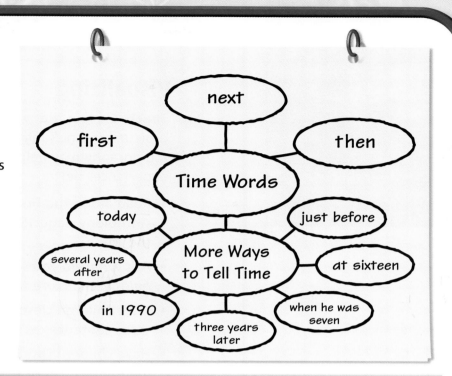

REREADING FOR UNDERSTANDING

Visualizing

Teach Explain that visualizing is using an author's words to create a picture in one's mind. Visualizing scenes or events described in a biography may help a reader to understand the person's life experiences better.

- Read aloud the first three sentences in the last paragraph on Anthology page 150 while children close their eyes and visualize the scene.

- Ask *What do you see? What do you know about relay races that helps you picture the scene?*

- Have children close their eyes again, in order to visualize the last three sentences as you read them aloud.

- Have children choose a part of the relay race and draw their mental pictures of it.

Practice/Apply Have children work in small groups. They can take turns reading sections of each biography and share what they visualize about those events.

REREADING FOR FLUENCY

Rereading the Biographies Have children choose one section of a biography to reread orally in small groups. If children are not reading with feeling and expression, you might model for them.

COMPREHENSION: Literature Discussion

Have a class discussion, using the questions below.

1. **MAKING JUDGMENTS** What are some characteristics you admire in people you know? (Answers will vary.)

2. **COMPARE AND CONTRAST** Do you think Ellen Ochoa, Wilma Rudolph, and Theodore Roosevelt are good role models? (Accept answers that show an understanding of positive traits.)

3. **COMPARE AND CONTRAST** In what ways are the time periods different in the biographies of Ellen Ochoa and Theodore Roosevelt? (Clothing styles were different. In the 1800s, when Roosevelt lived, there was no space travel. In the mid 1900s, women like Ellen took part in the space program.)

4. **COMPARE AND CONTRAST** How are most biographies alike? How are they similar to and different than fables? (Most biographies focus on true, key events in a person's life. Both biographies and fables can teach lessons about how to live, but fables usually involve animals and have a moral.)

GRAMMAR: Improving Writing

Proofreading for Capital Letters

Teach Display **Transparency F4–8**. Explain that each of these sentences needs a capital letter.

- Remind children that the first word in a sentence, the word *I*, and proper nouns begin with capital letters.

- Review that a proper noun names a specific person, place, or thing. Write and discuss these examples: Ellen Ochoa, New York City, and Space Shuttle Discovery.

- Have a child read the first sentence on the transparency, name the word that needs a capital letter, and tell why. Write the correction. Follow the same procedure for the remaining sentences.

Practice/Homework Assign **Practice Book** page 94. Have children review a sample of their own writing to see if they have used capital letters correctly.

Transparency F4–8

THEME 4 Focus on Biography
Grammar Skill Improving Writing

ANNOTATED VERSION

Proofreading for Capital Letters

1. ^Wwho would you like to read about?

2. Ellen Ochoa was born in ^Ccalifornia in 1958.

3. Reading is what ^Ii like to do!

4. ^Hhow was Theodore ^Rroosevelt's life different

   from yours?

5. ^Bbiographies are fun to read.

6. What did you learn about ^Wwilma Rudolph?

TRANSPARENCY F4–8
TEACHER'S EDITION PAGE T359

Practice Book page 94

Focus on Biography
Grammar Skill Improving your Writing

Name _____

Capital Letters Needed

Read the letter. Circle six words that should start with capital letters. Write the words correctly. (6 points)

May 5, 2004

Dear Grandma,
   I got a puppy for my birthday. I named it (rusty). (yesterday) we bought the puppy a collar that glows in the dark. (mom) takes the puppy for a walk on (maple) Street. My sister and (i) feed the puppy. I hope you can see the puppy soon.

Love,
(cora)

1. Rusty **(1 point)**   4. Maple **(1)**

2. Yesterday **(1)**   5. I **(1)**

3. Mom **(1)**   6. Cora **(1)**

- Spell words with the vowel + *r* sounds in *for* and *before.*
- Share biographies.

TEST

SPELLING: The Vowel + *r* Sounds in *for* and *before*

Test

Say each underlined word, read the sentence, and then repeat the word. Have children write only the underlined word.

Basic Words

1. When were you **born**?
2. Don't eat the apple **core**.
3. We took a **short** trip.
4. I jog every **morning**.
5. His **fork** is beside his plate.
6. Anna has **four** boxes.
7. The car **horn** beeped.
8. Is baseball the **sport** she likes?
9. One page in the book is **torn**.
10. They will **sort** the beads.
11. Do you **snore** every night?
12. My friends made a snow **fort**.

Challenge Words

13. They found **forty** shells.
14. We saw many trees in the **forest**.

EXTENSION

WRITING: Publishing a Biography

Ideas for Sharing

- Have children write final copies of their biographies.
- Children may read their biographies aloud to small groups. Have group members each write a fact they learned about the person. Have them share the facts with the group.
- Have children draw a picture of the person from the biography doing something memorable.
- Invite children to take their biographies home to share with their families.

LISTENING & SPEAKING: Making Introductions

OBJECTIVES

- Understand how to make introductions.
- Introduce themselves and others.

❶ Teach

Discuss why introductions are a polite and useful custom.

- Ask children what they might like to know about visitors to their school.

- Ask what Dr. Ellen Ochoa might say if she introduced herself. (Sample response: *Hello, class. My name is Dr. Ellen Ochoa. I am an astronaut, and I was the first Hispanic woman in space.*)

- Ask children why providing information about people might be helpful when introducing them to each other. (Learning about each other will help them begin a conversation.)

Model how to introduce others. Say *Sue, this is Mark. Mark likes to play soccer. Mark, this is Sue. She likes to sing.*

Share these tips for making introductions.

⭐ Look at the person or people to whom you are speaking.

⭐ Say each person's name clearly.

⭐ Try to tell something interesting about each person you are introducing.

❷ Practice/Apply

Have groups of three complete the activity below.

Hello, My Name Is . . .

Introduce Yourself

- Tell the group your name.
- Say two interesting things about yourself; for example tell what you like to do most.

Introduce Others

- Introduce your group members to one another.
- Say the name of each person. Tell interesting details about him or her.

Florence Griffith Joyner Olympic Champion

Summary *Florence Griffith Joyner won her first race at the age of seven, and she continued to run—and to win—throughout her childhood. At the 1988 Olympics, Joyner won three races and became an Olympic gold-medal champion.*

Vocabulary

Introduce the Key Vocabulary and ask children to complete the **BLM**.

college a school that a student can attend after high school, *p. 7*

coach a person who helps athletes improve their skills, *p. 7*

champion the person whose skills are judged to be the best, *p. 7*

Olympics the Olympic Games, an event at which great athletes from all over the world compete, every four years, *p. 7*

medal a metal disk awarded as a prize for first, second, or third place in a race or game, *p. 10*

● BELOW LEVEL

Building Background and Vocabulary

Explain that this book is a biography, a true story about a real person, Florence Griffith Joyner. Ask children to share any knowledge they have about Joyner. Use some of the language of the book and key vocabulary as you guide children through the text.

Writing Skill: Writing a Biography

Have children read the Strategy Focus on the book flap. Remind children to use the strategy and to think about the elements of a biography as they read the book. (See the Leveled Readers Teacher's Guide for **Vocabulary and Writing Practice Masters**.)

Responding

Have partners discuss how to answer the questions on the inside back cover.

Think About What You Have Read Sample answers:

1. She loved running when she was young. She won her first race when she was seven.

2. Possible response: She felt proud because she had worked hard. She felt happy because her hard work had paid off.

3. Possible response: I would practice, train, and work hard.

Making Connections Responses will vary.

Building Fluency

Model Read aloud pages 2–4. Ask students to identify the repetition of the forms of the word *race* (race, races, racing).

Practice Ask a volunteer to read aloud the selection. Ask the class to read in unison whenever a form of the word *race* appears.

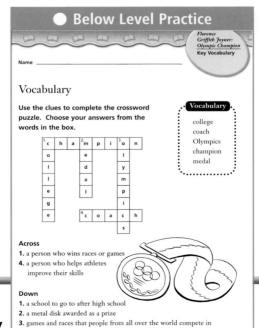

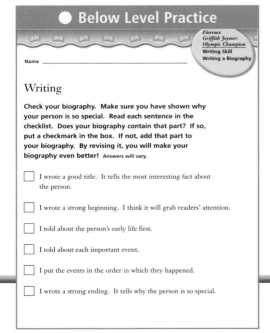

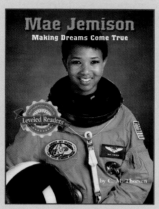

*Mae Jemison: Making
Dreams Come True*

Summary *As a child, Mae
Jemison had one great ambition:
she wanted to become an astronaut.
In 1987, she was accepted to
NASA's astronaut program. She flew
on the space shuttle* Endeavour *in
1992. As the first African American
woman to fly into space, Jemison
proved that hard work and determi-
nation can make a person's dreams
come true.*

Vocabulary

Introduce the Key Vocabulary and
ask children to complete the BLM.

launched took off; started to
move, *p. 2*

astronauts men and women
who travel into space, *p. 2*

voyage to travel, *p. 3*

curiosity an eagerness to
learn, *p. 4*

universe all of the planets
and stars that exist, *p. 5*

weightlessness the feeling of
having little or no weight,
due to a lack of gravity, *p. 15*

Building Background and Vocabulary

Explain that this book is a biography about Mae Jemison. Ask children what
would be fun or exciting about being an astronaut. Discuss the types of special skills that astronauts need to have. Use some of the language of the
book and key vocabulary as you guide children through the text.

Writing Skill: Writing a Biography

Have children read the Strategy Focus on the book flap. Remind children to
use the strategy and to think about the elements of a biography as they read
the book. (See the Leveled Readers Teacher's Guide for **Vocabulary and
Writing Practice Masters.**)

Responding

Have partners discuss how to answer the questions on the inside back cover.

Think About What You Have Read Sample answers:

1. When she was young, she read many books about outer space. When space
   missions were launched, she became interested in traveling in space.

2. She was the first African American woman to fly in space.

3. She studied chemical engineering. She became a medical doctor.

4. Possible responses: She might work with people to improve their health; she
   might work to develop better foods and medicines; she might design a space
   station.

Making Connections Responses will vary.

Building Fluency

Model Read aloud page 2, demonstrating how to read a date within text.

Practice Have children find the other pages on which dates and/or years
appear (pages 4, 11, 12, 13, and 15) and read them aloud.

▲ On Level Practice

Name _____

*Mae Jemison:
Making Dreams
Come True*
Key Vocabulary

Vocabulary

Use the words from the box to complete
the sentences.

Vocabulary
launched
astronauts
voyage
curiosity
universe
weightlessness

1. The ____astronauts____ flew into space.

2. NASA ____launched____ the space shuttle.

3. The men and women on board would
   ____voyage____ to the moon.

4. The moon, planets, and stars are all part
   of the ____universe____.

5. In space, people float because of ____weightlessness____.

6. Each astronaut felt great ____curiosity____
   about what they might find on the moon.

▲ On Level Practice

Name _____

*Mae Jemison:
Making Dreams
Come True*
Writing Skill
Writing a Biography

Writing

Check your biography. Make sure you have shown why
your person is so special. Read each sentence in the
checklist. Does your biography contain that part? If so,
put a checkmark in the box. If not, add that part to
your biography. By revising it, you will make your
biography even better! Answers will vary.

☐ I wrote a title that tells an interesting fact about the person.

☐ I wrote an interesting beginning. I think it will grab the readers'
attention.

☐ I presented the facts in the right order.

☐ I told about the person's early life.

☐ I told about each important event.

☐ I put the events in the order in which they happened.

☐ I wrote a strong ending. It tells why I think that this person
is special.

Focus on Biography

■ ABOVE LEVEL

Theodore Roosevelt: Friend of Nature

Summary *Theodore Roosevelt had a life-long interest in, and respect for, nature. After two terms as president, Roosevelt explored wilderness areas on other continents. He died in 1919.*

Vocabulary

Introduce the Key Vocabulary and ask children to complete the **BLM**.

specimens scientific objects, such as bones or rocks, that are studied or exhibited, *p. 5*

lumber wood that has been cut into boards for building supplies, *p. 6*

destruction the process of ruining or destroying something, *p. 7*

president the leader of a national government, *p. 7*

politician a person who runs for, or holds, an elected office, such as a mayor or president, *p. 8*

sanctuary a safe place, *p. 11*

Building Background and Vocabulary

Explain that this book is a biography about Theodore Roosevelt. Explain that Roosevelt was very active in preserving our wilderness areas. Use some of the language of the book and key vocabulary as you guide children through the text.

⟳ Writing Skill: Writing a Biography

Have children read the Strategy Focus on the book flap. Remind children to use the strategy and to think about the elements of a biography as they read the book. (See the Leveled Readers Teacher's Guide for **Vocabulary and Writing Practice Masters**.)

Responding

Have partners discuss how to answer the questions on the inside back cover.

Think About What You Have Read Sample answers:

1. Roosevelt watched, sketched, and collected things in nature.
2. He saw the damage people were doing to the natural areas.
3. Possible responses: He set up the Pelican Island Bird Reservation; he created the Grand Canyon National Monument.
4. Possible response: Our country's forests might not have been saved.

Making Connections Responses will vary.

⟳ Building Fluency

Model Read aloud pages 2–3. Draw attention to the use of President Roosevelt's first name, *Theodore*. Brainstorm consequences of the use of this rather than his full or last name.

Practice Ask small groups to find the places where Roosevelt is referred to by something other than *Theodore* (9, 13, 14, 15, 16). Have them read aloud those sentences.

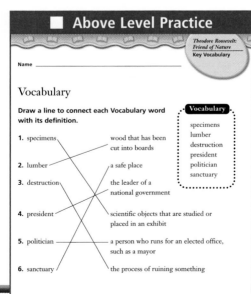

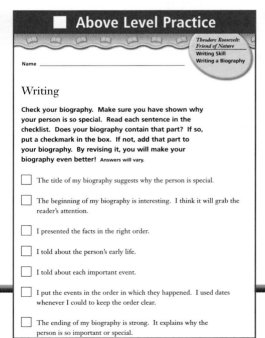

Leveled Readers

Florence Griffith Joyner Olympic Runner

Summary *Florence Griffith Joyner won her first race at the age of seven. She started training for the Olympics in college and won a silver medal in 1984. In 1988, she realized her dream when she took home three Olympic gold medals.*

Vocabulary

Introduce the Key Vocabulary and ask children to complete the BLM.

prizes something offered or won in competitions, games, or contests, *p. 6*

coach a person who trains athletes, *p. 7*

champion the winner of a game or contest, *p. 7*

Olympics an international athletic competition held every four years, *p. 8*

team a group of people who work or play together, *p. 8*

medal a small piece of metal with a design, awarded to honor a person, an action, or an accomplishment, *p. 10*

◆ LANGUAGE SUPPORT

Building Background and Vocabulary

Ask children to share what they know about the Olympics. Line up three volunteers and have them cross a "finish line" one at a time in slow motion. Then act out awarding the bronze, silver, and gold medals for the race. Distribute the **Build Background Practice Master** and have children complete it independently. (See the Leveled Readers Teacher's Guide for **Build Background** and **Vocabulary Masters**.)

Reading Strategy: Evaluate

Have students read the Strategy Focus on the book flap. Ask students to decide how well the author tells about Florence Griffith Joyner as they read.

Responding

Have partners discuss how to answer the questions on the inside back cover.

Think About What You Have Read Sample answers:

1. Florence liked short, fast races called sprints.
2. Answers will vary but should indicate that Florence had achieved her dream.
3. Answers will vary.

Making Connections Answers will vary.

Building Fluency

Model Read aloud page 12 as children follow along in their books. Remind them that an exclamation point at the end of a sentence means that the author is telling about something exciting, and that readers can show that excitement.

Practice Lead a choral reading of the same page. Have the class read the page together several times, using voices and volume to show excitement.

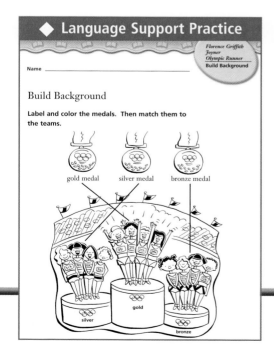

◆ **Language Support Practice**

Florence Griffith Joyner Olympic Runner **Build Background**

Name _____

Build Background

Label and color the medals. Then match them to the teams.

gold medal   silver medal   bronze medal

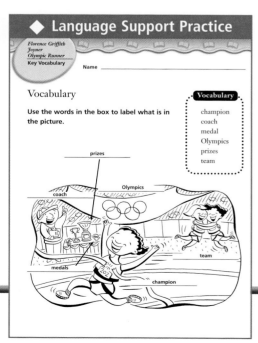

◆ **Language Support Practice**

Florence Griffith Joyner Olympic Runner **Key Vocabulary**

Name _____

Vocabulary

Use the words in the box to label what is in the picture.

Vocabulary
champion
coach
medal
Olympics
prizes
team

Resources for Theme 4

Contents

From Caterpillar to Butterfly

by Deborah Heiligman

Today a caterpillar came to school in a jar. It is eating green leaves. It is climbing and wiggling. This tiny caterpillar is going to change. It will change into a beautiful butterfly.

Caterpillars usually turn into butterflies out-doors. They live in gardens and meadows and yards. But we will watch our caterpillar change into a butterfly right here in our classroom. This change is called metamorphosis.

Our caterpillar started out as a tiny egg. The mother butterfly laid the egg on a leaf.

When the caterpillar hatched out of the egg, it was hungry. It ate its way out of its own eggshell! Then it started to eat green plants right away.

A caterpillar's job is to eat and eat and eat, so it will grow and grow and grow.

Each day when we come into school, we look at our caterpillar. Each day it is bigger.

Our skin grows with us. But a caterpillar's skin does not grow. When the caterpillar gets too big for its skin, the skin splits down the back. The caterpillar crawls right out of its own skin. It has new skin underneath. This is called molting. Our caterpillar will molt four or five times.

After many days our caterpillar is finished growing. It is much bigger than when it first

came to school. It is almost as big as my little finger now.

Our caterpillar is making a special house. First it makes a button of silk. It uses this but-ton to hang upside down from a twig. Then it molts for the last time. Instead of a new skin, this time there is a hard shell. This shell is called a chrysalis. Our caterpillar will stay inside the chrysalis for a long time.

Every day the chrysalis looks the same. We can't see anything happening. But inside the chrysalis our caterpillar is changing.

Will our caterpillar ever turn into a butter-fly? Will it ever come out of its chrysalis? We can hardly wait. But we do. We wait and wait and wait.

Then, one day, during snack time, somebody shouts, "Look!" And we all rush over to see.

The chrysalis is cracking.

We see a head, a body, and then . . . wings! It's a butterfly!

The tiny caterpillar who came to school in a jar turned into a Painted Lady butterfly! And we saw it happen.

Our butterfly is damp and crumpled. It hangs on to the chrysalis while its wings flap, flap, flap. Blood pumps into its wings. The wings straighten out and dry. Soon our butterfly will be ready to fly.

Our butterfly cannot stay in the jar. It needs to be outside with flowers and grass and trees and other butterflies.

It is a warm spring day. I put my finger into the jar. The butterfly sits on my finger. I pull it out and our butterfly goes free. We feel a little sad and a little happy.

We watch our butterfly land on a flower. It will sip the flower's nectar through a long, coiled tube called a proboscis. Maybe it is a female butterfly.

Maybe someday she will lay an egg on a leaf.

I know just what will happen then. That egg will hatch into a caterpillar. And that caterpillar will turn into a beautiful butterfly.

On My Way
Practice Readers

THEME PAPERBACKS

Sandy Goes to the Vet

by Becky Cheston
illustrated by Kathryn Mitter

Houghton Mifflin

Sandy Goes to the Vet

Summary *Ling thinks his dog, Sandy, is nothing special compared to the chameleons, kittens, parrots, and snakes he sees around him. However, when Sandy is injured and missing, Ling discovers just how special his dog really is.*

Vocabulary

tired p. 1: impatient or bored

zing p. 3: excitement or interest

loafing p. 5: spending time in a lazy way

romp p. 7: play; frolic

croaked p. 9: made a low, hoarse sound

boasting p. 10: describing with pride; bragging

unusual p. 22: not common or ordinary

● BELOW LEVEL

Preparing to Read

Building Background Briefly discuss what children know about dogs and their behavior. Have children relate any experiences they have had with dogs or with other pets. Encourage children to use the Monitor/Clarify strategy to check their understanding of the story.

Developing Key Vocabulary Preview with children the meanings of the Key Vocabulary words listed at the left for each section of the book. Encourage children to provide examples from their own lives that relate to each word.

Previewing the Text

Sandy Goes to the Vet may be read in its entirety or in two readings, pages 1–13 and pages 14–24. Before reading, discuss the title and cover illustration with children and talk about what they think the book will be about. Have them use the illustrations to make predictions about what will happen in the story.

Supporting the Reading

pages 1–13

- Why does the author write, "Sandy was nothing special"? (The author wants readers to understand that Ling thinks of Sandy as a regular, run-of-the-mill dog.)

- Why does Ling find Carlo's lizard interesting? (The lizard changes color to match its surroundings.)

- What animals does Ling see at the vet's office? Why does he find these animals interesting? (He sees a parrot, a golden retriever, and a snake. The parrot can talk, the retriever is a prizewinner, and the snake is unusual.)

- What words does the author use to describe Sandy? ("dull color somewhere between sand and toast," "bland as a bowl of oatmeal")

- What does Dr. Farmer do during Sandy's visit? (She checks his legs and listens to his heart. She gives him a cookie and says he's good and strong.)

R4   **THEME 4: Amazing Animals**

pages 14–24

- How does Ling realize that Sandy is missing? (It's dinnertime, and Sandy is nowhere to be found.)

- What has happened to Sandy? (He's been hit by a car. He's run away.)

- How do you know that Ling and his mother are worried about Sandy? (They call for Sandy, search the neighborhood, and ask people if they have seen him.)

- Point out the term *rolled into* on page 19, and explain that this term means that the car was moving slowly.

- What does Sandy do that proves he is a special dog? (Sandy seems to realize he needs the vet's help after he is injured.)

Responding

Ask children whether the predictions they made about the book were accurate. Discuss how they used Monitor/Clarify, one of the focus strategies for this theme. Then have them summarize the story, talking about what happens first, next, and last in the story. Have children draw a picture of an activity that would be fun to do with a dog. Tell them to include a caption with their drawings.

English Language Learners

Language Development

Be sure children understand the descriptive language and idiomatic expressions used in the story, including *big deal, kittens the color of coal, dart around, she crowed, gave him a wink,* and *back to the same old grind.*

Leveled Theme Paperbacks

Raptors!

Summary *This nonfiction book describes the appearance and habits of the raptor, a fearsome and cunning creature that was one of the last dinosaurs to become extinct.*

Vocabulary

pounced p. 5: jumped on suddenly

prey p. 5: a creature that is hunted

cunning p. 12: smart

predators p. 12: hunters

ferocious p. 16: dangerous, scary

extinct p. 26: no longer existing

▲ ON LEVEL

Preparing to Read

Building Background Briefly discuss what children know about dinosaurs. Have children name and describe any dinosaurs they know about. Tell them they will be reading about one type of dinosaur, the raptor. Encourage children to use the Monitor/Clarify strategy to check their understanding of the story.

Developing Key Vocabulary Preview with children the meanings of the Key Vocabulary words listed at the left for each section of the book. Point out and pronounce the dinosaur names *Tyrannosaurus* and *Protoceratops,* and the era name, *Cretaceous.*

Previewing the Text

Raptors! may be read in its entirety or in two readings, pages 1–15 and pages 16–30. Before reading, discuss the title and cover illustration with children and talk about what they think the book will be about. Have them use the illustrations to make predictions about what they will learn from the book.

Supporting the Reading

pages 1–15

- How did raptors kill their prey? (Raptors used their claws to slash at and kill their prey.)

- Why does the author compare the size of the raptors to that of the *Tyrannosaurus*? (The *Tyrannosaurus* is likely to be familiar to readers, so the author compares the raptor to something the reader may know.)

- Point out the term *packs* on page 12 and explain that it is used to describe a group of animals who live and hunt together.

- What made raptors such deadly hunters? (the placement of their eyes, their long fingers, their speed, and the fact that they hunted in packs)

- Why could raptors attack and kill animals that were much bigger? (Raptors attacked as a group, so the bigger animal had to fight off several of them at once.)

pages 16–30

- **What have scientists learned from the skeletons found in the Gobi Desert?** (Scientists believe that the *Protoceratops* could kill only one raptor when it was attacked by several raptors. The remaining raptors killed the Protoceratops.)

- **What was the importance of the dinosaur's skin color and patterns?** (Skin colors and patterns probably helped dinosaurs blend in with their surroundings so they could hide from enemies; they may also have helped the dinosaurs attract mates.)

- **Point out the word *period* on page 26, and explain that in this sentence the word is used to describe an amount of time or a series of years.**

- **Why does the author end the book by discussing why raptors may have become extinct?** (The author wants the reader to understand that scientists still have more to learn about dinosaurs.)

Responding

Ask students whether the predictions they made about the book were accurate. Discuss how they used Monitor/Clarify, one of the focus strategies for this theme. Then have students summarize what they learned about raptors from reading this book.

English Language Learners

Language Development

Be sure children understand the colloquial expressions that are used throughout the book. Examples include *spotted a victim, end up like this, went on their way,* and *left behind.*

THEME PAPERBACKS

Leveled Theme Paperbacks

A Toad for Tuesday

Summary This animal fantasy tells the story of Warton the Toad's efforts to bring a gift to his aunt by traveling through the woods on skis. His journey is interrupted twice: first, he is befriended by a mouse; later, an owl named George imprisons him. George plans to eat Warton in five days, as a birthday treat. In spite of their situation, the toad and the owl become friends. But Warton still doesn't want to be eaten, so aided by the mouse, he escapes. When George is attacked by a fox, both Warton and the mouse try to save his life. George shows his gratitude and friendship by flying Warton the rest of the way to his aunt's home.

Vocabulary

brittle p. 9: a sweet, hard candy

bid p. 19: told

peered p. 20: looked carefully

dreary p. 25: dull and dark

hobbled p. 33: walked with a limp

unraveling p. 37: taking apart

■ ABOVE LEVEL

Preparing to Read

Building Background Briefly discuss what children know about animal fantasy stories. Have children describe any fantasy stories they know about. Encourage them to use the Summarize strategy to check their understanding of the story.

Developing Key Vocabulary Preview with children the meanings of the Key Vocabulary words listed at the left for each section of the book. Have children relate as many words as possible to their own experiences.

Previewing the Text

A Toad for Tuesday may be read in its entirety or in three sections, pages 9–21, pages 22–46, and pages 47–64. Before reading, discuss the title and cover illustration with children and ask what they think the book will be about. Make sure children understand that the story is a fantasy. Have them use the illustrations to make predictions about the book.

Supporting the Reading

pages 9–21

- How does Warton decide to travel to Aunt Toolia's home? (He decides to ski.)

- Point out the word *skimming* on page 14 and explain that it is used to describe how Warton glides over the snow.

- Why does Warton decide to continue through the woods in spite of the mouse's warning? (Warton believes he can move fast enough on his skis to avoid the owl.)

pages 22–46

- Why does George stay up so late talking to Warton? (He enjoys talking about himself and his life. He's energized by Warton's interest in him.)

- Point out the word *talons* on page 43, and explain that it refers to the claws of a hunting bird.

- Why does the author have Warton stay in George's home for five days, instead of having George eat him right away? (The five days give George and Warton a chance to get to know one another and become friends.)

pages 47–64

- Why do you think the mouse works so hard to save Warton? (Warton saved the mouse when it was stuck upside down in the snow, and the two became friends during their lunch.)

- Point out the word *tattered* on page 59, and explain that the word describes wings that are torn and hanging from George's struggles with the fox.

- Why does the author end the book with George flying Warton to his aunt's home? (The author wants to show that the two have become friends.)

Responding

Ask children whether the predictions they made about the book were accurate. Discuss how they used the Summarize strategy, one of the focus strategies for this theme. Then have children tell the key events of the story.

Bonus Have students role-play a scene in which Warton brings his new friend George home to meet his brother, Morton.

English Language Learners

Language Development

Be sure children understand the descriptive language used in the story, including *dark mouse eyes filled with gratitude, like a tiny rocket, he swept along the valley, weaving a ribbon that wound swiftly though the trees, zipped along,* and *slimmest chance.*

RETEACHING

r-Controlled Vowel ar

Teach

Tell children to listen closely to these words: *arm, jar, scarf, target, carnival.* Ask what vowel sound these words have in common. /är/ Then say sets of words such as *am, aid, arm; hate, hand, harm; cave, carve, cove.* Have children raise their hands each time they hear a word with the /är/ vowel sound.

Display the **Sound/Spelling Card** *artist,* and remind children that the letter *a* followed by *r* makes the sound /är/ as in the word *artist.* Have children repeat the sound /är/ each time you point to the *ar* spelling. Write the word *card* on the board. Use **Blending Routine 2** to help children blend the word. For each sound, point to the letter(s), say the sound, and have children repeat it. Have children say the sound for *c,* /k/, then the sound for *ar,* /är/, then blend /kär/. Finally, have them say the sound for *d,* /d/, and blend /kärd/, *card.* Repeat the blending procedure with *hard* and *dark.*

Write *garden.* Help children divide the word into syllables between the *r* and *d* (VCCV pattern). Underline the *ar* and point out how the letters stay together in the same syllable; they will make the /är/ sound. Help children blend the sounds in each syllable and then blend the syllables to read the word. Repeat with *starting* and *target.*

Practice

Display the punchout letter cards *a* and *r.* Show children how to make words by putting other letter cards before and after the two cards that make the /är/ sound. Then have children use their punchout letters to make words such as *arm, art, tar, part, cart, yarn, harm, farm.* As children form the words, write them down, underline the *ar,* and have children repeat the word, listening for the /är/ sound.

Apply

Have children work in pairs as they read *A Park for Parkdale.* Ask them to make a list of words that they find in the story with *ar* in them. Have children write their lists for the class and compare them.

Monitoring Student Progress

If . . .	Then . . .
children need more practice with *r*-controlled vowels,	have them reread *A Park for Parkdale* from the Phonics Library and then read it again at home. As an alternative, assign **I Love Reading Book** 37.

CHALLENGE/EXTENSION:
r-Controlled Vowel *ar*

Silly Pictures

Have children brainstorm *ar* words. Then have them put *ar* words together in silly combinations. For example, they might pair *shark artist,* or *art farm.* Have children choose a favorite combination and illustrate it. Bind the illustrated pages into a book for the classroom library. Then challenge children to give the book a title using at least one *ar* word.

CHALLENGE

Rhyming *ar* Words

Have children brainstorm rhyming *ar* words. Then have them write rhyming riddles or couplets using those words. For example:

What's scarier than the dark?
A very hungry shark!

Ask children to write their couplets on the board and read them aloud to the class.

r-Controlled Vowels *or*, *ore*

OBJECTIVES

- Identify the letters *or* and *ore* as spelling the /ôr/ sound.
- Independently read and write words with *or* and *ore*.

Target Skill Trace

- *r*-Controlled Vowels *or, ore*, p. T35

Materials

- **Sound/Spelling Card** *orange;* **Blending Routines Card 2**

Teach

Tell children to listen to these words: *corn, torch, shore, order, morning.* Ask children what vowel sound these words have in common. /ôr/ Say these pairs of words, and ask children to identify the word with the /ôr/ sound: *cone, corn; torch, touch; pot, port.*

Display the **Sound/Spelling Card** *orange* and have children repeat the /ôr/ sound several times. Point out the *or* spelling of this sound on the card. Next, write the word *fork* on the board and use **Blending Routine 2** to help children blend the word. For each sound, point to the letter(s), say the sound, and have children repeat it. Have children say the sound for *f*, /f/, then the sound for *or*, /ôr/, and then blend /fôr/. Finally, have them say the sound for *k*, /k/, and blend /fôrk/, *fork.*

Write *more* and point out the *ore* spelling of the /ôr/ sound. Then follow the same blending procedure as above to blend the sounds in the word *more.*

Write *horse,* and say the word. Have children repeat it. Underline the *or* and *e;* circle the *s.* Then point out that sometimes a consonant comes between the *or* and the *e.* The letters *or* still make the /ôr/ sound, which is followed by the consonant sound.

Practice

Display these sentences:

> The waves hit the <u>shore</u> with <u>force</u>.
> We used a <u>torch</u> to see until <u>morning</u>.
> Linda was <u>born</u> <u>before</u> Josh.
> The <u>horse</u> had a <u>sore</u> leg.

For each underlined word, call children to circle the spelling of the /ôr/ sound and blend the word. After children have correctly sounded out the underlined words in each sentence, have them read the sentence in its entirety.

Then have children brainstorm a list of other *or* and *ore* words. Challenge them to include words with more than one syllable. Record the words for the class.

	One Syllable	Two or More Syllables
<u>or</u>	fort north	formula forklift
<u>ore</u>	sore score chore	before scoreboard shoreline

Apply

Have children work in pairs to write short stories using words from the list. Tell children to underline words that have the *or* spelling of the /ôr/ sound and to circle words that have the *ore* spelling of the /ôr/ sound. Invite children to read their stories to the class.

Monitoring Student Progress

If . . .	Then . . .
children need more practice with *r*-controlled vowels *or, ore,*	have them read *A Park for Parkdale* from the Phonics Library. As an alternative, assign **I Love Reading Books** 38–39.

CHALLENGE/EXTENSION:
r-Controlled Vowels *or, ore*

Illustrating Words

Have children brainstorm *or* and *ore* words. List the words as they are suggested. Then have children choose three words from the list. Children should write each word on a separate sheet of paper and then illustrate the word. Place all the sheets of paper in a stack, and have children randomly choose a page. The child must then write a sentence using the word that is written and illustrated on the page. Repeat until children have each written three sentences.

forest

CHALLENGE

Building Word Ladders

Have children build word ladders that begin with *or* or *ore*. Each word must use the same letters in the same order and be longer than the one before it.

For example:

or	ore
port	tore
important	store

Words with *nd, nt, mp, ng, nk*

OBJECTIVES

- Listen for final *nd, nt, mp, ng, nk.*
- Identify words with *nd, nt, mp, ng, nk.*
- Independently read and write words with *nd, nt, mp, ng, nk.*

Target Skill Trace

- Words with *nd, nt, mp, ng, nk,* p. T120

Materials

- punchout letter cards *a, b, c, d, e, g, i, k, l, m, n, o, p, r, s, t, u, w, y;* **Blending Routines Card 2**

Teach

Have children listen for and identify the final sound in words ending with a single consonant, such as *cap, light,* and *knob.* (/p/, /t/, /b/) Then have them listen for and repeat the final consonant sounds in each of these words: *sand, lamp, pant, went, hand, dump.* (/nd/, /mp/, /nt/, /nt/, /nd/, /mp/) Finally, challenge children to listen for and repeat the final consonant sounds in *think* and *song.* (/nk/, /ng/)

Remind children that *n* sometimes joins together with another consonant at the end of a word or syllable. Write *sand,* circle the *nd,* and say the word. Have children repeat it and then say the /nd/ sounds several times. Note how the two sounds blend together. Next, write the word *land* and use **Blending Routine 2** to help children blend the word. For each sound, point to the letter, say the sound, and have children repeat it. Have children say the sound for *l,* /l/, then the sound for short *a,* /ă/, and then blend the two sounds. Next, have them say the sound for *n,* /n/, and blend the three sounds, /lăn/. Finally, have them say the sound for *d,* /d/, and blend all the sounds to say *land.*

Follow the same procedure, using these words and consonants:

pant for the letters *nt*   *long* for the letters *ng*
lamp for the letters *mp*   *pink* for the letters *nk*

Practice

Have children place their punchout letter cards for *n* and *d* together on their desk. Then ask children to make words by adding other letters. Have volunteers tell the words they are making, and write the words for the class. Repeat with *nt, mp, ng,* and *nk.*

Apply

Have children work in pairs as they read *Hank's Pandas.* Have them find words with *nd, nt, mp, ng, nk.* Create a chart with each pair of letters as a column heading. Then ask children to take turns writing their words beneath the appropriate heading.

nd	nt	mp	ng	nk
sand	point	lump	sing	pinkest
bond	plant	lumpy	brings	oink
panda	paint	damp	stung	blank
pound	print	camper	string	drink

Monitoring Student Progress

If . . .	Then . . .
children need more practice with words having *nd, nt, mp, ng, nk,*	have them reread *Hank's Pandas* from the Phonics Library and then read it again at home. As an alternative, assign **I Love Reading Books** 40–44.

CHALLENGE/EXTENSION: Words with *nd, nt, mp, ng, nk*

Silly Consonants Book

Have children brainstorm words with the consonants *nd, nt, mp, ng,* and *nk*. Then have them copy these sentence frames on a sheet of paper.

The _____ to the _____.
The _____ on the _____.
The _____ about the _____.

Children should use words with the letters *nd, nt, mp, ng,* and *nk* to complete their sentences. Most of their sentences will be silly. Have the children choose their silliest sentence and illustrate it. Bind the pages together to make a Silly Consonants Book for the classroom library.

The <u>lamp</u> <u>sang</u> to the <u>sink</u> .

CHALLENGE

Building Words

Write the consonants *nd, nt, mp, ng,* and *nk*. Have children work in pairs to brainstorm words in which the consonants appear in the middle of the word. Have children read their words to the class and write them down. Some suggestions to help them get started might be *ending, mountain, hungry*.

Base Words and Endings in Nouns (-s, -es, -ies)

OBJECTIVES

- Listen to words to identify endings -s, -es, -ies (nouns).
- Independently read and write words with -s, -es, and -ies endings.

Target Skill Trace

- Base Words and Endings -s, -es, -ies (nouns), p. T121

Teach

Write the words *cat, watch, wife,* and *city*. Point out that each of these nouns names one thing. Explain that to name more than one thing of each noun, you must make the noun plural by adding -s, -es, or -ies.

Write *cats* beneath *cat*. Explain that people add -s to most nouns to make them plural.

Write *watches* beneath *watch*. Explain that when nouns end in *ch, s, x,* or *sh*, people add -es to make them plural.

Write *cities* beneath *city*. Explain that when nouns end in a consonant plus *y*, people change the *y* to *i* and add -es.

Practice

Recite the following phrases. Have children write the phrases down. You may need to recite each phrase several times. Then have volunteers write the phrases for the class. Review the spellings of the singular and the plural nouns with children.

One hand, two hands,
One kiss, two kisses,
One mix, two mixes,
One march, two marches,
One wish, two wishes,
One fly, two flies.

Apply

Have children write sentences for three pairs of nouns they have written, using the singular noun in the first sentence, and the plural noun in the second sentence. You may wish to have children write their sentences for the class.

Monitoring Student Progress

If . . .	Then . . .
children need more practice with base words and endings -s, -es, and -ies (nouns),	have them read *Hank's Pandas* from the Phonics Library.

CHALLENGE/EXTENSION: Base Words and Endings in Nouns (-*s*, -*es*, -*ies*)

Numbering Book with *ss, ch, sh, x,* and *y* words

List the following words: *dress, ax, box, stitch, arch, patch, peach, bush, brush, family, baby, fairy, city.* Have children make a number book for the numbers 1–10. Have them illustrate the number of items for each page, labeling the page with the number and the noun. For example, page one might show a picture of one dress, with the label *one dress;* page two might show a drawing of two boxes, with the label *two boxes,* etc. Allow children to pick from the words listed or think of their own words that end in the letters *s, x, ch, sh,* or *y.*

CHALLENGE

Building Words

Ask students to fold a plain sheet of paper into three columns and label the columns -*s,* -*es,* -*ies.* Have students choose a book or magazine, search for plural nouns, and write them under the appropriate headings.

Vowel Pairs *oa, ow*

OBJECTIVES

- Say the long *o* vowel sound when they see vowel pairs *oa, ow*.
- Independently read and write words with vowel pairs *oa, ow*.

Target Skill Trace

- Vowel Pairs *oa, ow*, pp. T190–T191

Materials

- **Sound/Spelling Card** *ocean*; **Blending Routines Card 2**; a large sheet

Clue	Word
You rest your head on it.	pillow
When something stays on top of the water	floats
Used to clean hands	soap
What the wind does	blows

Teach

Tell children to listen to and blend these sounds: /s/ /ō/ /p/. Have children repeat the sounds and say the word. (*soap*) Repeat with *glow*.

Display the large **Sound/Spelling Card** *ocean* and review the long *o* sound, /ō/, as heard in the word *ocean*. Have children repeat the long *o* sound back to you, /ō/ /ō/ /ō/. As you point to the various sound/spellings, remind children that you've already talked about the *o_e* spelling of the long *o* vowel sound. Tell children that the long *o* vowel sound can also be spelled with the letters *oa* or *ow*.

Write the word *boat*. Use **Blending Routine 2** to help children blend the word. For each sound, point to the letter(s), say the sound, and have children repeat it. Have children say the sound for *b*, /b/, then the sound for *oa*, /ō/, then blend /bōō/. Finally, have them say the sound for *t*, /t/, and blend /bōōt/, boat.

Write the word *row* and point out the *ow* spelling of the /ō/ sound. Follow the same blending procedure as above.

Provide clues about words spelled with *oa* and *ow* to help children generate a word list and record the words.

Practice

Have children choose one *oa* word from the list to write on a sheet of paper. Have them choose an *ow* word to write on the back of the paper. Next, lay a large sheet on the floor. Tell children it is a boat. Have children take turns holding up their *oa* words and reading them. After each word is read correctly, respond, *Come into the boat*. Tell children to bring their papers with them.

After all children are in the boat, they take turns reading their *ow* words. After each word is read correctly, respond, *Now row the boat*. Have children pantomime a rowing motion.

Apply

Have children work in pairs as they read *Crow's Plan*. Have them find words with vowel pairs *oa* and *ow*. Create a chart with each vowel pair as a column heading. Then ask children to take turns writing their words beneath the appropriate vowel pair.

Monitoring Student Progress

If . . .	Then . . .
children need additional practice with long vowel *o* spelled *oa* and *ow*,	have them reread *Crow's Plan* from the Phonics Library and then read it again at home. As an alternative, assign **I Love Reading Books** 45–46.

CHALLENGE/EXTENSION:
Vowel Pairs *oa, ow*

Silly Sentences

Have each child write one *oa* word and one *ow* word on paper. Then divide the class into groups of four. Have each group work together to write two silly sentences: one that incorporates all four of its *oa* words and one that uses all four *ow* words. Children may enjoy illustrating their sentences. Allow time for groups to share their work.

A toad took a loaf and a coat on the boat.

CHALLENGE

Crossword Puzzle Game

Have children work with partners, and give each pair a sheet of graph paper. Partners take turns writing words with long *o* vowel pairs *oa* and *ow* to form a crossword puzzle. Children can use a student dictionary for help with their definitions and word clues. Allow partners to have another sheet of graph paper if necessary to make a clean copy, which can be placed in a center with blank transparencies and waterproof markers. Children can solve the puzzles in their free time.

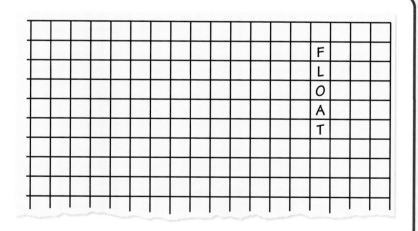

RETEACHING: High-Frequency Words

Words for Week 1

Teach

Write *board, listen,* and *told.* Ask *Where did I write these words?* (on the board) Ask *Which of these words is* board? Have children give other examples of what the word *board* can mean.

Ask *What do I need you to do when I am talking?* (listen)

Ask *Which of these words is* listen? Have children give examples of times when they listen.

Under the word *told,* write the words *cold* and *hold.* Have children read the two new words. Then point out that the word *told* ends the same way as *cold* and *hold.* Have the students read the word *told.* Then write the sentence *I told you a story yesterday.* Ask children how the sentence would change if *yesterday* became *now.* Encourage children to conclude that *told* is the past tense form of the verb *to tell.*

Practice

Write these sentence frames:

> Our teacher _____ us we should
>
> _____ when he talks.
>
> Then he wrote on the _____.

Have volunteers come up and complete the sentences using the High-Frequency Words.

Apply

Have children work in pairs to write a sentence for each High-Frequency Word. Then have the pairs trade sentences and read each other's work, circling the High-Frequency Words in the sentences. Have children read the sentences aloud to the class.

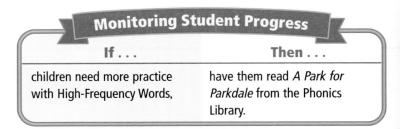

Monitoring Student Progress	
If . . .	**Then . . .**
children need more practice with High-Frequency Words,	have them read *A Park for Parkdale* from the Phonics Library.

CHALLENGE/EXTENSION:
High-Frequency Words

Complete the Sentences

Write these sentence starters:

> I listen to _____.
> My mother told me _____.
> I can use a board to _____.

Have children copy and complete the sentence starters. Then encourage children to write a second sentence to develop the idea of each sentence starter. Have children read their sentences aloud to the class.

CHALLENGE

A Day at School

Write the High-Frequency Words *board, listen,* and *told.* Have children write a diary entry that tells about their school day so far, using these words as many times as they wish. Children may want to share their diary entries with the class.

RETEACHING: High-Frequency Words

Words for Week 2

OBJECTIVE

- Read and write new High-Frequency Words *between, care, weigh.*

Target Skill Trace

- High-Frequency Words Lesson, p. T122

Teach

Write *between.* Then draw a vertical line between the *be* and the *tween.* Cover *tween* and ask children to read *be.* Then cover *be* and ask children to read *tween.* Remind them that a double *e* makes the sound /ē/. Then uncover the whole word and have children read it. Have children give examples of sentences with the word *between* in them.

Write the word *care,* read it, and have children repeat it. Ask volunteers for examples of sentences with the word *care.*

Write the word *weigh,* read it, and have children repeat it. Tell children that this word has an unusual spelling and have them spell it aloud with you. Ask volunteers for examples of sentences with the word *weigh.*

Practice

Write the following sentence frames:

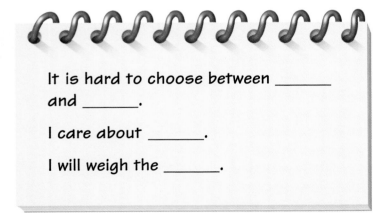

It is hard to choose between _____ and _____.

I care about _____.

I will weigh the _____.

Have children copy the sentence frames and complete them. Then have children read their answers aloud. You may wish to make lists of the different words and phrases used to complete each sentence.

Apply

Have children write one sentence for each word. Then have them exchange papers and take turns reading the sentences.

Monitoring Student Progress

If . . .	Then . . .
children need more practice with High-Frequency Words,	have them read *Hank's Pandas* from the Phonics Library.

CHALLENGE/EXTENSION:
High-Frequency Words

Independent Activities

Answering the Questions

Write the following questions, and have children copy each question onto a separate piece of paper. Then have them write a sentence to answer each question, and have them illustrate their answers.

What is between the tree and the house?

Who will care for the cat?

How much does an ant weigh?

CHALLENGE

Rhyming Words

Have students write the words *between, care,* and *weigh* at the top of a page. Then have them identify words that rhyme with each of these words. List the rhyming words for the class, then encourage children to notice different ways of spelling the sounds found in these words.

RETEACHING: High-Frequency Words

Words for Week 3

Teach

Hold up the word card *war* and read it aloud. Tell children that they are going to play tug-of-war. Next, hold up the *field* card. Read the word and tell children where they are going to play the game. Then, hold up the *half* card. Divide the children into equal teams. Point out that half the class is on each team. Finally, line up children. Hold up the *ago* card. Tell children that a short time *ago* you explained the details of the tug-of-war activity, and now it is time to play.

Take the children and the word cards outside or clear a space inside. Hold up each card and cue children to say the word at the appropriate time as children prepare to play the game. (We are going to play tug-of-. . . [war]. We are going to play on the . . . [field].)

Practice

Display the High-Frequency Word cards. Have children draw pictures of the class playing tug-of-war. Ask them to write descriptions underneath their drawings, using the High-Frequency Words.

Apply

Have children show their pictures to the class and read aloud their descriptions.

I played tug-of-war a short time ago. We went to a field. Half of the class was on the green team. The other half was on the red team. The red team won. I was on the red team.

Monitoring Student Progress

If . . .	Then . . .
children need more practice with High-Frequency Words,	have them read *Crow's Plan* from the Phonics Library.

CHALLENGE/EXTENSION:
High-Frequency Words

Tug-of-War

Take children outside to play tug-of-war. Afterward, tell children that a newspaper article answers five questions: Who, What, When, Where, How. Have children write newspaper stories about the class tug-of-war. Ask them to use the High-Frequency Words in their articles. Have children draw pictures to accompany their stories.

CHALLENGE

A Sports Broadcast

Divide the class into pairs. Have each pair write and perform a "live," play-by-play broadcast of a tug-of-war sports event. Remind children to use the High-Frequency Words in their scripts. Children may read their scripts for the class or record them on audiotape or videotape.

Drawing Conclusions

OBJECTIVES

- Draw conclusions about events in a story.
- Identify feelings based on actions in role plays.

Target Skill Trace

- Drawing Conclusions, pp. T70–T71

Teach

Show children pictures of people in various uniforms, such as a police officer, firefighter, nurse, soldier, or dentist. Or you might simply want to begin with a description of a person in an occupation: *She drives me and all of my schoolmates to school in the morning. She beeps the horn. She turns the wheel. Who is she?* Ask *What do you think this person's occupation is? What clues do you see (or hear) that help you reach this conclusion?*

Point out that children used the details in the pictures or sentences to *draw conclusions.* Tell them that they can use their skill in drawing conclusions to understand something that may not be stated directly in a story. Use the following Think Aloud:

Think Aloud *I am in line at the grocery store. The woman in front of me is buying hot dogs, buns, potato chips, sodas, charcoal, and lighter fluid. From the items that I see in her shopping cart, I draw a conclusion that she is going to have a cookout.*

Tell children that you are going to read a list of items. Ask them to draw a conclusion about what they can do with the items.

flour, sugar, eggs, frosting, candles (make a birthday cake)

mop, bucket, scrub brush, ammonia (mop the floor)

lettuce, tomatoes, carrots, cucumber, ranch dressing (make a salad)

Practice

Tell children that they are going to use clues from the text and illustrations in the story *Officer Buckle and Gloria* to figure out some things that happened that the author did not tell them directly.

Direct children to page 22 of the story. Read the text aloud. Ask *What do you see?* (children are sleeping, someone is throwing airplanes) Ask *Based on what the story says and what the picture shows, how do you think the students at Napville School were feeling?* (bored) Ask *Did the author SAY the students were bored?* (no) Explain that they used the story clues to figure out how the children were feeling.

Use other examples in the story, such as the following:

Page 35 *How does Officer Buckle feel about all the phone calls?* (he looks happy, or proud)

Pages 42–43 *How does Officer Buckle feel when he sees himself on the news?* (surprised) *How does Gloria feel?* (worried, nervous)

Conclude by saying *Being able to figure things out that are not stated in the story will help you to understand the meaning of the story. This will make you a better reader.*

Apply

Have children take turns acting out different feelings that characters in the story have. Ask the other children to guess the mood or emotion. Some examples of different moods include the following: *bored, happy, proud, friendly, loving, grumpy* or *unhappy.*

Monitoring Student Progress

If . . .	Then . . .
children need more practice with drawing conclusions,	suggest that they read the text and look at the pictures to figure out the meaning in other stories they read.

CHALLENGE/EXTENSION:
Drawing Conclusions

 ## Write Riddles About Community Workers

Discuss the important job that Officer Buckle does in his community. Have children work together in small groups and make up riddles about other kinds of community helpers, for example, firefighters, teachers, postal workers, sanitation workers, and so on. On one side of large index cards, have children write riddles that list contributions each helper makes to a community. Ask children to write the answer (the kind of worker) on the back. Then have them ask classmates to guess the answers to their riddles.

> I work at school.
> I make sure everyone is well.
> I take care of children if they do not feel well.
> Who am I?

> School Nurse

CHALLENGE

 ## Learn About Different Breeds of Dogs

Have several books on dogs and dog breeds available, or copy information on several breeds of dogs from the encyclopedia or the Internet. Ask students to use the text and illustrations from the story to make a list of details about the dog Gloria, such as her color and size, to see if they can determine the kind of dog Gloria is. Then have children write a description and draw pictures of other kinds of dogs. Based on their pictures and what they have written, have classmates try to guess the breed of the dog.

 ## Make and Model Safety Rules

Have each pair of children generate a list of safety rules for the home. Tips might include the following:

- Never put anything into an electrical outlet.
- Clean up spills so no one slips.
- Have a smoke alarm in every bedroom.

Have each child select one rule and think about what kind of trick Gloria might do to represent that safety tip. Have children take turns acting out the tips for their partners, and have the partners guess the tip.

RETEACHING: Comprehension Skills

Text Organization

OBJECTIVES

- Identify main ideas in text organization.
- Locate pages in the story with main ideas.

Target Skill Trace

- Text Organization, pp. T152–T153

Teach

Write the following story on six sentence strips:

> I woke up when my alarm went off.
> Next, I put on my red shirt.
> I got to school on time.
> I ate a banana and cereal.
> First, I took a shower.
> Then I got on the school bus.

Read the story to children. Ask *Does my story make sense?* (no) Have children help you organize the story in a way that makes sense by rearranging the sentence strips.

Tell children that when we tell a story, we have to organize it in a way that makes sense. We might organize it by which things happened first, as the story organization above.

Tell children that authors also have to organize their information in a way that makes sense. Explain that, as readers, we use the author's organization to decide which ideas are the most important and how ideas relate to each other.

Practice

Tell children that they are going to find out how the author organized the story *Ant*. Begin on page 63. Together, read the text aloud. Ask *What is the main idea?* (You hardly ever see just one ant.)

Direct children to pages 64–65 of the story. Read the text aloud. Ask *What is the main idea of these pages?* (ants live in colonies) Say *So far, we have seen that the author has a main idea for each set of pages. Did she tell us there would be a main idea?* (no) Ask *How did we find out what the main idea was?* (read the words, looked at the pictures, listened for repeated words) Explain that they used clues in the text to figure out how the author organized the text.

Using the same procedure, have children identify how the text is organized on these pages:

Pages 66–67 (ant antennae)

Pages 68–69 (ants help each other)

Repeat that children used the information given on each set of pages to help them figure out how the story is organized—by main ideas.

Apply

Write the following words: *leafcutter ants, army ants, farmer ants, carpenter ants, weaver ants.* Have children copy the words, and tell them that each one is a main idea. Ask them to find the pages on which each main idea is described, and write the page numbers next to it.

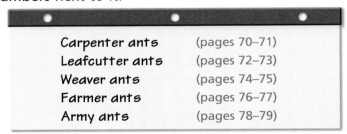

Carpenter ants	(pages 70–71)
Leafcutter ants	(pages 72–73)
Weaver ants	(pages 74–75)
Farmer ants	(pages 76–77)
Army ants	(pages 78–79)

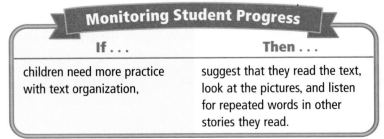

Monitoring Student Progress

If . . .	Then . . .
children need more practice with text organization,	suggest that they read the text, look at the pictures, and listen for repeated words in other stories they read.

CHALLENGE/EXTENSION: Text Organization

Independent Activities

CHALLENGE

Organize Information for a Report

Have children cut out a picture of an animal they like from a magazine or newspaper. Ask them to think about writing a report about the animal. Ask *What information would you include? How would you organize it?*

Have children glue their animal picture on a piece of paper. Next, have them write a list of headings for topics they might include in their report on the animal. You might want to show children a sample list such as:

> What it is
>
> Where it lives
>
> What kind of group it lives in
>
> What it eats
>
> How long it lives
>
> Interesting facts about the animal

Have children research the animal chosen and write the answers to the topics they chose.

Determine Main Idea of a Picture Book

Display several picture books. Show one book to the group and point out how the pages are organized so they tell a story even though the story doesn't have words. Have children suggest a main idea for each page.

Have children choose partners. Give each pair a picture book. Have them write the page number and a main idea for each page on a sheet of lined paper.

Locate Regions on a World Map

On chart paper, list the four areas of the world listed here. Have maps or atlases available for children. Ask them to find a picture or kind of ant from the story that belongs in each geographical area. Have groups see if they can locate other places mentioned in *Ants*.

> Africa
>
> South America
>
> Asia
>
> North America

Cause and Effect

OBJECTIVES

- Identify cause-and-effect key words *because, so, since,* and *as a result.*
- Make a cause-and-effect chart about the story.

Target Skill Trace

- Cause and Effect, pp. T220–T221

Teach

Write the following sentences:

> The flowers grew because we had a lot of rain.
>
> We had a lot of rain, so the flowers grew.
>
> Since we had a lot of rain, the flowers grew.
>
> As a result of the rain, the flowers grew.

Explain that in each of these sentences one event makes another event happen. Tell them when one event causes another event it is called a *cause and effect.*

Ask *What happened in each of those sentences?* (the flowers grew) Explain that the part of the sentence that tells what happened is the effect. Ask *Why did the flowers grow?* (because of the rain) Explain that the part of the sentence that tells why something happened is the cause.

Read the sentences aloud again. Point out *so, since, because,* and *as a result.* Tell children that these words signal a cause-and-effect relationship.

Practice

Remind children that there are many events in the story *The Great Ball Game.* Identify each of the following events as the cause, and let the children tell the effect:

- The Birds and Animals have an argument, so _____.
  (they decide to have a ball game to settle it)

- The Birds are on one team because _____. (they all have wings; they can fly)
- The Animals are on the other team since _____. (they all have teeth)
- Bat doesn't know where to go because _____. (he has teeth and wings)
- As a result of Bat's playing, _____. (the Animals win)

Tell the children that when they read they can look for the words *so, because, since,* and *as a result* to help them see how the events flow in a story.

Apply

Copy the cause-and-effect chart below. You may want to add sentences from other story details. Have children complete the chart with partners or as a class. Remind them that a cause tells why something happened and an effect tells what happened.

Cause	Effect
The Birds are swifter, so	(they keep stealing the ball.)
(The Birds don't want him, so)	Bat joins the Animal team.
(Because he could see better,)	Bat flies when it gets dark.
(Because the Birds lose the game,)	they have to leave for half of every year.

Monitoring Student Progress

If . . .	Then . . .
children need more practice with cause and effect,	suggest that they look for the words *so, because, since,* and *as a result* in other stories they read.

CHALLENGE/EXTENSION: Cause and Effect

 ## Explain Animal Traits or Behaviors

Have children use the birds and animals from the story *The Great Ball Game* (crane, bear, bat, fox, deer, hawk, squirrel, rabbit, sparrow or other small bird) to write a list of cause-and-effect animal behaviors. Have children list one trait or behavior of each animal, and then write a sentence telling why the animal needs that particular characteristic. For example, *Crane has long legs because . . . he needs to wade in the water.*

CHALLENGE

 ## Make Story Problems

Have children work in pairs to make story problems involving doubling. Use animals from the story for the problems. Here are two examples:

If 1 crane has 2 legs, then 2 cranes have _____ legs.

If 2 foxes have 2 tails, then 4 foxes have _____ tails.

Encourage children to draw simple illustrations for their story problems. Allow children to exchange papers and solve other story problems.

Have children make story problems that involve multiplying by 3s, 4s, or 5s. For example: *If 2 bears have 4 legs, then 5 bears have _____ legs.*

Choose a Favorite Animal

Have each child select a favorite animal from the story *The Great Ball Game.* Instruct children to think of a cause-and-effect statement explaining why that animal is their favorite. Allow each child to tell their statement to the group. You may want to model some sample statements, such as:

*The bear is my favorite because he plays hard.
Since the bat wins the game, he is my favorite animal.*

RETEACHING: Grammar Skills

Words for Nouns

OBJECTIVES

- Replace naming words with pronouns in the story.
- Write sentences with pronouns.

Target Skill Trace

- Words for Nouns (Pronouns), p. T41

Materials

- index cards with *He, She, They, I, We,* and *Them;* tape

Teach

Ask children what they did after school yesterday. Using their names, write sentences similar to these:

> Jorge played baseball.
>
> Ashley watched television.
>
> Jason and Michelle rode bikes.
>
> Natalie rode bikes with Jason and Michelle.

Prepare some index cards with these pronouns written on them: *He, She, They, I, We,* and *Them.* Tell children that sometimes we use other words in place of naming words. Show the index cards, and have the children read the pronouns aloud. Tell children that the names of the people in the sentences can be replaced with these words. Hold up pronoun cards for each name or pair of names, and read the sentence with the substituted pronouns. Ask *Which word makes more sense in this sentence? Does the word* He *replace* Jorge? Tape the pronoun over the name or names in the sentence. Continue until you have placed a pronoun over each name or pair of names.

Practice

Direct children to *Officer Buckle and Gloria.* Choose sentences from the story, and have the children replace nouns with pronouns. Read each sentence aloud, and then have the children say the pronoun that they think belongs in that sentence. Some of the following examples could be used:

"Officer Buckle shared his safety tips with the students at Napville School." (He)

"Gloria obeys my commands." (She)

"The children sat up and stared." (They)

"Officer Buckle loved having a buddy." (He)

Apply

Have children find sentences in the story that already contain pronouns. Instruct them to write the sentences and circle the pronoun. Then have children work with a partner to identify the story character that the pronoun refers to in the story.

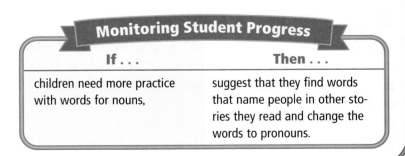

Monitoring Student Progress	
If . . .	Then . . .
children need more practice with words for nouns,	suggest that they find words that name people in other stories they read and change the words to pronouns.

Singular Possessive Nouns

OBJECTIVES

- Write names as singular possessive nouns.
- Identify singular possessive nouns in the story.
- Form singular possessive nouns in their writing.

Target Skill Trace

- Singular Possessive Nouns, p. T127

Teach

Display a list of your students' names. Ask each child to name his or her favorite toy. Write the name of the toy next to the child's name, leaving space to add *'s*. Tell children *When I want to show that an object belongs to someone, I add an apostrophe and an -s to the name.* Go down the list and add *'s* to each child's name.

Have each child write his or her name on an index card and add an apostrophe and -*s*. Assemble a small pile of objects such as crayons, pencils, and books. Hand an object to a child and ask *Whose crayon is this? It is Bob's crayon.* Have the child hold up his or her name card. Continue with this process until each child's name has been used as a possessive noun.

Practice

Direct children to page 67 in *Ant*. Read aloud the last sentence. Ask *Where do you see an apostrophe and -s in this sentence?* (queen's eggs) *Who do the eggs belong to?* (the queen)

Write the following sentences:

> The ant tunnels filled the colony.
> (ant's tunnels)
>
> The ant antennae are like a nose and fingers. (ant's antennae)
>
> A worker job is to find food. (worker's job)

Apply

Have children write and complete the following sentences about ants:

> An _____ home is called an anthill. (ant's)
>
> The _____ job is to lay eggs. (queen's)
>
> An _____ colony is a lot like a city. (ant's)

Have children share their completed sentences as you write them down. You might want to have children write other sentences related to what they have read about ants and have them draw pictures to illustrate the concepts.

Monitoring Student Progress

If . . .	Then . . .
children need more practice with singular possessive nouns,	suggest that they make lists of things they and other people own, adding *'s* to names to show ownership.

Plural Possessive Nouns

> **OBJECTIVES**
> - Identify plural possessive nouns.
> - Punctuate plural possessive nouns in sentences.
>
> **Target Skill Trace**
> - Plural Possessive Nouns, p. T197

Teach

Write the following sentences with plural nouns:

> The boys will bring the hockey sticks.
> The boys' hockey sticks are in the gym.

Read the sentences with children. Explain that in the first sentence, the word *boys* is a plural noun; it ends in *-s*, and it tells us that there is more than one boy. Then explain that in the second sentence, the word *boys'* is a plural possessive noun. It has an apostrophe to show that the hockey sticks belong to all the boys. You might want to review singular possessive nouns by adding the sentence *John's hockey stick is broken*.

Practice

Direct children to page 100 in the story *The Great Ball Game*. Read aloud this sentence: *On the Animals' side Fox and Deer were swift runners, and Bear cleared the way for them as they played.* Ask *Where do you see an apostrophe in this sentence?* (Animals' side) *Where is the apostrophe in the word Animals'?* (after the *s*)

Write the following sentences for the class:

> The Birds wings made them better than the Animals.
>
> The Animals teeth made them better than the Birds.
>
> The Birds penalty was to leave the land for a half of each year.

Read the sentences aloud. Tell children that each possessive noun is missing an apostrophe. Ask them to tell you where they think the apostrophe should go in each sentence, and add the apostrophe. (Birds' wings, Animals' teeth, Birds' penalty)

Apply

Have children punctuate the possessive nouns in the following sentences about the animals in the story.

> Birds wings help them to fly. (Birds')
> Animals teeth help them to eat and catch prey. (Animals')
> The Birds penalty was given because they lost the game. (Birds')

Have children copy the sentences and draw pictures to illustrate the concepts. Then have them share what they have drawn and written. Ask children how the meaning of the sentences would change if they were written, *The Bird's wings, An Animal's teeth,* or *The Bird's penalty.* Help children to see that when written this way, the *'s* means just one bird or animal.

Monitoring Student Progress	
If . . .	**Then . . .**
children need more practice with plural possessive nouns,	suggest that they identify both singular and plural possessive nouns in other stories they read.

board

listen

told

story

bought

hear

never

stand

Use for Theme 4, Week 1.

carry

together

climb

between

important

letter

word

piece

Use for Theme 4, Weeks 1 and 2.

busy

head

across

great

care

weigh

world

pull

Use for Theme 4, Weeks 2 and 3.

field

half

war

during

soon

ago

Use for Theme 4, Week 3.

most

behind

once

more

Use for Theme 4, Week 3.

Name _____

Word Search

Find and circle each word from the box.

Word Box			
put	three	sure	shoes
four	listen	about	letter
bought	move	watch	school
girl	live	touch	never

Theme 4: **Amazing Animals**

Directions:
Have children look across and down to find and circle the words.

Name _____

Using a Dictionary

Look at the dictionary guide words on the book pages below. Write each word from the box on the dictionary page where it can be found.

Word Box		
city	carpenter	chew
big	branch	anthill
antennae	bunch	colony

amaze • bridge

_____

_____

_____

_____

_____

_____

bug • corner

_____

_____

_____

_____

_____

_____

Theme 4: **Amazing Animals**

words. Then ask them to write the entry words on the pages with the appropriate guide words.

anthill, big, branch; **bug/corner:** bunch, carpenter, chew, city, colony

Find the Exact Word

**Choose a word from the box that describes
the animal sound. Then complete the sentence
to tell what happens next.**

Word Box
bellowed   howled   roared   hooted   squeaked

Example: The moose <u>bellowed</u>, and <u>the birds flew before him</u>

<u>in a panic</u>.

1. The lion _____, and _____

    _____ .

2. The mouse _____, and _____

    _____ .

3. The owl _____, and _____

    _____ .

4. The dog _____, and _____

    _____ .

Now draw a picture to go with one sentence.

Theme 4: **Amazing Animals**

Exact Words: 1. roared; 2. squeaked; 3. hooted; 4. howled Sentence length will vary.

Directions: Have children choose a word from the box that describes the sound an animal makes. Ask them to write the word and complete the sentence to tell

Name _____

S is for Space

Read each sentence. Look for a *different* definition of the underlined word in a dictionary. Then write the new definition on the lines.

Materials

dictionary

1. Ellen Ochoa was an astronaut on the space <u>shuttle</u> *Discovery.*

   _____

   _____

2. Dr. Ochoa was one of five astronauts on <u>board</u> *Discovery.*

   _____

   _____

3. The astronauts used to <u>store</u> their equipment on the shuttle in a cargo bay.

   _____

   _____

4. *Discovery* spent nine days in <u>space</u> before coming back to Earth.

   _____

   _____

Theme 4: **Focus on Biography**

Daily Routines Activity Masters **R43**

[sidebar, rotated] sentence. Then ask them to use a dictionary to find and write alternative meanings to the underlined words.

that moves people back and forth quickly;
2. **board:** a long, flat piece of wood;
3. **store:** a place where things are sold;
4. **space:** empty places

Reading-Writing
Workshop

Research Report
Conference Master

Writing Conference

What Should I Say?

In a writing conference, a writer reads a draft to a
partner or a small group. A listener can help the writer
by asking questions.

If you're thinking . . .   *You could say . . .*

- How does the writer know that?
- This part is hard to understand.

- Where did you find this information?
- Can you give more facts to make this part clearer?

More Questions a Listener Might Ask

Read these questions before you listen. Then discuss
your thoughts with the writer.

1. What do you like about the writer's research report?

2. What topic is the writer telling about? Retell what
   you heard.

3. What facts did you find most interesting?

4. Where does the writer need to add more facts?

Theme 4: **Amazing Animals**

WORD LIST

THEME 4, WEEK 1

Phonics Skills:
r-Controlled Vowel *ar*; r-Controlled Vowels *or, ore*

Phonics Review Skill:
Common Syllables *-tion, -ture*

High-Frequency Words:
board, listened, told

Day 1

Phonics Library: *A Park for Parkdale*

Phonics Practice Words: Barkway, Bart, farms, garden, March, market, Martin, pardon, park, Parkdale, smart, start; Cora, Doctor, for, Horn, important, mayor, more, morning, Short, stores, an, and, at, ate, but, came, can, cleaned, did, everyone, everything, except, feel, fine, first, fun, good, had, happen, has, he, help, helps, houses, how, is, it, know, land, led, let's, liked, lot, made, make, me, meeting, Miss, named, need, needs, nice, no, nodded, now, on, opened, out, pay, plan, planted, played, proud, right, say, see, sells, shouted, so, speech, spot, stood, tend, that, then, thing, think, this, town, trash, up, very, we, weedy, we'll, when, will

High-Frequency Words: board, listen, told, a, are, began, everyone, have, I, idea, nearly, old, one, opened, others, our, people, said, someone, something, the, to, together, what, work

Day 2

Anthology: *Officer Buckle and Gloria*

Phonics Practice Words: auditorium, before, department, enormous, favorite, for, Gloria, more, morning, snoring, star, star-shaped, started, storms; *attention, imagination, station*

High-Frequency Words: board, listened, told, *bought, hear, never*

Key Vocabulary: accident, attention, audience, commands, officer, safety

Day 4

Phonics Library: *Arthur's Book*

Phonics Practice Words: attention, fiction, section, creature, creatures, mixture, *about, act, an, and, Arthur, asked, at, back, be, book, books, brain, by, can, cat, chases, chasing, desk, did, dog, drop, fact, felt, for, frightful, from, funny, get, got, had, hard, he, helpful, him, himself, his, how, hurt, in, is, it, jumped, just, kept, know, look, looked, lots, made, might, missing, my, need, needed, new, out, outside, own, not, pens, picked, question, raced, run, saw, sea, see, shelf, stacks, started, starting, story, tale, tell, that, that's, then, thing, things, thinking, this, three, time, tree, up, very, went, white, will, window, write, writing, yelled*

High-Frequency Words: *a, could, do, I, I'll, idea, of, one, paper, said, the, they, to, told, wanted, was*

This list includes all words in Phonics Library and words from the Anthology selections that apply skills taught and reviewed. Words in roman apply skills for the week; words in italics apply previously taught skills. High-Frequency Words are practiced in Phonics Library and Anthology selections and in Practice Book and Word Wall activities. Reading Strategy notes provide practice in using the Phonics/Decoding Strategy with familiar phonics elements.

WORD LIST

THEME 4, WEEK 2

Phonics Skills:
Words with *nd, nt, mp, ng, nk*;
Base Words and Endings in Nouns
(*-s, -es, -ies*)

Phonics Review Skill:
r-Controlled Vowels *ar, or, ore*; Base Words and
Endings in Nouns (*-s, -es, -ies*)

High-Frequency Words:
between, care, weigh

Day 1

Phonics Library: *Hank's Pandas*

Phonics Practice Words: hand, lends, panda,
pandas, pond, plants, chomp, kingdom, drink,
Hank, Hank's; chores, foods, parts, tells, sees,
takes, stories, *and, animal, arms, as, at, away,
baby, back, be, big, by, can, clean, cleans, close,
dad, day, eat, feeding, for, fur, go, groom, he, her,
his, if, in, is, it, just, learn, light, likes, look, me,
might, mom, my, named, new, nice, on, park, see,
sits, sleep, snow, so, soon, that, then, we, wild,
will, with, work, zoo*

High-Frequency Words: between, care, weigh,
*a, about, begins, brother, every, have, hold, I,
quietly, small, the, their, they, think, to, want,
watches, water, what*

Day 2

Anthology: *Ant*

Phonics Practice Words: and, ant, anthills,
around, bend, bring, fingers, fungus, going,
ground, long, munching, plant, rubbing, strong,
tending, things, think, turning, waving; ants,
branches, bugs, chains, cities, cows, eggs, experts,
fingers, groups, houses, insects, jobs, leaves, legs,
logs, lots, nests, piles, plants, rocks, sunshades,
teams, things, trees, tunnels; *army, carpenter,
carpet, farmer, for, hardly, larva, march, more, or,
part, shortcut, York; anthills, ants, branches, bugs,
chains, cities, cocoons, colonies, cows, eaters,
eggs, experts, fingers, groups, houses, insects,
jobs, leaves, legs, logs, lots, nests, piles, plants,
sunshades, teams, things, trees, tunnels*

High-Frequency Words: between, care, weigh,
*across, busy, carry, climb, even, head, piece, pull,
together, world, year, young*

Key Vocabulary: antennae, cocoons, colonies,
fungus, larvae, tunnels

Day 4

Phonics Library: *Marta's Larks*

Phonics Practice Words: arms, bark, dart,
farm, garden, hard, hardly, harm, large, larks,
larks', March, Marta, Marta's, part, smart, start,
yard, yarn, born, torn, chore, chores, *and, at, ate,
back, best, big, birds, bits, blades, bug, bugs, by,
carry, close, day, each, eat, every, exclaims, fat,
feeding, feel, felt, find, finding, food, for, from,
get, glad, grass, hands, her, in, is, leaf, likes, looks,
lot, lots, making, nests, on, perch, picks, place,
safe, seeds, sees, she, sing, sky, swoop, take,
teamwork, that, them, then, these, things, thinks,
those, trees, try, turn, up, when, will, wow*

High-Frequency Words: *a, any, are, away,
even, friends, has, have, hear, I, into, little, never,
of, others, pull, the, they, to, under, was, watching,
what, work, works, working, would*

WORD LIST

THEME 4, WEEK 3

Phonics Skills:
Vowel Pairs *oa, ow*

Phonics Review Skill:
Words with *nd, nt, mp, ng, nk*

High-Frequency Words:
ago, field, half, war

Day 1

Phonics Library: *Crow's Plan*

Phonics Practice Words: croak, croaked, Crow, floats, goal, moan, Oak, oath, rowboat, toad, below, bellowed, fellow, flow, flowed, follow, hollow, now, show, throw, *about, and, animals, around, at, ate, be, before, big, back, beak, came, can, cans, care, clean, dad, don't, dove, dropped, everyone, family, finished, flash, flew, for, good, got, had, he, help, his, hit, how, if, in, is, it, keep, make, let's, little, looks, mad, make, me, met, more, must, my, now, on, other, picked, picnic, problem, out, raccoon, rest, see, side, so, someone, something, soon, speak, spoke, take, tale, that, this, then, think, tossed, trash, tree, up, wait, way, we, went, when, why, will, with, won't, yelled, yes, you*

High-Frequency Words: ago, field, half, war, *a, about, again, have, hear, I, long, of, once, one, or, our, said, the, their, they, to*

Day 2

Anthology: *The Great Ball Game*

Phonics Practice Words: goal, goalposts, *and, argument, end, flying, land, long, sank, want, went, wings*

High-Frequency Words: ago, field, half, war, *across, between, even, great*

Key Vocabulary: accept, advantage, argument, guarded, penalty, quarrel

Day 4

Phonics Library: *Brent Skunk Sings*

Phonics Practice Words: and, behind, found, Granddad, hand, land, Brent, Brent's count, counted, dentist, plant, went, lamp, slumped, stumped, bring, sang, sing, string, blinking, Frank, Skunk, think, stunt, stunts, yanked, *about, asked, be, best, bird, bit, but, came, can, can't, chance, check, checked, clean, cleaned, closed, did, down, fine, for, get, go, got, had, has, he, him, his, How, hurt, is, it, I've, just, kept, let, like, make, me, mouth, much, my, need, new, nice, not, on, opened, opens, out, over, pass, please, quite, room, sat, set, so, see, still, take, teeth, that, them, then, this, those, three, tight, time, toy, trip, try, up, visit, waiting, we, we'll, when, wide, with, will, won't, you, you'll, yo-yo*

High-Frequency Words: *a, afraid, are, behind, do, first, in, laugh, long, open, said, the, there, through, to, was, what, your*

FOCUS ON BIOGRAPHY

Phonics Review Skills:
r-Controlled Vowels
Final Syllables and Endings

High-Frequency Words:
General Review

Day 1

Phonics Library: *Where Do I Start?*

Phonics Practice Words: *closer, creatures, dark, horses, large, loudly, Mr. Parks, nature, pictures, questions, sandbar, sharks, start*

High-Frequency Words: *floor, kitchen, special, story (stories)*

Day 2

Anthology: *Focus on Biography*

Phonics Practice Words: *after, arm, before, birthday, born, cargo, carved, church, Conservation, determined, discovery, doctors, ever, every, everyone, exercises, exercising, fastest, favorite, first, for, forests, forty-two, Foundation, girl, hard, her, history, important, interested, limitations, makers, member, meter, more, morning, national, nature, nearly, never, North, November, occur, orchestra, other, parks, part, permission, return, runner, several, sports, stars, started, starts, stronger, teacher, Theodore, third, whatever, wore, work, York, youngest*

High-Frequency Words: *beautiful, believed, board, important, later, moved, surprised, story, year, years*

Key Vocabulary: astronaut, biography, champion, event, fact, president

HIGH-FREQUENCY WORDS

Word	Taught as High-Frequency Word THEME/WEEK	Decodable THEME/WEEK	Word	Taught as High-Frequency Word THEME/WEEK	Decodable THEME/WEEK
across	2/3	2/2	kitchen	1/1	3/1
ago	4/3	n/a	lady	3/4	2/3
air	5/4	n/a	later	2/2	5/1
alphabet	6/2	n/a	letter	1/3	5/1
aunt	5/3	n/a	lion	3/1	n/a
beautiful	2/1	n/a	listen	4/1	n/a
behind	3/3	n/a	middle	5/1	5/2
believe	3/4	n/a	million	5/3	n/a
below	6/3	4/3	mind	6/2	n/a
between	4/2	n/a	move	1/3	n/a
board	4/1	n/a	neighbor	6/3	n/a
bought	1/1	n/a	order	3/2	4/1
brother	2/3	n/a	pair	5/3	n/a
brought	1/2	n/a	poor	1/3	n/a
busy	2/2	n/a	quiet	2/1	n/a
care	4/2	n/a	reason	1/2	3/4
child	5/4	n/a	roll	1/1	n/a
clothes	3/2	n/a	should	6/3	n/a
different	1/3	2/3	soldier	3/3	n/a
during	3/1	n/a	special	1/2	n/a
early	5/2	n/a	stand	2/3	2/3
even	2/1	2/3	story	3/3	4/1
fair	6/1	n/a	straight	2/1	5/4
field	4/3	n/a	surprise	1/2	1/3
floor	1/3	n/a	told	4/1	n/a
front	1/1	n/a	touch	2/2	n/a
gold	6/1	n/a	trouble	5/1	n/a
great	2/3	n/a	uncle	5/1	5/2
guess	3/2	n/a	until	1/1	1/2
hair	5/2	n/a	war	4/3	n/a
half	4/3	n/a	weigh	4/2	n/a
heard	3/1	n/a	whole	3/4	n/a
heart	6/2	n/a	winter	3/1	5/1
heavy	5/4	n/a	woman	6/1	n/a
hour	5/4	n/a	word	1/3	n/a
important	2/2	4/1	year	2/1	3/4
instead	5/2	n/a	young	2/2	n/a

These words or forms of these words appear on the 800 Base Words of Highest Frequency of Occurrence in the American Heritage Computerized Study of the Vocabulary of Published Materials Used in Public Schools or on the Dolch list.

TECHNOLOGY RESOURCES

American Melody
P.O. Box 270
Guilford, CT 06437
800-220-5557
www.americanmelody.com

Audio Bookshelf
174 Prescott Hill Road
Northport, ME 04849
800-234-1713
www.audiobookshelf.com

Baker & Taylor
100 Business Center Drive
Pittsburgh, PA 15205
800-775-2600
www.btal.com

BDD Audio/Random House
400 Hohn Road
Westminster, MD 21157
800-733-3000

Big Kids Productions
1606 Dywer Ave.
Austin, TX 78704
800-477-7811
www.bigkidsvideo.com

Books on Tape
P.O. Box 25122
Santa Ana, CA 92799
800-541-5525
www.booksontape.com

Broderbund Company
1 Martha's Way
Hiawatha, IA 52233
www.broderbund.com

Filmic Archives
The Cinema Center
Botsford, CT 06404
800-366-1920
www.filmicarchives.com

Great White Dog Picture Company
10 Toon Lane
Lee, NH 03824
800-397-7641
www.greatwhitedog.com

HarperAudio
10 E. 53rd St.
New York, NY 10022
800-242-7737
www.harperaudio.com

Houghton Mifflin Company
222 Berkeley St.
Boston, MA 02116
800-225-3362

Informed Democracy
P.O. Box 67
Santa Cruz, CA 95063
800-827-0949

JEF Films
143 Hickory Hill Circle
Osterville, MA 02655
508-428-7198

Kimbo Educational
P.O. Box 477
Long Branch, NJ 07740
800-631-2187
www.kimboed.com

Library Video Co.
P.O. Box 580
Wynnewood, PA 19096
800-843-3620
www.libraryvideo.com

Listening Library
P.O. Box 25122
Santa Ana, CA 92799
800-541-5525
www.listeninglibrary.com

Live Oak Media
P.O. Box 652
Pine Plains, NY 12567
800-788-1121
www.liveoakmedia.com

Media Basics
Lighthouse Square
P.O. Box 449
Guilford, CT 06437
800-542-2505
www.mediabasicsvideo.com

Microsoft Corp.
One Microsoft Way
Redmond, WA 98052
800-426-9400
www.microsoft.com

National Geographic School Publishing
P.O. Box 10597
Des Moines, IA 50340
800-368-2728
www.nationalgeographic.com

New Kid Home Video
P.O. Box 10443
Beverly Hills, CA 90213
800-309-2392
www.NewKidhomevideo.com

Puffin Books
345 Hudson Street
New York, NY 10014
800-233-7364

Rainbow Educational Media
4540 Preslyn Drive
Raleigh, NC 27616
800-331-4047
www.rainbowedumedia.com

Recorded Books
270 Skipjack Road
Prince Frederick, MD 20678
800-638-1304
www.recordedbooks.com

Sony Wonder
Dist. by Professional Media Service
19122 S. Vermont Ave.
Gardena, CA 90248
800-223-7672
www.sonywonder.com

Spoken Arts
195 South White Rock Road
Holmes, NY 12531
800-326-4090
www.spokenartsmedia.com

SRA Media
220 E. Danieldale Rd.
DeSoto, TX 75115
800-843-8855
www.sra4kids.com

Sunburst Technology
1550 Executive Drive
Elgin, IL 60123
800-321-7511
www.sunburst.com

SVE & Churchill Media
6677 North Northwest Highway
Chicago, IL 60631
800-829-1900
www.svemedia.com

Tom Snyder Productions
80 Coolidge Hill Road
Watertown, MA 02472
800-342-0236
www.tomsnyder.com

Troll Communications
100 Corporate Drive
Mahwah, NJ 07430
800-526-5289
www.troll.com

Weston Woods
143 Main St.
Norwalk, CT 06851-1318
800-243-5020
www.scholastic.com/westonwoods

PRONUNCIATION GUIDE

In this book some unfamiliar or hard-to-pronounce words are followed by respellings to help you say the words correctly. Use the key below to find examples of various sounds and their respellings. Note that in the respelled word, the syllable in capital letters is the one receiving the most stress.

Dictionary letter or mark		Respelled as	Example	Respelled word
ă	(pat)	a	basket	BAS-kiht
ā	(pay)	ay	came	kaym
âr	(care)	air	share	shair
ä	(father)	ah	barter	BAHR-tur
ch	(church)	ch	channel	CHAN-uhl
ĕ	(pet)	eh	test	tehst
ē	(bee)	ee	heap	heep
g	(gag)	g	goulash	GOO-lahsh
ĭ	(pit)	ih	liver	LIHV-ur
ī	(pie, by)	y	alive	uh-LYV
		eye	island	EYE-luhnd
îr	(hear)	eer	year	yeer
j	(judge)	j	germ	jurm
k	(kick, cat, pique)	k	liquid	LIHK-wihd
ŏ	(pot)	ah	otter	AHT-ur
ō	(toe)	oh	solo	SOH-loh
ô	(caught, paw)	aw	always	AWL-wayz
ôr	(for)	or	normal	NOR-muhl
oi	(noise)	oy	boiling	BOYL-ihng
o͝o	(took)	u	pull, wool	pul, wul
o͞o	(boot)	oo	bruise	brooz
ou	(out)	ow	pound	pownd
s	(sauce)	s	center	SEHN-tur
sh	(ship, dish)	sh	chagrin	shuh-GRIHN
ŭ	(cut)	uh	flood	fluhd
ûr	(urge, term, firm, word, heard)	ur	earth	urth
			bird	burd
z	(zebra, xylem)	z	cows	kowz
zh	(vision, pleasure, garage)	zh	decision	dih-SIHZH-uhn
ə	(about)	uh	around	uh-ROWND
	(item)	uh	broken	BROH-kuhn
	(edible)	uh	pencil	PEHN-suhl
	(gallop)	uh	connect	kuh-NEHKT
	(circus)	uh	focus	FOH-kuhs
ər	(butter)	ur	liter	LEE-tur

Glossary

Visit www.eduplace.com for
e • Glossary and e • Word Game.

This glossary can help you find the meanings of some of the words in this book. The meanings given are the meanings of the words as they are used in the book. Sometimes a second meaning is also given.

A

accept
To say yes to: *I accept your offer of a new puppy.*

accident
Something you did not want or expect to happen: *Harry had an accident on his bicycle and fell down.*

advantage
Anything that is a help in getting what someone or something wants: *Frogs have the advantage of long, sticky tongues to catch fast flying insects.*

angry
Unhappy with someone; mad: *Tyler got angry when his sister dropped his glass.*

antennae
A pair of thin organs on the head of insects that can be used to touch and smell: *An ant's antennae can help it find food.*

antennae

argument
A talk between people who do not agree and are mad at each other: *Miko had an argument with Leah over whose painting was better.*

472

attention
The act of looking and listening with care: *We paid close attention to the teacher as she read the story.*

audience
The people who gather to hear or see something: *A large audience sat in the theater waiting to see the movie.*

B

bakery
A place where foods such as bread and cake are made or sold: *The new bakery makes the best doughnuts.*

bakery

bolt
A flash of lightning: *The bolt of lightning was so bright it lit up my bedroom.*

C

chalk
A writing tool made mostly from seashells and used to write on blackboards or other surfaces: *Keisha used green chalk to draw pictures on the board.*

chalk

473

---

cocoon
Silky covering made by some insects to protect themselves until fully grown: *The caterpillars curled up in their cocoons and waited to grow.*

cocoon

colony
A group of animals, plants, or people living or growing together: *Ants live together in large colonies.*

command
An order: *I taught our dog the commands, "sit" and "speak."*

copy
To make another of something: *Everyone had to copy the letters of the alphabet from the board.*

crayon
A stick of colored wax used for drawing or writing: *Each box had eight crayons in it.*

crayons

474

culture
The things that a group of people do and think and the laws that the group lives by: *Sports like baseball are a part of our culture.*

customer
Person who often buys goods or services: *Ms. Ames is one of the customers who come into the coffee shop every morning.*

D

deaf
Unable to hear: *Mrs. Li watches your lips when you speak to her because she is deaf.*

distract
To make someone less interested in one thing and more interested in another: *My mother has to distract me from looking at the needle when I get my flu shot.*

dough
A thick mixture of flour and liquid that is used to make bread and other baked foods: *We cut the cookie dough into animal shapes.*

dough

E

event
Something that happens: *The first event of the party was a game of tag.*

475

Glossary continued

F

fungus
A group of living things that are not plants or animals and have no flowers, leaves, or green coloring: *A mushroom is a type of fungus.*

fungus

fuss
To complain needlessly: *My aunt used to fuss about getting dirt on the porch.*

fussed
Form of **fuss**: *Jorge fussed about not getting any ice cream.*

G

groan
To make a deep sound low in the throat to show pain or anger: *I groan when I have an earache.*

groaned
Form of **groan**: *Kai groaned when the dentist told her she had a cavity.*

grumble
To say things in an unhappy tone: *We heard our dad grumble when he found the broken lamp.*

grumbled
Form of **grumble**: *Jenny grumbled when she was sent to bed early.*

grumpily
Acting in a cranky or upset way: *Andre grumpily got out of the pool when his mother called him to go to bed.*

476

guard
Watch over and keep safe: *My sister likes to eat my cookies, so I guard them when she's around.*

guarded
Form of **guard**: *The dog guarded the front door so no one could get past it.*

H

hearing
The sense by which sound is picked up; ability to hear: *My dog's sense of hearing is very good.*

horizon
The line along which the earth and the sky appear to meet: *Before night fell, the sun sat like a big orange ball on the horizon.*

I

ingredient
Part that makes up a mixture: *We bought all the ingredients we needed to make pumpkin pie.*

instrument
Thing that is used in making music: *Flutes are instruments that make high and soft sounds.*

L

larvae
Newly hatched insects that have no wings and look like worms: *Caterpillars are larvae that grow into butterflies and moths.*

larva

477

lightning
The flash of light in the sky in the middle of a storm: *The bright lightning lit up the sky.*

lightning

M

mural
A painting that is done on a wall or a ceiling: *The mural on the classroom wall was drawn by the students.*

N

newborn
Just brought into life: *My newborn baby brother hasn't left the hospital yet.*

O

officer
A member of a police force: *The officer made sure everyone at the parade was safe.*

officer

478

P

penalty
A punishment for breaking a rule or losing a game or sport: *The penalty for breaking the fire drill rules is no after-school sports.*

percussion
Musical instruments that create a special sound when struck: *Drums are percussion instruments.*

percussion

pest
A person or thing that is not nice to be around: *That fly is a pest because it keeps buzzing around my head.*

powder
Very small pieces of something: *That clown's face is covered with many different colored powders.*

practice
To do something over and over in order to be good at it: *Lelia and Rashawn practice jumping rope every day.*

pride
A feeling of happiness about something you or someone close to you has done: *Gino's parents were full of pride because he had learned to read so quickly.*

project
A special study or experiment done by students: *The class made a model of a volcano for their science project.*

promise
Say that you will do something: *I promise that I will always pick up my room.*

479

promised
Form of **promise**: *We **promised** to wash the car next Saturday.*

Q

quarrel
A talk between people who cannot agree and are mad at each other: *Marta and Joe had a **quarrel** about cleaning up after dinner.*

R

recipe
A set of directions for making something, usually food: *Gia wrote the **recipe** for oatmeal cookies on the board.*

recipe

ruin
To harm something so that it cannot be fixed: *Grape juice can **ruin** a white shirt.*

rumble
Make a deep rolling sound: *We listen to the train **rumble** by our house every night.*

rumbled
Form of **rumble**: *The big truck **rumbled** down the highway.*

S

safety
Freedom from danger or harm: *We follow school **safety** rules so that no one gets hurt.*

scene
Place, picture, or drawing of a place or thing as seen by a viewer: *The postcards from Grandpa have **scenes** from Italy on them.*

sign
Use hand motions to express thoughts: *I will **sign** the news to the children, since they can't hear it for themselves.*

signs
Form of **sign**: *Sam **signs** with his hands to tell stories to children who can't hear.*

sketch
A picture drawn with lines but not colored in: *My parents made many **sketches** of our house before it was built.*

smock
A long shirt or apron worn over clothes to keep them clean: *We used an old shirt as a **smock** when we painted.*

spread
To cover something with something else: *Shaily **spread** butter on her toast.*

T

teenage
Between the ages of thirteen and nineteen: *Since Mary started going to her new school, she has lots of **teenage** friends.*

thunder
The deep, loud noise that comes from the sky during a storm: *The **thunder** was so loud we couldn't hear each other.*

tunnel
Underground or underwater passageway: *Some animals dig **tunnels** underground.*

tunnel

twin
Two children born at one birth: *My cousins are **twins**, and they look exactly like each other.*

twins

V

vibration
Rapid movement back and forth or up and down: *The **vibration** of the table was caused by the earthquake.*

W

weather
The state of the atmosphere at a given time or place, including heat, cold, rain, and wind: *Since the **weather** was warm and sunny, we had a picnic in the park.*

Acknowledgments

Main Literature Selections

Ant, by Rebecca Stefoff. Text copyright © 1998 by Rebecca Stefoff. Reprinted by permission of Benchmark Books, Marshall Cavendish, New York.

The Art Lesson, by Tomie dePaola. Copyright © 1989 by Tomie dePaola. Reprinted by permission of G.P. Putnam's Sons, a division of Penguin Putnam Inc.

Brothers & Sisters, by Ellen B. Senisi. Copyright © 1993 by Ellen B. Senisi. Reprinted by permission of Scholastic Inc.

Carousel, by Pat Cummings. Copyright © 1994 by Pat Cummings. Reprinted with permission of Simon & Schuster Books for Young Readers, Simon & Schuster Children's Publishing Division. All rights reserved.

"A Curve in the River" from *More Stories Julian Tells*, by Ann Cameron. Copyright © 1986 by Ann Cameron. Used by permission of Alfred A. Knopf, an imprint of Random House Children's Books, a division of Random House, Inc., and the Ellen Levine Agency.

The Great Ball Game: A Muskogee Story, by Joseph Bruchac, illustrated by Susan L. Roth. Text copyright © 1994 by Joseph Bruchac. Illustrations copyright © 1994 by Susan L. Roth. Reprinted by permission of Dial Books for Young Readers, a division of Penguin Putnam Inc.

Jalapeño Bagels, text by Natasha Wing, illustrated by Robert Casilla. Text copyright © 1996 by Natasha Wing. Illustrations copyright © 1996 by Robert Casilla. Reprinted with permission of Simon & Schuster Books for Young Readers, Simon & Schuster Children's Publishing Division. All rights reserved.

"Join the Circus!," by Zhang Jin as told to Mike McLeod, from the March 2001 issue of *National Geographic World*. Copyright © 2001 by the National Geographic Society. Reprinted by permission of the National Geographic Society.

Selection from *Little Grunt and the Big Egg*, by Tomie dePaola. Copyright © 1990 by Tomie dePaola. All rights reserved. Reprinted by permission of Holiday House, Inc. and Whitebird, Inc.

Excerpt from *Mighty Dinosaurs: Young Discoveries*, written by Judith Simpson. Copyright © 1996 by Weldon Owen Pty Ltd. Reprinted by permission of Weldon Owen Pty Ltd.

Moses Goes to a Concert, by Isaac Millman. Copyright © 1998 by Isaac Millman. Reprinted by permission of Farrar, Straus and Giroux, LLC.

Officer Buckle and Gloria, by Peggy Rathmann. Text and illustrations copyright © 1995 by Peggy Rathmann. Reprinted by permission of G. P. Putnam's Sons, a division of Penguin Putnam Inc.

Selection from *Raymond's Best Summer*, by Jean Rogers. Text copyright ©1990 by Jean Rogers. Used by permission of HarperCollins Publishers.

The School Mural, by Sarah Vázquez, illustrated by Melinda Levine. Copyright © 1998 Steck-Vaughn Company. Reprinted by permission from Steck-Vaughn Company. All rights reserved.

"Slippery Siblings" from the March 2001 issue of *Jack and Jill* magazine. Copyright © 2001 by Children's Better Health Institute, Benjamin Franklin Literary and Medical Society, Inc., Indianapolis, Indiana. Used by permission.

Talent Show, by Tomie dePaola. Copyright © 2005 by Tomie dePaola. Published by arrangement with Whitebird Inc. All rights reserved.

Thunder Cake, by Patricia Polacco. Copyright © 1990 by Patricia Polacco. Reprinted by permission of Philomel Books, a division of Penguin Putnam, New York.

Focus Selections

The Cool Crazy Crickets, by David Elliott, illustrated by Paul Meisel. Text copyright © 2000 by David Elliott. Illustrations copyright © 2000 by Paul Meisel. Reproduced by permission of Candlewick Press Inc., Cambridge, MA.

Links and Theme Openers

"Bat Attitude," by Lynn O'Donnell from the October 1997 issue of *3 2 1 Contact* magazine. Copyright © 1997 by Children's Television Workshop. Reprinted by permission of the publisher.

Glossary **G3**

Calvin and Hobbes comic, by Bill Watterson, reprinted in the School Comics Media Link. Calvin and Hobbes © Watterson. Reprinted with permission of Universal Press Syndicate. All rights reserved.
"Carousel Designed for Kids," by Kathy Kranking from the June 1998 issue of *Ranger Rick* magazine. Copyright © 1998 by the National Wildlife Federation. Reprinted by permission of the National Wildlife Federation.
"Do Not Enter" from *Oh Grow Up!*, by Florence Parry Heide and Roxanne Heide Pierce. Text copyright © 1996 by Florence Parry Heide and Roxanne Heide Pierce. Reprinted by permission of Orchard Books, New York.
"Go to a Concert" from *Kids Make Music!*, by Avery Hart and Paul Mantell. Copyright © 1993 by Avery Hart & Paul Mantell. Reprinted by permission of Williamson Publishing Company.
"I Did Not Eat Your Ice Cream" from *Something Big Has Been Here*, by Jack Prelutsky. Copyright © 1990 by Jack Prelutsky. Reprinted by permission of HarperCollins Publishers.
"Little sister" from *Something on My Mind*, by Nikki Grimes. Copyright © 1978 by Nikki Grimes. Reprinted by permission of Dial Books for Young Readers, a division of Penguin Putnam Inc., and Curtis Brown Ltd.
Peanuts comics reprinted in the School Comics Media Link are reprinted from *Nothing Echoes Like an Empty Mailbox*, by Charles M. Schulz. PEANUTS © United Feature Syndicate. Reprinted by permission of United Feature Syndicate.
"The Story of Owney" from *Postal Pack for Elementary School Students*, published by the National Postal Museum at the Smithsonian Institution. Reprinted by permission.
"Sun & Ice" reprinted from *Out of the Bag: The Paper Bag Players Book of Plays*, by The Paper Bag Player. Text © 1997 by The Paper Bag Players. Reprinted by permission of Hyperion Books for Children and the Paper Bag Players.
"Welcome to the Kitchen," from *Young Chef's Nutrition Guide and Cookbook* by Carolyn Moore, Ph.D. R.D., Mimi Kerr and Robert Shulman,

PhD. Copyright © 1990 by Barron's Educational Series. Reprinted by permission of the Barron's Educational Series.
"What is a family?" from *Fathers, Mothers, Sisters, Brothers: A Collection of Family Poems*, by Mary Ann Hoberman. Copyright © 1991 by Mary Ann Hoberman. Reprinted by permission of Little, Brown and Company (Inc.) and the Gina Maccoby Literary Agency.

Credits

Photography

1 (t) © Bob Anderson/Masterfile. (m) Hemera Technologies Inc. (b) Creatas/PictureQuest. **3** © Bob Anderson/Masterfile. **4** (l) NASA. (m) Archive Photos/PictureQuest. (r) Jerry Cooke/Life Magazine © TIME Inc. **6** Hemera Technologies Inc. **9** © Creatas/PictureQuest. **10-11** (bkgd) © Tim Flach/Stone/Getty Images. **11** (m) © Bob Anderson/Masterfile. **12** Courtesy of Joseph Bruchac. **13** (tr) Courtesy of Joseph Bruchac. (bl) Courtesy of Joseph Bruchac. (br) James Balog/Stone/Getty Images. **14** Courtesy of Joseph Bruchac. **18-9** (bkgd) G. K. & Vikki Hart/The Image Bank/Getty Images. **18** Brooke Forsythe **52** Myrleen Ferguson/PhotoEdit. **54-5** Smithsonian National Postal Museum. **56** Corbis/Dan Guravich. **57** (t) Corbis/Dan Guravich. **60-1** (bkgd) © Damir Frkovic/Masterfile. **60** (t) Remy Amann-Bios/Peter Arnold, Inc. (l) Zefa Germany/Corbis Stock Market. (inset) Courtesy Marshall Cavendish. **61** (inset) Raymond A. Mendez/Animals Animals. **62-3** Hans Pfletschinger/Peter Arnold, Inc. **63** (r) Gary Retherford/NASC/Photo Researchers, Inc. **64** (t) Len Rue Jr. /NASC/Photo Researchers, Inc. (b) Jerome Wexler/NASC/Photo Researchers, Inc. **65** Leonard Lee Rue/NASC/Photo Researchers, Inc. **66-7** J. H. Robinson/NASC/Photo Researchers, Inc. **68** (t) Hans Pfletschinger/Peter Arnold, Inc. (b) Leonide Principe/NASC/Photo Researchers, Inc. **69** Rudolph Freund/NASC/Photo Researchers, Inc. **70** S. J. Krasemann/NASC/Photo Researchers, Inc. **71** John Dommers/NASC/Photo

Researchers, Inc. **72** Gary Retherford/NASC/Photo Researchers, Inc. **73** (t) Philip K. Sharpe/Animals Animals. (b) S. J. Krasemann/Peter Arnold, Inc. **74** (l) K. G Preston-Mafham/Animals Animals. (r) Gregory D. Dimijian/NASC/Photo Researchers, Inc. **75** Gregory D. Dimijian/NASC/Photo Researchers, Inc. **76** Donald Specker/Animals Animals. **77** Mantis Wildlife Films, Oxford Scientific Films/Animals Animals. **78-9** Gary Retherford/NASC/Photo Researchers, Inc. **80-1** Hans Pfletschinger/Peter Arnold, Inc. **82-3** Varin/Jacana/NASC/Photo Researchers, Inc. **84** (inset) Raymond A. Mendez/Animals Animals. **85** (l) Bob Anderson/MASTERFILE. **88** (icon) © PhotoDisc/Getty Images. **88-9** (bkgd) Ed Bock/Corbis Stock Market. **89** (t) Corbis/Hulton-Deutsch Collection. **90** (t) Mike Greenlar/Mercury River Gallery/PictureQuest. **90** (l) Lawrence Migdale/Mira. **90-1** (bkgd) © ImageState/Panoramic Images. **90** (t) Mike Greenlar/Mercury Pictures. (b) Courtesy Penguin Putnam. **111** (l) © Planet Earth Pictures 1998/FPG International. **112** (t) Jens Rydell/Natural Selection. **113** (l) Robin Thomas. (tr) John Serrao/Photo Researchers, Inc. (br) Corbis/Joe McDonald. **114-5** Stephen Dalton/Photo Researchers. **116-7** (bkgd) © Gail Shumway/Taxi/Getty Images. **116** (b) © Bob Anderson/Masterfile. **136** NASA. **137** Roger Ressmeyer/Corbis. **138** (t) Corbis. (b) NASA. **139** Corbis. **140** (t) © PhotoDisc/Getty Images. (b) NASA. **141** AFP/Corbis. **142** (bkgd) © PhotoDisc/Getty Images. (b) Archive Photos/PictureQuest. **143** Corbis **144** (t) Dave G. Houser/Corbis. (b) Corbis/Bettmann. **145** Tom Bean/Corbis **146** (l) Kim Sayer/Corbis. (r) Wood River Gallery/PictureQuest. **147** (t) © PhotoDisc/Getty Images. (b) Jerry Cooke/Life Magazine © Time Inc. **148** Mark Kauffman/Life Magazine © Time Inc. **148-9** AP/Wide World Photos. **150** Corbis/Bettmann. **151** Corbis/Bettmann. **152** Corbis/Bettmann. **153** (t) Robert Maass/Corbis. (b) AP/Wide World Photos. **154** (tl) © Ziggy Kaluzny/Stone/Getty Images. **154-5** (tr) © Jose Luis Pelaez/CORBIS **154-5** (br) © Ronnie Kaufman/CORBIS **154** (bl) © Arthur Tilley/Taxi/Getty Images **155** (m) Hemera

Technologies Inc. **156** (t) Courtesy of Pat Cummings, © HMCo./Ken Karp. **157-158** Courtesy of Pat Cummings. **162-3** (bkgd) David Perry/Taxi/Getty Images. **162-80** Ellen B. Senisi. **181** Mike Greenlar/Mercury Pictures. **182** Ellen B. Senisi. **183** (l) Courtesy Trisha Zembruski. (cl) Michael Newman/PhotoEdit. (cr) David Young-Wolff/PhotoEdit. **190** (t) StockByte. (b) John & Eliza Forder/Stone/Getty Images. **190-1** Don Smetzer/Stone/Getty Images. **191** Don Smetzer/Stone/Getty Images. **192-3** (bkgd) © Royalty-Free/CORBIS. **192** (t) Courtesy Natasha Wing. (b) Tom Iannuzzi/Mercury Pictures. **220-1** (bkgd) © Roy Ooms/Masterfile. **220** Courtesy Pat Cummings. **254-7** Photographs © 1997 Christopher Hornby. **258-9** Corbis Royalty Free. **260-1** (bkgd) © Daryl Benson/Masterfile. **260** Lawrence Migdale. **298-9** (bkgd) © Lori Adamski Peek/Stone/Getty Images **298** (b) Hemera Technologies Inc. **307-309** Courtesy of Danny Bryant. **344-5** (bkgd) © Eyewire/Getty Images. **345** (m) © Creatas/PictureQuest. **346** (t) Courtesy of Tomie DePaola. **351** (artwork) *Sunflowers*, Vincent Van Gogh, 1853–90, Dutch, National Gallery, London/SuperStock. **352** (bkgd) Elizabeth Simpson/Taxi/Getty Images. **379** © 1997 Suki Couglin. **382-3** *Tamalada (Making Tamales)*, 1987. Carmen Lomas Garza. **384** *Guacamole*, 1989. Carmen Lmoas Garza. gouache, 9 x 5 1/2 inches, Collection of Antonia Castaneda and Arturo Madrid, Claremont, CA. **385** *Naranjas (Oranges)*, 1990. Carmen Lomas Garza. **386** Corbis Royalty Free. **388** Dave Schlabowske/TIME Inc. **390-1** (bkgd) Wayne Eastep/Stone/Getty Images. **390** Tom Iannuzzi/Mercury Pictures. **426** © PhotoDisc/Getty Images. **427** Rick Friedman/Black Star/PictureQuest. **428-9** Oliver Benn/Stone/Getty Images. **430-1** Jeffry W. Myers/IndexStock. **432** (bkgd) Ken Whitmore/Stone/Getty Images. **453** (t) John Redmond. (b) Kenneth Rice Photography **458** (b) © Creatas/PictureQuest. **458-9** (bkgd) © Euan Myles/Stone/Getty Images. **460** Ben Van Hook. **461** Ben Van Hook/National Geographic. **462** Ben Van Hook. **463** Ben Van Hook/National Geographic. **472** PhotoSpin. **473** Dick Luria/FPG International.

474 (l) © PhotoDisc/Getty Images. **475** Artville. **476** Artville. **477** Digital Vision/PictureQuest. **478** Corbis Royalty Free. **479** © PhotoDisc/Getty Images. **481** Corbis Royalty Free. **482** Donna Day/Stone/Getty Images.

Assignment Photography
16-7, 216-17, 294-7, 351, 389, 425 HMCo./Joel Benjamin. **53, 85** (r)**, 111, 183** (r)**, 253, 293, 381, 455** HMCo./Ken Karp. **133, 313, 471** © HMCo./Michael Indresano Photography

Illustration
12-15 Chris Lensch. **58-59** Carolyn Iverson. **84** Mike Reed. **86** William Brinkley & Associates. **86-87** Nancy Gibson-Nash. **127-130** (border) Patrick Gnan. **134-5** Ed Martinez. **158** Pat Cummings. **159** Annette Cable. **160-61** Dave Klug. **184-45** Eric Brace. **186-67** Copyright © 2001 by Raúl Colón. **192, 214** Tom Brenner. **214** (cl)**, 252** (cl)**, (b) 253** (t) Eileen Gilbride. **219** Clive Scruton. **260, 292, 293** Jason Farris. **301, 303-306** Gail Piazza. **314-5** Paul Meisel. **346-8** Tomie dePaola. **379, 380** (cl) **(bl)** Daniel Del Valle. **390, 424** (b) **425** George Ulrich. **432** (inset) **433-52** Melinda Levine. **453, 454** (b) **455** Jim Kelly. **465, 467, 468** Jessie Reisch.

Index

Boldface page references indicate formal strategy and skill instruction.

A

Abbreviations. *See* Mechanics, language.

Acquiring English, students. *See* English Language Learners. *See also* Reaching All Learners.

Activating prior knowledge. *See* Background, building.

Affixes. *See* Structural analysis.

Analyzing literature. *See* Literary analysis; Literature, analyzing.

Art activities. *See* Cross-curricular activities.

Assessment, planning for
Comprehension Check, *T69, T151, T217, T338*
End-of-Selection Assessment, *T69, T151, T219, T339*
Formal Assessment, *T14, T244*
Informal Assessment, *T14*
Monitoring Student Progress, *T34, T35, T36, T41, T56, T63, T71, T78, T104, T120, T121, T122, T127, T145, T153, T160, T191, T192, T197, T207, T213, T228, T316, T221, T244-T300, T261, T269, T296, T318, T323, T331, T337, T345, T352, R10, R12, R14, R16, R18, R20, R22, R24, R26, R28, R30, R32, R33, R34*
National Test Correlation, *T15*
Portfolio Opportunity, *T83, T104, T147, T165, T233, T250, T340, T351*
Scoring Rubric, *T105*
Selection Test, *T69, T151, T219, T339*
Self-Assessment, *T69, T105, T151, T219, T339*
See also Teacher's Assessment Handbook.

Assignment Cards. *T54, T56, T59, T135, T137, T141, T206, T207*

Audio-visual resources. *See* Technology resources.

Author's craft. *See* Writer's Craft.

Author's viewpoint. *See* Comprehension skills, author's viewpoint.

Authors of selections in Anthology
Alonso, Elena, *T328*
Berman, Stephen, *T332*
Bruchac, Joseph, *T203*
dePaola, Tomie, *T255*
Ellis, Veronica Freeman, *T334*
Rathmann, Peggy, *T48*
Simpson, Judith, *T266*
Stefoff, Rebecca, *T133*

Automatic recognition of words. *See* High-Frequency Words; Spelling; Vocabulary, selection.

B

Background, building
in a teacher read aloud, *T32, T118, T188, T314*
key concepts, *T44, T90, T91, T92, T93, T130, T172, T173, T174, T175, T200, T240, T241, T242, T243, T326, T329, T362, T363, T364, T365*
previewing. *See* Previewing.
prior knowledge, *T32, T118, T188, T314, R4, R6, R8*
See also English Language Learners, activities especially helpful for.

Bibliography, Leveled, *T6–T7*

Biography, focus on, *T302–T365*

Blending. *See* Decoding skills; Phonics.

Books for independent reading. *See* Independent and recreational reading; Leveled Readers; Leveled Theme Paperbacks, Leveled Readers.

Brainstorming, *T44, T340, R11*

C

Categorizing and classifying. *See* Comprehension skills.

Cause-effect relationships. *See* Comprehension skills.

CD-ROM diskettes, *T93, T175, T243, T244, T365*

Challenge. *See* Reaching All Learners

Character(s)
feelings, *T59, T62, T63,*
making inferences about, *T51, T54, T56,*
motives, *T48,*
as story element, *96*
traits revealed through action, *T58, T207, T212*

Cites evidence from text, *T46, T51, T53, T56, T59, T61, T63*

Classifying. *See* Comprehension skills.

Classroom management
Classroom Management Activities, *T28–T29, T114–T115, T184–T185, T250–T251*

groups, *T13, T29, T39, T56, T62, T69, T82, T86, T114, T125, T130, T137, T144, T145, T152, T152, T160, T168, T184, T195, T200, T211, T212, T213, T223, T226, T229, T231, T232, T236, T239, T251, T281, T293, T331, T337, T349, T310, T344, T353, T358, R19*
individuals, *T12, T28, T29, T56, T63, T115, T130, T137, T145, T162, T184, T185, T200, T202, T213, T250, T251, T277, T285, T293, T311*
partners, *T13, T28, T29, T37, T41, T69, T74, T78, T79, T80, T81, T87, T90, T91, T92, T93, T114, T115, T123, T127, T156, T160, T161, T164, T169, T172, T173, T174, T175, T185, T192, T193, T197, T200, T209, T210, T213, T215, T218, T222, T225, T228, T230, T236, T239, T240, T241, T242, T243, T250, T251, T269, T272, T280, T287, T288, T291, T292, T310, T311, T319, T321, T352, T354, T362, T363, T364, T365, R10, R12, R14, R15, R18, R19, R20, R22, R25, R27, R29, R30, R32*
whole class, *T56, T137, T145, T200, T207, T213, T331, T337*

Coherence in narrative text. *See* Comprehension skills, story structure.

Collaborative learning. *See* Cooperative learning activities.

Combination classroom, *T16*

Communication activities. *See* Listening; Speaking; Viewing.

Community-school interactions. *See* Home-Community Connections.

Compare/contrast, Comprehension skills, compare and contrast.

Comparing. *See* Connections.

Comprehension skills
author's viewpoint, *T144, T261,* **T284,** *T329, T331, T333, T335*
cause and effect, **T86,** *T139, T168,* **T188–T189, T202,** *T205, T208,* **T210, T220–T221,** *T240, T241, T242, T243, T258, T259, T296, R30–R31*
compare and contrast, *T76, T137, T150, T159, T206,* **T236,** *T257, T261, T267, T276, T284, T334, T336, T337, T338*
conclusions, drawing, **T32–T33, T46, T52,** *T54, T56, T58, T62, T68,* **T70–T71,** *T90, T91, T92, T93, T208, T227, T256, T257, T258, T262, T331, T334, T335, R26–R27*

Process writing. *See* Reading-Writing Workshop (process writing): Research Report; Writing skills.

Pronouns. *See* Grammar and usage; Speech, parts of.

Proofreading. *See* Reading-Writing Workshop, steps of; Writing skills, proofreading.

Publishing. *See* Reading-Writing Workshop, steps of; Writing skills, publishing.

Punctuation. *See* Mechanics, language.

Purposes for reading
find answers to questions, *T47, T133, T203*
think about careers, *T329*
reviewing, *T56, T137, T145, T205, T331*

Purpose setting for reading, *T32, T47, T118, T133, T188, T203, T314, T329*

Questions, formulating, *T87, T215, T210, T219, T254*

Quotations
direct, **T227, T346**
interpreting, **T227, T346**

Reaching All Learners
Challenge, *T62, T64, T76, T135, T137, T141, T144, T146, T212, T214, T257, T259, T336, T341, R11, R13, R15, R17, R19, R21, R23, R25, R27, R29, R31*
English Language Learners, *T33, T49, T50, T53, T60, T61, T69, T76, T119, T130, T134, T139, T143, T144, T151, T159, T189, T200, T204, T208, T219, T258, T269, T286, T315, T326, T334, T335, T339, R4, R6, R8*
Extra Support, *T40, T47, T51, T55, T59, T62, T69, T133, T136, T142, T151, T158, T196. T203, T205, T206, T219, T226, T256, T260, T267, T286, T322, T329, T330, T333, T339*
On Level Students, *T62, T137, T219*
Special Needs, *See* Teaching and management.

Reading across the curriculum. *See* Content area, reading in the.

Reading fluency. *See* Fluency.

Reading log. *See* Journal.

Reading modes
cooperative reading, *T56, T137, T207, T280, T287, T288, T296, T331*
guiding comprehension. *See* Critical thinking.
independent reading, *T56, T137, T207, T280, T331, R4–R5, R6–R7, R8–R9*
oral reading, *T30, T37, T39, T42, T66, T74, T80,*

T81, T84, T86, T90, T91, T92, T93, T116, T123, T125, T128, T134, T148, T156, T158, T159, T162, T163, T166, T168, T172, T173, T174, T175, T186, T193, T195, T198, T202, T216, T224, T226, T231, T234, T236, T240, T230, T319, T241, T242, T243, T252, T256, T261, T264, T274, T280, T282, T287, T290, T296, T310, T312, T321, T324, T342, T348, T362, T363, T364, T356, T358, T365
paired reading, *T56, T137, T207, T280, T287, T288, T296*
teacher read aloud, *T32–T33, T118–T119, T188–T189, T314–T315, R2–R3*
See also Rereading.

Reading strategies. *See* Strategies, reading.

Reading traits
Decoding Conventions, *T153, T345*
Developing Interpretations, *T71*
Integrating for Synthesis, *T221*

Reading-Writing Workshop (process writing); Research Report
conferencing, **T102**
evaluating, **T104**
reading as a writer, **T97**
steps of
drafting, **T101**
prewriting, **T98–T100**
proofreading, **T102–T103**
publishing and sharing, **T104**
revising, **T102**
student model, **T96–T97**
topics
research report, **T94–T105**
See also Writing skills.

Reads on and rereads. *See* Strategies, reading, Monitor/Clarify.

Reference and study skills
electronic sources
Internet, *T13,* **T29,** *T151,* **T251,** *R27*
graphic sources. *See* Graphic information, interpreting.
information skills. *See* Information and study skills.
reference resources
books, *T115, T151, T340, R27*
dictionary, **T78**
encyclopedia, *T12, T13, T115, T151, T340, R27*
glossary, **T169**
thesaurus, *T281, T283*
study strategies
notes, taking, *T29, T340*
See also Dictionary Skills.

Rereading
cooperatively, *T39, T81, T125, T163, T195, T231, T288, T296, T321*
for comprehension, *T86, T154, T168, T222, T226, T236, T310, T339, T346, T358*
for fluency, *T86, T168, T236, T280, T288, T296*

for extra support, *T226, T277, R10, R12, R14, R16, R18*
to support answer, *T159, T210*
orally, *T39, T81, T125, T163, T195, T231, T320*
with feeling and expression, *T39, T81, T86, T125, T163, T168, T195, T231, T236, T240, T241, T242, T243, T280, T288, T296, T321, T358*

Research activities, *T12, T13, T29, T151, T169, T219, T251, T259, T277, T291, T340, R27, R29*

Responding to literature, options for discussion, *T56, T90, T91, T92, T93, T137, T150, T151, T172, T173, T174, T175, T207, T212, T240, T241, T242, T243, T338, T350, T362, T363, T364, T365, R5, R7, R9*

Internet, *T69, T151, T219, T339*

personal response, *T33, T69, T119, T151, T189, T315, T339*

writing, *T68, T150, T151, T218, T338*

Reteaching, *R4, R6, R8, R10, R12, R14, R16, R18, R20, R22, R24, R26, R28, R30, R32–R34*

Retelling, *T69, T269, T335, T345*

Revising. *See also* Reading-Writing Workshop, steps of; Writing skills, revising.

Rhyme, rhythm. *See* Poetic Devices.

Routines
Daily, *T30–T31, T42–T43, T66–T67, T74–T75, T84–T85, T116–T117, T128–T129, T148–T149, T156–T157, T166–T167, T186–T187, T198–T199, T216–T217, T224–T225, T234–T235, T252–T253, T264–T265, T274–T275, T282–T283, T290– T291, T312–T313, T324–T325, T342–T343, T348–T349, T356–T357*
Daily Message, *T30, T42, T66, T74, T75, T84, T116, T128, T129, T148, T156, T166, T186, T198, T216, T224, T234, T252, T264, T274, T282, T290, T312, T324, T342, T348, T356*
instructional, *T11*
management, *T10*

Science activities. *See* Cross-curricular activities.

Selecting books. *See* Independent and recreational reading.

Selections in Anthology
article
"Bat Attitude," from *3-2-1 Contact*, biography
"The Ellen Ochoa Story," by Elena Alonso, *T328–T331*
"President Theodore Roosevelt," by Stephen Berman, *T332–T334*

Student self-assessment. *See* Assessment, planning for; Self-Assessment.

Study skills. *See* Reference and study skills.

Study strategies. *See* Reference and study skills.

Summarizing.
oral summaries, *T55, T62, T63, T136, T144, T206, T212, T213, T260, T330, R5, R7, R9*

Syntactic cues. *See* Structural analysis.

Syntax. *See* Decoding skills, context using.

Take-Home Books, *T39, T81, T125, T163, T195, T231, T321*

Teacher Read Aloud
biography
    "Meet Dr. Seuss," by Sarah M. Healey, *T314–T315*
fiction
    "Little Fly and the Great Moose, The," by Janeen R. Adil, *T188–T189*
nonfiction
    "Aero and Officer Mike: Police Partners," by Joan Plummer Russell, *T32–T33*
    From Caterpillar to Butterfly, by Deborah Heiligman, *R2–R3*
    "Octopus Is Amazing, An," by Patricia Lauber, *T118–T119*

Teacher-guided reading. *See* Critical thinking.

Teaching across the curriculum. *See* Content areas, reading in the; Cross-curricular activities; Links, content area.

Teaching and management
managing assessment, *T14–T15*
managing instruction, *T8–T9*
managing program materials, *T20–T23, T106–T109, T176–T179, T302–T305*
parent conferences. *See* Home-Community Connections.
special needs of students, meeting. *See* Reaching All Learners.

Technology resources
address list, *R49*
Internet, *T69, T151, T219, T339*
www.eduplace.com, *T69, T151, T219, T339*

Test-Prep, *T46, T71, T132, T153, T202, T221, T345*

Tests, taking
Vocabulary items, *T270, T278, T286, T294*

Text organization and structure
captions, **T140,** *T152–T153, T280, T355*
headings, **T140,** *T152–T153, T280, R29*
timelines, *T355*
See also Comprehension skills, text organization.

Theme
Amazing Animals, *T16–T297*

Theme, Launching the, *T16–T19*

Theme paperbacks. *See* Leveled Theme paperbacks.

Theme Skills Overview, *T8–T9*

Think Aloud. *See* Modeling.

Thinking
creatively. *See* Creative thinking.
critically. *See* Critical thinking.

Topic, main idea, and supporting details. *See* Comprehension skills.

Topics, selecting. *See* Reading-Writing Workshop, steps of, prewriting; Research activities.

Usage. *See* Grammar and usage.

Venn diagrams. *See* Graphic Organizers.

Viewing
illustrations or photographs, *T61,* **T154, T222,** *R29*

Visual literacy
descriptive photographs, **T154**
illustrator's craft, **T72**
perspective, **T222**

Visualizing, T358

Vocabulary expansion
action words, **T43, T209**
animals, **T117, T149, T157, T187, T199,** *T207, T211,* **T217, T235, T253, T265**
ball games vocabulary, *T204*
dinosaurs, parts of, *T269*
direction words, **T239**
everyday activities, *T211*
exclamations, **T61**
kinds of antennae, **T135**
kinds of leaders, **T167**
multiple-meaning words, **T343**
noun/verb words, **T60**
rhyming words, **T217,** *T315, R23*
time order words, *T239,* **T351,** *T357*
verbs, exact, **T313,** *T237*
volcano, parts of, *T259*
words for things having to do with letter writing, **T85**
word webs, *T235, T253, T265, T33, T119, T357*
See also Language concepts and skills.

Vocabulary, selection
high-frequency words. *See* High-frequency words.
key words, *T45, T50, T51, T53, T57, T75, T90, T91, T92, T93, T130, T131, T134, T135, T136, T138, T139, T141, T157, T158, T172, T173, T174, T175, T201, T204, T205, T208, T209, T225, T240, T241, T242, T243, T255, T256, T257, T258, T259, T260, T266, T267, T268, T327, T328, T330, T331, T332, T349, T362, T363, T364, T365, R4, R6, R8*
See also Daily Language Practice; Decoding skills; context clues.

Vocabulary skills
abbreviations, **T352**
categorizing, *T325*
dictionary entry words, **T78, T228,** *T272, T288*
genre vocabulary, *T327*
using a thesaurus, **T160,** *T281, T283*
See also Dictionary skills, Tests, taking; Vocabulary expansion; Vocabulary, selection.

Vowels. *See* Phonics, vowels; Spelling, vowels.

Word analysis. *See* Structural analysis; Vocabulary, extending.

Word Wall, *T30, T36, T42, T66, T74, T75, T84, T116, T122, T128, T129, T148, T156, T166, T186, T198, T216, T224, T234, T252, T264, T274, T282, T290, T312, T318, T324, T342, T348, T356, R35–R39*

Word list, *R47–R49*

Word webs. *See* Graphic organizers.

Writer's craft
idioms, *T143, T187, T258, R5, R7, R9*
paragraphs and topic sentences, **T346**
poetic devices. *See* Poetic devices.
quotations, **T227, T346**

Writer's log. *See* Journal.

Writing activities and types
animal ABC book, **T13**
animal award, **T293**
animal dictionary, **T293**
biography, *T326,* **T340,** *T360*
broadcast of sports event, *R25*
character sketch, *T43, T149*
cooperative writing. *See* Cooperative Learning activities.
creative. *See* Writing modes, creative.
description, *T67, T117, T129, T187, T199, T277, T349, R27*
definitions, *T293, T341*
diagram with labels, *T67*
dialogue in speech balloons, *T339*
diary entry, **T311,** *T357, R21*
directions, **T239**

drawing with caption, *R5*
explanation, *T157, T225, T275, T313, T343, T250*
fact/fantasy animals, describing, ***T277***
folktale, ***T219, T229***
invitation, *T28,* ***T65,*** *T253*
letters
  advice, *T217*
  thank-you, *T69*
math problems based on story, *R31*
news article, ***T215,*** *T275, R25*
persuasive speech, ***T206***
poem, *T31,* ***T115, T147,*** *T167, T265*
poster to advertise theme selection, ***T285***
questions, *T133, T210, T227*
report on nonfiction reading, *T157, T339*
report, research, ***T94–T105,*** *T151, T277, T283, T291*
rhymes, *T273, T315,* ***T325,*** *R11*
riddles, ***T216,*** *R27*
safety tips, ***T29,*** *T44, T54, T64, T89, T75*
sentences, *T36, T41, T197, T273, T275, T285, T293, T315, T340, R20, R21, R22, R23, R31*
stories
  new ending/sequel, *T185, T235, T250*
summary. *See* Summarizing, oral summaries.
tongue twisters, *T146*
verses for a song, *T158*
See also Author's craft; Reading-Writing
  Workshop (process writing); Research Report;
  Writer's craft.
Writing as a process. *See* Reading-Writing
Workshop.

Writing conferences. *See* Reading-Writing
Workshop.
Writing modes
  classificatory, *T13,*
  creative, *T31, T43, T115, T147, T149, T167, T185, T219, T229, T235, T250, T265, T273, T311, T315, T325, T326, T339, T340, T360, R21*
  descriptive, *T67, T117, T129, T187, T199, T277, T349, R27*
  evaluative, *T157, T339*
  expository, *T157, T225, T239, T275, T313, T343, T250*
  expressive, *T31, T115, T147, T167, T265, T273, T311, T315, T325, T357, R21. See also* Journal.
  functional, *T28, T65, T69, T239, T253, T293*
  informative, *T67, T94–T105, T151, T157, T215, T275, T277, T283, T291, T293, T339, R5, R25*
  narrative, *T43, T149, T185, T219, T229, T235, T250, T326, T339, T340, T360*
  persuasive, *T206, T217, T285*

Writing skills
  biographies, writing, ***T340,*** *T362–T363*
  computer tools
    See Technology resources.
  drafting skills
    answering the five W's, *T215*
    facts and details, using, ***T233***
    paragraphs, ***T346***
    research report, *T291*
    topic sentences, ***T346***
    writing times, ***T83***
  formats. *See* Writing, activities and types.

prewriting
  brainstorming, *T340*
  labeling picture of subject, *T334*
  listing possible subjects, *T326*
  organizing and planning, *T65, R29*
process writing, steps of. *See* Reading-Writing
  Workshop.
proofreading skills
  apostrophes in possessives, ***T170***
  capital letters, *T359*
publishing skills
  class newspaper, *T215*
  illustrate original writing, *T277, T285, T292, T293*
  read aloud, *T360*
revising skills
  adding details, ***T233***
  exact nouns, using, *T227*
  pronouns, writing clearly with, ***T88, T323***
  using *I* and *me,* ***T165***
See also Author's craft; Reading-Writing
  Workshop (process writing); Research Report;
  Writer's craft.

Writing traits
  conventions, *T83, T165, T105*
  ideas, *T95, T98, T105, T233*
  organization, *T95, T105, T351*
  presentation, *T105*
  sentence fluency, *T105*
  voice, *T105*
  word choice, *T105*